DAVID

His Life and Times

A Biographical Commentary

Books by Ivor Powell

Bible Cameos
Bible Gems
Bible Highways
Bible Names of Christ
Bible Nuggets
Bible Oases
Bible Pinnacles
Bible Promises
Bible Windows
Matthew's Majestic Gospel
Mark's Superb Gospel
Luke's Thrilling Gospel
John's Wonderful Gospel
The Amazing Acts
The Exciting Epistle to the Ephesians
David: His Life and Times
Heaven: My Father's Country
What in the World Will Happen Next?

DAVID

His Life and Times

A Biographical Commentary

IVOR POWELL

kregel
PUBLICATIONS

Grand Rapids, MI 49501

David: His Life and Times, by Ivor Powell.

Copyright © 1990 by Kregel Publications, a division of Kregel, Inc., P.O. Box 2607, Grand Rapids, Michigan 49501. All rights reserved.

Cover photograph: POSITIVE IMAGES/Patricia Sgrignoli
Cover design: Alan G. Hartman

Library of Congress Cataloging-in-Publication Data
Powell, Ivor, 1910-
    David: his life and times / Ivor Powell.
    Includes index.
    1. David, King of Israel. 2. Bible. O.T.—Biography.
3. David, King of Israel—Sermons. 4. Bible. O.T. Samuel,
1st, XVI, 1-Kings, 1st, II. 11—Homiletical use. 5. Bible.
O.T. Psalms—Homiletical use. 6. Sermons, American.
I. Title.
BS580.D3P68   1990 222'.4092—dc20   90-36487
                                                                CIP
ISBN   0-8254-3532-3 (pbk.)

            6 7 8 9 10 Printing/Year 99 98 97 96 95

Printed in the United States of America

To
Bowdre Lucian Carswell, M.D.,
who, with God's help,
prolonged my life. I have
been enriched by his fellowship,
helped by his counsel, and
inspired by his witness for Christ.
To him, this book is gratefully dedicated.

Contents

Contents

Index of Homilies

Preface

Many years ago, when I was a small child attending a Sunday school in Wales, I was fascinated by the story of David, who slew a Philistine giant. Enthralled, I listened to the account of how a boy selected pebbles from a brook and accomplished the impossible. Later, as an evangelist, I visited the Presbyterian churches of North Scotland and admired the fervor of the highland congregations as they sang the psalms of David. Some church people refused to sing other compositions, stating that David's words were inspired by God and should never be replaced by the lyrics of other writers. I did not always agree with what I was told, but now I am able to appreciate the sentiments of those delightful Scottish Christians. They deepened my interest in the ancient psalmist and prepared my soul for the writing of this book. During the last eighteen months I have spent many hours with my Bible and David, and what I discovered has now been written.

Sometimes it was difficult to understand the actions of the king of Israel. I was perplexed by his indiscretions and disappointed by his stubbornness. Nevertheless, the sweet singer of Israel never bowed before idols and, in this matter, was supreme among the potentates of his generation. I have traveled, so to speak, from the fields of Bethlehem to the palace in Jerusalem; from the cave of Adullam to the cave in which Saul consulted a witch. I have seen David's face wet with the tears of repentance and aglow with a resplendence which came from God. If I have written as a minister with alliterated headings, understand that such expression has been my style for over sixty years. It is my prayer that others will be helped as they prepare their sermons.

I could never adequately express how much I owe to my wife, Betty. With great care and endless patience, she studied and improved my manuscript. I tried, with God's assistance, to produce a diamond; my partner cut and polished it!

I would like to express sincere thanks to Mrs. Eleanor Dzuro, who typed this manuscript and six others which preceded it. She never complained of the magnitude of her task, for this was her way of serving the Savior. I thank the Lord for Eleanor's continuing assistance.

As this volume commences its ministry, I pray that it will bring David into the hearts and homes of all its readers.

Santa Barbara, California   IVOR POWELL

Introduction

BETHLEHEM - David's Birthplace

Some theologians believe that there were two Bethlehems in ancient Palestine. The first was mentioned in the book of Joshua (Josh. 19:15) and was possibly the burial place of Ibzan, one of the earliest judges in Israel (Judg. 12:8). This was situated approximately seven miles from Nazareth. Josephus disagrees with this conclusion. He wrote: "Now when Jepthah was dead, Ibzan took the government, being of the tribe of Judah, and of the city of Bethlehem. He had sixty children, thirty of them sons, and the rest daughters; all of whom he left behind him. The daughters he gave in marriage to husbands, and took wives for his sons. He did nothing in the seven years of his administration that was worth recording, or deserved a memorial. So he died an old man and was buried in his own country" (Josephus, *The Antiquities of the Jews.* Book 5, Chap. 7, Paragraph 13).

Other writers, disagreeing with this statement, believed that two cities existed with the same name and affirmed that this explains why Micah indicated which of the two would be the birthplace of the Savior. The prophet wrote: "But thou, Bethlehem *Ephratah*, though thou be little *among the thousands of Judah*, yet out of thee shall he come forth unto me that is to be ruler in Israel; whose goings forth have been from of old, from everlasting" (Mic. 5:2).

David's birthplace was situated about six miles from the city of Jerusalem (see early reference in Josh. 19:15). It was founded by Salma, one of Caleb's sons, who, after the conquest of Canaan, began to colonize the land. This man was described as "the father of Bethlehem" (see 1 Chron. 2:51). It was set in the midst of very fertile plains where crops were abundant. This probably accounts for its name, which means "The House of Bread." Only on the rare occasions when drought and famine ravaged the area (see Ruth 1:1), did the citizens of Bethlehem experience hardship. The city was normally a small but very prosperous place close to the important centers of the nation. It was considered to be a very strategic center and, at a later date, became a garrison for Philistine soldiers. Bethlehem was frequently mentioned by biblical writers (2 Sam. 23:14; 1 Chron. 11:16, and 2 Chron. 11:6).

It should be remembered that, at that time, Israel's only sanctuary was the tabernacle erected by Moses in obedience to the command of Jehovah. Special commemorative feasts were convened each year and all Hebrews, able to attend, were expected at the celebrations. Nevertheless, because priestly indiscretions had aroused the disgust and anger of the nation, Samuel had become God's only spokesman. The revered man of God was an excellent administrator who resided at Ramah, which was near to the house of God at Shiloh. Each year he visited Bethel, Gilgal, and Mizpah. Samuel was the supreme judge in the nation, and all matters of jurisprudence were brought to him at the various centers.

Saul reigned over the nation, but rumors circulated throughout the country that something had gone wrong within the heart and home of the monarch. His deteriorating morality, his tempestuous moods, and his flaming anger were discussed by every family. The respect of the population had been offered upon the altar of the king's ego, and even Samuel was apprehensive concerning the future. Surrounding nations recognized the unrest and anxiety within the country, and their arrogant demands caused dismay among the people of Israel, whose crops were either destroyed or confiscated. Saul made wonderful promises to his people, but did little to fulfill them. Unlike the halcyon days, when the glory of God hovered above the tabernacle, the clouds of mistrust and gloom spread over the land. No one knew or cared what would happen next. It was amid such conditions that David was born. As he developed and understood, at least to a degree, what was taking place around him, it would have been interesting to know what he thought of Israel's spiritual and moral depravity. At that period in history, Samuel was the only man whom God could trust.

When the time arrived for the annual visit of the prophet, each city made special preparation for his hospitality, and those with grievances prepared to state their case before him. At any other time, if Samuel visited a city in Israel, the people became apprehensive and questioned his reason for coming. Had they offended Jehovah? Would the arrival of the prophet be the harbinger of doom? David certainly must have listened when the members of his family discussed these possibilities. The city of Jebus (later to be known as Jerusalem) lay six miles to the north of Bethlehem; beyond were Ramah and Shiloh, and further still, in almost every direction, were ruthless enemies who delighted in tormenting their victims. When the spiritual importance of Shiloh declined (see 1 Sam. 2:13-17), citizens who detested the hypocrisy of the priests preferred to stay away from the sanctuary. The land was very small, and the people were aware of the moral and religious laxity of their generation.

King Saul had become a puppet in the hands of circumstance, while his counselors and associates left much to be desired. Only Samuel remained resolute and unchangeable. He resembled Moses among the decadent tribes of Israel. When he frowned, the nation's sun was eclipsed and shadows of apprehension spread across the land. The survival of the people was considered to be linked with the pleasure of Jehovah. If He were pleased, Israel could expect divine assistance; if He were not, their future was in jeopardy. Samuel was the only means by which Israel could understand God; he reflected the feelings of the Almighty.

The national picture was not attractive, and when the citizens of Bethlehem became aware of Samuel's unexpected visit, "the elders of the town trembled at his coming, and said, Comest thou peaceably? And he said, Peaceably" (1 Sam. 16:4-5). They did not know the prophet was searching for a new king.

Episode 1

THEME: *The Boy From the Field*

SCRIPTURE: 1 Samuel 16:1-13

KEY VERSES:

> And he sent, and brought him in. Now he was ruddy, and withal of a beautiful countenance, and goodly to look to. And the LORD said, Arise, anoint him: for this is he. Then Samuel took the horn of oil, and anointed him in the midst of his brethren: and the spirit of the LORD came upon David from that day forward. So Samuel rose up, and went to Ramah (vv. 12-13).

OUTLINE:
    I. A Boy Sought (Verses 1-11)
   II. A Boy Brought (Verse 12)
  III. A Boy Taught (Verse 13)

Expository Notes on Samuel's Disappointment in Saul

And the LORD said unto Samuel, How long wilt thou mourn for Saul, seeing I have rejected him from reigning over Israel? fill thine horn with oil, and go, I will send thee to Jesse the Bethlehemite: for I have provided me a king among his sons (v. 1).

It is not difficult to understand why the prophet grieved over the rejection of Israel's first king. Samuel had crowned the young farm worker and had rejoiced over his protege's triumphs. He had been as a father to the king, and to see him falling from grace and being rejected by God was the greatest disappointment in the prophet's life. Samuel had momentarily taken his eyes from God to gaze sorrowfully at a rejected monarch. It would have been wiser if he had considered that God's work is always greater than the people who represent it. Empires may rise and fall, but the kingdom of God remains eternally intact. When Moses was buried, Joshua continued his work. When Saul was rejected by God, David was already being prepared to succeed him. Many years later when Judas betrayed the Savior, there were other dedicated disciples ready to embrace the responsibility which the traitor had forgotten. It is never safe to idolize men, for even the best of them have feet of clay!

A BOY SOUGHT

The citizens of Bethlehem were anxious; their elders were evidently worried. News had reached the quiet, rural town that Samuel, the prophet of God, was approaching. Grim apprehension of trouble banished smiles from the faces of the Bethlehemites. The forthcoming visit could mean anything, but the Man of God was possibly, about to denounce something which had displeased the Almighty. Bethlehem was not one of the places included in the annual circuit of the great judge. He had not been invited; why then was he coming? What had they done to offend the Almighty?

Samuel resided at Ramah which was only twelve miles from Bethlehem, and some traveler had probably seen the prophet walking down the dusty road. The fear was groundless. Shiloh, Israel's national place of worship, had lost some of its importance, for the sacred ark of the covenant had been in the home of Abinadab at Kirjath-jearim for several years (see 1 Sam. 6:20—7:2). The once-sacred tabernacle had become an empty shell. Therefore, in order to preserve the religious life of the nation, Samuel was accustomed to offering sacrifices in various centers throughout the land. It was no cause for amazement when God's servant said to the apprehensive elders of the city: "I am come to sacrifice unto the LORD: sanctify yourselves, and come with me to the sacrifice. And he sanctified Jesse and his sons, and called them to the sacrifice" (v. 5). This was done in accordance with the Mosaic commandment (see Exod. 19:14-15). "The word used is *zebach* and means a sacrifice followed by a feast, at which all the elders of the town, and with them Jesse and his elder sons, would be present by the prophet's invitation" (*The Pulpit Commentary*, vol. 4, p. 295).

It should be remembered that the king was only a few miles away within that small country, and any suspicious movement of the prophet would arouse the attention of the melancholy ruler. Even Samuel was aware of the violent reactions which could follow his visit to Bethlehem. The prophet was not untruthful when he explained his intention; this was to be another attempt to maintain and spread the faith of their fathers. The people were therefore commanded to bathe, change their attire, and consider the approaching festivities an opportunity to present themselves before Jehovah.

It was customary to slay the sacrifice and then to roast and eat the flesh. This procedure presented the opportunity for Samuel to rest in the home of one of the town's most celebrated leaders. Most likely, Jesse was considered to be among that elite company. He was probably a wealthy farmer, and the fact that he had eight sons increased his prestige. Their existence was considered to be an evidence of divine blessing upon their father. It is not known to what extent Jesse was aware of Samuel's intentions, but at least he realized that the man of God was about to bestow a great honor upon one of his family. The absence of the youngest son, David, presented no problem, for the lad was thought to be unimportant. He spent most of his time with the sheep on the hills and in any case was considered too young to appreciate the significance of this religious occasion.

And it came to pass, when they were come, that he looked on Eliab, and said, Surely the LORD's anointed is before him. But the LORD said to Samuel, Look not on his countenance, or on the height of his stature; because I have refused him: for the LORD seeth not as man seeth; for man looketh on the outward appearance, but the LORD looketh on the heart. Then. . . . Jesse made seven of his sons to pass before Samuel. And Samuel said unto Jesse, The LORD hath not chosen these (1 Sam. 16:6–10).

It is not difficult to imagine the ancient scene. Silently, speculatively, Samuel watched as a proud father presented his sons. Beginning with the eldest one, whose name was Eliab, Jesse introduced seven of his boys, and there is reason to believe their appearance was magnificent. Work on the farm had developed their physique, their muscles were prominent and their complexion was admirable. They were wonderful specimens of healthy, attractive humanity, a fact which probably explains why the three eldest went to oppose the invading Philistines (see 17:13). Jesse was perplexed and disappointed when he saw the frown on the face of his spiritual leader. His sons had not found favor in the eyes of the prophet; his best was unacceptable. Jesse could not have known the significance of the occasion; only Samuel knew that God was looking for a new king. The nation was aware that Jehovah had called a small child named Samuel, who had grown to be God's official representative in the nation after special training in the sanctuary. Jesse believed that some special commission would be given to one of his sons, but his parental pride suffered irreparable damage when he saw indecision upon the face of the prophet. It was inconceivable to him that his magnificent sons should be rejected for any reason. It became obvious then, as it is now, that God's answer to human need does not always come from expected sources. The Lord loves to surprise His people, and sometimes when our carefully made plans are apparently overlooked or rejected, we fail to see that help is only a prayer away. God has His own special way of supplying our needs. There have been times when He did far more with an insignificant David than He ever could have with a magnificent Eliab!

And Samuel said unto Jesse, Are here all thy children? And he said, There remaineth yet the youngest, and, behold, he keepeth the sheep. And Samuel said unto Jesse, Send and fetch him: for we will not sit down till he come hither. And he sent, and brought him in. Now he was ruddy, and withal of a beautiful countenance, and goodly to look to. And the LORD said, Arise, anoint him: for this is he (vv. 11-12).

A BOY BROUGHT

It is impossible to be conclusive about David's age at this time of his life. Josephus states that he was ten years old, but some commentators believe that he was about fifteen or sixteen. He was considered to be the baby of the family and had no part in deciding policy. He was relegated to the task of being a shepherd boy and spent most of his time caring for his father's flocks. In verse 12, the word for "ruddy" in the ancient Vulgate version of the Scripture is *refus*, and the translation therefore should be: "He had reddish or auburn hair." The lad had bright, attractive eyes, a beautiful complexion, and a pleasing disposition. He was "goodly to look to." It was said of Saul that he was "a choice young man, and a goodly: and there was not among the children of Israel a goodlier person than he; from his shoulders and upwards he was higher than any of the people" (1 Sam. 9:2). David was considerably shorter, and yet, in the sight of God, he was taller! Evidently, Saul was measured from his shoulders; David was measured from his heart.

Someone hastened to the fields in search of David. There was no time to "sanctify" David in preparation for the meeting with the prophet. He came as he was and found favor in the sight of God. It was later said that he was a mighty man of valor (see 1 Sam. 16:18). The entire world is now aware that David became the sweet singer of Israel, and that under his guidance, the nation climbed to heights of magnificence. A teen-age boy could hardly have possessed such talents. He was an attractive, but unprepared child. God saw not what he was, however, but what he would become. Samuel also realized the boy's potential. Wise are they who believe that God can take the insignificant people and perform the impossible with them. See the homily, "God's Love for Little Boys," at the end of this section, p. 25.

> **Then Samuel took the horn of oil, and anointed him in the midst of his brethren: and the spirit of the LORD came upon David from that day forward. So Samuel rose up and went to Ramah (v. 13).**

A BOY TAUGHT

It was customary for travelers to take a supply of water on every journey in a land where it was always scarce. It was commonly carried in a horn or a goatskin. That Samuel had been seen carrying a horn was not a matter of concern either to Saul or his officers. The prophet, however, used it to carry anointing oil, and not water. This action was to indicate that the Holy Spirit would be commissioning a designated servant for an appointed task. David's seven brothers watched as the prophet anointed their baby brother, but maybe thought that this was an act of choosing the boy to become a student in the school which Samuel had possibly established at Ramah (see 1 Sam. 19:18).

There appears to be a break in the continuity of the story of David. Later, one of Saul's servants referred to him as: "*a mighty, valiant man, and a man of war*" (1 Sam. 16:18). This could not have been said of David when he was leading sheep in the wilderness. When the lad appeared before King Saul, he said, "Thy servant kept his father's sheep, and there came a lion, and a bear, and took a lamb out of the flock: And I went out after him, and smote him, and delivered it out of his mouth: and when he arose against me, I caught him by his beard, and smote him, and slew him" (1 Sam. 17:34-35). David's act of bravery could hardly identify him as "a man of war." It, therefore, seems evident that between his anointing with oil and the conquest of Goliath, David's skills had been improved under the supervision of Samuel. During his time of caring for the sheep, the boy carried a harp, and when the animals were peacefully grazing, he learned to play the simple melodies which echoed the symphonies within his soul. The soothing influence of his music calmed the sheep and assured them that David had not left them. Later, that boy became known as the sweet singer of Israel, and his collection of psalms enriched an appreciative world. It may never be known how much David owed to his aged mentor. Samuel taught the boy, and with every passing day, a strange ecstasy filled the soul of the developing student. God was preparing a boy to fill a role beyond human comprehension.

C. Morris wrote an entrancing paragraph in which he said: "The morning of his day this extraordinary man spent not in colleges, nor camps, nor courts, but in following the sheep among the pastures of Bethlehem. There, under the breathings of spring and the blasts of winter; there, in fellowship with fields and flocks and silent stars; there, with the spirit of nature and of God fresh upon him; there in the land of vision, miracle and angels—there it was that his character was formed, a character which afterwards exhibited so rare a combination of simplicity and grandeur, sensibility and power" (*The Pulpit Commentary*, vol. 4, p. 307).

HOMILIES FOR PREACHERS AND TEACHERS

Study No. 1

GOD'S LOVE FOR LITTLE BOYS

Solomon said: "There be four things which are little upon the earth, but they are exceeding wise" (Prov. 30:24). He had become a student of diminutive things and was probably emulating his father's example. David had been taught similar truth by Samuel the prophet. Many people only consider the greatness of God when they compare Him with the vastness of the world He created. To some observers it appears inconceivable that the Creator of heaven and earth should be interested in commonplace things of life. Nevertheless, it is to be expected that God should care for ordinary things for He made so many of them! Those writers who gave the Bible to the world described how the Lord carefully protected small children and prepared them to receive the highest honors He could bestow. It must be admitted that the Maker of the universe was more interested in children than with conquerors!

MOSES . . . The Liberator Who Survived (Exod. 2:19)

The Jewish captives in Egypt were troubled; their expectant mothers were terrified. Pharaoh had commanded the midwives to destroy every male baby, but although those brave women refused to cooperate, fear spread relentlessly through the homes and hearts of the Jews. "And there went a man of the house of Levi, and took to wife a daughter of Levi. And the woman conceived, and bare a son: and when she saw that he was a goodly child, she hid him three months. And when she could not longer hide him, she took for him an ark of bulrushes, and daubed it with slime and with pitch, and put the child therein; and she laid it in the flags by the river's brink. And his sister stood afar off, to wit what would be done to him" (Exod. 2:1-4).

Thus did Moses, the famous liberator of Israel, commence his illustrious career. At first, that baby seemed alone and helpless, but actually he lay safely in the Creator's hand. Momentarily, God seemed to forget the needs of His vast world; His eyes were focused on a condemned infant adrift on a meandering river. The Lord carefully controlled every ripple of that waterway; He aroused yearnings in the heart of a princess preparing to bathe in the Nile. As a result, when that day terminated, the child was resting comfortably in the arms of his adoring mother. "And the child grew, and she brought him unto Pharaoh's daughter, and he became her son. And she called his name Moses: and she said, Because I drew him out of the water" (Exodus 2:10). That delightful princess paid for the child's upkeep, directed his training, and unwittingly became God's handmaiden in preparing Moses for the greatest task ever given by God to man. That small boy was destined to bring Jehovah's benediction to millions of people. God knew exactly what He was doing when He arranged the survival of a helpless baby.

SAMUEL . . . The Listener Who Served (1 Sam. 3:10)

He was only a small lad who was, at times, confused. His wonderful mother visited him every year, but for the rest of the time, he had to be content to live with an old man named Eli. Samuel had heard how he had been given to God, but it is doubtful whether or not he understood the implications of that account. The old priest taught him about the law of God and superintended every facet of his training, but it was always a relief to retire to his bed at night and forget the problems which remained in his mind.

One night, as he lay peacefully in his bed, he was awakened by a strange voice which called his name. "And he ran unto Eli, and said, Here am I; for thou calledst me. And he said, I called not; lie down again. And he went and lay down. . . . Now Samuel did not yet know the LORD, neither was the word of the LORD yet revealed unto him. And the LORD called Samuel again the third time. And he arose and went to Eli, and said, Here am I; for thou didst call me. And Eli perceived that the LORD had called the child" (1 Sam. 3:5-8).

Many years later, when that boy had become an aged man, he was able to reminisce, and say, "God led me all the way." Samuel came to know that that voice belonged to his daily Companion. The more he listened, the more he heard. As his knowledge of God increased, the greater became his desire to serve the Lord. And when his long and illustrious ministry terminated, he resembled Enoch of whom it was said, "Enoch walked with God: and he was not; for God took him" (Gen. 5:24).

DAVID . . . The Lyricist Who Sang (1 Sam. 16:18)

He was just an insignificant lad who spent most of his time caring for sheep and playing a harp. When the flock peacefully grazed, he often sat on a boulder and softly sang his songs. When Samuel visited Bethlehem, the lad was not even invited to meet him until the prophet insisted that he be summoned to appear before him. David was a nonentity; only God knew that he was destined to become the king of Israel. The psalmist expressed his greatest desire when he wrote: "I will bless the LORD at all times: his praise shall continually be in my mouth" (Ps. 34:1). As an acorn grows to become a great tree, so David's talent developed until his sonnets became the joy of his nation and an inspiration to an enchanted world. He was only a boy, but God took "the foolish things of the world to confound the wise; and . . . the weak things of the world to confound the things which are mighty" (1 Cor. 1:27). David was a dreamer who recognized no horizons. His vision encompassed creation and went beyond to see the Lord of heaven and earth. His mind was challenged, his soul inspired. Thus, it was to be expected that from his excited soul arose the melodies which calmed his sheep and fascinated his friends. Jesse's youngest son became God's most trusted servant. It is impossible to overestimate the great things which become possible when a young life is surrendered to Almighty God.

JOASH . . . The Lad Who Studied (2 Kings 11:1-3)

"And when Athaliah the mother of Ahaziah saw that her son was dead, she arose and destroyed all the seed royal. But Jehosheba, the daughter of king Joram, sister of Ahaziah, took Joash the son of Ahaziah and stole him from among the king's sons which were slain; and they hid him, even him and his nurse, in the bedchamber from Athaliah, so that he was not slain" (vv. 1-2). The account of the events which surrounded the life of this little boy is one of the most sensational stories in the Scriptures. The ancient writer was careful to explain that he was hid with his nurse in the house of the LORD *six years* (v. 3). During that time, he never saw another child, he never played in the streets, and his few companions were elderly folk. If the lad ever looked through a window, he probably saw soldiers guarding every entrance to the sanctuary; if he ever asked why this should be, his instructors were very careful in explaining the reign of terror which made his concealment necessary.

Evil stalked as a monster through the land. The people were terrorized, and their only hope of survival lay with the small child for whom his guardians were willing to die. Joash, who was also called Jehoash, was only seven years old when he began to reign. It is written: "And Jehoash did that which was right in the sight of the LORD all his days wherein Jehoiada the priest *instructed him*" (2 Kings 12:2). Those early lessons returned great dividends, for that young man became instrumental in restoring the house of God to its former grandeur. Unfortunately, in his later years, he compromised with his enemies, but as long as he practiced what he had been taught from the Scriptures, he proved continually that "Happy is that people, whose God is the LORD" (Ps. 144:15).

JESUS . . . The Lord Who Saved (Luke 2:25-32)

Perhaps Mary was somewhat embarrassed when an old man's excited outburst of praise echoed through the silence of the sanctuary. Unwelcome noise in any place of worship can be an offense! Joseph, Mary's husband, might also have been a little perturbed, for unexpected events threatened to ruin their visit to Jerusalem. They had brought their Baby to be circumcised, but an old man named Simeon had interfered with their intentions. "And it was revealed unto him by the Holy Ghost, that he should not see death, before he had seen the Lord's Christ. And he came by the Spirit into the temple: and when the parents brought in the child Jesus, to do for him after the custom of the law, then took he him up in his arms, and blessed God, and said, Lord, now lettest thou thy servant depart in peace, according to thy word: for mine eyes have seen thy salvation, which thou hast prepared before the face of all people; a light to lighten the Gentiles, and the glory of thy people Israel."

Other worshipers had paused to watch and listen, and everyone was nonplused when a very old lady, a permanent resident of the temple, "coming in that instant gave thanks likewise unto the Lord, and spake of [the baby Jesus] to all them that looked for redemption in Jerusalem" (v. 38). Many years later, Paul referred to that Child when he wrote to Timothy, saying: "God was manifest in the flesh, justified in the spirit, seen of angels, preached unto the Gentiles, believed on in the world, received up into glory" (1 Tim. 3:16). How can finite minds grasp the infinite and any writer express the inexpressible? Unquestionably, Mary thanked God for her child, but at that moment God was resting in her arms. Yes, God was always interested in children, and if for no other reason, all babies should be considered as gifts sent from heaven.

Episode 2

THEME: *The Boy and His Harp*

SCRIPTURE: 1 Samuel 16:14-23

KEY VERSE:

> Then answered one of the servants, and said, Behold, I have seen a son of Jesse the Bethlehemite, that is cunning in playing, and a mighty valiant man, and a man of war, and prudent in matters, and a comely person, and the LORD is with him (v. 18).

OUTLINE:
I. A Reasonable Request (Verses 14-17)
II. A Revealing Recommendation (Verse 18)
III. A Remarkable Reception (Verses 19-21)
IV. A Royal Resolve (Verses 22-23)

But the Spirit of the LORD departed from Saul, and an evil spirit from the LORD troubled him. And Saul's servants said unto him, Behold, now, an evil spirit from God troubleth thee (vv. 14-15).

Expository Notes on Saul's Despondency

This concise and very deliberate statement reflects the fact that, among ancient people, any type of mental illness was attributed to the work of evil spirits. This belief is evident throughout the New Testament era, and it survives today in certain parts of the world. I was informed in New Guinea that the native people believed that the "Great Spirit" lived above their villages and that sacrifices would prevent his sending catastrophic storms upon the communities. Identical beliefs survive in the Middle East, where people paint parts of their homes *blue*, believing this color to be a protection against evil spirits. Nevertheless, problems arise from the fact that in Saul's case, it was said: "an evil spirit *from the LORD* troubled him." It is difficult to believe that anything evil emanates from God. It must, therefore, be concluded that this was made possible by the *permissive* will of God. God *allowed* this to happen because Saul had forfeited his right to rule over Israel. The desperate monarch had opened his mind to evil, and as a result,

God permitted certain catastrophes to occur in order to preserve an entire nation.

Josephus, the Jewish historian, wrote an interesting summation of those events. "The Divine Power departed from Saul and removed to David, who, upon this removal of the Divine Power to him, began to prophesy; but as for Saul, some strange and demoniacal disorders came upon him, and brought upon him such suffocations as were ready to choke him; for which the physicians could find no other remedy but this, That if any person could charm those passions by singing, and playing upon the harp, they advised them to inquire for such a one, and to observe when those demons came upon him and disturbed him, and to take care that such a person might stand over him, and play upon the harp, and recite hymns to him." (Josephus, *The Antiquities of the Jews*. Book 6, Chap. 8, Paragraph 2).

A REASONABLE REQUEST

And Saul's servants said unto him, Behold now, an evil spirit from God troubleth thee. Let our LORD now command thy servants, which are before thee, to seek out a man, who is a cunning player on an harp: and it shall come to pass, when the evil spirit from God is upon thee, that he shall play with his hand, and thou shalt be well. And Saul said unto his servants, Provide me now a man that can play well, and bring him to me (vv. 15-17).

Expository Notes on the Strange Faith of the Ancient People

King Saul had become a piece of human wreckage and was only a shadow of his former self. The bright, attractive faith of earlier days had vanished. His unclouded vision of the majesty of God was only a memory. He had become churlish, suspicious, envious, jealous, moody, irritable, and very dangerous. The withdrawal of God's Spirit had left the monarch a bewildered, disillusioned ruler who hardly believed in himself. His melancholy moods and fanatical behavior brought increasing apprehension to his court, and even his closest friends feared for his future.

When the king was absent, the servants considered his problem and evidently discussed how he could be helped. They were convinced that Jehovah had sent the evil spirit. But in spite of that ominous supposition, they believed that there existed a way by which the anger of God could be evaded. They had faith that God's judgments were always overshadowed by His mercy. If someone played softly upon the strings of a harp, the music would soothe the tortured mind of the king. God could be influenced, and in some mysterious way, His anger would disappear.

They probably waited until Saul was approachable, and to their relief, the monarch listened to their suggestion. It might have been a moment of great peril to remind the king that he had been forsaken by Jehovah; he could have ordered the execution of men who were endeavoring to help him. Carefully, gently, they suggested how he could be helped and emphasized that they desired the return of his health. Saul listened, and as tranquillity and hope returned to his soul, he said: "Provide me now a man that can play well, and bring him to me."

A REVEALING RECOMMENDATION

Then answered one of the servants, and said, Behold, I have seen a son of Jesse the Bethlehemite, that is cunning in playing, and a mighty valiant man, and a man of war, and prudent in matters, and a comely person, and the LORD is with him (v. 18).

Expository Notes on the Servant's Opinion of David

Saul's servant was an expert judge of character unequaled in the art of condensing facts. Never did any man say so much with so few words. He described in about fifteen seconds the secret of David's success. He knew exactly what he wanted to say and said it in the shortest possible time. That unknown reporter set an example for all long-winded preachers! He seemed to have obeyed an old precept which said: "If you have anything to say, say it; if you have nothing to say, remain silent." His statement: "Behold, I have seen a son of Jesse the Bethlehemite," suggested that somewhere in the fields of Bethlehem, he had paused to watch and listen to the young minstrel and had never forgotten the charm of those moments. It was impossible to forget when God desired him to remember what he had heard and seen. That servant was a lowly pawn on the chessboard of history; God directed his movements. (See the homily, "The Type of Man God Uses," p. 35.)

A REMARKABLE RECEPTION

Wherefore Saul sent messengers unto Jesse, and said, Send me David thy son, which is with the sheep. And Jesse took an ass laden with bread, and a bottle of wine, and a kid, and sent them by David his son unto Saul. And David came to Saul, and stood before him: and he loved him greatly; and he became his armorbearer (vv. 19-21).

Expository Notes on Saul's Desire for David

The throne room was very silent; the king and his captains were expecting the lad from Bethlehem. The monarch was, to say the least, fascinated; his friends were hopeful. A servant entered to announce: "Master, he is here. He brought presents from his father; bread, wine, and a kid from the flock. These I have accepted in your name, and they are outside waiting for you." All eyes were focused on the teen-age boy who shyly, timidly, walked toward Saul. He carried his harp and wondered what this was all about. He was exceedingly beautiful; his speech was gentle and attractive; he brought with him a breath of the countryside. More than likely, the king remembered how he also had worked in the fields. Saul looked at the boy and liked what he saw. David was different from all the others present. He had no uniform, no weapon of war, no pretense, no sophistication. He did not pretend to be what he was not. He was clean, good, and wholesome; the longer Saul gazed at the boy, the more he smiled. He probably felt better at that moment than he had in days or weeks. Somehow, the burdens evaporated, the clouds parted, and ecstasy began filling the soul of the troubled ruler. He liked the young Bethlehemite, and when David gave an exhibition of his musical ability, Saul smiled with the result that every man present breathed a sigh of relief. The dawn of a new day was banishing the gloom of the night they had endured. When the king asked David to work for him, the lad must have surely smiled and said, "Yes, Sir!" "And he became his armorbearer."

Thus did God prepare his young servant for a future role in Israel. This kind of thing had happened earlier in the history of the Hebrew people. When Moses was adopted by a princess in Egypt, he was introduced to the life and characteristics of the royal court. He began to learn all kinds of military secrets, and long afterward, his acquired skills were of invaluable assistance as he led Israel against the armies of their enemies.

It was essential that a shepherd boy should know something of the higher counsels of the nation, and since he was an apt student, his proximity to Saul and the counselors was of incalculable worth. God was preparing His servant for the coming rigors of later years. When Paul contemplated such things centuries later, he wrote: "And we know that all things work together for good to them that love God, to them who are the called according to his purpose" (Rom. 8:28).

A ROYAL RESOLVE

And Saul sent to Jesse, saying, Let David, I pray thee, stand before me; for he hath found favor in my sight. And it came to pass, when the evil spirit from God was upon Saul, that David took an harp, and played with his hand: so Saul was refreshed, and was well, and the evil spirit departed from him (vv. 22-23).

Expository Notes on David's Influence on Saul

It is remarkable how David's haunting melodies charmed his royal listener and the way that smiles replaced frowns on the monarch's face. Matthew Henry, the famous commentator, wrote: "Music cannot work upon the devil, but it may shut up the passages by which he has access to the mind" (*Matthew Henry's Commentary*, vol. 2, p. 369). Although Saul eventually hated David, he found no other person could help him as did the young musician. It should be recognized that, although great forces of evil may be arrayed against the people of God, entrance into the mind of individuals is only possible when men and women open the doors of their intellect. That God permitted David's artistry to dispel Saul's gloom suggests that help is seldom beyond the reach of men and women. There is reason to believe that God never ceases to love people. He may remove them from office when they are no longer fit for service, but His love is eternal. It is worthy of attention that during the years which followed, the Lord was extremely patient with the petulant king, but unfortunately, Saul was so self-centered and sinful that God could do nothing for him. The story and fate of Saul should be a constant warning to people who emulate his example.

HOMILIES FOR PREACHERS AND TEACHERS

Study No. 2

THE TYPE OF MAN GOD USES

King Saul was very excited when he instructed his servants, "Provide me now a man that can play well, and bring him to me" (1 Sam. 16:17). The monarch had suffered long periods of acute depression when the royal physicians had failed to dispel fear from his mind. Now, after he heard advice from trusted servants, a light seemed to appear at the end of the tunnel! Their counsel had been good, their sincerity unquestionable. He urgently needed a musician to produce soothing music. Surely, somewhere in Israel, such a man could be found.

> **Then answered one of the servants, and said, Behold, I have seen a son of Jesse the Bethlehemite, that is cunning in playing, and a mighty valiant man, and a man of war, and prudent in matters, and a comely person, and the LORD is with him"** (1 Sam. 16:18).

When that servant said, "I have seen a son of Jesse", he indicated that he possessed first-hand knowledge of the subject at hand. Perhaps, he had paused on a journey through the fields of Bethlehem to watch and listen to the young harpist and had learned of the boy's ability to protect flocks. Evidently, David had rescued a sheep from a lion and a bear, and such exploits could not have been unknown among the inhabitants of Bethlehem. Neighbors talked about the son of Jesse so that the lad had become a local hero. Saul's servant had surely heard their opinions concerning the notorious shepherd boy, and a deep impression had evidently been made upon the man's mind. His testimony may be divided into five categories: He said David was *clever, courageous, commendable, conspicuous,* and *consecrated.* All preachers should find help in the following suggestions.

DAVID WAS CLEVER

The unknown servant described David as being "cunning in playing." The word "cunning" is provocatively attractive. The five Hebrew words translated "cunning" in the Old Testament describe: "an artist, faithful and trustworthy in his art" (Gen. 25:27; Exod. 28:6); "to understand or be wise" (1 Kings 7:14); "to think, devise, or be skillful and ingenious in any work" (Isa. 3:3); "to know or be knowledgeable" (1 Sam. 16:18; Dan. 1:4). (William Wilson, *New Wilson's Old Testament Word Studies,* p. 105.)

It must therefore be recognized that the Old Testament word did not mean excellence in deception. It described the quality of being wise, capable, resourceful in every facet of conduct. The term "cunning" now means an ability to entice and trap birds and animals. During his many hours in the wilderness, David might have had a similar opportunity to snare animals and could have been described as "cunning." The boy also had opportunity to practice his musical talents in the sanctuary at Shiloh, where, most likely he took part in the devotional services. His skills had been refined and perfected under the supervision of Samuel, and all of his acquired knowledge was afterward available to God.

DAVID WAS COURAGEOUS

He was described as "a mighty valiant man, and a man of war." This statement presents problems, for David was only a youth. It was true that he had overcome marauding animals, but that would hardly qualify him to be a "man of war." Furthermore, if the lad had become famous for some outstanding conquest of an enemy, that fact would have been known to Saul. Some theologians express the belief that David might have assisted this royal servant in some act of bravery and had convinced his companion that he had the *makings* of a man of war! It is difficult to be conclusive in interpreting this passage of Scripture. Nevertheless, for a teen-age boy to seize the beard of an angry lion indicates that he was fearless.

Another statement should be considered with this verse. When David addressed King Saul concerning former exploits, he said: "Thy servant slew both the lion and the bear: and this uncircumcised Philistine shall be as one of them, seeing he hath defied the armies of the living God. David said moreover, The LORD that delivered me out of the paw of the lion, and out of the paw of the bear, he will deliver me out of the hand of this Philistine" (1 Sam. 17:36-37). It was evident, even at that part of his life, that *faith in God* was the strongest weapon in David's arsenal. He believed that with God, all things were possible.

DAVID WAS COMMENDABLE

David was described as being "prudent in matters." The marginal reading (AV) corrects the translation by stating that it meant "prudency, or carefulness in speech." As a lad he spoke when he was addressed; he never claimed nor thought himself to be wise. He was dignified in his demeanor and thoughtful in his approach to every matter under consideration so that whatever he said was worth hearing. William Wilson states in his book *New Wilson's Old Testament Word Studies* (p. 332), that the Hebrew word translated "prudent" means "to consider; to balance; to weigh things in the mind; to form a judgment; to have judgment and discretion." The boy's manners were excellent, and Samuel was possibly responsible for this commendable feature in the lad's life. Young men who believe and act as if they are omniscient are irritating; adolescents who have no respect for their peers are an embarrassment to their parents. It was said of Jesus: "And he went down with them, and came to Nazareth, *and was subject unto them*: . . . And Jesus increased in wisdom and stature, and in favor with God and man" (Luke 2:51-52). Even Jesus had much to learn as a child, and there is no record that He ever contradicted or criticized His parents. A beautiful, well-mannered child is always attractive.

DAVID WAS COMELY

The Old Testament use of the word "comely" is exceptionally interesting. William Wilson, an authority on ancient Hebrew words, states its meanings as an "honor, majesty, beauty, splendor," or anything which "commanded reverence or praise." It was used to express "beauty; glowing; vigor and grace of form or figure of the body" (*New Wilson's Old Testament Word Studies*, p. 86). David was evidently a very beautiful young man. His red, or auburn hair contrasted strangely with the dark hair and sallow complexion of the Eastern people. His appearance and eyes commanded attention so that the maidens of Israel considered David to be exceedingly attractive. His bright eyes revealed that he was a visionary, and the psalms, which he subsequently wrote, indicated that the lad from the fields considered the marvelous things found in God's world. David wrote: "The heavens declare the glory of God; and the firmament sheweth his handywork. Day unto day uttereth speech, and night unto night sheweth knowledge. There is no speech nor language, where their voice is not heard" (Ps. 19:1-3). His fresh, cheerful countenance suggested a dawn in contrast to the perpetual gloom of Saul's depression. His presence was exhilarating, his voice and harp produced exquisite music, and his general demeanor was a benediction in a palace where criticism, fear, and suspicion had banished happiness.

DAVID WAS CONSECRATED

"And the LORD is with him." This was the most important facet of the servant's recommendation of David. Whether or not that conclusion was reached after a brief encounter with the shepherd boy, or whether it was formed after hearing the opinions of the citizens, we may never know. Saul's servant was convinced that David was God's man! The boy from Bethlehem was not only attractive, courageous, polite, and well-spoken; above all else he was good, reverent, and completely devoted to God. This was evident when he said to Goliath: "This day will the LORD deliver thee into mine hand . . . that all the earth may know that there is a God in Israel" (1 Sam. 17:46).

When the LORD spoke to Samuel about Eliab, the eldest son of Jesse, He said: "Look not on his countenance, or on the height of his stature; because I have refused him: for the LORD seeth not as man seeth; for man looketh on the outward appearance, but the LORD looketh on the heart" (1 Sam. 16:7). This passage explains how David found favor in the sight of God. The lad was beautiful without *and within.* His eyes reflected the serenity of his soul; his conduct revealed the purity of his thinking. David was a boy who pleased the Almighty, and it was no cause for amazement when Jehovah made him the king of Israel. The Lord never changes His methods. His servants need clean hands and hearts. Even the greatest of intellectual acquisitions are futile unless they are inspired by the Spirit of God. David recognized these facts and later in his life wrote: "Who shall ascend into the hill of the LORD? or who shall stand in his holy place? He that hath clean hands, and a pure heart; who hath not lifted up his soul unto vanity, nor sworn deceitfully. He shall receive the blessing from the LORD, and righteousness from the God of his salvation" (Ps. 24:3-5).

Episode 3

THEME: *A Boy and His Sling*

SCRIPTURE: 1 Samuel 17:1-58

KEY VERSES:

> Then said David to the Philistine, Thou comest to me with a sword, and with a spear, and with a shield: but I come to thee in the name of the LORD of hosts, the God of the armies of Israel, whom thou hast defied. This day will the LORD deliver thee into mine hand; and I will smite thee, and take thine head from thee; and I will give the carcases of the hosts of the Philistines this day unto the fowls of the air, and to the wild beasts of the earth; that all the earth may know that there is a God in Israel (vv. 45-46).

OUTLINE:
   I.   An Intriguing Explanation (Verses 1-12 and 16)
   II. An Insulting Enemy (Verses 4-11)
   III. An Important Errand (Verses 13-22)
   IV. An Inspired Encounter (Verses 40-51)
   V.   An Interesting Enquiry (Verses 52-58)

Expository Notes on Some Confusing Problems

Now the Philistines gathered together their armies to battle, and were gathered together at Shochoh, which belongeth to Judah, and pitched between Shochoh and Azekah, in Ephes-dammim. And Saul and the men of Israel were gathered together, and pitched by the valley of Elah, and set the battle in array against the Philistines. And the Philistines stood on a mountain on the one side, and Israel stood on a mountain on the other side: and there was a valley between them. And there went out a champion out of the camp of the Philistines, named Goliath, of Gath, whose height was six cubits and a span. . . . And the Philistine drew near morning and evening, and presented himself forty days (vv. 1-4 and 16).

The story of David's conquest of Goliath is one of the most interesting accounts ever told. Nevertheless, a careful examination of its absorbing details suggests questions of great importance. At first glance, certain discrepancies become obvious, and all who believe in the inspiration of the Scriptures become concerned with the statements of the ancient writer.

AN INTRIGUING EXPLANATION

It should never be forgotten that the description of David's encounter with the Philistine giant was written many years after the event took place. The writer, in retrospect, was describing events which, to some of the earliest readers, were a lifetime away! Some theologians believe that his *order of events* became confused. Vital questions may be asked concerning three issues and may be summarized under the following headings: (1) A Delayed Attack, (2) A Disturbing Astonishment, and (3) A Definite Announcement.

A Delayed Attack

The historian stated that Goliath continued his challenge to the men of Israel for forty days. The question must be asked, "Why did the opposing armies remain inactive for such a long time?" Neither the Philistines nor the Hebrews had regular, full-time armies; their soldiers were drawn from citizens who spontaneously left their homes and occupations to respond to their ruler's call for volunteers. Within our modern world, regular armies are maintained continually, and their food and wages are supplied by the government. This standing army was not customary in ancient times. Men worked in their fields and only abandoned their daily routine when peril threatened their country. The fact that Goliath taunted Israel for forty days resulted in great hardship for depleted families whose sons and laborers had been absent for nearly six weeks. It was to be expected, therefore, that Jesse should be apprehensive concerning his three sons (see vv. 17-18).

During the last generation, Palestine, which is now called Israel, has completely changed. The developing policies of Israel's agricultural efforts have altered the countryside. The desert has literally blossomed as the rose, and in many areas, what once was, no longer exists. It becomes absorbingly interesting to read the books of Claude Reignier Conder, the famous surveyor, archaeologist, and author, if for no other reason than to learn of this dramatic transformation. He described Palestine as he saw it in the nineteenth century and explained why Goliath taunted Israel for forty days (see the notes in the section, "An Important Errand," p. 42.)

A Disturbing Astonishment

The ancient writer stated that David was instrumental in assisting Saul when "the evil spirit from the Lord" troubled the melancholy monarch. At that time Saul made the young harpist "his armor-bearer" (see 1 Sam. 16:14, 21). Yet, after the conquest of Goliath, neither the king nor Abner, the captain of the host, knew the new hero. "And when Saul saw David go forth against the Philistine, he said unto Abner, the captain of the host, Abner, whose son is this youth? And Abner said, As thy soul liveth, O king, I cannot tell" (1 Sam. 17:55). This might suggest that neither of the two men had seen David previously. On the other hand, if several years had elapsed since David played before the king, he might have grown a beard. This could explain the inability of Saul and Abner to recognize the daring young fellow who accepted the Philistine's challenge.

Dr. W. M. Thomson in his book, *The Land and the Book*, comments: "We do not know how long a period intervened between the return of David to his father's house, and his appearance before the king on the morning of the duel with Goliath. If it were two or three years, it is possible that David had, in the meanwhile, suddenly shot up from boyhood to youth, tall and robust, and his personal appearance might have so changed as to bear little resemblance to the ruddy lad who played skillfully on the harp. It is a fact that lads of this country, particularly of the higher classes, are often very fair, full and handsome until about fourteen years of age. During the next two or three years, a surprising change takes place. They not only spring into full-grown manhood as if by magic, but all their former beauty disappears; their complexion becomes dark, their features harsh and angular, and the whole expression of countenance, stern and even disagreeable. I have often been accosted by such persons, formerly intimate acquaintances, but who had suddenly grown entirely out of my knowledge, nor could I, without difficulty, recognize them. David had become a shepherd after leaving the king's palace, an occupation which of all others would most rapidly change his fair complexion into a dirty bronze. He appeared before Saul in his shepherd's attire, not in the dress of a courtier in the king's palace, and he *may*, therefore, not have been recognized."

A Definite Announcement

"And David took the head of the Philistine, and brought it to Jerusalem; but he put his armor in his tent" (1 Sam. 17:54). This statement offers persuasive evidence that the ancient writer was describing events which were not placed in chronological order. At the time of his slaying of Goliath, David had no tent, except perhaps for a small covering which he may have erected to supply shade from the sun. He did not go to Jerusalem until many years later when a captain crawled through a tunnel to make possible the capture of the Jebusite stronghold (see 2 Sam. 5:6-9).

AN INSULTING ENEMY

And there went out a champion out of the camp of the Philistines, named Goliath of Gath, whose height was six cubits and a span. And he had an helmet of brass upon his head, and he was armed with a coat of mail; and the weight of the coat was five thousand shekels of brass. And he had greaves of brass upon his legs, and a target of brass between his

shoulders. And the staff of his spear was like a weaver's beam; and his spear's head weighed six hundred shekels of iron: and one bearing a shield went before him. And he stood and cried unto the armies of Israel, and said unto them, Why are ye come out to set your battle in array? Am not I a Philistine, and ye servants to Saul? Choose you a man for you, and let him come down to me. If he be able to fight with me, and to kill me, then will we be your servants: but if I prevail against him, and kill him, then shall ye be our servants, and serve us. And the Philistine said, I defy the armies of Israel this day; give me a man, that we may fight together. When Saul and all Israel heard those words of the Philistine, they were dismayed, and greatly afraid (vv. 4-11).

The fear of the Israelites was justified, for Goliath was of immense proportions. "Whose height was six cubits and a span" (v. 4). "The word *cubit* signifies the length from the *cubitus*, the elbow, to the top of the middle finger, a distance generally measured at eighteen inches. The span, ordinarily nine inches, is the distance from the top of the middle finger to the end of the thumb when they are extended as far as they can reach. The height of this Philistine would then be nine feet, nine inches, which is a tremendous height for a man." (Adam Clarke, *The Bethany Parallel Commentary on the Old Testament*, p. 542.)

It was said that Goliath's suit of armor weighed five thousand shekels of brass. This would mean copper, for brass was unknown at that time. It is estimated that a shekel was equal to two-thirds of an ounce and therefore the corselet, or literally the "shirt of scales", would weigh at least two hundred pounds—a huge load for any man to carry. The description of his other equipment is truly awe-inspiring, and through the youthful eyes of the shepherd boy, Goliath probably appeared to be a man-mountain.

When David had delivered the parcels of food to his brothers and the captain of their brigade, he suddenly became aware of the thunderous voice of the giant echoing across the valley. He was both interested and astounded to hear the blasphemous words of the heathen, but when he saw Saul's men fleeing in terror, his youthful soul was stirred and dismayed. He asked questions concerning the situation, an action that annoyed his brothers. Their rebuke brought forth David's response: "What have I now done? Is there not a cause?" (v. 29). Doubtless, the rewards offered by Saul aroused David's interest, but the lad was more concerned with the apparent helplessness of Israel. David was able to see the strength and presence of the God who made the mountains; Goliath only saw his own importance to the cause of the Philistine army. Had he been a wiser man, he would have known that a small lad with God could accomplish more than ten thousand armies without Him.

AN IMPORTANT ERRAND

And Jesse said unto David his son, Take now for thy brethren an ephah of this parched corn, and these ten loaves, and run to the camp to thy brethren; And carry these ten cheeses unto the captain of their thousand, and look how thy brethren fare, and take their pledge. Now Saul, and they, and all the man of Israel, were in the valley of Elah, fighting with the Philistines. And David rose up early in the morning, and left the sheep with a keeper, and took, and went, as Jesse had commanded him; and he came to the trench, as the host was going forth to the fight, and shouted for the battle. For Israel and the Philistines had put the battle in array, army against army. And David left his carriage in the hand of the keeper of the carriage, and ran into the army, and came and saluted his brethren (vv. 17-22).

Jesse was worried because his three eldest boys had been absent from the farm for six weeks; their absence was becoming a burden. Furthermore, because so many laborers had responded to Saul's appeal for help, it was impossible to hire additional workmen. He also was concerned for the welfare of his family. The possibility existed that his sons might never return to their home. When the battle commenced, there would be many casualties and his sons might be slain. The uncertainty of the future was more than the anxious parent could bear, and his charge to David was to be expected. The shepherd boy was given a carriage and driver, and the journey to the battle area commenced.

During the middle of the nineteenth century, Claude Reignier Conder, the famous explorer, surveyor, and archaeologist camped near the site of the battle and to say the least, his reports are exceedingly interesting. He wrote: "It is interesting to observe that the scene of David's victory over Goliath is distant only eight miles from the cave at *Aid el Ma*. It was in the valley of Elah, between Shochoh and Azekah, that the Philistines encamped in 'Ephes Dammim,' or 'the Boundary of Blood.' Saul, coming down by the highway from the land of Benjamin, encamped by the valley (see 1 Sam. 17:2), on one of the low hills, and between the two hosts was the *Gai* or *'ravine.'* Two points require to be made clear as to the episode of David's battle with Goliath; one was the meaning of the expression *Gai* or *'ravine'*; the other was the source from which David took the 'smooth stones'. A visit to the spot explains both. In the middle of the broad open valley we found a deep trench with vertical sides, impassable except at certain places—a valley in a valley, and a natural barrier between the two hosts. The sides and bed of this trench were strewn with rounded, waterworn pebbles, which would have been well fitted to David's sling.

"Here, then, we may picture to ourselves the two hosts, covering the low rocky hills opposite to each other, and half hidden among the lentisk bushes; between them was the rich expanse of ripening barley and the red banks of the torrent with its white shingly bed. Behind all were the distant, blue hill-walls, whence Saul had just come down. The mail clad champion advanced from the west, through the low corn, with his mighty lance perhaps tufted with feathers, his brazen helmet shining in the sun. From the east, a ruddy boy in his white shirt and sandals, armed with a goat's hair sling, came down to the brook, and according to the poetic fancy of the rabbis, the pebbles were given voices, and cried, 'By us shalt thou overcome the giant.' The champion fell from an unseen cause, and the wild Philistines fled to the mouth of the valley, where Gath stood towering on its white chalk cliff, a frontier fortress, the key to the high road leading to the corn lands of Judah, and to the vineyards of Hebron." (Conder, *Tenting in Palestine*, vol. 2, pp. 159-161).

With the aid of this observation, we begin to understand the strange inactivity of the two armies over a long period of time. Between the two hosts was a broad valley, and in the middle of this was a trench impassable except at certain places. Had either army attacked, the defenders would have had a definite advantage, for they would have been shooting down at enemies trying to scale very difficult cliffs. This fact led to a stalemate and explains why the Philistines were willing to risk their future on the efforts of a single combatant.

AN INSPIRED ENCOUNTER

The late F. B. Meyer, in his wonderful book, *Great Verses Through the Bible* referred to the armies of the living God as follows: "This made all the difference between David and the rest of the camp. To Saul and his soldiers, God was an absentee—a name, but little else. They believed He had done great things for His people in the past, and that at some future time, in the days of the Messiah, He might be expected to do great things again. But no one thought of Him as being *present*. Keenly sensitive to the defiance of the Philistine, and grieved by the apathy of the people, David, on the other hand, knew that God was *alive*. He had lived alone with Him in the solitude of the hills, until God had become one of greatest realities of his young existence. As the lad went to and fro among the armed warriors, he was sublimely conscious of the presence of the living God amid the clang of the camp."

When Saul entertained fears regarding the ability of the young man to oppose Goliath, David rehearsed what had taken place on the hills when, in protecting sheep, he had slain both the lion and the bear. Unashamedly, he confessed that he owed his victories to the presence and power of God. Rejecting the cumbersome armor of Saul, David ran down into the valley, chose some rounded pebbles suitable for his sling, and then confidently went to meet his enemy. Responding to the insults of Goliath, David said: "Thou comest to me with a sword and with a spear, and with a shield: but I come to thee in the name of the LORD of Hosts, the God of the armies of

Israel, whom thou hast defied. This day will the LORD deliver thee into mine hand . . . that all the earth may know that there is a God in Israel. And all this assembly shall know that the LORD saveth not with sword and spear: for the battle is the LORD's, and he will give you into our hands" (vv. 45-47).

David's wisdom is seen in three areas. (1) *He rejected Saul's armor.* A suit of armor would have hindered movement. David preferred to depend upon the faithfulness of God. (2) *He chose FIVE stones!* He recognized that although he could depend upon Jehovah, he could not always depend upon himself. If his first shot failed to reach its objective, he had four spare pebbles in his shepherd's bag. It was wise not to be overconfident. (3) *He desired only that God should be glorified.* He wished that all the earth should be aware of God's presence in Israel and especially that *this* assembly should be revived in its knowledge of the reliability of Jehovah. Smaller men might have enjoyed the prospect of becoming a national hero.

AN INTERESTING ENQUIRY

> **And when Saul saw David go forth against the Philistine, he said unto Abner, the captain of the host, Abner, whose son is this youth? And Abner said, As thy soul liveth, O king, I cannot tell. And the king said, Inquire thou whose son the stripling is. And as David returned from the slaughter of the Philistine. . . . Saul said to him, Whose son art thou, thou young man? And David answered, I am the son of thy servant Jesse the Bethlehemite (vv. 55-58).**

Mention has already been made of Saul's inability to recognize David. Apparently, neither he nor Abner had knowledge of the identity of the youthful warrior. Dr. R. Payne Smith, the former Dean of Canterbury, points out that the Hebrew word translated "stripling" means "a young man fully grown, and arrived at the age to marry" (*The Pulpit Commentary*, vol. 4, p. 325). Whether or not this was actually Saul's first encounter with David has been a matter of interest to theologians in all ages. Most teachers agree that David's beard provided sufficient disguise that neither Saul nor Abner could recognize the youthful harpist who might have performed earlier in the royal court.

HOMILIES FOR PASTORS AND TEACHERS

Study No. 3

DAVID . . . and His Habit of Slaying Giants

The scene was awe-inspiring; the man-mountain had appeared again from the tents of the Philistines. He sneered and asked: "Why are ye come out to set your battle in array? Am not I a Philistine, and ye servants to Saul? Choose you a man for you, and let him come down to me. If he be able to fight with me, and to kill me, then will we be your servants: but if I prevail against him, and kill him, then shall ye be our servants, and serve us. . . . I defy the armies of Israel this day" (1 Sam. 17:8-10). As David heard the challenge, he looked expectantly toward his countrymen. Surely this blasphemous heathen should be taught a lesson. *What! Is there no man willing to fight him? Then I will.* It was unbelievable; even Israel stood aghast. A mere boy had performed the impossible. They surged forward to reap the reward of his deed. They overtook and slew many Philistines, but Goliath had strange relatives who lived to fight another day.

THE GIANT OF REGAL FURY (1 Sam. 18:11)

Saul was desperately angry; hidden fires smoldered within his breast. This upstart had bewitched and stolen the hearts of Israel. What were they singing? "Saul hath slain his thousands, and David his ten thousands" (18:7). Bah! Jealousy made him furious, his hands clenched at his sides. David was a menace. The boy's smiles were maddening. His music thrilled the soul, but everything was wrong. Suddenly, volcanic fires erupted in Saul's soul. "And Saul cast the javelin; for he said, I will smite David even to the wall with it. . . . And David behaved himself wisely in all his ways; and the LORD was with him" (18:11-14). Saul repeatedly revealed the same inexcusable ferocity of purpose, but on each occasion David overcame bitterness with kindness. Then another giant came forward.

THE GIANT OF PERSONAL REVENGE (1 Sam. 24:4)

Poor David had been driven from all his friends. He was homeless and went in danger of his life, but God smiled upon the fugitive. The camp of Saul was wrapped in slumber, for the men, weary with the pursuits of the day, had lain down to rest. Even the sentries slept at their posts. David smiled in the shadows. A little care and his enemy would be at his mercy. David calmly watched the camp and deliberately planned his approach to the royal tent. Then he began the most perilous journey of his career. It was done; his enemy lay at his feet. David heard the suggestions of evil: "Smite him now and remove your enemy. Israel will acclaim your deed. The LORD has delivered him into your hands. This is the chance of a lifetime. Seize it." The youthful captain shook his head. King Saul was the Lord's anointed. David silently severed a piece of the sleeper's skirt and then disappeared into the blackness of the night. He had conquered another giant. The reactions in the realm of evil were very considerable; this David was a great warrior. Was there another volunteer to challenge this Israelite? Certainly, a giant was already on his feet.

THE GIANT OF TORMENTING GUILT (2 Sam. 12:13)

He was clever—ruthlessly clever. He avoided open conflict with the dynamic fighter, for he knew David had to be trapped. Were there openings in the royal armor? Were there any weak spots in the king's rugged defenses? Could any dart pierce to the heart of the invincible? What about a little bewitching beauty? What about an illegitimate affection? Could this impregnable human citadel be destroyed by fire—the fire of unholy passion kindled by a spark of lust? It was worth trying.

The giant planned his campaign, and David was soon fighting for his life. Apollyon had hands of toughened steel, and those hands were choking him. His eyes blurred, his heart was bursting. The devil of lust had ruined his fighting qualities. Adultery, villainy, and murder had filled the music of his soul with vibrating discords. David reeled back under the pressure of the enemy and was haunted by the memory of his disgraceful conduct. A man lay in his grave; the fair name of a beautiful wife had been eternally stained; he himself was guilty before God. And Giant Guilt sneered at his helpless victim. It was the monster's first mistake, for it gave David an opportunity to get on his knees. The guilty man prayed (Psalm 51), and the oppressor had the shock of his life. The battle continued for a long time, but the end was no longer in doubt. Ultimately, the giant was overcome. He had been so near to triumph, but had thrown away his chances of victory. David never gave him another opportunity, for he knew those giants and liked them as much as they liked him. (Homily reprinted from the author's book, *Bible Treasures*, pp. 25-26.)

Episode 4

THEME: *David's Increasing Influence In Israel*

SCRIPTURE: 1 Samuel 18

KEY VERSE:

> And David behaved himself wisely in all his ways; and the LORD was with him (v. 14).

OUTLINE:
      I.   David's Friend (Verses 1-4)
     II. David's Foe (Verses 5-13 and 22-25)
   III. David's Fame (Verses 7, 16 and 30)

This is the unfolding of an early chapter in the experiences of the young shepherd from Bethlehem. It quickly became evident that "the LORD was with him" (see vv. 12, 14 and 28). Here are described three unmistakable facts, and since they reappear at intervals throughout David's story, it might prove to be beneficial to consider them in detail. It has often been claimed that every ominous cloud has a silver lining and that even the darkest night leads to a dawn. A terrible catastrophe threatened to overwhelm the young Bethlehemite, but God prepared two very special people to help him through the crisis. David's experiences provide a perfect example of the truth written by Paul. "There hath no temptation taken you but such as is common to man: but God is faithful, who will not suffer you to be tempted above that ye are able; but will with the temptation also make a way to escape, that ye may be able to bear it" (1 Cor. 10:13).

DAVID'S FRIEND

And it came to pass, when he had made an end of speaking unto Saul, that the soul of Jonathan was knit with the soul of David, and Jonathan loved him as his own soul. . . . And Jonathan and David made a covenant because he loved him as his own soul. And Jonathan stripped himself of the robe that was upon him, and gave it to David, and his garments, even to his sword, and to his bow, and to his girdle (vv. 1-4).

Expository Notes on Jonathan's Love for David

This delightful story describes the love of a charming young prince for a lad from the fields of Bethlehem. Within a palace where hatred, suspicion, and other forms of evil were commonplace, the affection which united those young men shone as a beacon on a very dark night. It was so spontaneous and exciting; it surpassed anything previously known in the history of man.

It was said of Abraham that he became the friend of God (see 2 Chron. 20:7 and Isa. 41:8). It was also said of Moses that the Lord spoke to him "face to face, as a man speaketh unto his friend" (see Exod. 33:11). Those relationships were, to say the least, very special. To find the same thing existing between humans was rare. Three things became evident: (1) jealousy was outlawed, (2) joy was overflowing, and (3) justice was outraged.

Jealousy Was Outlawed

Jonathan was heir to the throne of Israel; all the splendor associated with royalty would be his by right of succession. It would have seemed justified had he resented the intrusion of another man who would prevent his becoming king of Israel. When Saul heard the maidens of the country singing their songs of adulation for David, he became enraged and his ever-increasing jealousy ruined his happiness. That Jonathan, his son, should willingly and gladly relinquish his claim to the throne provided a strange contrast to the attitude of his father. Jonathan's gesture was remarkable, for he gave to his friend everything which attested to the fact of his regal status. It was a concise but clear indication that he was bestowing upon his friend his choicest treasures. His action and attitude remind modern readers of John the Baptist's words. When the wilderness preacher spoke of the LORD, he said, "He must increase, but I must decrease" (John 3:30). John had been the center of the religious life of Israel; his meetings drew immense congregations; his name was known throughout the nation. All this changed when Jesus of Nazareth began His memorable ministry. John's popularity came to an abrupt end when he was incarcerated in Herod's prison; yet, never for a moment did the evangelist become jealous of his successor. Jonathan was a perfect example of that kind of grace when he rejoiced that God had chosen David to become the king of Israel.

Joy Was Overflowing

When David heard of the death of his beloved friend, he said, "I am distressed for thee, my brother Jonathan: very pleasant hast thou been unto me: thy love to me was wonderful, passing the love of women" (2 Sam. 1:26). When a man falls in love with a woman, something happens within his soul which defies description. He discovers a person with whom he desires to share his life. Thereafter, in accordance with the wishes of God, they are joined in matrimony to share a unique relationship which, hopefully, lasts a lifetime. David was destined, for better or for worse, to share his affections with many women, but in a very special sense, nothing surpassed his love for Jonathan. Each loved to be in the presence of the other; mutual joys and disappointments were always shared. When David was overwhelmed with fear and despondency, he wept on Jonathan's shoulder. When danger threatened the life of the fugitive, the prince proved to be a friend who stayed "closer than a brother" (Prov. 18:24). Abraham Lincoln was once criticized by an associate regarding his attitude toward enemies. He was asked: "Why do you always try to make friends of them? You should destroy them." Lincoln replied: "Am I not destroying my enemies when I make them my friends?" (Doan, *The Speaker's Sourcebook*, p. 108).

Justice was Outraged

Later in the story, Jonathan explained to his father how he had permitted David to attend a feast in Bethlehem. "Then Saul's anger was kindled against Jonathan, and he said unto him, Thou son of the perverse rebellious woman, do not I know that thou hast chosen the son of Jesse to thine own confusion, and unto the confusion of thy mother's nakedness? For as long as the son of Jesse liveth upon the ground, thou shalt not be established, nor thy kingdom. . . . And Saul cast a javelin at him to smite him. . . . So Jonathan arose from the table in fierce anger, and did eat no meat the second day of the month: for he was grieved for David, because his father had done him shame" (1 Sam. 20:30-34). True friends are faithful at all times. It is significant that, although David was not present to hear what was being said, Jonathan faithfully defended his friend. Sometimes people remain silent so that they do not encourage unpleasant repercussions. Jonathan ignored such reactions and proudly upheld the honor of David. The apostle Paul surely appreciated the qualities found in Jonathan and David, for he wrote: "[Love] suffereth long, and is kind; [love] envieth not; [love] vaunteth not itself; is not puffed up. Doth not behave itself unseemly, seeketh not her own, is not easily provoked, thinketh no evil; Rejoiceth not in iniquity, but rejoiceth in the truth" (1 Cor. 13:4-6). A true friend is worth his weight in gold!

DAVID'S FOE (vv. 5-13 and 22-25).

And it came to pass . . . when David was returned from the slaughter of the Philistine, that the women came out of all cities of Israel, singing and dancing, to meet king Saul, with tabrets, with joy, and with instruments of music. And the women answered one another as they played, and

said, Saul hath slain his thousands, and David his ten thousands. And Saul was very wroth, and the saying displeased him. . . . And Saul eyed David from that day and forward. . . . And Saul cast the javelin; for he said, I will smite David even to the wall with it. And David avoided out of his presence twice. And Saul was afraid of David, because the LORD was with him, and was departed from Saul (vv. 6-12).

Expository Notes on Saul's Continued Animosity Toward David

A careful study of the Scriptures reveals that Saul's anger was more than a spasmodic outburst of temper. What appeared to be a manifestation of temporary insanity was actually a premeditated act of unrestrained violence. The king was apparently a hypocrite who used religion to hide his evil intentions. The scholarly Adam Clarke, referring to the statement "Saul prophesied", wrote: "He prophesied in the midst of the house. He was beside himself; made prayers; supplications and incoherent appreciations. But let us examine the original [Scriptures] more closely. It is said that Saul prophesied in the midst of his house, that is, *he prayed in his family*, while David was playing on the harp. Then suddenly he threw his javelin intending to have killed David. Let it be observed that the word *vaiyithnabbe* is the third personal singular of the future *hithpael*, the sign of which is not only to do an action, on or for oneself, but also to "feign or pretend to do it." The meaning seems to be, Saul pretended to be praying in, or with his family, the better to conceal his murderous intentions, and to render David unsuspicious, who was probably at this time, performing the musical part of the family worship. This view of the subject makes the whole case natural and plain" (*The Bethany Parallel Commentary on the Old Testament*, p. 546).

A Sudden Attack

There is no deeper despair than that found in the soul for whom there is no hope. When a man has experienced God's blessing in life, the loss of that hallowed benediction leads to an indescribable emptiness within his soul. Saul's knowledge that God had rejected him filled him with frustration, bitterness, helplessness, and a deepening anger. During the day, his mind was a maelstrom of bitterness, and throughout the night, sleep was elusive as he dreamed of the man he desired to destroy. Apparently, his struggles reached a climax during the family devotions.

It is not known how many people were present at the time. Somewhere close at hand, the young musician played his soothing music and perhaps even led the small congregation in the singing of an ancient melody. Saul uttered words of gratitude and praise to Jehovah, but his heart was not in tune with what he said. Frequently, he looked at the harpist, and his eyes became slits. How he detested that young man whose serenity mocked him! His anger increased until there was no escape. As a man bereft of his senses, the king threw his javelin, but alas, he failed to recognize the impossibility of killing what God was determined to preserve. Some theologians believe Saul only pretended to throw his weapon—there is an alternative rendering of the Hebrew words—but since at a later time the king's javelin entered the wall, the interpretation is at least questionable (see 1 Sam. 19:10). People may find it difficult to understand why David did not retaliate, but it should be remembered that the young shepherd believed Saul to be *the Lord's anointed.* To strike the king would have been tantamount to striking Jehovah.

A Sincere Attachment

"And David behaved himself wisely in all his ways; and the LORD was with him. Wherefore when Saul saw that he behaved himself very wisely, he was afraid of him. But all Israel and Judah loved David, because he went out and came in before them" (see vv. 14-16). It is thought-provoking that in the midst of all the problems, God arranged for David to win the affections of the entire nation. Some very bright stars began to shine in the firmament of the young man's life. First, there was Jonathan's friendship, and at a later time the love of Michal, Saul's daughter, became one of David's most cherished joys. The affection of these noble people spread throughout the land; "all Israel and Judah loved [him]."

A man cannot be alone when he abides in the center of God's will. The sense of the Almighty's continuing presence is inescapable. Elijah appeared to be alone when he lived in a cave, but when the ravens brought food twice a day, it became evident that God was superintending the prophet's survival (see 1 Kings 17:5-6). Paul seemed to be one of a kind when he was confronted on a storm-tossed vessel by an inevitable shipwreck. Yet, he was able to say to the frightened crew, "There stood by me this night the angel of God, whose I am, and whom I serve" (see Acts 27:23). John Bunyan was the only occupant of his cell in the prison at Bedford, England, but no person can read *The Pilgrim's Progress* and not realize that every moment of that incarceration was shared with the living Christ. David was evidently appreciative of excellent company when he was alone on the hills of Bethlehem.

A Smoldering Anger

Although Saul appeared at intervals to be repentant, the continuation of his hatred of David proved that he had become a reprobate. First, his own attempts at assassination failed, and he then deceived David in regard to a marriage with the princess, Merab. He suggested an attack on the Philistine garrison, hoping his rival would be among the casualties. On each occasion, however, David "behaved himself more wisely than all the servants of Saul; so that his name was much set by" (v. 30). The experiences of Saul suggest that it is possible for an unrepentant sinner to reach a time when even God can do little to help him. Close to the beginning of human history, God said: "My Spirit shall not always strive with man" (see Gen. 6:3), and in various ways His justice has been demonstrated throughout the ages. The people who perished in the flood; Pharaoh, who persistently disobeyed the commands of Moses; and many others have learned that there is an end even to the patience of God.

"His mercy is from everlasting to everlasting *upon them that fear Him.*" God's offer of mercy gives added importance to other texts in the Bible. God said through Isaiah: "Come *now*, and let us reason together, saith the LORD, Though your sins be as scarlet, they shall be as white as snow; though they be red like crimson, they shall be as wool" (see Isa. 1:18). The writer to the Hebrews quoted the Scriptures when he said: "*Today*, if ye will hear his voice, harden not your hearts, as in the provocation" (see Heb. 3:15).

A Stubborn Awareness

"And Saul saw and knew that the LORD was with David, and that Michal, Saul's daughter loved him. And Saul was yet the more afraid of David; *and Saul became David's enemy continually*" (vv. 28-29). There seems to be no limit to the treachery of the deranged monarch. When Saul recognized that the Lord was with David, he repeatedly attempted to slay God's servant. He clearly refused to obey the commandments of God and dug a grave for himself. When he died a very lonely and dejected leader on Mount Gilboa, he had no one else to blame but himself (see 1 Sam. 31).

DAVID'S FAME

> ... and [David] was accepted in the sight of all the people and also in the sight of Saul's servants" (v. 5). " ... the LORD was with him" (v. 12). But all Israel and Judah loved David" (v. 16). "And Michal Saul's daughter loved David" (v. 20).

Expository Notes on the Increasing Popularity of David

Perhaps the psalmist considered these preceding truths when he wrote, "For the LORD God is a sun and shield: the LORD will give grace and glory: no good thing will he withhold from them that walk uprightly" (see Ps. 84:11). At this point in his life, David had progressed tremendously. Much had taken place since the days when he lived with his sheep in the vicinity of Bethlehem. Then he had been a young, inexperienced lad who practiced with his sling. Most people would have considered him to be an ordinary young man who possessed no skills of outstanding worth. Many years later, Paul wrote: "But God hath chosen the foolish things of the world to confound the wise; and God hath chosen the weak things of the world to confound the things which are mighty; and base things of the world, and things which are despised, hath God chosen, yea, and things which are not, to bring to nought things that are: That no flesh should glory in his presence" (1 Cor. 1:27-29).

> Oh, to be nothing, nothing:
>   Simply to lie at His feet.
> An emptied and broken vessel,
>   For the Master's use made meet.
> Emptied that He might fill me,
>   As forth to His service I go:
> Broken that so unhindered,
>   His life through me might flow.

Episode 5

THEME: *God's Continued Protection of David*

SCRIPTURE: 1 Samuel 19:1-24

KEY VERSE:

> And Saul sent messengers to take David: and . . . the Spirit of God was upon the messengers of Saul, and they also prophesied (v. 20).

OUTLINE:
  I. A Delightful Intercession (Verses 1-8)
  II. A Dastardly Instigation (Verses 9-10; 14-17)
  III. A Deceptive Image (Verses 11-14)
  IV. A Divine Intervention (vv. 18-24)

And Jonathan spake good of David unto Saul his father, and said unto him, Let not the king sin against his servant, against David; because he hath not sinned against thee, and because his works have been to theeward very good: For he did put his life in his hand, and slew the Philistine, and the LORD wrought a great salvation for all Israel: thou sawest it, and didst rejoice: wherefore then wilt thou sin against innocent blood, to slay David without a cause? And Saul hearkened unto the voice of Jonathan: and Saul sware, As the LORD liveth, he shall not be slain. And Jonathan called David, and Jonathan shewed him all those things. And Jonathan brought David to Saul, and he was in his presence, as in times past (vv. 4-7).

Expository Notes on Jonathan's Defense of David

A DELIGHTFUL INTERCESSION

This incident in the life of David is one of the most attractive stories in the Bible. The strange contrasts among three men provides food for thought. That Jonathan was able to influence his obstinate father reveals the selfless devotion of a young man who was about to lose the throne of Israel. David's frustration and fear indicates that he sometimes allowed circumstances to influence his actions. He never feared Goliath, yet was constantly afraid of Saul who was, in many ways, a less formidable foe. When Saul

responded to the entreaty of his son, he indicated that he was still susceptible to reason and compassion. Evidently, he had not yet reached the point
of no return, and if he had sincerely repented of his indiscretions and sins,
a more attractive account of his life might have been written for posterity.
If the citizens of this world knew how to love as did Jonathan, wars and
other forms of brutality would be only unpleasant memories.

Expository Notes on Saul's Increasing Infamy

A DASTARDLY INSTIGATION

There appears to be a progression in the evil intentions of King Saul.
The writer says at first that "he eyed David from that day and forward."
Every day he looked suspiciously at the young musician who had been
summoned to the court. Any kindness was a mask hiding the jealousy
which dominated the king's soul. Saul was mentally and emotionally sick,
but when he refused to accept the guidance of God, he contributed to his
own downfall. Then, if the interpretation offered by some commentators is
accepted, Saul *pretended* to throw his javelin. It may never be known
whether or not, at first, he restrained himself from the vicious act. In any
case, however, it was to no avail as ultimately, the javelin was thrown with
such force that its head pierced the wall of the room where the king sat.

Cancer is one of the greatest physical menaces of our time, yet, the
medical profession often announces that *if discovered in time, it can be
cured.* Delay in treating the disease is dangerous. Could the same thing be
said about the ailment which destroyed Saul's life? It was a long and
lonely road which reached from the days when Saul was the protege of the
prophet to the time when that same prophet rebuked—even from his grave—
the man who had become the greatest figure in Israel (see 1 Sam. 28:11-20).
Sin resembles a quicksand. If a man continues to play along its edges, he is
in danger of sinking into oblivion.

Expository Notes on the Subtlety of Saul's Daughter

A DECEPTIVE IMAGE

> **Saul also sent messengers unto David's house, to watch him, and to slay
> him in the morning: and Michal David's wife told him, saying, If thou
> save not thy life tonight, to morrow thou shalt be slain. So Michal let
> David down through a window: and he went, and fled, and escaped. And
> Michal took an image, and laid it in the bed, and put a pillow of goat's
> hair for his bolster, and covered it with a cloth. And when Saul sent mes-
> sengers to take David, she said, He is sick (vv. 11-14).**

The princess was a very brave woman; her deception could have led to her death. Her father was incensed; even family members might have been executed because of their disobedience. Evidently, Jonathan and his sister desired David's safety, and when the prince informed his sister of Saul's intentions, she devised a way by which her fugitive husband would be able to make his escape. The *teraphim* or "image" was a carving that was thought to assure protection and good fortune for households. Such objects frequently led to idolatry. Some were large like the one used by Michal, but others were small. For example, when Rebekah stole Laban's teraphim, she hid it in her baggage, placed it on her camel, and then sat on it (see Gen. 31:34). It is not known why this object was found in David's home. Perhaps his wife was interested in wood carvings, or maybe it was a part of their furniture. Confronted by the problem of providing time for David to escape, Michal conceived the idea of deceiving the messengers of Saul. She took the manlike form of the carving, placed it in David's bed, and covered it to suggest the form of a sleeping man. The Hebrew word *beged*, translated "cloth", was frequently used in the ancient records. It referred to a loose mantle often worn over a tight-fitting undergarment. During the night it was a blanket supplying warmth; during the day it was just a covering. It is interesting to note that even when David was approaching his death, he still used such a garment (see 1 Kings 1:1 where the same word is translated "clothes").

In Eastern countries, a bed is usually a piece of carpet; peasants lie on the floor. It would have been easy for Michal to deceive the messengers of Saul because they would respectfully stand at a distance. When Saul commanded David to be brought *in his bed*, he was merely instructing his men to pick up the carpet and bring David to the palace. To hide complicity in her husband's escape, Michal lied, for she feared the wrath of her father. Saul probably knew about her deception, but could not punish his daughter for a crime he could not prove. It seemed at that point in time that everybody had lost sight of God except the prophet who lived at Ramah. It has often been said that "God helps those who help themselves," but when self-preservation becomes so important that even God is forgotten, the survivor might be in jeopardy. God overruled circumstances and used the wiles of a woman to protect His servant. Nevertheless, a question should be considered: Is God dependent upon the questionable conduct of any man or woman? Samuel handled a similar situation very differently. He knew his safety did not depend upon a lying tongue, but upon the faithfulness of God.

A DIVINE INTERVENTION

So David fled, and escaped, and came to Samuel to Ramah, and told him all that Saul had done to him. And he and Samuel went and dwelt in Naioth (v. 18).

Expository Notes on the Exciting Events at Naioth

This follows one of the strangest accounts ever written about David. Armed and hostile guards, who were sent to apprehend a fugitive, became so enthralled with what they saw and heard that they either forgot or ignored their commission. An arrogant, stubborn monarch, who was determined to assassinate David, succeeded only in losing his dignity. Saul "lay down naked all that day and all that night" and was probably despised by his followers.

The Safe Sanctuary . . . How Desirable

David apparently believed that he was alone! King Saul had become his greatest enemy. Jonathan was undoubtedly doing his best, but his efforts were doomed to fail. Although the common people loved and admired the youthful hero, they were still the subjects of Saul and would not disobey his commands. If David returned to his former occupation, he would bring danger to his family. Where could he go to seek refuge? Samuel was an old man whose activities were curtailed. He lived at Ramah where he had established a school for the prophets, and was fully occupied with that project. He was the only accredited representative of God. David anxiously considered the alternatives. Even if the old prophet were unable to grant him asylum, at least he would offer advice and thereby give guidance to the young man whose life was being threatened. David hurried to Ramah to meet his old friend.

Several of David's psalms have been associated with this period, but it should be recognized that, perhaps with a few exceptions, it is impossible to say with certainty when or where David completed his poems. Probably, the psalms were written during times of reminiscing when, in the seclusion of his palace, he remembered various episodes in his career. For example, what better time could there have been to write: "I will lift up mine eyes unto the hills, from whence cometh my help" (Ps. 121:1) or, "God is our refuge and strength, a very present help in trouble" (Ps. 46:1). When Hannah's heart was troubled, she went to the tabernacle to pray (see 1 Sam. 1:10). When the disciples of John the Baptist realized their master was dead, they "took up the body, and buried it, *and went and told Jesus*" (see Matt. 14:12). After Toplady crept into a cleft of the rock to shelter from a storm, he wrote,

> Rock of Ages, cleft for me
> Let me hide myself in Thee.

The story has been told of the time when a small bird, chased by a hawk, flew through a window to find shelter in the waistcoat of John Wesley. Fascinated and thrilled by that incident, the famous preacher wrote:

Jesus, Lover of my soul
Let me to Thy bosom fly.

Isaiah evidently had known such experiences. He wrote: "For thou hast been a strength to the poor, a strength to the needy in his distress, a refuge from the storm, a shadow from the heat, when the blast of the terrible ones is as a storm against the wall" (see Isa. 25:4). A modern hymn asks an important question. "Where can we go but to the Lord?"

The Sacred Seminary . . . How Delightful

"And he and Samuel went and dwelt in Naioth" (v. 18). It is generally believed that Samuel established a school for the prophets at Ramah. Concerned about the spiritual state of the nation and realizing he would soon die, the aged prophet trained men to lead Israel in the paths of righteousness. As his students increased, additional dormitories and classrooms were built so that the education of the students could proceed without interruption. The word *Naioth* or *Nevaioth* means "dwellings" or "lodgings". The Chaldean scriptures translate this term "house of study" or "students' lodgings." Samuel evidently had erected these buildings in a small suburb of Ramah.

When David came to see the prophet, perhaps both men stayed in the college buildings, and the reasons for that decision were varied. Naioth offered better and possibly safer accommodation. There were numerous buildings, and in the event of physical danger, there would have been many young men to offer assistance. Maybe Samuel recognized the value of fellowship, and the students would encourage David, who was still a young man. There had to be some organization or people responsible for feeding the students, and David could join the students at mealtimes. His physical needs could be supplied in the dining hall; his weary soul could be refreshed in their company.

Samuel's college was probably the most spiritual center in Israel. The priests lived and worked in Shiloh, but God was in Ramah! The arrival of Samuel with his young friend could not have remained a secret, and it is not surprising, therefore, that the king was informed of David's hiding place.

The Surprised Servants . . . How Disturbed

"And Saul sent messengers to take David: and when they saw the company of the prophets prophesying, and Samuel standing as appointed over them, the Spirit of God was upon the messengers of Saul, and they also prophesied" (v. 20). This prophesying was repeated on two other occasions, but the king failed to recognize the obvious implications of the strange events in Naioth. There has been prolonged discussion concerning the events among the students, and certain conclusions have not been based on fact. To prophesy not only means *to predict the future*; it also means *to proclaim the praises of God.* There was probably nothing sensational about the conduct of the young prophets. They were engaged in the usual devotional routine and were singing the praises of Jehovah. Samuel was presiding over the assembly when the presence of God's Spirit transformed the gathering into a revival service.

It is easy to imagine what happened that day. The choir of graduate students was at its best! The clarity of their notes and the sweetness of their voices had produced a crescendo of praise never surpassed in their history. Perhaps even angels had paused to listen. Whether or not the devotions were being held in the open air or within a building is not a matter of importance. Every person within hearing stopped and smiled. Then, along the street came the messengers of Saul. It was said that "all Israel loved David;" yet Saul's anger was something to be feared. It was regrettable for the soldiers, but if David had to be apprehended, it was their duty to do as they had been commanded. Enquiries were made, the captain smiled, all was in order, and there would be no problem. David was unarmed and was worshiping with a congregation. Then, suddenly came the sound of the heavenly anthem, and the arresting officers came to an abrupt halt.

Doubtless, they had heard choirs many times, but this one was different. Young voices were singing as if the Spirit of God was upon them. Maybe the song was an ancient melody, and at first, the messengers quietly joined the outburst of praise. Their enthusiasm increased until the purpose of their errand was completely forgotten. Utterly spellbound, the men sang with enthusiasm; Saul was forgotten; they were in the presence of the King of kings.

Centuries later, servants of the law were sent to arrest a Carpenter from Nazareth, but they made one mistake. They paused to listen to His message, and their response was unimaginable. Swayed by what they heard, they returned to their employers to say: "Never man spake like this man" (John 7:46).

The Subdued Saul . . . How Demoralized

"Then went [Saul] also to Ramah . . . and he asked and said, Where are Samuel and David? And one said, Behold they be at Naioth in Ramah. And he went thither to Naioth in Ramah: and the Spirit of God was upon him also, and he went on, and prophesied, until he came to Naioth in Ramah. And he stripped off his clothes also, and prophesied before Samuel in like manner, and lay down naked all that day, and all that night. Wherefore they say, Is Saul also among the prophets?" (vv. 22-24). When Saul heard the exciting songs of the inspired choir, he too became exuberant, and being completely overwhelmed, he emulated the example of his servants by joining in the proceedings. He therefore discarded his armor as the weight of it was too restrictive to facilitate freedom of movement. Finally, utterly exhausted, he lay down in his undergarments, a condition which suggested nakedness to onlookers. That God did something special cannot be denied. The man's soul was in jeopardy; he needed to be taught that he was helpless without God. Perhaps there was a compulsion which temporarily deprived him of propriety. He had ignored the fact that three groups of messengers had failed to intimidate Samuel and David. If he had been a wiser man, he would have known that his sending of the last two armies was just as futile as his sending of the first one. God's judgments are always overshadowed by mercy. Even though He sees the end from the beginning, it is incumbent upon the Almighty to "go the extra mile" so that guilty people would never say: "If you had tried once more, we might have repented." God never abandons anyone until further effort is useless.

The statement "Is Saul also among the prophets?" is doubtless a reference to an earlier, happier time when, as a young man, he had been pleasing to Jehovah. The story of King Saul is a reminder that people who turn their backs on the light inevitably live in darkness.

HOMILIES FOR PREACHERS AND TEACHERS

Study No. 4

SAUL ... Who Seemed to Be Hypnotized

Dear David,

It is strange that we are thinking of you when we should be thinking of Saul, but that's just the way of things. You two always seem to be getting in each other's way, and whenever we read of King Saul, we expect you to appear on the page. No, no, do not misunderstand us; we are glad, very glad, for action is always to be expected when you and Saul come together. You are not too busy to answer a few questions? Good. You remember those troublesome days when Saul hunted you from pillar to post, when life was a nightmare, when death threatened to overtake you at any moment? Did you laugh when your wife put an image in your bed, covered it with a sheet, and then tucked it in as if she were caring for her husband? No wonder Saul was mad when he discovered what she had done.

HOW INVITING

We have often read: "So David fled, and escaped, and came to Samuel to Ramah, and told him all that Saul had done to him. And he and Samuel went and dwelt in Naioth" (see 1 Sam. 19:18). David, that verse appeals to us a great deal, for Samuel was the mouthpiece of God. Amid all the decadent conditions of his day, he stood for truth and goodness. To be near him was to stand in the Lord's presence. His home was a sanctuary, his smile a benediction. You felt safe with him. God's man was your friend; he was a refuge in the storm. We know how you felt, for we have often acted similarly. When ugly circumstances follow us day after day, we flee for refuge to Another One, who is also God's Man.

HOW IRRESISTIBLE

Were you just a little scared when the group of soldiers came to take you away? Did you tremble and look expectantly toward your kind benefactor? Were you amazed when he quietly smiled and when "the Spirit of God was upon them and they prophesied"? David, were you not astonished when this procedure was twice repeated? Samuel—assured, dignified—stood at your side. His eyes were pools of inscrutable mystery; the smile playing about his lips held just a trace of mockery and scorn. Who were these stupid men that they should challenge the authority of the Most High? Yes, the messengers of Saul were swayed by eternal powers; they spoke words of praise and extolled the name of the Almighty. David, you knew a thing or two, didn't you, when you sought shelter with Samuel!

HOW INVINCIBLE

And then King Saul arrived (v. 22). Wasn't he stupid? Yes, he would show Samuel that other people, as well as he, could act and speak with authority! "Men, seize that scoundrel, David, and allow no interference!" Samuel's eyes merely flickered. Imperceptibly, the lines around his mouth deepened; his beard twitched as if suppressed mirth was trying to find expression. Gravely, the prophet inclined his head, and, behold, "the Spirit of God was upon Saul also, and he went on and prophesied, until he came to Naioth in Ramah. And he stripped off his clothes also, and prophesied before Samuel in like manner, and lay down naked all that day, and all that night. Wherefore they say: Is Saul also among the prophets?" And still Samuel watched him. David, do you know what the worldly-wise people of our generation would say about that event? They would declare that Samuel was a hypnotist and that Saul was impressionable and went into a trance! Not that it matters, for if God desired, He could paralyze an army of kings!

HOW INSPIRING

What happened after the demonstration ended? It must have been comical to see Saul awakening. Surely he was disconcerted when he discovered his need of clothing. Was he any wiser, or did he become morose and sullen? He was a strange man. But, David, we cannot understand why you fled from Samuel. You were very fearful when you found Jonathan and said, "What have I done? What is mine iniquity, and what is my sin before thy father, that he seeketh my life?" (see 1 Sam. 20:1). Of course, we may be all wrong in our thinking, but it seems to us that if the presence of Samuel afforded glorious protection, you would have been well-advised to have remained with him. Were you afraid that he might die and leave you at the mercy of your enemy? What a pity you are so far away, David. You could tell us so much. Anyhow, we have a Savior who will never die. We fled for refuge to Him and felt so much at home in His presence that we decided to stay forever. What do you think of that, David? (Homily reprinted from the author's book, *Bible Treasures*, pp. 27-28.)

Episode 6

THEME: *David's Covenant With Jonathan*

SCRIPTURE: 1 Samuel 20:1-42

KEY VERSES:

> So Jonathan made a covenant with the house of David. . . . for he loved him as he loved his own soul (vv. 16-17).

OUTLINE:
      I.   The Prince and His Friend (Verses 1-24)
     II. The Problem at the Feast (Verses 25-34)
   III. The Pathos in the Field (Verses 35-42)

THE PRINCE AND HIS FRIEND

And David fled from Naioth in Ramah, and came and said before Jonathan, What have I done? what is mine iniquity? and what is my sin before thy father, that he seeketh my life? And he said unto him, God forbid; thou shalt not die: behold, my father will do nothing either great or small, but that he will shew it me: and why should my father hide this thing from me? is it not so. . . . Whatsoever thy soul desireth, I will even do it for thee (vv. 1-4).

Expository Notes on David's Departure from Naioth

The question is raised in the preceding homily, "Saul . . . Who Seemed to Be Hypnotized" (p. 63), which follows whether David was wise to leave his sanctuary with Samuel at Naioth. Did he consider the approaching decease of his friend and wonder what would happen when the prophet could no longer protect him? The events at the seminary had demonstrated the superiority of Samuel over Saul. Why then did David forsake his refuge? Did his act reflect *fear of Saul*, or *obedience to Samuel*? David was without confidence when he said to Jonathan, "There is but a step between me and death" (20:3). It appears that David did not want to leave Naioth. Therefore, the only reasonable conclusion is that Samuel evidently advised him to go. The advice was excellent since David needed to rely increasingly on the Lord and less on his friends. Later, when David became the king of Israel, many battles would be fought against the Philistines and other nations, and it would be vitally necessary to know every ravine, hill, valley, and cave in the country. He would have to be acquainted with the terrain—how and where to retreat or advance—and such knowledge would never have been acquired had he remained with his aged friend. Some lessons are only learned in the school of experience. Samuel was aware of that fact, but David was not.

And David said unto Jonathan, Behold, to morrow is the new moon, and I should not fail to sit with the king at meat: but let me go, that I may hide myself in the field unto the third day at even. If thy father at all miss me, then say, David earnestly asked leave of me that he might run to Bethlehem his city: for there is a yearly sacrifice there for all the family. If he say thus, It is well; thy servant shall have peace: but if he be very wroth, then be sure that evil is determined by him. Therefore thou shalt deal kindly with thy servant; for thou hast brought thy servant into a covenant of the Lord with thee; notwithstanding, if there be in me iniquity, slay me thyself; for why shouldest thou bring me to thy father? And Jonathan said, Far be it from thee: for if I knew certainly that evil were determined by my father to come upon thee, then would not I tell it thee? (vv. 5-9).

Expository Notes on David's Request to Jonathan

The Continuing Frustration

When David fled from Naioth, it must have seemed that only a few people worthy of trust remained in the country. His brothers had already expressed disapproval of his actions; his professed admirers were willing to obey the commands of Saul; only Jonathan and Samuel remained. Therefore, it was to the prince that David went to seek comfort and reassurance. Since King Saul was capable of deception, his vows to Jehovah were meaningless. If David were to elude the continual nationwide search for him, he needed special help. Jonathan alone was able to supply this assistance.

The Customary Feasts

Throughout Israel the appearance of a new moon was always celebrated with sacrifices and feasting (see Num. 28:11). Evidently on this occasion, special festivities were to be held. Dr. Payne Smith, writing in *The Pulpit Commentary* (vol. 4, p. 377), says: "A yearly sacrifice was made for all the family—for all the *mishpachah*, i.e. not only for Jesse's household, but for all that subdivision of the tribe of Judah to which Jesse belonged; for a tribe was divided into families, and again into fathers' houses (Josh. 7:16–

17). The occasion would thus be a grand one." Friends from near and far would gather to celebrate the appearance of the new moon, and within the palace of Saul, every member of the royal family would be expected. David realized that attendance at the feast could be disastrous. His request for Jonathan's help reveals the fear which gripped his soul.

The Consenting Friend

The fact that Jonathan was willing to cooperate and to do as David suggested indicates that he was ready to place his own life in jeopardy. His father expected obedience from the family, and if Jonathan disobeyed the edict issued by the king, he could be accused of treason. This is the story of a man who could be trusted. When David eventually occupied the throne of Israel, he was able to remember a friend who never disappointed him. David was a fortunate man, for in the emergencies of his life, there were always men who helped him (see 2 Sam. 19:31-37). The same thing might be said of the Savior. Unfortunately, most of the Lord's professed friends deserted·Him when they were needed most. Nevertheless, throughout the gospel story, mention is made of the Savior's special friends. The plan made by Jonathan and David supplies exciting reading. The hiding place, the shooting of the arrows, and the unwavering confidence both men had in each other provides drama of the most intense kind. When viewed against the depravity of sinful people, love remains indestructible.

THE PROBLEM AT THE FEAST

So David hid himself in the field: and when the new moon was come, the king sat him down to eat meat. And the king sat upon his seat, as at other times, even upon a seat by the wall: and Jonathan arose, and Abner sat by Saul's side, and David's place was empty. Nevertheless, Saul spake not anything that day: for he thought, Something hath befallen him, he is not clean; surely he is not clean. And it came to pass on the morrow . . . Saul said unto Jonathan his son, Wherefore cometh not the son of Jesse to meat, neither yesterday nor to day? And Jonathan answered Saul, David earnestly asked leave of me to go to Bethlehem. . . . Then Saul's anger was kindled against Jonathan. . . . And Saul cast a javelin at him to smite him: whereby Jonathan knew that it was determined of his father to slay David. So Jonathan arose from the table in fierce anger, and did eat no meat . . . for he was grieved for David; because his father had done him shame (vv. 24-34).

Expository Notes on the Continuing Anger of King Saul

The Empty Seat . . . Disturbing

". . . and David's place was empty" (v. 25). The royal dining hall was silent except for people who engaged in "small talk." Every person was aware that trouble was brewing. David was not present, and the king's furtive glances in the direction of the empty seat were evidence that a domestic storm was approaching. Guests of honor sat with members of the royal family at a lavishly-spread lower table; above them at another table sat Abner and Jonathan; in the far corner next to the wall sat Saul. It was the first day of the new-moon celebrations, and every person there knew the king's son-in-law should have been present. Saul tried to ignore the empty seat, but the task was too difficult. His apparent unconcern lasted a whole day, but an enquiry was inevitable. He doubtless tried to be a good host, but every few moments he thought, "Something has happened to him so that he has become unclean; surely, he is unclean." With these conclusions Saul tried to pacify himself. Certain laws had to be observed before a man could attend such a banquet, and the possibility existed that David had somehow become defiled (see Lev. 15:2-16).

The Explanatory Statement . . . Describing

"And Jonathan answered Saul, David earnestly asked leave of me to go to Bethlehem. . . . Then Saul's anger was kindled against Jonathan." The listeners were shocked because the king had lost his sense of decency by insulting the heir to the throne! He could not mean what he said; their hearing must have been impaired! Jonathan had only done what any master would have done for a slave. David had asked permission to do what they were doing themselves: merely to attend family celebrations in his home city. They looked at the young prince and smiled; he was willing to help anybody. Why was Saul so enraged?

Jonathan said that David had been *commanded* by his brother—possibly, the eldest brother who would be authorized to act on behalf of an aged parent. There was nothing wrong with going home for a few days, for this celebration was a national holiday! Even the king under similar circumstances would have asked such a favor. Could it be that his motives were impure? Had he planned another assassination attempt, and was he angry because his plans had been ruined?

The Explosive Saul . . . Denouncing

"Then Saul's anger was kindled against Jonathan, and he said unto him, Thou son of the perverse rebellious woman, do not I know that thou hast chosen the son of Jesse to thine own confusion, and unto the confusion of thy mother's nakedness. . . . And Saul cast a javelin at him to smite him." To abuse the name of a mother was probably the greatest insult known in the Middle East. Saul's reprehensible statement explains why Jonathan was so infuriated when he left the room. The Hebrew text might be translated: "Thou art the son of an unjust rebellion," or "Thou art a rebel against thine own father." It has been suggested by some that the statement "Unto the confusion of thy mother's nakedness," could be translated: "Thy mother will feel ashamed and disgraced at having borne such a son." It was evident that Saul was now on a collision course with disaster. His periods of penitence were false; his vows to God were without value. He cared only for himself and was convinced he could do no wrong.

THE PATHOS IN THE FIELD

And it came to pass in the morning, that Jonathan went out into the field at the time appointed with David, and a little lad with him. . . . And when the lad was come to the place of the arrow which Jonathan had shot, Jonathan cried after the lad, and said, Is not the arrow beyond thee? . . . And Jonathan gave his artillery unto his lad, and said unto him, Go, carry them to the city. And as soon as the lad was gone, David arose out of a place toward the south, and fell on his face to the ground, and bowed himself three times: and they kissed one another and wept one with another, until David exceeded. And Jonathan said to David, Go in peace, forasmuch as we have sworn both of us in the name of the LORD, saying, The LORD be between me and thee, and between my seed and thy seed for ever. And he arose and departed: and Jonathan went into the city (vv. 35-42).

Expository Notes on a Tearful Farewell

This incident was basically the final farewell for these young men. Later, Jonathan went into a forest to speak with his friend for the last time, but this was the final occasion when they were able to weep in secret on each other's shoulder. Their hearts were filled with tenderness and sorrow; their tears were copious. There was a finality about their farewell; perhaps they thought they would never see each other again. Their love was complete and overflowing.

Love Protecting

"And Jonathan's lad gathered up the arrows, and came to his master. But the lad knew not anything; only Jonathan and David knew the matter." The arrangement by which David would learn of his danger was a carefully-kept secret. The prince doubtless loved his young companion, but refrained from letting the youth understand what was transpiring that morning. The lad unwittingly could have made known what had happened. Jonathan was determined to protect David from his enemies.

Love Promising

"We have sworn both of us in the name of the LORD." The covenant made between Jonathan and David was destined to last throughout their lifetime. Even after the death of the prince, David was kind to Jonathan's descendents. For example, he did for Mephibosheth all that his own father would have loved to do (see 2 Sam. 9). Love is timeless, immortal, and wonderful. Maybe Jonathan had premonitions of his imminent death; a realization which added depth to the statement, "The LORD be between me and thee, and between my seed and thy seed *forever*." He always thought of others. Happy are they who learn from his example.

Love Preparing

"And [David] arose and departed: and Jonathan went into the city." The prince went back to be with his father and at the same time continued his service to David as his friend at court. David went his way, and the Spirit of the Lord went with him. The two men were destined to meet again, but it is thought-provoking to discover that the final meeting was made possible because Jonathan risked his life to see his friend. "And Jonathan Saul's son arose, and went to David into the wood, and strengthened his hand in God. And he said unto him, Fear not: for the hand of Saul my father shall not find thee; and thou shalt be king over Israel, and I shall be next unto thee; and that also Saul my father knoweth. And they two made a covenant before the LORD" (see 1 Sam. 23:16-18). Unfortunately, Jonathan was killed in battle and never lived to see the realization of his dream. Nevertheless, he remained loyal to David even until he died with his father on Mount Gilboa. It is refreshing to know that of him the Lord might have said: "Be thou faithful unto death, and I will give thee a crown of life" (see Rev. 2:10). Perhaps in a very real sense, Jonathan exchanged an earthly crown for another which was eternal!

Episode 7

THEME: *David Becomes a Fugitive*

SCRIPTURE: 1 Samuel 21:1-9

KEY VERSE:

> So the priest gave him hallowed bread: for there was no bread there but the shewbread, that was taken from before the LORD, to put hot bread in the day when it was taken away (v. 6).

OUTLINE:

    I.   An Inexcusable Deception . . . *Worrying* (Verses 1-2)
    II. An Insistent Demand . . . *Weakening* (Verses 3-6, 8-9)
    III. An Insolent Detainee . . . *Watching* (Verses 7-9)

Then came David to Nob to Ahimelech the priest: and Ahimelech was afraid at the meeting of David, and said unto him, Why art thou alone, and no man with thee? And David said unto Ahimelech the priest, The king hath commanded me a business, and hath said unto me, Let no man know any thing of the business whereabout I send thee, and what I have commanded thee: and I have appointed my servants to such and such a place (vv. 1-2).

Expository Notes on David's Lies to the Priest

AN INEXCUSABLE DECEPTION . . . Worrying

The Lord's Center . . . Disturbed

It is important to remember the great changes which had occurred in Israel. Shiloh, the center of all religious activities, had become deserted and desolate. The sins of the priests had brought Shiloh into disrepute so that most of the religious activities had been transferred to Nob, which was on the Mount of Olives, close to Jerusalem. The name *Nob* means "a knoll or hill." The sacred treasures of the nation probably had been transferred to the new sanctuary. Remembering what had happened to the ancient shrine, the psalmist wrote of the people and the place: "For they provoked [God] to anger with their high places, and moved him to jealousy with their graven images. When God heard this, he was wroth, and greatly abhorred Israel: so that he forsook the tabernacle of Shiloh, the tent which he placed among men; and delivered his strength into captivity, and his glory into the enemy's hand" (see Ps. 78:58-61). It is believed by some that, with the help of Saul and Samuel, the new center of worship was established at Nob where at least eighty-five priests were assembled to revive and strengthen their monotheistic religion. Ahimelech was the high priest, and there is reason to believe the rituals previously practiced at Shiloh were performed at Nob.

David was aware of these changes, and when he was confronted by the urgent necessity of leaving the country, he decided to visit the sanctuary. Since he and his followers needed supplies of food, David hoped the priest would be cooperative. "Then came David to Nob to Ahimelech the priest: and Ahimelech was afraid at the meeting of David." Literally, the Scriptures mean, "he went *trembling* to meet him." The mind of the old priest stirred with the realization that something was wrong, for David was apparently traveling alone. The king's son-in-law usually had a military escort, but these men had been left at a distance. Why had David come alone to the sanctuary? Rumors of Saul's animosity had circulated through the country, and Ahimelech feared Saul might even then be approaching to slay his suspected enemy. David must have anticipated the question asked by Ahimelech, "Why art thou alone, and no man with thee?"

The Lost Confidence . . . Disrupting

"And David said unto Ahimelech the priest, The king hath commanded me a business, and hath said unto me, Let no man know any thing of the business whereabout I send thee" (v. 2). The lies told on that occasion were destined to haunt David throughout his life. He temporarily lost sight of all that Jehovah had done for him, and his lies led to the slaughter of innocent people. His actions were completely shameful and despicable. David must have remembered this incident later in his life when he wrote: "My soul melteth for heaviness: strengthen thou me according unto thy word. *Remove from me the way of lying*: and grant me thy law graciously" (see Ps. 119:28-29).

David and his men were hungry because they had not eaten for days. As a result, provisions had to be obtained if they were to continue their flight from Saul. The priest answered David's request for bread by explaining that he had none to offer except the shewbread. Dr. Kitto explains that this occurrence was perfectly natural, for David arrived on the Sabbath a few hours after the loaves had been removed from the table in the tabernacle (*Kitto's Daily Bible Illustrations*, vol. 1, p. 698). Josephus also wrote: "Upon this table, which was placed on the north side of the temple, not far from the most holy place, were laid twelve unleavened loaves of bread, six upon each heap, one above another. . . . . Now after seven days other loaves were brought in their stead, on the day which is by us called *The Sabbath*; for we call the seventh day *The Sabbath*" (Josephus, *The Antiquities of the Jews*. Book 3, Chap. 6, Paragraph 6).

On any other day, there would have been an abundant supply of bread. However, because Jewish law prohibited working on the holy day, the only bread available on that day was that which had just been replaced on the table of shewbread. Normally, this stale bread was eaten by the priests, but even Ahimelech recognized that human need is more important than observing the letter of the law. This great fact was also upheld by the Savior when He said: "Have ye not read what David did, when he was an hungered, and they that were with him; how he entered into the house of God, and did eat the shewbread, which was not lawful for him to eat, neither for them which were with him, but only for the priests?" (see Matt. 12:3-4). That high priest was a staunch supporter of David and certainly would have helped the fugitive without David's lie. It was wrong for David to deceive the high priest of God, and David's lies led to a savage massacre (see 1 Sam. 22:16-19).

The Last Chance . . . Disappearing

David was unarmed and needed weapons; he and his men were hungry and needed food. That is understandable, but why did he go to Nob when he could have so easily received supplies from any farmer in the district? Wild animals lived in the hills, crops were abundant in the valleys, and food was therefore close at hand. David knew that he was soon to leave Israel and, however great his indiscretions, remembered that God had been his refuge and strength. Maybe he momentarily forgot that he was destined to become the new king and was afraid that he might never again see the sanctuary. Perhaps it was sentiment; maybe his faith, though weak, was not dead. His convictions led him unerringly to the tabernacle. It is regrettable that instead of sharing his problems with Ahimelech, he resorted to subterfuge and brought disaster on many innocent people.

AN INSISTENT DEMAND . . . Weakening

And David said unto Ahimelech, And is there not here under thine hand spear or sword? for I have neither brought my sword nor my weapons with me, because the king's business required haste. And the priest said, The sword of Goliath the Philistine, whom thou slewest in the valley of Elah, behold, it is here wrapped in a cloth behind the ephod: If thou wilt take that, take it: for there is no other save that here. And David said, There is none like that; give it me (vv. 8-9).

Expository Notes on David's Request for Goliath's Sword

At this period in his life, David was only a shadow of his former self. The glorious faith which enabled him to defeat the Philistine giant was weak; his vision of God's invincibility had been impaired. Unfortunately, the young man from Bethlehem now depended entirely upon his own prowess; his request for the sword of Goliath was one of the most pitiable demands ever made. The weapon, which had failed to protect the heathen champion, would be useless in the hand of David. The sword, which had been wrapped in a cloth—possibly to prevent rust—had been a trophy in the Lord's presence. To express his gratitude to God, David had placed it near the altar. Now, without asking the Lord's permission, he demanded that it be returned to replace what had been lost. Since he no longer depended upon God, he was compelled by circumstances to do what he could. He assumed that God's provision evident in the valley of Elah would no longer be available.

If David and his friends urgently needed weapons, they could have borrowed, stolen, bought, or even made them. Spears, swords, and shields were owned by every farmer in the locality. The people realized that assisting fugitives could be dangerous, but David had many friends who would have willingly helped their beloved hero. Unfortunately, having commenced to wander away from God, David went from bad to worse. Had he become a little superstitious? Did he imagine that the sword of Goliath could do what other weapons could not? His disregard of other people caused the massacre of an entire city; eighty-five priests with their families and homes were ruthlessly destroyed. Although David later endeavored to make restitution to a lone survivor named Abiathar (see 1 Sam. 22:22-23), it is evident that he had become an expert at getting into trouble.

Some readers might think that he was exploiting the kindness of God. Whenever he was indiscreet, he asked God to forgive his indiscretions. Unfortunately, however, he seldom learned from his moral and spiritual deficiencies. If one might use modern terminology, David climbed out of one ditch only to fall into another, and then another. The Lord needed great patience to instruct a very slow learner! It remains a mystery how God accomplishes so much through such imperfect servants. He can change history suddenly, but often takes longer transforming people. It has often been said that "God brought Israel out of Egypt in one day, but it took forty years to remove Egypt out of Israel!"

Several of David's psalms might have come from his memories of these events. Many years probably elapsed before the poems were composed, but the earlier years could not be forgotten. David reminisced later in his life and the immortal psalms came into being. What did David feel when he remembered his earlier indiscretions? It is generally believed that he wrote Psalm 51 after the prophet Nathan denounced his illicit intercourse with Bath-sheba and the murder of her husband, Uriah. Yet, when he wrote, "Deliver me from bloodguiltiness, O God, thou God of my salvation" (see Ps. 51:14), he might also have thought of other occasions when innocent blood was needlessly shed.

It is thought-provoking to remember that when David came into prominence, he was a lad who implicitly trusted God; as a man he left his country because his scintillating faith had disappeared. It seemed to him that he was now alone, but was he? Even during his most regrettable moments, somewhere in the shadows, God lingered, awaiting an opportunity to bring pardon and comfort to a distraught, unhappy man. This part of David's life might be summarized under three headings: (1) His faltering faith, (2) His fermenting fear, and (3) His frightening future. He appears to have reached the place where he believed that God helps those who help themselves!

AN INSOLENT DETAINEE . . . Watching

Now a certain man of the servants of Saul was there that day, detained before the LORD; and his name was Doeg, an Edomite, the chiefest of the herdmen that belonged to Saul (1 Sam. 21:7). And David said unto Abiathar, I knew it that day, when Doeg the Edomite was there, that he would surely tell Saul: I have occasioned the death of all the persons of thy father's house (1 Sam. 22:22).

Expository Notes on the Treachery of Doeg the Edomite

David's actions at Nob led to one of the greatest sorrows of his life. Until he died he was haunted by the memory of his stupidity. Nothing could bring back from the grave the eighty-five priests who were slaughtered by an embittered Edomite. A knowledge of this Edomite's experiences might help readers understand why he hated the priests of the Lord.

The Edomites were descendants of Esau, who was robbed of his birthright by his brother, Jacob. The fierce animosity of Esau was shared by his descendents, who occupied the southern extremities of Palestine. King Saul had recently defeated this nation in battle (see 1 Sam. 14:47), and the possibility exists that after the conflict, for undisclosed reasons, Doeg became a servant of his former enemy. He could not have been a prisoner-of-war since he was permitted to go wherever he desired in Israel. He was promoted to the chief of the king's herdmen, and in some ways resembles Judas Iscariot, who also sold himself to enemies. When Doeg began to serve the Israelites, he would have been considered a traitor to his race. He evidently had no regard for Jehovah or the priests, since he willingly and enthusiastically superintended the slaughter of the inhabitants of Nob and, not satisfied with his brutality, proceeded to destroy the city. He was disagreeable, detestable, and defiant. His mood did not improve when he was detained by the priests, whom he eventually murdered.

A Detaining Suspension

The reason for Doeg's detention is never revealed. He had possibly violated some law and was held in seclusion until the requirements for cleansing had been provided. Some theologians believe that he was suspected of having leprous symptoms. Perhaps, he had unwittingly violated a ceremonial law and was instructed to remain in seclusion until pronounced clean by an ecclesiastical official. It does not seem reasonable that he was a leper, for he was ultimately released and became Saul's infamous executioner.

His incarceration wounded his pride and kindled within him a fire of resentment. He hated those priests and vowed that someday they would pay for this unnecessary interference in his affairs. It is extremely unfortunate that this embittered man heard David's request for food and weapons.

A Disturbing Suspicion

During the conversation with the high priest, David saw Doeg becoming increasingly interested in what was being said and done, and a terrible premonition of approaching betrayal overwhelmed his soul. Had he been more dependent upon God, something might have been done, even then, to prevent the tragedy which eventually filled Israel with sorrow. Unfortunately, David was too self-concerned to heed the warning of the Holy Spirit. At a later time he remembered those moments of apprehension and sorrowfully exclaimed, "I have occasioned the death of all the persons of thy father's house" (22:22). Had he been a wiser man, he would have known the folly of "crying over spilt milk"! At another point in his life, David heard God saying, "Be still, and know that I am God: I will be exalted among the heathen, I will be exalted in the earth" (Ps. 46:10).

When a man is running away from God, he has no time to listen and cannot be still. When Elijah fled from Jezebel, he was unable to hear the voice of God. Nevertheless, as he sat in the quietness of a mountain cave, he heard a still small voice speaking to him. Alas, he had lost the greatest opportunity of his career. The nation, which had been brought to its knees, would now scoff at his preaching. His ministry terminated when God took him to heaven. He and David both needed to be still—and listen!

A Devastating Sorrow

David's eyes were moist, his heart was heavy. He had been told of the massacre at Nob. As he stared into space, he saw the blood-stained garments of the priests and the bodies of God's servants lying in the street. He saw the charred homes where his friends had lived and the animals lying dead in the fields. Sighs shook his body and soul. Why had he been so thoughtless? He had destroyed the Lord's cause; there was now no sanctuary, no intercessors, and—for many people—no God. David whispered, "Of course God lives, but what does He think of me? I, who fought the Philistine, could not conquer myself. I not only took the shewbread and the sword from Ahimelech's hands, I took life from his body and blood from his veins."

David put his face into his hands, and tears perhaps ran down his cheeks. Of course he would be blamed for the tragedy so that all Israel would hate him. He had abandoned his country and had left behind a trail of innocent blood. Could he ever return again? There was neither sanctuary nor priest; perhaps for him, there would be no God, for how could he ever pray to One so grievously offended? It was said of Judas, "He . . . went immediately out: and it was night" (see John 13:30). David experienced a similar darkness, but it preceded a glorious dawn.

Episode 8

THEME: *David Becomes an Actor*

SCRIPTURE: 1 Samuel 21:10-15

KEY VERSE:

And he changed his behavior before them, and feigned himself mad in their hands, and scrabbled on the doors of the gate, and let his spittle fall down upon his beard (v. 13).

OUTLINE:
     I.   David's Faith Weakens (Verse 10)
    II. David's Foes Wonder (Verses 11-12)
   III. David's Frenzy Works (Verses 13-15)

And David arose, and fled that day for fear of Saul, and went to Achish the king of Gath (v. 10).

Expository Notes on David's Departure from Israel

It is difficult to appreciate the details of David's flight to Gath unless one possesses a knowledge of the geographical details of southern Palestine. Gath was one of five important cities of the Philistines. The others were Ashdod, Ashkelon, Gaza, and Ekron, which were cities of the Canaanites which survived the Hebrew invasion of their country. Although Joshua was commanded to slay the inhabitants of Canaan, these five cities survived and remained to be thorns in the flesh of the conquerors. These places were surrounded by walls and were situated on or near the coastline of southern Palestine. The inhabitants were nomads; their flocks grazed the land around their strongholds. During periods of peace, the shepherds and their animals could be seen everywhere, since their homes were tents which could be moved easily to other localities. When an enemy threatened the community, the shepherds retired within their fortress and prepared to withstand a siege. It should be remembered that David was seldom more than sixty or seventy miles from his home, but to a lonely man that distance seemed to be far away. He was well acquainted with the Philistine cities, for their citizens were notorious. The men whose height was enormous came from the Anakim people who resided in Gath (see 1 Sam. 17:4). The Scriptures speak of another giant living in Gath who had six fingers on his hands and six toes on his feet (see 2 Sam. 21:18-22). Some teachers believe that these men of abnormal size were descendants of "the nephilim," the sons of God who married the daughters of men in the days of Noah (see Gen. 6:2-4). The result was that their children were "giants." Each of the cities had its own king (see Josh. 13:3 and 1 Sam. 6:16-17). It is also interesting to remember that when the ark of Jehovah was captured by the Philistines, it was kept in Askelon, Gath, or Ekron until the people were punished by God. It was only after severe calamities that the Philistines placed the ark on a new cart and watched as two milking cows took it back to the place from which it had come (see 1 Sam. 5 and 6). David knew of the Philistine strongholds and, believing his need to find a sanctuary was urgent, decided he would appeal to Achish, the king of Gath. The exact location of this ancient city has never been authoritatively established, but a possible identification places it close to the other four cities—about sixty-five miles from Jerusalem. It might have been closer.

DAVID'S FAITH WEAKENS

For the first time in his life, David had left his native land. His eyes were probably filled with tears; his heart was heavy. His vision of God's invincibility had been blurred. Poor man, he was running away from his problems, and difficulties are seldom removed by such action. In more senses than one, the fugitive had turned his back on the sanctuary. His actions had left Nob in shambles; his stupidity eventually stained its streets with the blood of God's priests (see 1 Sam. 22:16-19). At that time David probably believed that he had reached the end of his career and considered, as did Jonah, that the safest thing to do was to run away. It is extremely fortunate for both men that they failed to outrun God! It is stimulating to know that the Lord is always a step ahead of His disappointing servants. Throughout this section of David's story, God's *perception, planning,* and *power* are very evident. The story of Jonah, the prophet, provides an excellent illustration of these facts.

To revert to an earlier study, when David looked at Jehovah, Goliath seemed to be a midget; when he lost sight of God, King Saul appeared to be an invincible menace against whom no one could prevail. Poor David! His experiences are informative to all who claim to be servants of the Lord. When Joshua's spies returned from Canaan, their testimony was conflicting. Ten of their number had been so horrified as they gazed at the inhabitants of the land that, when they made their report, they fearfully exclaimed, "And there we saw the giants, the sons of Anak, which come of the giants: and we were in our own sight as grasshoppers, and so we were in their sight" (see Num. 13:33). The two remaining spies, Joshua and

Caleb, provided a different viewpoint when they said, "The land which we passed through to search it, is an exceeding good land. If the LORD delight in us, then he will bring us into this land, and give it us; a land which floweth with milk and honey" (see Num. 14:7-8). Perhaps the writer to the Hebrews had similar thoughts in his mind when he wrote: "Wherefore seeing we also are compassed about with so great a cloud of witnesses, let us lay aside every weight, and the sin which doth so easily beset us, and let us run with patience the race that is set before us, *Looking unto Jesus* the author and finisher of our faith; who for the joy that was set before him endured the cross, despising the shame, and is set down at the right hand of the throne of God" (Heb. 12:1-2).

DAVID'S FOES WONDER

And the servants of Achish said unto him, Is not this David the king of the land? did they not sing one to another of him in dances, saying, Saul hath slain his thousands, and David his ten thousands? And David laid up these words in his heart, and was sore afraid of Achish the king of Gath (vv. 11-12).

Expository Notes on the Questions of the Philistine

It is not difficult to decide why David fled to Gath. Other adjacent nations or cities had made their peace with Israel and would have been reluctant to welcome a fugitive sought by Saul. They feared the repercussions which would follow if they annoyed their powerful neighbor. On the other hand, the Philistines were perennial foes of the Hebrews, and David probably believed that they were his only chance of survival. He possibly believed that Achish would be thrilled about Saul's loss of his greatest warrior's services. Nevertheless, neither David nor any other person could argue effectively against a guilty conscience. The fugitive should never have gone to the Philistine city, and the fact that he was quickly in trouble is not a cause for amazement. He failed to consider that his countrymen would denounce him as a traitor. Fraternizing with the enemies of the nation was never permitted, and at a much later period in history, even Simon Peter learned the folly of sitting at the enemies' fire. Perhaps David believed that he could remain unrecognized and that the usual courtesy shown to strangers would be given to him. He was filled with dismay when the Philistine leaders expressed their disapproval and repeated what the maidens of Israel had sung. Their spies had evidently been very active, and their information concerning Israel was correct.

David quickly became aware of the hostility of the people, and when they criticized the king's acceptance of David, his fear increased. The inscription at the beginning of Psalm 34 describes it as "a Psalm of David when he changed his behavior before Abimelech (Achish); who drove him away, and he departed." The words written at that time enable readers to understand the emotions of the worried author. David wrote: "This poor man cried, and the LORD heard him, and saved him out of all his troubles. The angel of the LORD encampeth round about them that fear him, and delivereth them. . . . The LORD redeemeth the soul of his servants: and none of them that trust in him shall be desolate" (Ps. 34:6-7, 22). When David wrote, "The LORD is nigh unto them that are of a broken heart; and saveth such as be of a contrite spirit" (v. 18), he expressed the tremendous change which had taken place within his soul. Arrogance, selfishness, and fear had been removed by a sincere, genuine dependence upon God. Any defiance in his attitude had been replaced by a broken heart and a contrite spirit. There is hope for any man when he kneels before his Maker.

DAVID'S FRENZY WORKS

And he changed his behavior before them, and feigned himself mad in their hands, and scrabbled on the doors of the gate, and let his spittle fall down upon his beard. Then said Achish unto his servants, Lo, ye see the man is mad: wherefore then have ye brought him to me? Have I need of mad men, that ye have brought this fellow to play the mad man in my presence? shall this fellow come into my house? (vv. 13-15).

Expository Notes on David's Act of Madness

David's predicament at that time was exceedingly dangerous. He had trusted that God's providential care protected him at all times, but when he felt deprived of this assistance, David was afraid of imminent danger. If the king of Achish had commanded his execution, his servants would have immediately carried out the sentence. His peril was obvious. What could he do to offset such a threat to his existence? Two thoughts suddenly came to his mind. He remembered how Saul had acted when "an evil spirit troubled him"; he had become so agitated that even his closest friends believed that he was completely irresponsible. At the same time, David was aware of the common belief that all insane people were controlled by demons and that interference of any kind might anger the spirit and cause unpleasant repercussions. No one had sufficient courage to meddle in affairs which basically did not concern him. David apparently believed that faking insanity was the only way to solve his problem. He therefore "changed his behavior before them, and feigned himself mad in their hands, and scrabbled on the door of the gate, and let his spittle run down upon his beard." He resembled an irresponsible dervish by waving his arms and trying to climb the walls and doors while frothing at the mouth. The horrified onlookers were astonished, and their report to the king elicited an immediate response. "Have I need of mad men . . . shall this fellow come into my house?" (v. 15).

This electrifying episode in the life of David commands attention in every age. Was David pretending to be insane, or was he subject to epileptic seizures? Commenting on the king's statement, John Kitto writes, "The Jewish writers think that there was more emphasis than we are aware of in the king's asking if *he* had need of insane people. They tell us that the king's wife and daughter were both insane, and that while David was simulating madness outside, they were exhibiting madness inside. Thus, poor Achish might have thought that he had already had enough of this. We should like to be able to entertain the belief that this epileptic madness of David was real, and not feigned. . . . Both the Septuagint and the Vulgate versions intimate that it was real. . . . To us, it seems that the plain meaning of the text is that the madness was assumed; but we are ready to admit, that were the text less explicit, we could see no improbability in a sudden attack of epilepsy under such circumstances" (*Kitto's Daily Bible Illustrations*, vol. 1, p. 702).

The gate or the door upon which David scrawled, scratched, or made indentations was probably in the chamber adjacent to the throne room. There the noblemen, courtiers, and distinguished visitors awaited an audience with the king. David's desperate fear added reality to his performance. When he frothed at the mouth and permitted his saliva to desecrate his beard, the watching Philistines decided that their visitor was mentally deranged. They believed that no sane person would ever spoil his personal appearance by defiling his beard. David, in their estimation, had now reached the depth of human degradation. He who was destined to become the king of Israel had become a disgusting sight, clawing at doors and dribbling spittle over his chin, beard, and clothing. David desperately hoped that the viewers would be deceived by his antics. To compare this man with the simple, trusting, dignified lad who fearlessly went to meet Goliath, confounds the mind.

Josephus, the Jewish historian, agrees with many commentators. He wrote: "David was afraid the king would put him to death, and that he would experience that danger from him, which he had escaped from Saul: so he *pretended* to be distracted and mad, so that his spittle ran out of his mouth; and he did other like actions before the king of Gath which might make him believe that they proceeded from such a distemper. Accordingly, the king was very angry at his servants that they had brought him a mad man, and he gave orders that they should eject David immediately out of the city." (Josephus, *The Antiquities of the Jews*. Book 6. Chap. 12. Paragraph 2).

The Bible is a revelation of the grace of God; it supplies irrefutable evidence that the Lord's kindness supersedes anything known by humanity. Paul wrote: "For ye see your calling, brethren, how that not many wise men after the flesh, not many mighty, not many noble, are called: but God hath chosen the foolish things of the world to confound the wise; and God hath chosen the weak things of the world to confound the things which are mighty; And base things of the world, and things which are despised, hath God chosen, yea, and things which are not, to bring to nought things that are: That no flesh should glory in his presence" (1 Cor. 1:26-29). The Bible tells of sheep herders, fishermen, vine dressers, and many other ordinary people who responded to the call of God; but when they failed in their duties, the Lord graciously forgave their indiscretions and restored them to His favor. David was just an unknown lad who made innumerable mistakes. Yet, God never forsook him, and in the light of these facts, there is hope for everybody.

HOMILIES FOR PREACHERS AND TEACHERS

Study No. 5

DAVID . . . and the Madness Which Suggested a Psalm (Psalm 36)

David sat in the cave of Adullam and quietly watched the surrounding countryside. The days were perilous because a price had been placed on his head. Away through the trees, rugged men guarded the trails; in the secrecy of their stronghold, other men prepared a meal; but all the while their brave young leader dreamed and watched. In thought he still saw the hazardous flight into the country of Gath, and he involuntarily shuddered as he recalled the narrowness of his escape in that foreign land. David smiled when he remembered his desperate acting. In retrospect it appeared strangely comical, but, of course, grim tragedy had stalked his every movement. The enemies had watched as he clawed at the walls; they had frowned with disgust as spittle ran down his beard while this immature actor was forced into a more convincing display of his acting skills. He had traced fantastic patterns on the walls, and his laughs had been those of an idiot. His actions had been so grotesque and revolting that finally his enemies had pronounced him insane. They had driven the lunatic away, but had failed to see the relief which suddenly appeared in his eyes. David took his writing material, lifted his face to the sky, and as gratitude filled his soul, he wrote Psalm 34.

DAVID'S GREAT SALVATION

Slowly he wrote his testimony—"This poor man cried, and the LORD heard him, and saved him out of all his troubles" (v. 6). Maybe he paused awhile and put down his pen, for he realized that his statement fitted many episodes in his eventful career. The words "this poor man" seem to indicate that every vestige of David's self-confidence had disappeared before an overwhelming sense of personal need. He had desperately cried to God for help, and his petition had been heard.

Verse six suggests a proposition: *A man must recognize his need before God can save him.* This is one of the basic laws of Holy Scripture and human experience. When a man has unlimited confidence in his own ability, he feels no need for God. A sense of insufficiency causes a desire to pray, and prayer is the key which unlocks heaven's resources.

DAVID'S GREAT SECURITY

David's pen is moving again. "The angel of the LORD encampeth round about them that fear him, and delivereth them" (v. 7). Once again the scenes of recent days appeared before David's eyes. But except for the explanation provided by his own words, how else could he have escaped from his enemies? King Saul was probably an expert javelin thrower who seemingly could not have missed a sitting target at such a short distance. David had been playing his instrument at Saul's feet. Then the escape from Gath had been most providential. That a one-time shepherd boy should, without rehearsal, develop into a first-rate actor seems impossible. Even David could scarcely believe his own memories. Surely in his successive hours of need, the angel of the Lord had encamped around him. God had been his refuge and strength, a very present help in trouble. Verse seven suggests another proposition: *God is never far from a man who needs help.* And that is as true today as it was in David's day.

DAVID'S GREAT SATISFACTION

"O taste and see that the LORD is good: blessed is the man that trusteth in him" (v. 8). The story of testimony halts as this spontaneous expression of praise rises unchecked from a thankful heart. God had been exceedingly kind and gracious, and David knew the blessedness of the man whose trust is in the Lord. Eventually, before he laid aside his pen, he wrote that "none of them that trust in Him shall be desolate" (v. 22).

The birds were singing in the trees, and the sun, a ball of flaming glory, had filled the sky with crimson. The evening meal was ready, and the men were waiting. David stood up. He was a prince indeed, for his meditation had taken him into the presence of the eternal King. Yes, all was well, and he went to join his followers. In thought we watch him; and then, recalling his third great statement, we recognize our final proposition: *Concerning the things of God, to taste for a moment means to trust for ever.* (Homily reprinted from the author's book, *Bible Pinnacles*, pp. 69-70.)

Episode 9

THEME: *The Massacre of the Priests of Nob*

SCRIPTURE: 1 Samuel 22

KEY VERSE:

And the prophet Gad said unto David, Abide not in the hold; depart, and get thee into the land of Judah. Then David departed, and came into the forest of Hareth (v. 5).

OUTLINE:
  I.   A Thoughtful Provision (Verses 1-4)
  II. A Terrible Plight (Verses 5-16)
  III. A Treacherous Performance (Verses 17-19)
  IV. A Thrilling Promise (Verses 20-23)

Expository Notes on David's Care for His Family

David therefore departed thence, and escaped to the cave Adullam: and when his brethren and all his father's house heard it, they went down thither to him. And every one that was in distress, and every one that was in debt, and every one that was discontented, gathered themselves unto him; and he became a captain over them: and there were with him about four hundred men. And David went thence to Mizpeh of Moab: and he said unto the king of Moab, Let my father and my mother, I pray thee, come forth, and be with you, till I know what God will do for me. And he brought them before the king of Moab: and they dwelt with him all the while that David was in the hold (vv. 1-4).

Poor David! It might be said he leapt out of the frying pan into the fire! Haunted by fears that would not disappear concerning his immediate future, he surely asked the questions: "Where shall I go? What can I do?" At that time in his life he was apparently without a friend and had reached "rock bottom." Then, he thought of the cave of Adullam which was close to the city bearing the same name. Believing that it offered a chance of survival, he "departed thence, and escaped to the cave of Adullam."

It is interesting to note that this place was one of the oldest cities in the world and was mentioned in Genesis 38:1-2. Judah had associated with an Adullamite woman who bore his sons. It had become one of the most formidable strongholds of the Philistines and has been identified with Khibit-eld el-Ma, which is halfway between Lachish and Jerusalem. Describing the area, Conder wrote: "East of Ziph is a prominent hill on which is the ruined town of Cain; hence the eye ranges over the theatre of David's wanderings. On the south are the wilds of the original plateau, with the plains of Beersheba beyond; on the East is the 'Solitude' with white peaks; cones of chalk, and deep narrow watercourses terminated by the great pointed cliff of Ziz above Engedi, and by the precipices over the Dead Sea, two thousand feet high. Here, among the rocks of the wild goats, the herds of ibex may be seen bounding, and the partridge are chased on the mountains, as David was followed by the stealthy hunter, Saul. The blue sea is visible in its deep chasm and is backed by the dark precipice of Kerak, scarred with a hundred wintry watercourses" (Conder, *Tenting in Palestine*, vol. 2, p. 90). "The site of Adullam is ruinous, but not deserted. The sides of the tributary valley are lined with rows of caves, and these we found inhabited and full of flocks and herds; but still more interesting was the discovery of a separate cave, on the hill itself, a low, smoke-filled, blackened burrow which was the home of a single family. We could not but suppose as we entered the gloomy abode that our feet were standing on the very footprints of the Shepherd-King, who here encamped between the Philistines and the Jews. Here, he was but three miles distant from the thickets of Hareth" (Conder, *Tenting in Palestine*, vol. 2, p. 159).

It was to this desolate area David fled, and in his moments of deepest despair, his soul seemed as barren as his place of refuge. His fears resembled enemies who lived and lurked in the shadows of the blackened caves. Yet, all was not lost. Even though David apparently had lost sight of God, Jehovah continued to see His erring servant and was already sending assistance to him.

A THOUGHTFUL PROVISION

A Family Reunion

> . . . and when his brethren, and all his father's house heard it, they went down thither to him (v. 1).

The question might be asked, "Why were his relatives anxious to join the fugitive when they had earlier been indifferent and even antagonistic toward him?" Perhaps they felt threatened by the continuing animosity of the frustrated king. Saul had searched everywhere to find David, but even his best efforts had failed to locate the wanted man. He was not favorably disposed toward the family of Jesse and probably believed they were aiding and abetting a criminal. During his more irrational moments, he was capable of using force to obtain desired information. Since they feared an ominous future, Jesse and his family decided that it would be wise to seek refuge with David. To do this, their farm had to be sold, rented, or abandoned. Their arrival at Adullam brought pleasure and problems. It was wonderful to enjoy fellowship with his kinsfolk, but David became contemplative when he considered the future. His brothers, if they chose, could join his army, but the noncombatants in the group would be a liability if Saul's forces attacked David's followers. What then could be done with the women and children who had unexpectedly arrived at Adullam?

A Faithful Regiment

And everyone that was in distress, and everyone that was in debt, and everyone that was discontented, gathered themselves unto him; and he became a captain over them: and there were with him about four hundred men (v. 2).

Thus did David begin the formation of his army, and it would be difficult to imagine a more incompetent group of soldiers. Is it possible to see in this incident foreshadowings of another Captain, who encouraged people to enlist in His army by announcing, "And whosoever will, let him take the water of life freely"? (see Rev. 22:17).

It is significant that there were no important people among those who came to David. The ancient writer mentioned three classes: the troubled, the threatened, and the tormented. The reason for the perplexity of the people is never explained. Unrevealed circumstances had ruined their happiness, and since they believed that David was their only hope, they decided to follow him whatever the cost might be. The men had to choose between slavery to Saul or freedom as servants of David. They were evidently unable to meet the demands made against them and desperately sought safety with David's army.

The word translated "discontented" means "bitter in soul." Hannah, who prayed at Shiloh, exhibited similar characteristics (see 1 Sam. 1:10-11). Even though she was desperate, she believed that God alone could satisfy the yearnings of her soul. Perhaps some of the men who came to David believed that their new leader could provide them with justice. No man-made laws could prevent their coming, and those who came were never turned away.

To say the least, David's first army was neither pretentious nor overpowering. They had no great array of weapons, possessing only those brought with them. They had no glittering uniforms nor shiny buttons and never received any promise of financial remuneration. Their only reason for coming was a tremendous faith in David's ability to help them. His need was as great as those of his new friends. They needed each other. He was no longer alone!

Could God build a kingdom on such unreliable foundations? David, at least, intended to give Him that opportunity. Centuries later, another group of people sought the aid of David's far-greater Son. Lepers, fishermen, impoverished folk from all walks of life, and people who were frightened and depressed were willing to leave their possessions to answer the call of the Savior. Could God build a church with such poor material? He evidently made the attempt, and today after two thousand years that church stands supreme—against it, even the gates of hell cannot prevail!

A Firm Request

And David went thence to Mizpeh of Moab: and he said unto the king of Moab, Let my father and my mother, I pray thee, come forth, and be with you, till I know what God will do for me (v. 3).

Perhaps David sought assistance from the king of Moab because he could not trust any other leader. Nevertheless, the question is unavoidable: Why did he entrust his parents to people who were the perpetual enemies of Israel? Did he believe that the king of Moab would gladly assist anyone who was hated by Saul? Did the king believe that a grateful David would assist in the continuing warfare against the Hebrews? Many answers might be given, but probably the most intriguing has its roots in history. The Bible states that Ruth, the Moabitess, married Boaz of Bethlehem and became the grandmother of Jesse, David's father. Furthermore, the other daughter-in-law of Naomi was also a Moabitess who loved her mother-in-law. That young woman decided to remain with her people, but the possibility exists that her strong affection for the woman of Israel was shared by her descendants. Orpah would have died, but her relationship with Naomi might have been known among her people. David realized the difficulty of finding a safe shelter, but of all the possibilities, Moab appeared to be the most promising.

A Friendly Response

And [David's parents] dwelt with [the king of Moab] all the while that David was in the hold (v. 4).

The *Amplified Bible* interprets the term "hold" as "the mountain fastness." David remained a fugitive in his hillside stronghold near the city of Adullam. Liberated from the responsibility of protecting his aged parents, he stayed with his men. "The hill is about five hundred feet high; it commands a fine view eastward over the broad valley (up which runs the high road to Hebron); its course dotted with terebinth, and rich with corn; in the distance are high, rocky mountains, dark with brushwood, and steeply sloping, with a small village here and there. These are perched on a great knoll, gleaming white. There is ample room to have accommodated David's four hundred men in the caves, and those, as we have seen, are still inhabited" (Conder, *Tenting in Palestine*, vol. 1, pp. 159-160).

The reasons for the king's friendly response to the Moabites have already been considered. David's relief about his family's safety was instantaneous, but when he returned to the solitude of his cave, loneliness dominated his thoughts. It is possible that at this time he wrote Psalm 142. The introduction to this sonnet reads: "A prayer when he was in the cave." It must be admitted that his words could belong to many other experiences in his life. He was being systematically sought by Saul, and this psalm can justifiably be connected with all his hiding places. His words supply a reflection of the writer's soul.

PSALM 142

David was convinced that he had reached the end of his usefulness. His message may be divided into three sections.

Despondency and Despair

The psalm is an expression of a man overwhelmed by fear, a person who felt helpless among ruthless enemies. His confession that no man cared for his soul indicates that he was almost without hope. It is tragic that the person who slew Goliath should have fallen so low, that his faith in God had become meaningless. It is not difficult to imagine him sitting in the cavern, his face resting in his upturned hands, with despair in his soul.

Years later, another man had a similar experience. Running from his problems and overwhelmed by fear, Elijah heard God asking: "What doest thou here Elijah?" (see 1 Kings 19:9). The great prophet, who had successfully challenged the king of Israel, had unfortunately succumbed to terror. Long after that incident, Paul also believed that his ministry was terminating as he sat in prison. His intense desire to attend a feast in Jerusalem has caused his disregard for the inspired warnings of the Holy Spirit. Finally, when it was too late to correct his mistake, the Apostle to the Gentiles was so despondent that God had to encourage His servant (see Acts 23:11). It is better to shelter in the Rock of Ages than to run before a storm.

Dependency and Desire

"I cried unto thee O LORD : I said, Thou art my refuge, and my portion in the land of the living. Attend unto my cry; for I am brought very low: deliver me from my persecutors; for they are stronger than I" (vv. 5-6).

David seemed aware of the repercussions resulting from his pitiable conduct. His pretending to be insane had only brought temporary deliverance; his ability to find a refuge for his endangered parents had not provided peace for his troubled soul. When a man sinks to the lowest point of degradation, there is only one direction in which he can gaze—upward. Slowly, David began thinking about God; he saw a light in the distance which reminded him of the fellowship he had previously enjoyed. When he cried, "O Lord", it is evident that he had ceased thinking about himself. Then he confessed, "Thou art my refuge, and my portion in the land of the living." Is it not significant that he wrote neither "Thou *hast been*" nor "Thou *wilt be* my refuge"? He could safely rest in the everlasting arms of God's kindness.

It may be recalled that when he accompanied his parents to the palace of the king of Moab, he said, "Let my father and my mother, I pray thee, come forth, and be with you, *till I know what God will do for me*" (1 Sam. 22:3). His use of that preposition was very suggestive. He did not say, "till I see what God will do *in me*"; neither did he say, "what God will do *with me*." David thought only of self-preservation and confessed that unless God intervened on his behalf, all other efforts would be useless. It has been said that until a man reaches rock bottom, he has no chance of reaching the Rock of Ages. When David wrote this psalm, he had evidently plumbed the depths of his insufficiency.

Deliverance and Delight

"Bring my soul out of prison, that I may praise thy name: the righteous shall compass me about; for thou shalt deal bountifully with me" (v. 7). Once again the sun was shining into the bleakness of David's soul; God's refreshing raindrops were reaching the parched areas of his life. As he prayed, his vision improved and his faith deepened. He even contemplated praising God's name. Forgetting, at least momentarily, the nearness of his foes, David exultantly cried, "The righteous shall compass me about." His loneliness was ending; his desolation was turning to glorious fellowship. God would surround him with reliable friends. Such faith brings its own reward, and it is extremely interesting to read the next verse in the narrative.

And the prophet Gad said unto David, Abide not in the hold; depart, and get thee into the land of Judah. Then David departed, and came into the forest of Hareth (1 Sam. 22:5).

It was never explained how, when, or where the prophet reached David's camp, but his timing was perfect. He arrived at the correct and crucial moment since the Lord directed his movements. David's lapse of faith had not changed the omnipotence of God, who remained upon His throne and thus could never forget His own. Many Christians unfortunately resemble David in that they permit circumstances to ruin their happiness. It is refreshing to remember that God is too wise to make mistakes and too loving to be unkind. At all times He knows what He is doing! The timely appearance of the prophet Gad suggests three things: (1) vision—God had not lost sight of David, (2) virtue—God showed that He still cared by commissioning the prophet to assist the worried fugitive, and (3) victory—if God had assumed responsibility for David's preservation, then the ultimate triumph was assured. Was it then that the psalmist wrote: "A thousand shall fall at thy side, and ten thousand at thy right hand; but it shall not come nigh thee. . . . Because thou hast made the LORD, which is my refuge, even the most High, thy habitation; there shall no evil befall thee, neither shall any plague come nigh thy dwelling. For he shall give his angels charge over thee, to keep thee in all thy ways"? (Ps. 91:7-11).

"Then David departed and came into the forest of Hareth." The statement "the forest of Hareth" is intriguing in view of the rocky desolation of the entire area. To imagine a forest in that locality is tantamount to imagining a fountain of pure water in the middle of the Dead Sea! Conder, the archaeologist who surveyed the district, wrote: "Driven from these lairs, David went further south to the neighborhood of Ziph, and here our English version speaks of a forest—the wood (Choresh of Ziph) where David met with Jonathan. A moment's reflection will, however, convince any traveler that as the dry porous formation of the plateau must be unchanged since David's time, no wood or trees could then have flourished over this unwatered, sun-scorched region. The true explanation seems to be that the word *Choresh* is a proper name with a different significance, and such is the view of the Greek scriptures and also of Josephus. We were able to strengthen this interpretation by the discovery of the ruin of *Khorisa* and the valley of *Hiresh* (the same word under another form), closer to Ziph the first of which may well be thought to represent the Hebrew *Choresh Ziph*. Should this word appear as a proper name in the new English Version, a very marked improvement will be made in what might be called the orientalization of the Bible. This substitutes the actual language of the land for that essentially English tone which has been imparted to the narrative by translators, to whom the East was less familiar than their own fair country." (Conder, *Tenting in Palestine*, vol. 2, p. 89).

A Mischievous Resolve

When Saul heard that David was discovered, and the men that were with him (now Saul abode in Gibeah under a tree in Ramah, having his spear in his hand, and all his servants were standing about him;) Then Saul said unto his servants that stood about him, Hear now, ye Benjamites; will the son of Jesse give every one of you fields and vineyards,

and make you all captains of thousands, and captains of hundreds; that all of you have conspired against me, and there is none that sheweth me that my son hath made a league with the son of Jesse, and there is none of you that is sorry for me (vv. 6-8).

History records many despicable acts of Saul, but this was one of his most villainous plans. Frustrated, bitter, and angry, he attempted to divide the nation. David belonged to the tribe of Judah, and recognizing this fact, the petulant king addressed his remarks to the men of Benjamin. He implied that remaining in royal favor would guarantee them prosperity in business and promotion in the military profession. Saul's contention was that, if David were given the opportunity, he would only reward the men of Judah. As a result, we see that in order to further his own schemes, Saul was willing to encourage a civil war.

A Malicious Report

Then answered Doeg the Edomite, which was set over the servants of Saul, and said, I saw the son of Jesse coming to Nob, to Ahimelech the son of Ahitub. And he inquired of the LORD for him, and gave him victuals, and gave him the sword of Goliath (vv. 9-10).

Doeg was an alien who had sold his services to the enemy of his nation. He had become the overseer of Saul's servants and was determined to increase his influence in the royal court. With a sinister smile on his face, he poured, as it were, gasoline on the fires of hate already burning in the king's soul. Treachery and a desire for revenge made Doeg a brutal murderer. Since he thought only of himself, he damned his soul.

A TERRIBLE PLIGHT

Saul's diatribe against the priests of Nob was as inexcusable as David's request to Ahimelech had been selfish and thoughtless. Human need was more important than ecclesiastical tradition, but in his uncontrollable fury Saul was determined to wreak vengeance upon any person who had assisted the elusive David. The reply given by the high priest was dignified, just, and commendable, and in defiance of his impending execution, the priest never apologized for his defense of his friend. He who lived in the house of God evidently had no fear of meeting Him face to face.

Some theologians emphasize that the execution was a fulfillment of the curse placed upon the descendants of Eli, whose sons desecrated the sanctuary at Shiloh (see 1 Sam. 2:31-36). This observation might be true, but it should be remembered that Ahimelech and his colleagues never flinched, even though they knew that the streets of their city would soon be stained with their blood.

Then Ahimelech answered the king, and said, And who is so faithful among all thy servants as David, which is the king's son in law, and goeth at thy bidding, and is honorable in thine house? Did I then begin to inquire of God for him? be it far from me: let not the king impute anything unto his servant, nor to all the house of my father: for thy servant knew nothing of all this, less or more. And the king said, Thou shalt surely die, Ahimelech, thou and all thy father's house. And the king said unto the footmen that stood about him, Turn, and slay the priests of the LORD; because their hand also is with David, and because they knew when he fled, and did not shew it to me (vv. 14-17).

Expository Notes on Saul's Denunciation of His Servants

The tragic death of the priests of Nob is only mentioned here because David was indirectly responsible for the tragedy. His selfish and perhaps arrogant stupidity placed the lives of the clerics in jeopardy. When the only survivor of that terrible massacre escaped, he carried the news of the event to David.

A Marvelous Refusal

And the king said unto his footmen that stood about him, Turn and slay the priests of the LORD, because their hand also is with David, and because they knew when he fled, and did not shew it to me. But the servants of the king would not put forth their hand to fall upon the priests of the LORD (v. 17).

Saul was surely livid with anger because rebellion and insubordination had appeared among his soldiers. He probably repeated and emphasized his commands by shouting, but it seemed that his men had been suddenly paralyzed. There are several possible explanations of their disobedience: (1) Were they secret admirers of David and thus among the "all Israel" reportedly in love with the fugitive? (2) Were they fearful of God's anger thus believing that His wrath would fall on any person who harmed the priests? (3) Were they disgusted with the king's conduct because they recognized that his vicious conduct had deprived him of the right to execute anyone? Had only one soldier refused to obey the king's command, he would have been slain immediately, but there was strength in unity. Confronted by their united refusal, Saul desperately commanded Doeg to complete what had been commenced.

A TREACHEROUS PERFORMANCE

And the king said to Doeg, Turn thou, and fall upon the priests. And Doeg the Edomite turned, and he fell upon the priests, and slew that day fourscore and five persons that did wear a linen ephod. And Nob, the

city of the priests, smote he with the edge of the sword, both men and women, children and sucklings, and oxen, and asses, and sheep, with the edge of the sword (vv. 18-19).

Expository Notes on the Brutality of the Edomite

When Doeg was given the opportunity to unleash the savagery within his embittered soul, he did not hesitate to plunge his sword into the chests of his defenseless victims. Within minutes the spotless linen of the priests' ephods were stained with infamy. Doeg appears to be a demon-possessed lunatic whose insatiable hunger for vengeance permitted no exceptions. Babies were dragged from the arms of screaming mothers, and the carnage did not end until the flocks and herds had all been slain. Then, breathless from his demoniacal displays of brutality, the Edomite paused, his face flushed with evil glee. Those filthy priests would never again humiliate him! He had vowed to punish the men whom he considered to be religious hypocrites; he had kept his word. He had annihilated everything that represented God and believed that no priests were still living! But he was mistaken. "And one of the sons of Ahimelech, the son of Ahitub, named Abiathar, escaped, and fled after David" (v. 20).

Doeg was an Edomite, a man without God. He had no sanctuary, no hope, and no friend. He was so full of himself that there remained no room for another. He had become the king's chief herdsman and was wealthy and bankrupt at the same time. He was also a very great fool. He was dead before he died!

A THRILLING PROMISE

And one of the sons of Ahimelech, the son of Ahitub, named Abiathar, escaped, and fled after David. And Abiathar shewed David that Saul had slain the LORD's priests. And David said unto Abiathar, I knew it that day, when Doeg the Edomite was there, that he would surely tell Saul: I have occasioned the death of all the persons of thy father's house. Abide thou with me, fear not: for he that seeketh my life seeketh thy life: but with me thou shalt be in safeguard (vv. 20-23).

Expository Notes on Abiathar's Coming to David

It may be asked how this man escaped when the massacre of the priestly family appeared to be complete. He possibly had been attending to duties within the sanctuary and had hidden when the executions commenced. The fact that he fled to David "with an ephod in his hand" (see 1 Sam. 23:6) might suggest that he had been attending to the vestments or uniforms used in the worship of Jehovah. Maybe he watched the horrifying scene and then left the building through some little-used exit. Thus was the priesthood preserved, and the ominously black clouds of adversity appeared to have a silver lining. David unexpectedly received a priest into his camp, and the ephod reopened lines of communication between Jehovah and a very needy captain.

The foreword to Psalm 52 reads, "A Psalm of David, when Doeg the Edomite told Saul, and said unto him, David is come to the house of Ahimelech." The words of this sonnet provide an insight into the soul of the author.

> **Why boasteth thyself in mischief, O mighty man? . . . Thy tongue deviseth mischiefs; like a sharp razor, working deceitfully. Thou lovest evil more than good; and lying rather than to speak righteousness. . . . God shall likewise destroy thee for ever. . . . Lo, this is the man that made not God his strength; but trusted in the abundance of his riches, and strengthened himself in his wickedness (Psalm 52).**

The Bible says that the way of transgressors is hard. Doeg unfortunately never discovered this fact until it was too late to correct his mistake.

HOMILIES FOR PREACHERS AND TEACHERS

Study No. 6

ABIATHAR . . . the Sole Survivor From a Massacred City
(1 Samuel 22:19-20)

Such a circumstance had never been known in Israel. King Saul had murdered a city of priests and had thereby sealed his doom. He had heard how they had helped David, and frustrated by his own inability to capture the young prince, he was furious. He snarled and demanded adequate reasons why the clerics should help the enemy of the throne. "Then Ahimelech answered the king, and said, And who is so faithful among all thy servants as David, which is the king's son in law, and goeth at thy bidding, and is honorable in thine house?" (1 Sam. 22:14). The calm, dignified answer annoyed Saul so much that he fiercely replied, "Thou shalt surely die, Ahimelech, thou, and all thy father's house. And the king said unto the footmen that stood about him, Turn, and slay the priests of the LORD. But the servants of the king would not. . . . And the king said to Doeg, Turn thou and fall upon the priests. And Doeg the Edomite . . . fell upon the priests, and slew on that day fourscore and five persons that did wear a linen ephod. And Nob, the city of the priests, smote he with the edge of the sword" (vv. 16-19). And the watching madman—for mad Saul must have been—could not see that his actions would become the greatest boomerang in history.

A GREAT DISTRESS

"And one of the sons of Ahimelech the son of Ahitub, named Abiathar, escaped, and fled after David" (v. 20). We do not know how the boy managed to evade the cruel sword of the Edomite. Possibly in the confusion he was able to dodge away through the ranks of sullen footmen. The soldiers were angry because their royal leader pronounced the despicable death sentence, and they risked their lives when they refused to obey a command. It is not too much to suppose, therefore, that they gladly assisted the fleeing boy. Abiathar ran for his life, and when he was able to rest for a few moments, he realized that he was alone and friendless in the world. Storm clouds filled his sky since Saul seemed likely to hound him to death. Then he remembered the fugitive prince. Yes, he would go to David and ask for help.

A GREAT DECISION

The young man slowly and carefully made his way toward the cave of Adullam. He quickly found the hillside trail and commenced the ascent, but a rough voice almost immediately commanded him to stand still. Startled, he obeyed, and a toughened sentry stepped from a hiding place to ask the cause of this intrusion. "Young man, where are you going, and why?" The boy told his story and confessed that he wished to reach David. The older man's eyes were filled with sympathy as he saw the boy's grief, and if Abiathar asked, "Do you think David will take me in?" the sentry hastened to dispel his fears. "Son, of course he will. He is the friend of all the needy. My boy, didn't you hear that there are about 400 of us who are in distress, in debt, or bitter about life that are following David as our captain? Son, I came to him, and I found a welcome. What he did for me, he will do for you. Go ahead. All is well."

A GREAT DELIVERANCE

"And Abiathar shewed David that Saul had slain the LORD's priests. And David said unto Abiathar. . . . Abide thou with me, fear not: for he that seeketh my life seeketh thy life: but with me thou shalt be in safeguard" (1 Sam. 22:21-23). That day the young man discovered three wonderful acts: (1) *A place to rest.* His own home had been destroyed, and the old surroundings were now prohibited to him. The birds had their nests, but he had no place to call home until he bowed before a charming prince who welcomed him into the fellowship of a new society, "My boy, stay here and rest." (2) *A promise to reassure.* "Fear not . . . with me thou shalt be in safeguard." Abide with me. I will be your protection, my words shall be your delight, my men shall be your brothers, and my presence shall be your home. (3) *A peace to enjoy.* As Abiathar looked into the face of his new friend, a new calm settled upon his tired spirit, and he lay down to rest. (Homily reprinted from the author's book, *Bible Pinnacles*, pp. 39-40).

Episode 10

THEME: *The Value of an Ephod*

SCRIPTURE: 1 Samuel 23

KEY VERSE:

> And it came to pass, when Abiathar, the son of Ahimelech fled to David to Keilah, that he came down with an ephod in his hand (1 Sam. 23:6).

OUTLINE:
   I. The Thrilling Intercession (Verses 1-14)
  II. The Tremendous Inspiration (Verses 15-28)
 III. The Timely Intervention (Verses 27-29)

Then they told David, saying, Behold, the Philistines fight against Keilah, and they rob the threshingfloors. Therefore David inquired of the LORD, saying, Shall I go and smite these Philistines? And the LORD said unto David, Go, and smite the Philistines, and save Keilah. And David's men said unto him, Behold, we be afraid here in Judah: how much more then if we come to Keilah against the armies of the Philistines? Then David inquired of the LORD yet again. And the LORD answered him and said, Arise go down to Keilah; for I will deliver the Philistines into thine hand. . . . And it came to pass, when Abiathar the son of Ahimelech fled to David to Keilah, that he came down with an ephod in his hand (vv. 1-6).

It was at this time that a startling change occurred in the life of David. Formerly, either because he had been wilfully independent or had forgotten to seek God's guidance, his impetuosity had created problems. He had become an expert at making wrong decisions and causing trouble for other people. The arrival of the young priest with an ephod changed everything. David had been prepared by the Lord for that moment. The fugitive had survived miraculously, but his greatest achievement was the discovery of his need to consult God about everything. Three times in nine verses it is said that David inquired of the LORD. He had reached the place where he desired to live in the center of God's will. His command to the young priest, "Bring hither the ephod," was probably his greatest request.

The ephod was a garment worn by priests. It was a close-fitting vest, possibly resembling the vest of a modern suit. It was of varying lengths, often reaching to the waist, where it was tied together by a woven girdle (see Exod. 28:27-28). It was held in place at the shoulders by special pieces designed for that purpose. Sewn to this garment were rings of gold by which the elaborate breastplate was held in place. The Bible indicates that the shoulders were gemstones upon which the names of the tribes were engraved. When the high priest entered the Holy of Holies, he represented the entire nation as he interceded before the mercy seat. Similar vestments were used by the other priests, but the Bible explains that these garments were used exclusively in communicating with the Almighty. The Urim and Thummim, which are frequently mentioned in the Scriptures, had some connection with the ephod, but mystery surrounds those sacred objects. Even the Hebrew writers failed to explain what they were or how they were used. This omission gave rise to speculations, few of which can be accepted as authentic.

The high priest wore his breastplate on the front of the ephod, and the breastplate had a pouch or "pocket" into which things could be placed. Some teachers believe the Urim and Thummim were gemstones with markings on either side and that these were taken out when guidance was needed from God. If both showed the one inscription, the answer was yes; if they showed the other, the answer was no. If they differed, the reply was inconclusive. Other writers express the belief that when the stones were used in the sanctuary, they glowed with a supernatural light, thus enabling the priest to understand what God wished to say. All this is speculative; no conclusive evidence has ever been forthcoming to prove the exact way in which these things operated. It is certain that Abiathar brought a vestment to David, and perhaps he also brought the Urim and Thummim. When David saw them, he realized that there remained an authentic way to commune with God.

The change which had taken place within David's soul was delightful. Formerly, he had hurriedly made decisions which brought disaster upon innocent people. Now, to know what God would say, he made the time to listen. It has often been claimed that fools rush in where angels fear to tread. David had unfortunately done this on several occasions, but he had become a much wiser man. When he heard of the Philistine attack on the city of Keilah, he inquired of the Lord saying, "Shall I go and smite these Philistines?" When his men expressed their fear, then David "inquired of the LORD yet again" (v. 4). When he heard of Saul's intention to continue his search, "he said to Abiathar the priest, Bring hither the ephod." At that period in his life, David would have appreciated the hymn which says, "I dare not go one step without Thine aid."

And David knew that Saul secretly practiced mischief against him. . . . Then said David, O LORD God of Israel, thy servant hath certainly heard that Saul seeketh to come to Keilah, to destroy the city for my sake. Will the men of Keilah deliver me up into his hand? Will Saul come down, as thy servant hath heard? O LORD God of Israel, 1 beseech thee, tell thy servant. . . . And the LORD said, They will deliver thee up. Then David and his men, which were about six hundred, arose and departed out of Keilah, and went whithersoever they could go (vv. 9-13).

The Persistent Petitioner

It is not surprising that David was fearful. Saul's spies were constantly seeking his hiding places. He was learning the dangers of trusting in men, and the ingratitude of the citizens of Keilah was becoming evident. David was worried when he decided to seek God's guidance. It is extremely interesting to recognize the persistence with which he conducted his inquiry. He continued to pray until he received the desired information. Could the men of Keilah be trusted? Would they deliver him to Saul in spite of the fact that he and his followers had risked their lives to protect their city? Would Saul continue his search and, if necessary, destroy the city to capture David? When the Lord only answered one of his questions, David immediately repeated his request. It was imperative that his movements be ordered by the Lord, for one false step could bring disaster upon his followers. His attitude had changed since the days when, relying upon himself, he did things which he regretted for the rest of his life.

The Passionate Persecutor

"And David knew that Saul secretly practiced mischief against him" (v. 9). "And Saul sought him every day" (v. 14). The king was like a bloodhound which relentlessly followed the scent of a fugitive and would not give up the search. It was necessary for David to watch and pray so that he would not enter into temptation (compare Mark 13:33). Thus did David exemplify the teachings of the Savior. During times of extreme danger, it is wise to pray with one's eyes open! A man who is driving an automobile should never pray with his eyes closed! If he does, he may not live to see his petitions answered! David realized that he was being sought by a relentless man who would never cease pursuing him. Christians also must remember their enemy. He tries to undermine the faith of believers and, given an opportunity, will destroy all that is of value in the Christian's life and testimony.

The Powerful Protector

"And Saul sought him every day, *but God delivered him not into his hand"* (v. 14). Poor Saul! He did not understand the stupidity of fighting against Jehovah, who knew his every movement. As Daniel said to king Nebuchadnezzar, "But [thou] hast lifted up thyself against the LORD of heaven . . . the God in whose hand thy breath is, and whose are all thy ways, hast thou not glorified" (Dan. 5:23). In spite of the dangers by which he was confronted, David should have had the kind of trust in God that is expressed in the words: "If God be for us, who can be against us?" (Romans 8:31). He suffered from a poor memory. God had promised to make him the king of Israel, and it was incumbent upon the Lord to preserve His anointed one until that promise was fulfilled. Unfortunately, David and many who succeeded him looked too much at threatening circumstances and too little at the Lord. Saul was fighting a losing battle, a fact that every person in Israel knew, except David.

THE TREMENDOUS INSPIRATION . . . The Making of a Covenant

And David saw that Saul was come out to seek his life: and David was in the wilderness of Ziph in a wood. And Jonathan Saul's son arose, and went to David into the wood, and strengthened his hand in God. And he said unto him, Fear not: for the hand of Saul my father shall not find thee; and thou shalt be king over Israel, and I shall be next unto thee; and that also Saul my father knoweth. And they two made a covenant before the LORD: and David abode in the wood, and Jonathan went to his house (vv. 15-18).

Expository Notes on Jonathan's Coming to David

"And David was in the *wilderness!*" This fact was true in a dual sense. He and his men were hiding in the wilderness of Ziph, but David's soul was unfortunately in a wilderness of a different kind. At another period in his life, the psalmist wrote, "The LORD is my shepherd; I shall not want. He maketh me to lie down in green pastures: he leadeth me beside the still waters" (see Ps. 23:1-2). Alas, in David's barren soul there was nothing green, and there were no still waters where he could quench his thirst. David was inconsistent; he would ask God for guidance, but at other times, permitted fear to destroy his confidence. God can supply a table in the wilderness, but Christians should always seek "the green pastures." Nevertheless, the patience of God supersedes human failure, and human messengers sometimes become angels in disguise.

A Rewarding Courage

"And Jonathan Saul's son arose, and went to David into the wood, and strengthened his hand in God" (v. 16). The night must have been very dark, because if the errand of the young prince had been discovered, his irate father might have executed him. In the stillness, Jonathan disappeared into the shadows. He knew the terrain and unerringly made his way through the desolation. Whether or not he was challenged by one of David's men is not revealed, but eventually, the courageous young man walked into the cave to meet his friend. Surprise, relief, and abounding joy were evident as they greeted each other. Tears were shed, and David might have scolded Jonathan for taking such a great risk in coming to visit him. The prince probably replied, "My brother, it was worth it. I had to see you." They embraced and wept in each other's arms. They sat in the shadows of that mountain hideout and talked long into the night. Jonathan did not realize at that time that he would never see the fulfillment of his prediction that David would become king. He was destined to die at his father's side fighting against the Philistines. Yet, the radiance of his glowing face and heart surely must have produced a remarkable change in the despondent David. After all, he was not alone; he had a friend in the royal household!

A Refreshing Contact

"Jonathan . . . went to David . . . and strengthened his hand in God." That simple statement is exceedingly thrilling. They could have spent half the night talking about unimportant things. The prince was a wise young man who spoke about the Lord's promises and his own certainty that God would complete what He had commenced. David's eyes became moist. It was wonderful that Jehovah had given him a true friend. There is no record of any other person being present during their conversation. When the young men emerged and David had said farewell to his friend, the onlookers saw on David's face something which had not been there earlier. Jonathan had performed a miracle; David exhibited a confidence which had been woefully absent prior to the arrival of Saul's son. The soldiers smiled and respectfully acknowledged the presence of the prince. They appreciated their leader's confidence. When he rejoiced, their fears disappeared.

A Renewed Covenant

"And they two made a covenant before the LORD: and David abode in the wood, and Jonathan went to his house" (v. 18). This action was possibly a renewal of the covenant which had already been made by the two men (see 1 Sam. 20:8). Nothing had changed in that their bond of friendship had not weakened. There is another reference to the phrase "before the LORD." It is found in 2 Samuel 5:3, a passage which seems to describe a binding contract between two parties with God endorsing the agreement. It was extremely important and permanent, but was never based on an emotional decision made without thought. Rather, it was a contract which neither party could violate. It resembled a wedding vow and was binding until death separated them. David had much for which to be grateful. He had a priest with an ephod, a God whose promises were reliable, an army which had increased to 600 men, and a true friend in Saul's household. He had reason to count his blessings. He was unfortunately very human, but God demonstrated inexhaustible patience with His doubting servant.

THE TIMELY INTERVENTION . . . The Miracle of Cooperation

Then came up the Ziphites to Saul in Gibeah, saying, Doth not David hide himself with us in strong holds in the wood, in the hill of Hachilah, which is on the south [right hand] of Jeshimon? Now therefore, O king, come down according to all the desire of thy soul to come down; and our part shall be to deliver him into the king's hand. . . . And they arose, and went to Ziph before Saul. . . . Saul also and his men went to seek him. And they told David: wherefore he came down into [from] a rock, and abode in the wilderness of Maon. . . . And Saul went on this side of the mountain: and David and his men on that side of the mountain; and David made haste to get away for fear of Saul. . . . But there came a messenger unto Saul, saying, Haste thee, and come; for the Philistines have invaded the land. Wherefore Saul returned from pursuing after David, and went against the Philistines: therefore they called that place Sela-hammahlekoth. And David went up from thence, and dwelt in strongholds at En-gedi (vv. 19-29).

Expository Notes on the Diversionary Tactics of the Almighty

An Unthinkable Ambition . . . Desiring

The Ziphites evidently came to Saul hoping that they would be rewarded for their cooperation. They endeavored to become prosperous at the expense of losing their souls. When their scheme failed, they repeated their suggestions at a later date (26:1) and indicated that repentance had no place in their lives. To gain material things, they sold their honor. They knew the terrain where David was hiding and were confident that they could help Saul capture his elusive son-in-law. Their assessment of the situation was accurate, and David was soon surrounded by his enemies. From his hiding place, he looked down upon the encircling forces, and the situation seemed desperate. Perhaps God was trying to teach him a lesson. He thought that his previous escapes were due to a combination of his own intelligence and the protection given by God. Maybe, he believed that God needed help! His philosophy might have been that "God helps those who help themselves!" It takes real faith to depend completely upon the Lord, but until that moment, there had been a great amount of self-centeredness in David's actions.

An Unparalleled Animosity . . . Destroying

The men of Ziph were satisfied; King Saul was delighted with their cooperation. He intended to catch that renegade if it were the last act of his life! His friends would be compensated handsomely so that their labor would not be in vain. Was it this incident that eventually suggested the second psalm? "Why do the heathen rage, and the people imagine a vain thing? The kings of the earth set themselves, and the rulers take counsel together, against the LORD, and against his anointed. . . . He that sitteth in the heavens shall laugh: the Lord shall have them in derision. Then shall he speak unto them in his wrath, and vex them in his sore displeasure" (Ps. 2:1-5). Saul's coordinated plans were destined to fail. As Charles Haddon Spurgeon said, "It would have been easier to lift an elephant out of a ditch with a toothpick!" Saul looked at the forbidding hills and was satisfied that his campaign would be victorious. David looked down at the threatening enemies and wondered if this would be the end of his promising career. Both men were misguided since the king lacked wisdom and David lacked faith.

An Unexpected Assistance . . . Delivering

"But there came a messenger unto Saul, saying, Haste thee, and come; for the Philistines have invaded the land. Wherefore Saul returned from pursuing after David" (vv. 27-28). That scene resembled a chessboard; the Master Player knew exactly what move was needed to win. If David's faith had enabled him to see the end from the beginning, he would have shouted with glee. It may seem incomprehensible that God could change the minds of men, but "he maketh the wrath of men to praise him." When problems encircle God's people and when defeat appears to be inevitable, the Lord is capable of performing special miracles. When Israel was helpless, Jehovah divided the Red Sea. When the walls of Jericho appeared to be impregnable, God instructed Joshua to walk around the city. When the Hebrew boys were thrown into the Babylonian fire, the Lord went ahead to give them a wonderful welcome (see Dan. 3:24-25).

> What a friend we have in Jesus:
> All our sins and griefs to bear;
> What a privilege to carry
> Everything to God in prayer.
> Oh, what peace we often forfeit,
> Oh, what needless pain we bear:
> All because we do not carry
> Everything to God in prayer.

Episode 11

THEME: *David's Refusal to Kill Saul*

SCRIPTURE: 1 Samuel 24

KEY VERSE:

> And David said unto his men, The LORD forbid that I should do this thing unto my master, the LORD's anointed, to stretch forth mine hand against him, seeing he is the anointed of the LORD (v. 6).

OUTLINE:

     I.   Caution in a Cave (Verses 1-7)
    II. Courage in a Confrontation (Verses 8-15)
   III. Concern in a Confession (Verses 16-22)

CAUTION IN A CAVE

Then Saul. . . . came to the sheepcotes by the way, where was a cave; and Saul went in to cover his feet: and David and his men remained in the sides of the cave. And the men of David said unto him, Behold the day of which the LORD said unto thee, Behold, I will deliver thine enemy into thine hand, that thou mayest do to him as it shall seem good unto thee. Then David arose, and cut off the skirt of Saul's robe privily. And it came to pass afterward, that David's heart smote him, because he had cut off Saul's skirt. And he said unto his men, The LORD forbid that I should do this thing unto my master, the LORD's anointed, to stretch forth mine hand against him, seeing he is the anointed of the LORD. So David stayed his servants with these words, and suffered them not to rise against Saul. But Saul rose up out of the cave, and went on his way (vv. 2-7).

Expository Notes on David's Kindness to Saul

A modern song suggests that "on a clear day, you can see forever"—an idea that would certainly be applicable to the place where David and his men were hiding. Apart from occasional sand or dust storms, visibility is broken only by the barren hills, which lift their forbidding peaks toward the skies. During the daytime the sky is always blue, and a small cloud of dust eloquently testifies to the movement of a desert animal. For some inscrutable reason, the Lord refrained from beautifying His handiwork in that part of the world, where barrenness is the predominant feature. Only expediency had made David and his men seek refuge in the rocky wilderness, where many caverns appear to be gaping holes in the rocky desolation. When the fugitives saw clouds of dust on the horizon, they knew that something unusual was taking place. Furthermore, when trained men placed their ears to the ground, they knew a large number of men were marching. As David analyzed the situation, he probably believed that he had committed a major error in permitting his men to be trapped in such hostile terrain. It would be unwise to retreat, for if they were able to see the dust disturbed by three thousand marching men, Saul's spies would also see similar evidence as David's men ran for their lives.

The young captain did not panic. Nearby was a large cave which had been made by centuries of erosion. It had been used by shepherds supplying shade for their sheep. "Quick" said David, "get into that cave, and remain silent." His company had hardly entered the cavern when Saul's army came into view. Desperately, David prayed that the intensity of the king's desires would make him continue his march, but it was not to be. It was difficult to remain alert when the sun relentlessly shone down upon weary men. Saul was tired, his eyes were heavy, and every muscle in his body demanded rest. David must have been petrified when he heard the royal command, "Stop; we will rest here." As he watched the king approaching the cave, death appeared to be imminent. If any man had coughed or sneezed, the enemy would have been alerted, and even the rolling of a small pebble would have been investigated. No man moved while they watched apprehensively as Saul's soldiers arranged a makeshift bed for their leader and then withdrew so as not to intrude upon his privacy. The silence was unbearable, but when Saul's heavy breathing was probably followed by his snoring, the worried watchers relaxed, and one whispered to David: "Master, here is your opportunity. The Lord has delivered the enemy into your hands. Kill him, and our problems will be over." Very carefully David moved toward the sleeping monarch to cut away a piece of Saul's skirt. Then pity suddenly overwhelmed his soul, and his eyes became moist. "And he said unto his men, The LORD forbid that I should do this thing unto my master, the LORD's anointed, to stretch forth mine hand against him, seeing he is the anointed of the LORD. So David stayed his men with these words, and suffered them not to rise against Saul" (vv. 6-7).

A strange calm had filled the cavern. The men were pensive because they could not understand David's motives. Yet, they admired the restraint which prevented his committing murder. The moments passed, but the night seemed to be endless. The rising sun ultimately challenged the chill of the night when, awaking from sleep, "Saul rose up out of the cave, and went his way." When David was assured that the enemy had left the immediate area, he and his men emerged from their hiding places. Perhaps they continued to question the wisdom of David's leniency toward Saul, but it became evident that he had won three major battles.

He Conquered Himself

This incident was David's greatest triumph. A man in his position ordinarily would have seized the opportunity to slay his enemy. He had been deprived of everything of value. His home, parents, wife, and liberty had been taken away, and every day his ruthless enemy continued to threaten him. Had the situation been reversed, Saul would not have hesitated for a single moment before plunging his sword into David's breast. The law said, "An eye for an eye; a tooth for a tooth; a life for a life." There was no law which forbade David's protecting himself; the majority of the people in Israel would have applauded had David killed the king. They knew the monarch had become a menace to the nation. At that time the idea of loving enemies was not practiced among combatants. Pity, compassion, and mercy for guilty people were unknown. David possessed qualities which were never fully expressed until the Prince of Peace began preaching in Galilee.

History describes many men who became famous by crushing the hopes of defenseless foes. Hitler was destroyed because he never conquered himself. David reached his finest hour when he refused to take advantage of his enemy's helplessness. "Blessed are the merciful: for they shall obtain mercy" (Matt. 5:7).

He Conquered His Followers

Throughout the following days, David's soldiers often recalled the incident in the cave. Maybe they questioned their leader's wisdom, but it was better to remember the pity in his eyes than the blood on his sword. Their master loved God intensely. God's will was more to be desired than the fulfillment of his own desires; honor was more important than fame. Yes, David was a good man, and they would follow him as long as they lived. That incident in the cave was destined to be remembered by people of every generation. David's deed was more eloquent than words. His immortal psalms won an abiding place in the affections of millions of people, not because of their profound philosophical or theological worth, but because they emanated from a soul in tune with the eternal God. David became immortal, not because he was a military genius, but because he was able to say: "One thing have I desired of the LORD, that will I seek after; that I may dwell in the house of the LORD all the days of my life, to behold the beauty of the LORD, and to inquire in his temple" (Ps. 27:4).

He Conquered His Enemy

Unfortunately, Saul was a man of moods, an irresponsible bigot who could not be trusted. His repeated acts of violence against David were inexcusable, but even he was overwhelmed by David's compassion. In the world of economics, financiers are often relentless in their endeavor to defeat competitors. Wealthy men crush their opposition and seldom express remorse when rival firms go bankrupt. Dictators celebrate victories by attacking weaker nations, and selfishness has become the outstanding characteristic of all kinds of people. Yet, Jesus revealed a better way of triumphant living. He said: "But I say unto you, Love your enemies, bless them that curse you, do good to them that hate you, and pray for them which despitefully use you, and persecute you; that ye may be the children of your Father which is in heaven: for he maketh his sun to rise on the evil and on the good, and sendeth rain on the just and on the unjust" (Matt. 5:44-45). A man who cannot discipline himself should never attempt to control others. Had David been as great outside the cave as he was within it, many of his subsequent problems would have been avoided.

COURAGE IN A CONFRONTATION

David also arose afterward, and went out of the cave, and cried after Saul, saying, My lord, the king. And when Saul looked behind him, David stooped with his face to the earth, and bowed himself . . . and said. . . . Moreover, my father, see, yea, see the skirt of thy robe in my hands for in that I cut off the skirt of thy robe, and killed thee not, know thou and see that there is neither evil nor trangression in mine hand, and I have not sinned against thee; yet thou huntest my soul to take it. The LORD judge between me and thee. . . . And [Saul] said to David, Thou art more righteous than I: for thou hast rewarded me good, whereas I have rewarded thee evil (vv. 8-17).

Expository Notes on David's Appeal to Saul

The statement "And when Saul looked behind him" may be interpreted in two ways.

(1) Some teachers believe that David was close behind the king when he shouted his message and that Saul turned around to see the hunted man only a few yards away. Such an explanation leaves much to be desired. At the time, David did not know how Saul would react to his questions. There was every possibility that the enraged monarch would fiercely resent David's interrogation and, using his advantage, seize the questioner. There was no way by which David could foresee any change in the intent of the murderer who sought him. Had the king remained hostile, David's men would have been slain within minutes. The young fugitive was an experi-

enced soldier whose exploits against the Philistines had already won rewards for valor. It is difficult to believe that such a strategist would risk the lives of his men on the unreliable feelings of an emotional murderer.

(2) Conder supplies a more acceptable answer. He writes, "The stronghold chosen by the fugitive was the hill Hachilah, in the wilderness of Ziph, south of Jeshimon. This I propose to recognize in the long ridge called El Kolah, running out of the Ziph plateau toward the Dead Sea desert, or Jeshimon. . . . On the north side of the hill are 'The Caves of the Dreamers,' perhaps the actual scene of David's descent on Saul's sleeping guards. Pursued to Hachilah, David descended farther south, to a rock or cliff in the wilderness of Maon, which was named Selahammahlekoth, or 'Cliff of Divisions'" (Conder, *Tenting in Palestine*, vol. 2, p. 91). Here he is represented as being on one side of the mountain, while Saul was on the other (1 Sam. 23:26). Now between the ridge of El Kolah, and the neighborhood of Maon, there is a great gorge called 'the Valley of Rocks,' a narrow but deep chasm, impassable except by a detour of many miles, *so that Saul might have stood within sight of David, yet quite unable to overtake his enemy.*" The possibility exists that if Saul went around that gorge, David would expect him to return within easy reach of his voice. Yet, adequate protection would be assured by the impassable valley between them. This appears to be the more reliable explanation, for David would never needlessly risk the lives of his men. The account of his conversation with Saul may be summarized under four simple words: *humility, honesty, humiliation,* and *hope.*

Humility

"And when Saul looked behind him, *David stooped with his face to the earth, and bowed himself. And David said to Saul. . . . After whom is the king of Israel come out? after whom dost thou pursue? after a dead dog, after a flea?*" (vv. 8, 9 and 14). It seems incomprehensible that he who had slain many Philistines should compare himself with a dead dog and a tiny flea. It is beyond expectation that he who had suffered much from the animosity of the king should bow in reverence before him. When David spoke in this way, he had neither self-esteem nor vengeance in his thoughts.

Honesty

"Behold this day thine eyes have seen how that the LORD had delivered thee to day into mine hand in the cave: *and some bade me kill thee: but mine eye spared thee; and I said, I will not put forth mine hand against . . . the LORD's anointed. . . .* The LORD judge between me and thee . . . *but mine hand shall not be upon thee*" (vv. 24:10-12). David neither enlarged on his grievances nor did he exaggerate what had taken place. He was willing for

God to arbitrate in any disagreement they had, but even though Jehovah decided against Saul, he would not even then lay his hand upon the king, nor would he help those who did. That Saul was the anointed of God was a situation that would continue throughout the king's reign as far as David was concerned.

CONCERN IN A CONFESSION

Humiliation

"And it came to pass, when David had made an end of speaking these words unto Saul, that Saul said, Is this thy voice, my son David? And Saul lifted up his voice, and wept" (v. 16). Perhaps it is not possible to assess the effect that Saul's weeping had upon his watching and listening soldiers. "Behold! the king is sobbing!" Neither is it possible to tell how sincere Saul's actions were. The fact that he soon quickly renewed his hostility suggests that he was never truly penitent. Did he put on an emotional show to retain the respect of his men? Was he mentally sick? Had his mind momentarily been freed from the elusions which ruined his life? Perhaps the answers to these questions will never be forthcoming. However, his acknowledgment that he knew David was to be the next king of Israel is truly startling. If God gave him this revelation, then his opposition to the king-elect was rebellion against the Almighty.

Hope

"And now, behold, I know well that thou shalt surely be king, and that the kingdom of Israel shall be established in thine hand. Swear now therefore unto me by the LORD, that thou wilt not cut off my seed after me, and that thou wilt not destroy my name out of my father's house. And David sware unto Saul" (vv. 20-22). Saul was a man who expected everything, but gave nothing in return. David honored his vow, for in later years he spared and assisted Mephibosheth, who was the king's grandson, but Saul maintained his hostility until the day he died on Mount Gilboa (see 1 Samuel 31).

What more can be said of Saul, the king of Israel. He was filled with such a diabolical hatred and such a terrible passion to kill his son-in-law that even God could do nothing with him in the end. There comes a time in the history of men and women when the Lord uses everything at His disposal to reclaim lost souls. Yet, even God admits that there is a point of no return beyond which unrepentant people are lost eternally. When sinners perish, they will do so, not because God's love is insufficient, but because they refused to allow Him to influence their lives. David evidently had no confidence in Saul's promises, for instead of returning to his homeland, "[he] and his men gat them up unto the mountain [stronghold]" (v. 22).

Chapter 12

THEME: *David Meets Abigail, the Wife of Nabal*

SCRIPTURE: 1 Samuel 25

KEY VERSE:

> And Samuel died. . . . And David arose, and went down to the wilderness of Paran (v. 1).

OUTLINE:
  I. A Request Is Refused (Verses 1-13)
  II. A Report Is Received (Verses 14-19)
  III. A Reputation Is Remembered (Verses 20-28)
  IV. A Remarriage Is Requested (Verses 39-42)

And Samuel died. . . . and all the Israelites were gathered together, and lamented him, and buried him in his house at Ramah. And David arose, and went down to the wilderness of Paran (v. 1).

Expository Notes on the Death of Samuel

When Moses died, Joshua survived. When Samuel died, David remained, but was a fugitive. When John the Baptist was executed, Christ continued his work, but was crucified. After the Lord's death, His disciples preached His gospel, but they were soon scattered through many lands. Nevertheless, throughout the ages, God's kingdom has remained unshaken because it has rested upon the Rock of Ages. His servants are dispensable, but the Lord remains indestructible, thus providing the guarantee that even the gates of hell cannot prevail against His efforts. The words "and Moses died" stand out as an epitaph in the cemetery of time. They testify to the termination of an era. The small child who heard God calling his name, Samuel, became one of Jehovah's most useful instruments. When Eli and his sons, the priests of Israel, became abhorrently disgusting at Shiloh, the spiritual welfare of the nation became the responsibility of the aging prophet. Each year, as long as he was able, Samuel went on a pilgrimage on which he provided justice to appointed cities in Israel. However, he had unfortunately become an old man and was evidently unable to prevent the murderous missions of Saul. Perhaps he was too old or too infirm to continue his activities in the political and religious life of the nation with the result that the people knew that his ministry was terminating.

When the news circulated through the country that their spiritual leader had gone, "all the Israelites . . . gathered together, and lamented him, and buried him in his house at Ramah." When David heard about the death of his old friend, he led his men deeper into the wilderness of Paran. There was now no restraining influence in Israel. Samuel had established schools in which young men were being trained, and Gad was probably one of the students who graduated from those seminaries. Yet, at the time of Samuel's decease, there was not another outstanding prophet in Israel, a fact that David knew. Therefore, fully aware that Saul would allow no interference in his plans, David sought sanctuary in the barren wastes of the wilderness of Paran.

The wisdom of his decision might be questioned. He appears to have been influenced by personal fears and instincts rather than by the promises, presence, and protective power of God. Any direction which takes a man away from the altar and sanctuary of the Lord generally leads to increasing problems, a result that became evident when David ran away from Saul.

A REQUEST IS REFUSED

And David heard in the wilderness that Nabal did shear his sheep. And David sent out ten young men, and David said unto the young men, Get you up to Carmel, and go to Nabal, and greet him in my name: and thus shall ye say to him. . . . I have heard that thou hast shearers: now thy shepherds which were with us, we hurt them not, neither was there ought missing unto them, all the while they were in Carmel. . . . give, I pray thee, whatsoever cometh to thine hand unto thy servants, and to thy son David. . . . And Nabal answered . . . Who is David? and who is the son of Jesse? . . . Shall I then take my bread, and my water, and my flesh that I have killed for my shearers, and give it unto men, whom I know not whence they be? (vv. 4-11).

Expository Notes on David's Request for Assistance

The time of sheepshearing was one of the most joyous periods of the year. Men came to assist in the labor, but the evenings were filled with dancing and rejoicing. It was customary for the host to provide ample provisions, and since Nabal, the farmer, had great possessions, his lavish banquets were never forgotten. It was on a similiar occasion that Absalom killed his half-brother, Amnon (see 2 Sam. 13:23-29). The entire countryside would have been aware of such a feast in Carmel, and therefore it was to be expected that David would also have known about it, even though he and his men were hiding in the nearby mountains.

His Restraint Had Been Remarkable

The feeding of hundreds of hungry men was not an easy task, and since the hills were unproductive except for animals which might be trapped, David was compelled to find sustenance wherever possible. When his men fought against the Philistines, they confiscated the enemies' sheep and cattle, but at other times food was difficult to obtain. It is extremely significant that David's men never took one sheep from the flocks which grazed around the hills of Carmel. Speaking of these plains, Conder wrote: "One is struck with the fitness which the plateau presents for the adventures of the fugitive, bandit chief who was destined to become the king of Israel. The inhabitants, like Nabal of Carmel, are rich in sheep and oxen. The villagers of Yuttah owned seventeen hundred sheep, of which 250 belonged to the Sheikh. All along the borders of the Jeshimon and Beersheba deserts, there is fine pasturage, to which the peasants descend in springtime, having made some sort of agreement with the neighboring Bedouins to protect them from other tribes. Thus we find perpetuated the old system under which David's hand protected the cattle of Nabal" (Conder, *Tenting in Palestine*, vol. 2, p. 88).

David's refusal to take any of Nabal's animals perhaps arose from the fact that he had been a shepherd. He knew the difficulties of protecting sheep from robbers and sympathized with the men responsible for guarding Nabal's flocks. There were probably times when his hungry followers said, "Master, there would be no harm in taking one beast; it would never be missed." Yet, David insisted that nothing would be stolen so that the shepherds would not be blamed for carelessness in attending to their task.

His Request Was Reasonable

The wealthy farmer would have lost many sheep if thieves had raided the flocks. The young man who spoke to Abigail, the wife of Nabal, said, "But the men were very good to us, and we were not hurt, neither missed we anything, as long as we were conversant with them, when we were in the fields. *They were a wall unto us, both by night and day, all the while we were with them keeping the sheep.*" It is significant that David likened himself to the son of the farmer, thus indicating that he had been pleased to be of service to one of his own people. To guard three thousand sheep and a thousand goats presented great problems, but David enjoyed being of assistance and believed that Nabal would reciprocate by allowing his men to share in the abundance of food. Nabal's insulting refusal was very foolish because his shepherds would continue to need David's help. A few kind words and a generous gift of food would have guaranteed all the protection Nabal would ever need.

His Reactions Became Reprehensible

> "So David's young men turned their way, and went again, and came and told [David] all those sayings. And David said unto his men, Gird ye on every man his sword. . . . and David also girded on his sword: and there went up after David about four hundred men; and two hundred abode by the stuff. . . . Now David had said, Surely in vain have I kept all that this fellow hath in the wilderness. . . . So and more also do God unto the enemies of David, if I leave of all that pertain to him by the morning light any that [urinates] against the wall" (vv. 12-22).

David was evidently enraged so much that he planned to kill every animal and human being connected with the man's family and business. Even guiltless people were to be slain. Had David carried out his intentions, his conscience would have been stained by the blood of innocent people, who knew little, if anything, of the ingratitude of their employer. David was a man out of touch with God, and any person who becomes enslaved to carnal desires cannot be a true representative of heaven. David knew nothing of those truths enunciated by Christ, who said: "Ye have heard that it hath been said, Thou shalt love thy neighbor, and hate thine enemy. But I say unto you, Love your enemies, bless them that curse you, do good to them that hate you, and pray for them which despitefully use you, and persecute you; that ye may be the children of your Father which is in heaven" (see Matt. 5:43-45). People who ignore the warnings of God inevitably get into trouble.

A REPORT IS RECEIVED

> But one of the young men told Abigail, Nabal's wife, saying, Behold, David sent messengers out of the wilderness to salute our master; and he railed on them. But the men were very good unto us, and we were not hurt, neither missed we anything, as long as we were conversant with them, when we were in the fields: they were a wall unto us both by night and day, all the while we were with them keeping the sheep. . . . Then Abigail made haste and took two hundred loaves, and two bottles of wine, and five sheep ready dressed, and five measures of parched corn, and an hundred clusters of raisins, and two hundred cakes of figs, and laid them on asses. . . . and, behold, David and his men came down against her; and she met them (vv. 14-20).

Expository Notes on Abigail's Confrontation with David

This is the story of an astute and courageous woman who was unfortunately married to a foolish man. Abigail probably had no part in arranging her wedding; in those days marriages were negotiated by parents. She and her husband were extremely different in that he was arrogant, selfish, and foolish, while she was friendly, intelligent, and resourceful. When an employee spoke of the threat to the farm and family, she immediately acted to preserve what her husband was about to destroy. Her confrontation with the irate David may be summarized under three suggestive headings.

Her Works Were Good

The speed with which Abigail gathered supplies is astonishing, but she realized there was no time to lose since David was already approaching her home. She made sure that there were sufficient provisions to supply the most sumptuous feast the men from the mountains would ever enjoy. The two bottles of wine were probably a gift for David. It was said centuries later that "faith without works is dead"! Abigail evidently knew that truth long before James wrote his letter (see James 2:20).

Her Words Were Better

The way in which that gracious woman talked David out of his deadly mission is extraordinary. It has often been said that the way to a man's heart is through his stomach. If that is true, Abigail was an ardent advocate of the idea. When David saw the supplies of food brought for his young men, he could only be pleased with the attention he was receiving. The result was that, as he listened to her speech, his bitterness began to disappear. She assured him that her husband was a fool and that the fault was really her own, for had she been alert, she might have intercepted the young messengers. Then she spoke about the future when David would be king of Israel and suggested that memories of a needless massacre would be as unpleasant as the deed he was about to commit. David, who was always attracted by beautiful women, began to respond to her entreaties. He recognized that when this lady spoke, she said something! Tenderness began to replace the hostility in his eyes, and even before he agreed with her desires, the battle against his militant project had been won.

Her Wisdom Was Best of All

It is difficult to decide whether or not this was a prepared speech; it was probably a spontaneous expression of her soul. She had acted in haste and could not have spent time preparing what she wished to say to David. Yet, all her words were wise. She made David feel that he was too great to be upset by a drunken fool. She insinuated that her husband was unworthy of his attention. She even spoke of the Almighty throwing out David's enemies "as stones out of the middle of a sling." The listener's ego was being inflated all the time she spoke; she knew how to make a man feel good! Perhaps if she lived in our day, she would be a professor of psychology in one of the great centers of learning. Her closing appeal was irresistible. She said, "When the Lord shall have dealt well with my lord, then remember thine handmaid." Her request was unnecessary because David had decided that she would never be forgotten! Those who heard that conversation could not have been surprised when David sought her hand in marriage a few weeks later. "Who can find a virtuous woman? for her price is far above rubies" (see Prov. 31:10).

A REPUTATION IS REMEMBERED

And Abigail came to Nabal; and behold, he held a feast in his house, like the feast of a king; and Nabal's heart was merry within him, for he was very drunken: wherefore she told him nothing, less or more, until the morning light. But it came to pass in the morning, when the wine was gone out of Nabal, and his wife had told him these things, that his heart died within him, and he became as a stone. And it came to pass about ten days after, that the LORD smote Nabal, that he died. And when David heard that Nabal was dead, he said, Blessed be the LORD, that hath pleaded the cause of my reproach (vv. 36-39).

Expository Notes on the Memories of David

Later, David's three memories were (1) the disgraceful conduct of the deceased, (2) the eloquent intercession of the woman who prevented his murderous mission, and (3) the overruling providence of God. As David reviewed his experiences, he could see the guiding hand of the Almighty in all the circumstances by which he had been surrounded. Even when he had been careless and wayward, the patience of the Almighty had never failed. He remembered Abigail's prediction that his enemies would be cast away like stones out of the middle of a sling. David saw clearly that all things had been made to work together for good for him because he loved the Lord (compare Rom. 8:28). As he thought of the death of Nabal, he realized that there was no need to worry about his enemies. The Lord was on his side so that he was safe. (See the homily, "Nabal . . . The Wealthy Pauper," p. 121).

A REMARRIAGE IS REQUESTED

And David sent and communed with Abigail, to take her to him to wife. . . . And she arose and bowed herself on her face to the earth. . . . And Abigail hasted, and arose, and rode upon an ass, with five damsels of hers that went after her; and she went after the messengers of David, and became his wife. David also took Ahinoam of Jezreel; and they were also both of them his wives. But Saul had given Michal his daughter, David's wife, to Phalti, the son of Laish, which was of Gallim (vv. 39-44).

Expository Notes on David's Marriage to Abigail

The motives behind David's marriage are highly questionable. Did he love the woman, or was he only infatuated by a beautiful and clever lady? If he truly loved Abigail, then it is difficult to explain why he married another woman at the same time. It should be remembered that it was lawful for a man to have as many wives as he could afford, and his stature in a community was often measured by the number of his sons. At the same time, it should be recognized that plurality of spouses did not guarantee happiness. Elkanah had two wives, but he only loved one (see 1 Sam. 1:1-6). On one notable occasion, David's association with another man's wife led to murder (see 2 Sam. 11). The ancient writer reminded his readers that Saul had illegally given David's first wife to another man; this knowledge might have encouraged David to seek additional wives. Abigail would have become a wealthy woman if she were the beneficiary of her husband's last will and testament. If she were alone and friendless, David might have felt obligated to assist her. He lived long before the Christian era when Christ taught that His followers should have one wife. Nevertheless, during the time that the law was a "schoolmaster to bring us unto Christ," even the most faithful of God's Old Testament servants would have been surprised to hear what the New Testament evangelists would later recommend. David could not have refused to offer shelter to the woman who had rendered such valuable assistance. Why he married the other woman was a secret known only to himself. That might have been another of many mistakes.

HOMILIES FOR PREACHERS AND TEACHERS

Study No. 7

NABAL . . . The Wealthy Pauper (1 Samuel 25)

If birth certificates had been issued in ancient times, the registrar would have had a great shock when he wrote the new baby's name—Nabal. He would have stared and then asked, "But why give such a silly name to the child? The lad will be the laughing-stock of all people with a name meaning 'fool.'" Yet, the parents for some unexplained reason remained adamant, and the new arrival began life with a name destined to be prophetical. Had it been the custom to erect tombstones over graves and to inscribe a true record of the person buried there, the sculptor responsible for Nabal's grave would have written, "His name was true. He was a great fool." Every act in the strange life of this wealthy farmer demonstrated folly of unprecedented dimensions. His foolish temper robbed him of his servants' respect, foolish drunkenness cost him his wife's love, foolish selfishness deprived him of a guardian's care, and sinning ruined his soul.

GRACE WATCHING

It was shearing time at Nabal's farm, and the bleating of the many sheep herded together in the sheepfolds echoed over the countryside. Nabal, the wealthy farmer, stood watching his perspiring slaves, and his foul temper was often evident in his dealings with the toilers. He wanted the maximum amount of work done for the least possible pay, and his brutal methods made one of the workmen say, "He is such a son of Belial that a man cannot speak to him." When David's men arrived to seek food in return for their untiring care of the flocks in the wilderness, Nabal raved and drove them away hungry. Revealing that gratitude was unknown in his heart, Nabal ignored the fact that God's servant had refrained from taking supplies. He was a wealthy pauper who possessed nothing but money. But in the final analysis, he did not possess money—it possessed him.

GRACE WORKING

Unknown to the ignorant man, retribution was swiftly descending upon his head as his loyal wife went forth to intercept the avenger. David's anger had been aroused and was hurrying to the scene of the insult when Abigail, Nabal's wife, fell at his feet. His heart was strangely stirred when she cried, "Upon me, my lord, upon me let this iniquity be" (v. 24). The sincere intercession of that great woman protected her sinful husband, for David refrained from carrying out his plans of vengeance. Had Abigail sought selfish interests, she would have allowed David to exact his vengeance. But she resisted any inclinations toward that end, interceded for her man, and succeeded beyond her wildest dreams. Nabal should have thanked God for the faithfulness of a good wife just as many other men should for he was not the last man to benefit from the prayers of a devoted woman. Alas, the foolish farmer was too short-sighted to recognize that, contrary to all that he deserved, the grace of God still worked on his behalf.

GRACE WAITING

"And Abigail came to Nabal; and, behold, he held a feast in his house, like the feast of a king; and Nabal's heart was merry within him, for he was very drunken." She wisely refrained from telling him of the events of the evening, but when "the wine was gone out of Nabal, and his wife had told him all these things, that his heart died within him, and he became as a stone." Either the fact that he had lost some of his possessions or that his wife had acted without his authority aroused his resentment to such a degree that, in modern parlance, he had a stroke. Yet, he did not finally die until another ten days had passed. During this respite he lay in his embittered helplessness, probably bemoaning the fate that had interfered with his freedom of movement. Perhaps he did not know how to pray, for he had been a long time without practice. At last, the soul of a fool was taken into the eternal shadows. Grace could not wait forever. In the closing moments of Nabal's life, all his former actions seemed futile and irresponsible to him. He had lived for self and had lived completely in vain. His money provided everything for an elaborate funeral, but it could not purchase a place in heaven. Eternal poverty provided a sad contrast to earthly luxury—and, alas, he had a very long time in which to study the difference. (Reprinted from the author's book, *Bible Cameos*, pp. 31-32).

Episode 13

THEME: *David's Last Meeting With Saul*

SCRIPTURE: 1 Samuel 26

KEY VERSE:

> So David took the spear and the cruse of water from Saul's bolster; and they gat them away, and no man saw it, nor knew it, neither awaked: for they were all asleep; because a deep sleep from the LORD had fallen upon them (v. 12).

OUTLINE:
   I.   The Continuing Problem (Verses 1-5)
   II. The Complete Protection (Verse 6-12)
   III. The Condemned Protagonist (Verses 13-24)
   IV. The Climactic Parting (Verse 25)

And the Ziphites came unto Saul to Gibeah, saying, Doth not David hide himself in the hill of Hachilah, which is before Jeshimon? Then Saul arose, and went down to the wilderness of Ziph. . . . David therefore sent out spies, and understood that Saul was come in very deed. . . . and David beheld the place where Saul lay, and Abner the son of Ner, the captain of his host: and Saul lay in the trench, and the people pitched round about him (vv. 1-5).

Expository Notes on Saul's New Crusade Against David

THE CONTINUING PROBLEM

The people of Ziph had tried earlier to betray David, but their efforts had failed. They were willing to try again, for they knew he was hiding in their part of the country. Saul, unchanged and unrelenting, was willing to pay any price for the realization of his greatest ambition—to catch the elusive David. Gratefully accepting the offer of the Ziphites and surrounded by three thousand chosen soldiers, the king commenced his new search. Saul was dominated by a single passion—to kill his supposed enemy. He set up camp in the hill of Hachilah, which was close to Jeshimon and within sight of the barren hills in which he expected to capture his enemy. He was attempting the impossible; to quote the words of David, he was attempting to "catch a flea in a wilderness" (See 1 Sam. 2:14; 26:20). To use his own words, he was "playing the fool" (See 1 Sam. 26:21), but at that time he was unfortunately unaware of his stupidity.

THE COMPLETE PROTECTION

Then answered David and said unto Ahimelech the Hittite, and to Abishai the son of Zeruiah, brother to Joab, saying, Who will go down with me to Saul to the camp? And Abishai said, I will go down with thee. So David and Abishai came to the people by night: and, behold, Saul lay sleeping within the trench, and his spear stuck in the ground at his bolster: but Abner and the people lay round about him (vv. 6-7).

Expository Notes on David's Repeated Refusal to Kill Saul

The term translated "trench" should be rendered "among the chariots." Saul was very insecure and therefore arranged to sleep in a place thought to be inaccessible to his enemies. Chariots guarded him on every side, and surrounded by armed warriors, he believed he was beyond the reach of any assassin. He was not sleeping in a ditch, as might be supposed from the translation in our Bible. It was to be expected that David would endeavor to gain all the information necessary for his preservation, and so, from a vantage point overlooking the camp of Saul, he gazed apprehensibly at his enemies.

When he had carefully considered his chances of bypassing the king's guards, David, accompanied by Abishai, who had volunteered for the mission, slowly approached the camp. He had no need to fear discovery, for "a deep sleep from the LORD was fallen upon them" (v. 12). God knew how to protect His servants and has never lost that ability. Once again, Saul lay helplessly at David's feet, and it is not a cause for amazement when Abishai said, "God hath delivered thine enemy into thine hand this day: now therefore let me smite him, I pray thee, with the spear even to the earth at once, and I will not smite him the second time" (v. 8). It was as though the young man said, "Master, this is our opportunity, but do not worry about killing the Lord's anointed; just leave the job in my hands, and I will not need to strike him twice." David had many faults, but to his credit it must be acknowledged that he never attempted to remove by force the man whom God had placed upon the throne of Israel. He seemed to say within his soul, "If Jehovah can tolerate Saul, who am I to complain?"

Frustrated, but obedient to his leader's command, Abishai quietly lifted Saul's spear and the cruse of water and, following his captain, carefully withdrew from the camp. Although surrounded by armed guards, the two men were completely safe. God had immobilized the soldiers, as He did the lions when Daniel was thrown into their den. Was it at this time that

David learned the truth expressed in Psalm 84:11, "For the LORD God is a sun and shield: the LORD will give grace and glory: *no good thing will he withhold from them that walk uprightly*"?

THE CONDEMNED PROTAGONIST

Then David went over to the other side, and stood on the top of an hill afar off; a great space being between them: and David cried to the people, and to Abner the son of Ner, saying, Answerest thou not, Abner? Then Abner answered and said, Who art thou that criest to the king? And David said to Abner, Art not thou a valiant man? and who is like to thee in Israel? Wherefore then hast thou not kept thy lord the king? for there came one of the people in to destroy the king thy lord. This thing is not good that thou hast done. As the LORD liveth, ye art worthy to die (vv. 13-16).

Expository Notes on David's Condemnation of Abner

The Powerful Accusation

When David's voice echoed across the valley to accuse Abner, his eyes were gleaming, and his words were like thrusts of a rapier which pierced the soul of Saul's Chief of Staff. That illustrious warrior was one of the greatest military personalities Israel possessed. Abounding in courage and proud of his achievements, Abner was the custodian of the king's safety. No person in the nation would have questioned his willingness to die in the service of Saul. It may have been his idea that the king should sleep amid the protecting chariots, and the positioning of the guards was arranged with utmost care. David was aware of these details, but taking advantage of the "deep sleep from the Lord", he continued to taunt the illustrious leader of the king's army. David surely smiled when he shouted, "Art thou not a valiant man? and who is like to thee in Israel?" If we may be permitted to use modern terms, David said, "Your conduct has been inexcusable. Abner, you slept at your post and permitted a would-be assassin to approach the king. If a watchman or sentry did that, you would execute him immediately. Abner, since you have committed a similar offense, will you order your own execution? What can you say in your defense?"

The Pointed Insinuation

"Abner, you are responsible for the king's safety. I am called the king's greatest enemy. Is that not the reason for your journey to this wilderness? You could have remained with your family, but, instead, at the king's command, you are doing your utmost to capture me. Now, Abner, would you like to tell all your men which is the greater friend of Saul? I came into your camp while you slept. I could have slain Saul and, had I so desired, could also have killed you. General, you slept; it did not seemingly matter to you what happened to Saul or anyone else. Yet, I decided to spare all of you. Abner, your men are listening. Tell us which one is the most reliable friend of your master?" Abner was speechless because the veiled accusations of the fugitive were irrefutable; David's questions could not be answered without damaging Abner's own prestige. The embarrassing silence which followed David's questions was difficult to endure. He knew what his men were thinking, and even Saul was impressed by David's words. "Yes, that upstart from Bethlehem deserves to die!"

The Potent Revelation

"Abner, will you do something for me? Now see where the king's spear is, and the cruse of water that was at his bolster. If you are unable to find them, look over here and I will show them to you. General, as easily as I lifted these things, I could have lifted your head! Is it possible that somewhere in your heart there exists a little gratitude?" A strange silence settled on that ancient scene; the soldiers were getting restless. Abner was embarrassed, but Saul suddenly said, "Is this thy voice, my son David? And David said, It is my voice, my lord, O king. . . . Wherefore doth my lord thus pursue after his servant? for what have I done? or what evil is in my hand? . . . If the LORD have stirred thee up against me, let him accept an offering: but if they be the children of men, cursed be they before the LORD; for they have driven me out this day from abiding in the inheritance of the LORD, saying, Go, serve other gods. . . . Then said Saul, I have sinned: return, my son David: for I will no more do thee harm . . . behold, I have played the fool, and have erred exceedingly" (vv. 17-21). Saul's confession apparently was sincere. Did he realize this would be his last meeting with David? Was he truly repentant? Had he been given the opportunity to continue his reign over Israel, would he have renewed his hostility toward his son-in-law? These are questions which can never be answered. He had unfortunately reached the point of no return where his fate should be a warning to others who might be tempted to emulate his example.

The Restricted Response

Even David probably found it difficult to accept the king's promises. He had trusted the monarch on many occasions and had become a victim of Saul's irascibility; he could not believe the king's word. Had he been able to do so, he could have returned the confiscated articles himself. However, realizing how unreliable Saul could be, David said: "Behold the king's spear! and let one of the young men come over and fetch it. . . . And, behold, as thy life was much set by this day in mine eyes, so let my life be much set by in the eyes of the LORD, and let him deliver me out of all tribulation" (vv. 22-24).

THE CLIMACTIC PARTING

Then Saul said to David, Blessed be thou, my son David: thou shalt both do great things, and also shalt still prevail. So David went on his way, and Saul returned to his place (v. 25).

Saul's last statement to David is pathetic. "Blessed be thou, my son David: thou shalt both do great things, and also shalt still prevail" (v. 25). It was at that time and with those words that their relationship ended. A broken, tired, and pitiable man, Saul returned to his home, but David, still a victim of fear and doubt, went back to his stronghold in the mountains. The sunlight of divine favor was shining for him, but David unfortunately continued to live in the shadows. A person who makes that choice is either sick in his soul or mentally deranged.

Episode 14

THEME: *David Seeks a New Home*

SCRIPTURE: 1 Samuel 27

KEY VERSE:

> And David said in his heart, I shall now perish one day by the hand of Saul: there is nothing better for me than that I should speedily escape into the land of the Philistines; and Saul shall despair of me, to seek me any more in any coast of Israel; so shall I escape out of his hand (v. 1).

OUTLINE:

      I.   A Diminishing Confidence (Verses 1-4)
     II. A Desired City (Verses 5-7)
   III. A Deceitful Crusade (Verses 8-10)
  IV. A Deadly Conclusion (Verses 11-12)

A DIMINISHING CONFIDENCE

And David arose, and he passed over with the six hundred men that were with him unto Achish, the son of Maoch, king of Gath. And David dwelt with Achish at Gath, he and his men, every man with his household, even David with his two wives, Ahinoam the Jezreelitess, and Abigail the Carmelitess, Nabal's wife (vv. 2-4).

Expository Notes on David's Extraordinary Lack of Faith

It is to be regretted that when David was close to the realization of his dreams, his diminishing faith caused him to falter. Saul would soon be dead, the crown of Israel would be placed upon David's head, and the night of oppression would be followed by the dawn of a new and glorious day. Yet, when he was so close to triumph, despondency overwhelmed him so that he murmured, "I shall now one day perish by the hand of Saul" (v. 1). If he had endured a few more days, some of his greatest tragedies would have been prevented. Why did he collapse when victory was near?

Prayerlessness

Other passages tell how he called for his young priest and the ephod to seek God's guidance. Yet, on this occasion, David left God out of his calculations. He never summoned Abiathar, but sought the aid of his nation's enemies. Many years later, Jesus said: "Men ought always to pray, and not to faint" (see Luke 18:1). Problems of many kinds harass the children of God, and people unfortunately depend on personal resourcefulness to relieve daily pressures. Many things may be of incalculable assistance, but if a man is too busy to pray, he is too busy! It is never safe to worry endlessly about personal problems; it is better and wiser to share them with God. David exchanged God for Gath, and subsequent experiences proved that he was exceedingly foolish.

Problems

David looked back and forward, but forgot to look up! His friends had failed him, twice the Ziphites had agreed to betray him, his enemies had been relentless, and he had grown tired. To use modern terminology, he had been in a rat race and believed it was time to quit! The promises of God seemed meaningless; let Israel look after herself; he was getting out! To protect his family he needed a home; a place where he could settle down and not be "a partridge hunted on the mountain." Poor David! He had become a self-centered, dissatisfied backslider. He believed that God moved too slowly and that he should look after himself. Years later, the young man Demas possibly had similar ideas when he deserted Paul to participate in the night life in Rome (see 2 Tim. 4:10).

Purposelessness

David was becoming older, but was getting nowhere! His home in Bethlehem belonged to other people; his parents were in Moab; everybody was getting along nicely except himself. Perhaps he had aspirations to become a wealthy farmer in Gath and thought that it might be wise to forget Israel and let Jehovah manage His own affairs! His small army could accompany him into the new land; he would arrange for their safety and prosperity; they could be his helpers as he commenced his new life. He would not have a sanctuary, but the house of God had been disappointing anyway! Why worry? He was as good as all those praying hypocrites in Saul's household. With these ideas firmly fixed in his mind, David commenced his sojourn in a land where happiness was elusive. He forsook God, but the Lord never left him! The poet was correct when he wrote: "O love that wilt not let me go."

A DESIRED CITY

And David said unto Achish, If I have now found grace in thine eyes, let them give me a place in some town in the country, that I may dwell there: for why should thy servant dwell in the royal city with thee? Then

Achish gave him Ziklag that day: wherefore Ziklag pertaineth unto the kings of Judah unto this day. And the time that David dwelt in the country of the Philistines was a full year and four months (vv. 5-7).

Expository Notes on David's Request for Sanctuary

A Regrettable Request

David's statement to the Philistine king "if I have found grace in thine eyes" is a clear indication of the state of his soul. It is a cause for regret that God's champion should ever have to beg from an idolater. He evidently considered the grace of God to be insufficient. When the servants of the Lord appeal for assistance from the enemies of their faith, they confess that God has not met their needs; when they accept help from unregenerate donors, they invariably become obligated, a circumstance that always leads to trouble. Paul's command to New Testament believers "Wherefore come out from among them" (2 Cor. 6:17) may be applied in more senses than one.

A Reasonable Recognition

"Why should thy servant dwell in the royal city with thee?" The reasons for this statement were varied. David was accompanied by six hundred men, and many of them had families. David may have believed that it would be an imposition to expect Achish to supply food for such a large company, and as a result, he possibly desired a more suitable place where his men could be self-supporting. If he had ambitions to settle permanently in Philistia, land would be more easily obtained "out in the country." Perhaps David did not trust the Philistine noblemen who coveted the king's favor. If they became jealous of the Hebrew intruder, their hostility would create problems for his party of refugees. Within the city, assassins could operate more easily; out in the country David's spies would have a better chance to detect the approach of enemies.

A Rebellious Region

It is interesting that Achish gave the city of Ziklag to David. Many years earlier when Joshua divided the land of Canaan, this place was allocated to the tribe of Judah (see Josh. 15:31). Later, it was transferred to the tribe of Simeon. There is no way by which we can discover if there were two places with the same name. The southern stronghold was never captured by Judah or Simeon. It continued to belong to the original inhabitants of the land and was situated at the southern extremity of Canaan. The people preserved their independence, either because of the difficulty of the terrain or because Joshua's followers could not be bothered to attack a stronghold when there were other territories which could easily be possessed. Achish, the Philistine king, completed what Joshua and his followers had only commenced.

A Repulsive Residency

"And the time that David dwelt in the country of the Philistines was a full year and four months [a year of days]." (v. 7). The alternate reading is very suggestive. Did every day seem to be a year? Did time appear to stand still? An evangelist was asked how long he had ministered in a very difficult church. He thought for a moment and then replied, "I was there for two weeks, which were six months!" David would have understood and sympathized with that weary preacher. Ownership of a city could not compensate for the loss of a home in Israel. Enormous wealth could not purchase the serenity known when as a lad he approached the Philistine giant. The idols of the heathen awakened within David's soul a yearning to see again the white vestments of the priests of God. It was then that David began to realize that somewhere along the road of life, he had lost his way.

A DECEITFUL CRUSADE

And David and his men went up, and invaded the Geshurites, and the Gezrites, and the Amalekites: for those nations were of old the inhabitants of the land, as thou goest to Shur, even unto the land of Egypt. And David smote the land, and left neither man nor woman alive, and took away the sheep, and the oxen, and the asses, and the camels, and the apparel, and returned, and came to Achish. And Achish said, Whither have ye made a road to day? And David said, Against the south of Judah, and against the south of the Jerahmeelites, and against the south of the Kenites (vv. 8-10).

Expository Notes on David's Military Expeditions

To understand this disappointing episode in the life of David, it is essential to remember that he was completely unaligned with the will of God. Jehovah had little, if any, part in the affairs of His wayward servant; the backslidden Israelite depended exclusively upon himself. With that fact before us, this scripture may be examined under four headings.

His Continuing Conflict

David had been given a city by the king of Gath, and the possibility existed that many repairs would have to be done to his new home. That situation would consume a great amount of time. The more urgent need was probably to find food and clothing; the people had been in the mountains for a considerable time. It was to be expected that David and his men would do their utmost to find provisions. The captain and his men carefully planned their course of action, but it is difficult to excuse the ferocity of the attacks made against women and children. It is impossible to excuse unjustifiable conduct. One sin led to another, and before he knew what was happening, David's future was threatened. He probably tried to justify his merciless attacks against his neighbors by remembering how God had told Joshua to annihilate the inhabitants of Canaan—a commission which was never fully obeyed. David triumphed over all the opposition and captured abundant supplies of food. He took the sheep, cattle, and camels back to his home in Ziklag; and sufficient clothing was obtained to replace the torn and dirty garments in which the people had endured in the mountains. How David would reconcile his conduct with the commandment "Thou shalt not steal" is unknown. All the dictates of the Lord were probably ignored by David and his entire army.

His Complete Conquest

It may be assumed that the combined forces of the Geshurites, the Gezrites, and the Amalekites would have outnumbered David's six hundred men. His plans included surprise attacks and the refusal to take prisoners. During World War II, this was known as the "scorched earth policy." Everything was destroyed so that the enemy would find nothing. When David had defeated the first of the Philistine strongholds, he proceeded to the next until he had finally destroyed three cities. Methods of communication were limited in those days, and since all the people were killed, there was no way by which the second and third cities could be warned of impending attacks. David's triumphs were complete.

His Consummate Cruelty

"And David left neither man nor woman alive." It is very difficult to condone such ferocious behavior. When murderous men dragged little children—even babies—from the arms of their screaming mothers, it is hardly indicative of the kindness of Jehovah. Expositors may persist in explaining that David was carrying out orders given to Joshua, but it is difficult to avoid the conclusion that David thought only of preserving the secrecy of his destructive mission. There is a difference between the permissive will of God and His perfect will. The Lord allowed certain things to happen in order to instruct His children, but when they abode in the shadow of the Almighty, those lessons were not needed. It is a cause for regret when innocent people suffer because of the mistakes of other folk. We are far removed from the ancient scene and do not know all the details connected with those savage massacres, but Christians can only frown when they consider these malicious murders.

His Concealed Conduct

"And [David] returned, and came to Achish" (v. 9). Why did the victorious David visit the Philistine monarch when he could have gone immediately to his waiting family? Did he wish to boast of his achievements? Did he desire the king to be aware of his value to the Philistine cause? It would have been far better had he refrained from entering the city of Gath; his presence created another situation in which he was compelled to lie. Once again he had forgotten or ignored the commandment "Thou shalt not bear false witness against thy neighbor" (see Exod. 20:16). In his backslidden state David unfortunately believed that it was necessary to do all kinds of prohibited things to justify his conduct. During those regrettable months in Philistinian territory, he spent a great amount of time looking at other people when he could hardly find a few moments to look into the face and heart of God. "And Achish said, Whither have ye made a road to day? And David said, Against the south of Judah, and against the south of the Jerahmeelites, and against the south of the Kenites" (v. 10). Poor David, he had become a very plausible liar who could not be trusted.

A DEADLY CONCLUSION

And Achish believed David, saying, He hath made his people Israel utterly to abhor him; therefore he shall be my servant for ever (v. 12).

A Terrible Fear

David was now living in the shadows; fear was his constant companion. Soon, a traveler would visit the destroyed cities, and news of the destruction would circulate throughout the land. When the evidence was considered, the king and his subjects would know the identity of the culprit. David's conduct had created increasing danger for himself and for those under his command. Perhaps that was the reason for his unexpected visit to Gath; maybe he wished to reassure himself that his lies would destroy the monarch's suspicion. David was now living by his wits, and his attitude could only be defined as reprehensible. He had made himself a god and was worshiping at his own shrine.

A Trusting Friend

"And Achish believed David." It was unlikely that David shared his spoils of war with the royal benefactor; the king of Gath would not need such gifts. He was probably delighted to see the prosperity of his protege and believed that it was advantageous to the Philistinian cause to shelter the refugee. He trusted his friend and could hardly justify any doubt which arose in his mind. As will be seen in the study of the next episode, his princes were not as gullible, and, apart from the overruling power of the Almighty, David might have died prematurely. He spoke from experience when he said, "It is better to trust in the LORD than to put confidence in man. It is better to trust in the LORD, than to put confidence in princes" (Ps. 118:8-9). Everyone should appreciate real friends since such people are hard to find.

A Tremendous Fallacy

And Achish believed David, saying, He hath made his people Israel utterly to abhor him [he hath made himself utterly to stink]; therefore he shall be my servant for ever (v. 12).

The motives of the king were evidently impure; he was kind to David because he expected his friendship to return good dividends. It is difficult to avoid the conclusion that he was a poor judge of character. Perhaps Solomon had this event in his thoughts when he wrote, "He that diggeth a pit shall fall into it" (Eccl. 10:8). There is never any affinity between light and darkness, and this applies to all unions between God's people and unbelievers. In the final analysis, neither can trust the other. Even at their worst, God's people are aware of higher laws. David and the king of Gath could never be life-long friends because their fellowship rested on an insecure foundation.

Episode 15

THEME: *David's Expulsion From the Philistine Army*

SCRIPTURE: 1 Samuel 28:1-2; 1 Samuel 29

KEY VERSE:

And the princes of the Philistines were wroth with him (the king); and the princes of the Philistines said unto him, Make this fellow (David) return, that he may go again to his place which thou hast appointed him, and let him not go down with us to battle, lest in the battle he be an adversary to us: for wherewith should he reconcile himself unto his master? should it not be with the heads of these men? (1 Sam. 29:4).

OUTLINE:
   I.   A Dangerous Situation (1 Samuel 28:2)
   II. A Deadly Suspicion (1 Samuel 29:4)
   III. A Disturbing Suggestion (1 Samuel 29:6-10)

A DANGEROUS SITUATION

And it came to pass in those days, that the Philistines gathered their armies together for warfare, to fight with Israel. And Achish said unto David, Know thou assuredly, that thou shalt go out with me to battle, thou and thy men. And David said to Achish, Surely thou shalt know what thy servant can do. And Achish said to David, Therefore will I make thee keeper of mine head for ever. . . . Then said the princes of the Philistines, What do these Hebrews here? And Achish said unto the princes of the Philistines, Is not this David, the servant of Saul the king of Israel, which hath been with me these days, or these years, and I have found no fault in him since he fell unto me unto this day? (1 Sam. 28:1-2 and 29:3).

Expository Notes on the Danger Confronting David

David was getting deeper and deeper into trouble; it could only be a matter of time before the Philistines became aware of his treachery. Knowing this, he and his followers wondered how much longer the deception of Achish could continue. It remains a mystery why the Philistine lords had not already heard of the destroyed cities which now disfigured the country-side. David was discovering that a land filled with idols was a poor substitute for his homeland; it could never be an effective haven for anyone running from Jehovah.

His friend Achish trusted him implicitly, but the request for assistance against Israel shocked him. The princes were annoyed by David's promotion to be the captain of the King's bodyguard. An Israelite, a potential enemy, had superseded them in obtaining that coveted honor. "Therefore will I make thee keeper of mine head for ever" (1 Sam. 28:2). There was every possibility that in the forthcoming conflict Saul and Achish might meet face to face in mortal combat and that David would ultimately need to choose which of the men he would protect. He had already refused to slay Saul, whom he believed to be the Lord's anointed. How could he slay Achish who had become an admiring friend? The Philistines would be watching him; he was "between a rock and a hard place." If he worried, he did so needlessly because God had already planned a way of escape. There was much more at stake than the survival of David and his followers; God had made covenant promises which could not be broken. David's extremity was God's opportunity. The Lord was able to make the wrath of men praise him.

A DEADLY SUSPICION

And the princes of the Philistines were wroth with [Achish] . . . and said unto him, Make this fellow return, that he may go again to his place which thou hast appointed him, and let him not go down with us to battle, lest in the battle he be an adversary to us: for wherewith should he reconcile himself unto his master? should it not be with the heads of these men? Is not this David, of whom they sang one to another, in dances, saying, Saul slew his thousands, and David his ten thousands? (1 Sam. 29:4-5).

Expository Notes on the Rejection of David

The Philistine lords were very angry; they were willing to risk their lives for the king, but were concerned by the possibility of having a traitor in their midst. They complained disdainfully to their leader, but he appeared to be biased. At first they could not believe the report that David had been made the captain of the royal bodyguard. Was Achish mad? Had he taken leave of his senses? David would be with their monarch at the rear of the battle zone. He would be protecting the king while they went ahead to confront the enemy. The situation was intolerable; they would not agree to such nonsense. Somebody expressed their unanimous opinion about David to Achish, who recognized the folly of antagonizing his officers.

"Then Achish called David, and said unto him . . . the lords favor thee not" (1 Sam. 29:6). Was there a gleam in David's eyes as he listened to the king's voice? Did he realize that a Higher Power was arranging his release from servitude to a cause he disliked? He continued to deceive when he asked, "What have I done . . . that I may not go fight against the enemies of my lord the king?" (1 Sam. 29:8). David had unfortunately become a great liar, a very bad habit which explains why he could have penned the words, "Remove from me the way of lying" (Ps. 119:29). The Philistine princes can hardly be blamed for their opposition to David; had the man from Judah been forced to make a choice between the Hebrews and their enemies, he would have betrayed his new allies.

So David and his men rose up early to depart in the morning, to return into the land of the Philistines. And the Philistines went up to Jezreel (1 Sam. 29:11).

A DISTURBING SUGGESTION

Then Achish called David, and said unto him . . . the lords favor thee not. Wherefore now return, and go in peace, that thou displease not the lords of the Philistines. Then David said unto Achish, But what have I done? . . . And Achish answered and said to David, I know that thou art good in my sight, as an angel of God: notwithstanding the princes of the Philistines have said, He shall not go up with us to the battle. Wherefore . . . as soon as ye be up early in the morning, and have light, depart (vv. 6-10).

Expository Notes on the Dismissal of David

A Word of Encouragement

"Thou art good in my sight, as an angel of God." It is beyond comprehension that David could have so charmed the king of Gath. Did the Hebrew truly love the Philistine; had that affection shown in their relationship? Had David improved his acting abilities to the point of being able to deceive the trusting monarch? Was the relationship real or false? There can be no doubt regarding the affection of the king of Gath; he had promoted his friend to a position of great honor and was ready to trust him with his life. He said, "You are like an angel of God in my sight." Achish possibly had mixed feelings when he did as his captains required. He would have been happier going to war if his new champion had been at his side, but he could not risk the antagonism of his princes. On the other hand, he was possibly greatly relieved when David departed. Even though the Philistines lost their battle against the Israelites, Achish at least could anticipate a reunion with his trusted friend.

A Way of Escape

It is interesting that Achish referred to David as being an angel of God. Did he really believe in Jehovah? Did the Philistine leader refer to "God" as being one of many worshiped in Philistia? He could hardly have been aware that the God of Israel had planned the expulsion of David. It was essential that David be rejected, for had he not returned to Ziklag immediately, he would have been too late to rescue his loved ones from a fate worse than death. The sovereignty of God is never at an impasse because, even though men may think they are indispensable, God remains on His throne. William Cowper was correct when he wrote:

> Deep in unfathomable mines
>   Of never-failing skill:
> God treasures up His bright designs,
>   And works His sovereign will.
> Ye fearful saints, fresh courage take:
>   The clouds ye so much dread:
> Are big with mercy and will break
>   In blessing on your head.

A Wish of Endearment

"And Achish answered and said, . . . Wherefore now rise up early in the morning with thy master's servants which are come with thee: and as soon as ye . . . have light, depart" (1 Sam. 29:9,10). His words "go in peace" expressed the deep desire of his soul; he wanted his friend to be in a safe place. The test of true fellowship is a desire to help others in all kinds of adversity. David was extremely fortunate that Achish loved him; without his assistance he would have been friendless during his stay among the Philistines. "A friend loveth at all times" (Prov. 17:17).

Episode 16

THEME: *The Destruction of David's City*

SCRIPTURE: 1 Samuel 30:1-31

KEY VERSE:

And David was greatly distressed; for the people spake of stoning him, because the soul of all the people was grieved, every man for his sons, and for his daughters: but David encouraged himself in the LORD his God (v. 6).

OUTLINE:
   I. David Reviews a Calamity (Verses 1-6)
   II. David Rescues a Castaway (Verses 11-18)
   III. David Rebukes His Critics (Verses 19-25)
   IV. David Rewards His Colleagues (Verses 26-31)

And it came to pass, when David and his men were come to Ziklag on the third day, that the Amalekites had invaded the south, and Ziklag, and smitten Ziklag, and burned it with fire; And had taken the women captives, that were therein: they slew not any, either great or small, but carried them away, and went on their way. . . . And David was greatly distressed; for the people spake of stoning him . . . but David encouraged himself in the LORD his God (vv. 1-6).

David's men were ecstatic that they were going home! The threat of war against Israel had miraculously vanished; the fear of being slain in battle had disappeared. Many of David's six hundred followers had wondered if they would ever see their families again, but now their homes were almost within sight. Then they suddenly saw the burnt-out buildings of Ziklag, and their anticipations died instantly. They desperately rushed toward what had been their city and frantically searched among the embers, but found nothing but ashes. A ruthless enemy had carried everyone and everything into captivity. Innumerable hoof-prints revealed how the cattle had been driven away. The men were desperate and angry; dread filled their souls. What would ruthless men do to the Hebrew women? It might have been better if the charred remains of the families had been found among the smoking remains of the city.

DAVID REVIEWS A CALAMITY

Expository Notes on David's Pain, Perception, and Purpose

David's Pain

During David's generation it was legal for any man to have as many wives as he could afford. The diversity of David's affections is never to be admired, but his greatest problem seems to have been his ever-recurring tendency to forget God. He was an expert at acting hastily and repenting leisurely. David's men rebelled because they had been involved in an expedition which was none of their business. They could have been at home defending their families against the attack of the Amalekites. They angrily questioned his decision to participate in an unnecessary crusade. David was aware they were planning to stone him, but what could any man do in those circumstances except pray? "[He] encouraged himself in the LORD his God" (1 Sam. 30:6).

David's Perception

"And David said to Abiathar the priest, Ahimelech's son, I pray thee, bring me hither the ephod. And Abiathar brought thither the ephod to David. And David inquired at the LORD, saying, Shall I pursue after this troop? shall I overtake them? And he answered him, Pursue; for thou shalt surely overtake them, and without fail recover all" (vv. 7-8). It is worthy of attention that in spite of everything that had happened, David paused to pray. He sent for the priest and the ephod. That was possibly the wisest thing he had done in a very long time. All his instincts suggested an immediate pursuit of the enemy; it seemed essential that he should hurry to the rescue of his wives. Yet, he paused to ask God for guidance. The statement that he encouraged himself in the Lord is very significant. How did he do this? Realizing his great danger, did he rest upon the everlasting arms of God's kindness? Did he secretly pray, or was his encouragement associated with the priest and the help obtainable through the ephod? It is difficult to answer these questions, but evidently David was more reassured after he consulted God. It has been said that "fools rush in where angels fear to tread." David had often unfortunately erred in this regard. The grief stricken captain realized that without the guidance of God, even his best plans would be useless. We are again reminded of the Savior's words, "Men ought always to pray, and not to faint" (Luke 18:1).

David's Purpose

"And [God] answered him, Pursue: for thou shalt surely overtake them, and without fail recover all. . . . So David pursued, he and four hundred men: for two hundred abode behind, which were so faint that they could not go over the brook Besor" (vv. 8-10). Three days of travel were followed by the search for missing families. The strain of these activities began to show on the faces of the pursuing soldiers. They were human; their bodies could not endure such hardship. Confronted by the necessity of crossing the brook Besor, they collapsed, and David realized they were incapable of further effort. His restraint in not compelling his men to continue is commendable. Yet, with or without them, he intended to overtake the Amalekites, and his mission demanded haste. It became evident later that other men who accompanied David disapproved of the action of their comrades' staying behind, so that some of the company accused the two hundred men of cowardice. They believed that the men feigned weariness to escape the ensuing battle. Throughout those difficult hours David acted with great restraint, which was made possible because he was a man under orders! God was directing his movements.

DAVID RESCUES A CASTAWAY

And they found an Egyptian in the field, and brought him to David, and gave him bread, and he did eat; and they made him drink water; And they gave him a piece of a cake of figs, and two clusters of raisins: and when he had eaten, his spirit came again to him: for he had eaten no bread, nor drunk any water, three days and three nights (vv. 11-12).

Expository Notes on the Providence of God

This is a story about the grace of God. The Lord moved in a mysterious way His wonders to perform. (1) He arranged for an *Egyptian* slave to become sick; had the man been an *Amalekite*, David's men would have been obliged to kill him (see Deut. 25:19). (2) Without realizing that he was the instrument of a higher power, the Amalekite master was pitiless when he abandoned his servant to certain death in a wilderness without shade. (3) Many people in similar circumstances would have succumbed. To be exposed to intense heat by day and chilling cold at night was an experience few people could have endured. (4) That he was found by David's men was not an accident. Those trackers were unerringly led to the place where the unconscious man lay. If they had failed to see his motionless body, he would have died.

It remains a mystery why David thought he needed a guide. The passing of herds of cattle and vast numbers of sheep, goats, and camels inevitably left tracks which any man could follow. The Amalekite army perhaps planned their retreat through rocky terrain, but it was inevitable that numerous signs of their journey would be visible. They knew that the Philistines were fighting the Israelites many miles away and believed that they had plenty of time to enjoy their victory celebrations.

Canst thou bring me down to this company? And he said, Swear unto me by God, that thou wilt neither kill me, nor deliver me into the hands of my master, and I will bring thee down to this company. And when he had brought him down, behold, they were spread abroad upon all the earth, eating and drinking, and dancing, because of all the great spoil that they had taken out of the land of the Philistines, and out of the land of Judah. And David smote them from the twilight even unto the evening of the next day: and there escaped not a man of them, save four hundred young men, which rode upon camels, and fled. And David recovered all that the Amalekites had carried away (vv. 15-18).

Expository Notes on David's Conquest of the Amalekites

It seems incredible that David's small army should so easily vanquish the Amalekite host. Those drunken soldiers probably felt that they were secure, for they had no knowledge of David's expulsion from the Philistine army. Neither sentries nor guards had apparently been posted, and the entire host was drinking and dancing. The description supplied by the ancient writer suggests a drunken orgy. There were no women present except the captives from Ziklag, and they would never willingly have participated in the revelry. Hilarious through the effects of wine, the invaders swayed their bodies, sang their songs, and waved their arms. The noise they made deadened the sound of David's approach. The rescued Egyptian evidently had supplied invaluable information which helped David complete his triumph. The story of the sin, salvation, and service of that revived slave makes exciting reading and illustrates what happens when a sinner is rescued by the grace of God. (See the homily, "The Nameless Slave . . . Who Made a Name for Himself," p. 149.)

DAVID REBUKES HIS CRITICS

And there was nothing lacking to them, neither small nor great, neither sons nor daughters, neither spoil, nor any thing that they had taken to them: David recovered all. . . . Then answered all the wicked men, and men of Belial, of those that went with David, and said, Because they went not with us we will not give them ought of the spoil we have recovered, save to every man his wife and his children, that they may lead them away, and depart. Then said David, Ye shall not do so, my brethren, with that which the LORD hath given us. . . . but as his part is that goeth down to the battle, so shall his part be that tarrieth by the stuff. . . . And it was so from that day forward, that he made it a statute and an ordinance for Israel unto this day (vv. 19-25).

Expository Notes on David's New Law

A Considerate Command

It is important to remember that the men who remained at the brook

Besor were *made* to do so. The Bible says: "And David came to the two hundred men, which were so faint that they could not follow David, whom they had *made* also to abide at the brook Besor." The men were not cowards; they wanted desperately to go to the battle, but their commander's experience warned them that they were physically unfit for combat. David not only recommended that they stay at the brook, but he *commanded* them so to do. This command is irrefutable evidence that he cared for his men. He was no longer self-centered. Even though he was depriving himself of the services of two hundred trusted men, he thought more of their welfare than he did of his own.

A Callous Covetousness

A serpent was in the Garden of Eden, a Judas was among the disciples of the Lord, and there were unfortunately "children of Belial" among the followers of David. Their inexcusable greed could have caused divisions among their comrades. That there was sufficient spoil for every man to have all that he required proves that they had personal grudges against their comrades when they wanted to keep the spoil for themselves. The Amalekites had not only confiscated the animals at Ziklag, but they had also raided the southern part of Israel. They had taken advantage of the fact that both the Hebrew and Philistine armies were fighting each other, and no opposition could consequently be forthcoming. When David captured all the animals, each citizen of Ziklag regained what had been stolen, plus much more. The fact that David was able to send large gifts to his friends in Judah proves that the complainers had impure motives. A captain with less grace might have been more severe in his treatment of these offenders.

A Charming Courtesy

It is to his credit that David never expressed annoyance with his disgruntled followers. When he replied, "Ye shall not do so, my brethren" (1 Sam. 30:23), he revealed a new attitude toward everybody. He was kind and considerate, restrained in his actions, slow to anger, and of great compassion. David was spending more time listening to God and less making his own decisions. Had he acted hastily or presumptuously, his army could have been divided and blood might have been shed. The joyous homecoming and glorious reunions could have been ruined if quarrelsome men argued and fought. David's thoughtfulness was destined to be remembered for ever. He set an example which was followed by succeeding generations. He was apparently aware of another great precept, "Give, and it shall be given unto you; good measure, pressed down, and shaken together, and running over" (Luke 6:38). The basic principles of virtue are ageless; like God, they are eternal.

A Continuing Custom

What David did became "a statute and an ordinance unto this day." An old Sankey hymn suggests that "one day we'll pass from the earth and its toiling, only remembered by what we have done." When Mary of Bethany broke her box of precious ointment, the Lord said of her: "Verily I say unto you, Wheresoever this gospel shall be preached in the whole world, there shall also this, that this woman hath done, be told for a memorial of her" (see Matt. 26:13). Blessed are the people whose testimony is remembered long after their labors cease. When I was a young preacher, I belonged to a party of itinerant evangelists known as the "Pilgrim Preachers." That company of laymen was led by a saintly man named Ernest Luff. He was one of the most dedicated men I ever knew; his white beard gave him the appearance of a patriarch! I shall always remember the day when a small child in the street looked into Mr. Luff's smiling face and asked "Mister, are you Jesus?" He replied, "No, son, but I am trying to be like him." That man left behind an immortal testimony.

DAVID REWARDS HIS COLLEAGUES

> **And when David came to Ziklag, he sent of the spoil unto the elders of Judah, even to his friends, saying, Behold a present for you of the spoil of the enemies of the LORD; To them which were in Bethel . . . Ramoth . . . Jattir . . . Aroer . . . Siphmoth . . . Eshtemoa . . . Rachal . . . and to them which were in Hebron, and to all the places where David himself and his men were wont to haunt (vv. 26-31).**

Expository Notes on David's Gifts to His Friends

The greatness of the spoil taken by David was never estimated. The Amalekites had plundered the southlands of Israel and other places in Philistia, and the number of confiscated animals was immense. It should be carefully noticed that David restored to each of his men that which had been lost and possibly gave them additional gifts to compensate for their trouble. Yet, he was very decisive when he indicated that the remaining animals belonged to him. He probably revealed what he intended to do with his share of the spoil, and his men understood that he had no personal ambition to become wealthy at their expense. What happened on that memorable occasion can be considered under three headings.

A Wonderful Relationship . . . Friendship

"He sent of the spoils unto all the elders of Judah. . . . and to all the places where David himself and his men were wont to haunt." He did not forget the friends who had provided help during times of adversity. When he sought shelter in the rugged mountains and when his company needed food, many people contributed to his cause. When Saul desperately sought to discover the various hiding places of the renegade band, thousands of Israelites could have been traitors, but none of David's friends betrayed him. David surely remembered that a true friend is closer than a brother and believed that he was indebted to many people. When the opportunity came to reward them, he was thrilled to do so.

A Welcome Restoration . . . Favor

David probably used his men to dispatch gifts to the distant cities of Israel. That scene was resplendent, for there were cattle-drives going in all directions. He was not obliged to give away what had been won in battle, but was motivated by the overflowing love in his soul. At that point, he could have established a farm and retired. His men could have been his neighbors, and their combined wealth and energy would have safeguarded their future. That retirement never happened because David was beginning to realize that he was not his own. God had plans for his life, and any decision unaligned with the divine will would be a mistake. When cattle began to arrive from Ziklag, the Hebrew recipients probably shouted for joy and remembered Saul's words: "Here now, ye Benjamites; will the son of Jesse give every one of you fields and vineyards, and make you all captains of thousands, and captains of hundreds?" (see 1 Sam. 22:7).

A Timely Reminder . . . Forethought

If David remembered that God had promised to give him the throne of Israel, he knew that his greatest opportunity was about to arrive. Even the removal of Saul could not guarantee his acceptance by all the tribes of Israel. It might take time to win the approval of the entire nation. Therefore, until that elusive goal was reached, it would be advisable to have many friends. David was beginning to cooperate with his Lord; the change in his attitude and efforts was overdue. Yet, in spite of the man's inconsistency, God never abandoned him. The Lord knew that the ultimate triumph was never in doubt.

HOMILIES FOR PREACHERS AND TEACHERS

Study No. 8

THE NAMELESS SLAVE . . . Who Made a Name for Himself
(1 Samuel 30:11-18)

So David and his men came to the city, and, behold, it was burned with fire; and their wives, and their sons, and their daughters, were taken

captive. Then David and the people that were with him lifted up their voice and wept, until they had no more power to weep (v. 4).

All around lay the ruins of their devastated city. A foul enemy had raided the place during the absence of the men, and every home had been destroyed by fire. The blackened timbers, the swirling clouds of smoke, and the awful silence broken only by the crackling of flames told their own poignant story. Somewhere beyond the horizon the triumphant enemy had driven the womenfolk into a captivity worse than death, and when the despairing men considered the untold horrors that would be employed to break the dauntless spirits of Israel's womanhood, they "wept until they had no more power to weep." "And David inquired at the LORD, saying, Shall I pursue after this troop? shall I overtake them? And He answered him, Pursue: for thou shalt surely overtake them, and without fail recover all. . . . And they found an Egyptian in the field" (vv. 8-11).

HOW SERIOUS HIS SITUATION

"And David said unto him, To whom belongest thou? and whence art thou? And he said, I am a young man of Egypt, servant to an Amalekite; and my master left me, because three days agone I fell sick. We made an invasion . . . and we burned Ziklag with fire" (vv. 13-14). The plight of that unfortunate slave had been most critical. Deserted by his slave owner, he had been left to perish in the merciless heat of an eastern sun. Friendless and forsaken, he had lain for days without food and water and had lost all hope of survival. Yet as he discovered the identity of the man who stood over him, his terror increased. He had helped to burn this stranger's home and had assisted in driving his family into unspeakable bondage. He deserved death, and if the Israelite captain decided to take the law into his own hands, there would be no court of appeal against his sentence. The dying Egyptian quickly realized that even death would be preferable to torture, and the outraged feelings of these distracted men would be capable of anything—even torture.

HOW SURPRISING HIS SALVATION

"And David said unto him, Canst thou bring me down to this company?" (v. 15). And as the young man looked up into the eyes of his questioner, he realized that in spite of the enormity of his crime, there was still a chance to escape execution. He looked at the listening men who had allowed the life-giving water to trickle down his parched throat, and their kindly smiles reassured him. This was neither dream nor trickery, for David was willing to offer mercy. It seemed too good to be true, but then he realized that this was not an unconditional offer of mercy. David's grace must be equaled by his own responsibility. Salvation would only be possible if he were willing to change masters. David required his services, and he had to therefore renounce the old task-master and seek rest in the service of a new lord. "And he said, Swear unto me by God, that thou wilt neither kill me, nor deliver me into the hands of my master, and I will bring thee down to this company." When he regained his strength and was able to stand, he knew that he had received a pardon he did not deserve.

HOW SPLENDID HIS SERVICE

He therefore determined to prove to his new master the extent of his gratitude. His best talents should be devoted to the cause of David to bring about the rescue of the other unfortunate men and women whose bondage would be as cruel as his own had been. "And when he had brought David down, behold, the Amalekites were spread abroad on the earth, eating and drinking and dancing. . . . And David smote them from the twilight even until the evening of the next day. . . . And David recovered all" (vv. 16-18). The young helper probably watched the emancipation of the slaves and rejoiced in the part he had been able to play in making their release possible. He had faithfully served the man who had graciously saved him from death. And thus once again the divine Author enshrined in an ancient story the triple truths of the Savior: *sin, salvation,* and *service.* Our debt to Christ is very great. We must therefore heed the words of Paul to "present our bodies a living sacrifice . . . which is your reasonable service" (see Romans 12:1). (Homily reprinted from the author's book, *Bible Cameos,* pp. 33-34.)

Episode 17

THEME: *David's Reaction to the News of Saul's Death*

SCRIPTURE: 2 Samuel 1:1-27

KEY VERSE:

> Saul and Jonathan were lovely and pleasant in their lives, and in their death they were not divided: they were swifter than eagles, they were stronger than lions (v. 23).

OUTLINE:
    I.   An Amalekite's Announcement (Verses 1-10)
    II. An Awesome Assassination (Verses 11-16)
    III. An Amazing Appreciation (Verses 17-27)

Two seemingly endless days had passed, and the impatient David hardly knew what to do. His men had made makeshift beds amid the wreckage of their burnt-out city, but the entire reconstruction of Ziklag was out of the question, for it had become evident David's sojourn there was ending. Every person was concerned about the battle fought between the Hebrews and the Philistines. David was very concerned, for Jonathan had been in the conflict. The fugitive captain walked among his men and watched the women preparing meals, but his thoughts were far away. Who had won the battle? What had happened to Saul and Jonathan? Why had no one arrived with news?

> It came even to pass on the third day, that, behold, a man came out of the camp from Saul with his clothes rent, and earth upon his head: and so it was, when he came to David, that he fell to the earth, and did obeisance. . . . And David said unto him, How went the matter? I pray thee, tell me. And he answered, That the people are fled from the battle, and many of the people also are fallen and dead; and Saul and Jonathan his son are dead also. . . . As I happened by chance upon mount Gilboa, behold, Saul leaned upon his spear; and, lo, the chariots and horsemen followed hard after him. . . . So I stood upon him, and slew him, because I was sure that he could not live after that he was fallen: and I took the crown that was upon his head, and the bracelet that was on his arm, and have brought them hither unto my lord (vv. 2-10).

AN AMALEKITE'S ANNOUNCEMENT

Expository Notes on the First Report of Saul's Death

David was speculative. The dust-covered messenger had evidently come from the war zone, for he held Saul's crown. That fact alone was sufficient to prove that a calamity had occurred. The king had to be dead; otherwise that crown would not have been in the hand of a stranger. But something was wrong with the report! King Saul would never have solicited aid from an uncircumcised heathen. There were other discrepancies which made David question the accuracy of the report. The messenger said: "I happened *by chance* on Mount Gilboa" where "chariots and horsemen followed hard after him." David asked himself: "How could a man be in the midst of the horrendous battle by chance?" The messenger quoted the king as having said: "Anguish is come upon me." The translation does not express the true meaning of the text. A better rendering of the original scripture would be: "My coat of mail and my embroidered coat hinder me." It seems that the king desired to die, but was incapable of committing suicide because his armor impeded action. The Amalekite inferred that Saul had been unable to place the head of the lance against a vulnerable part of his body. Yet, he said that Saul had leaned on his spear, and in doing so, the king could not have been totally incapacitated. Surely the monarch could have found an opening between the overlapping pieces of protective armor, and the weight of his falling body would have brought the desired end. David stared at the Amalekite and wondered if he were speaking the truth. Resentment suddenly began to increase within David's soul because Saul had been the Lord's anointed; the man chosen by God to be the king of Israel. David himself had repeatedly refused to harm the monarch, and now this heathen was proud of his achievement and hoped to be rewarded for his deed.

Then David speculated again. Why would an Amalekite be in the middle of the battle zone? He could not have been a conscript in Israel's army, since all men of his background were detested and executed. On the other hand, he could not have belonged to Achish, for if that were the case, David would have known him. Then who was he and from what place had he really come? David was nonplused. He knew that Saul had been exceedingly foolish; only a very stupid man would have worn a crown into battle. That action had made him a special target for the Philistine archers. Was he a fatalist? He knew he was about to die, for Samuel had predicted that sad event (see 1 Samuel 28:15-20). Had the king deliberately worn his crown to show that he was determined to die as he had lived? When David remembered Jonathan, his grief overwhelmed him.

AN AWESOME ASSASSINATION

Then David took hold on his clothes, and rent them; and likewise all the men that were with him: and they mourned and wept and fasted until

even, for Saul, and for Jonathan his son, and for the people of the LORD, and for the house of Israel; because they were fallen by the sword. And David said unto the young man that told him, Whence art thou? And he answered, I am the son of a stranger, an Amalekite. And David said unto him, How wast thou not afraid to stretch forth thine hand to destroy the LORD's anointed? And David called one of the young men, and said, Go near, and fall upon him. And he smote him that he died (vv. 11-15).

Expository Notes on the Amalekite's Execution

The Stricken Family . . . Pain Disturbing

It is worthy of commendation that David neither gloated nor rejoiced about the death of his most formidable enemy. His father-in-law, Saul, had been ruthless and unwavering in his hatred, but the hunted man never for a moment forgot that the king was the anointed of the Lord. It is extremely doubtful whether any other person of that generation would have possessed the restraining patience of the fugitive prince. Most people in a similar situation would have shouted for joy and hastened to take advantage of the situation. A majority of the Israelites would have probably accepted the new leadership, but David, for a time at least, was determined to follow God's directions. The rending of his clothes was a genuine expression of grief. His act was emulated by his followers, and their cries of anguish could be heard throughout the city. Perhaps the army could not share the intensity of their leader's grief, but the fact that Israel had been defeated in battle was a shame which everybody shared. "They wept; and fasted until even . . . for the people of the LORD, and for the house of Israel; *because they were fallen by the sword.*" Many years later, Paul wrote that when one member of the body suffers, all suffer (see 1 Corinthians 12:26). That truth was evident in Ziklag when the news of Israel's defeat devastated all the people. The entire nation had suffered a terrible setback when Saul and Jonathan died on Mount Gilboa, and their grief was intense.

The Stupid Fellow . . . Pretension Deceiving

Had the Amalekite been truthful, he might have received a reward for bringing Saul's crown and bracelet to David. He could have possibly been excused for not recognizing that Saul was the anointed of God. How could a stranger from Amalek be aware of customs and beliefs in Israel? Although Saul was a king, he was just another man who had been elected to high office. David could have overlooked the Amalekite's ignorance, but his lies and greed were unpardonable. The true account of Saul's demise is given in 1 Samuel 31:3-6.

And the battle went sore against Saul, and the archers hit him; and he was sore wounded of the archers. Then said Saul unto his armorbearer, Draw thy sword, and thrust me through therewith; lest these uncircumcised come and thrust me through, and abuse me. But his armorbearer would not; for he was sore afraid. Therefore Saul took a sword and fell upon it. And when his armorbearer saw that Saul was dead, he fell likewise upon his sword, and died with him. So Saul died, and his three sons, and his armorbearer and all his men, that same day together.

The Amalekite, for unrevealed reasons, was in the battle area and decided to capitalize on the tragic happenings. He seized the crown and bracelet and planned what he would say, hoping David would reward his act. Had he told the truth and offered those priceless things freely, he might have become a hero in Israel. He could have covered Saul's body with a cloak or some other garment to prevent its being desecrated or mauled by scavenger dogs. If he had only done anything which showed respect for the fallen, he would have been honored throughout the nation. His deception, greed, and irreverence infuriated David and led to his execution. Honesty is essential when a sinner approaches the Almighty. Many years later, Ananias and Sapphira committed a similar error before Simon Peter, and they also perished (see Acts 5:1-11).

The Solemn Fate . . . Punishment Destroying

It should be remembered that David lived in hard and difficult times when standards of justice and moral conduct were not what might be expected today. David was both the judge and jury, and there was no court of appeal. He held the powers of life and death in his hands, and no person could countermand or challenge the sentence of death passed upon that hypocritical courier. It has already been stated that there is a difference between the permissive and the perfect will of God. There are occasions when God allows things to happen—not primarily because He desires them to take place, but because in His omniscience, He knows that a specific procedure was the only way to teach Israel the value of righteousness.

When the Amalekite fell mortally wounded, the onlookers probably shuddered, but realized that neither God nor David would tolerate such disgraceful behavior. Afterward, if they were tempted to obtain illicit rewards through deception, they remembered the Amalekite's fate. The Scriptures endorse David's action, for during the conquest of Canaan, a similar event took place. Achan coveted and stole valuable items which belonged to the citizens of Jericho and lied concerning his conduct. He was sentenced to death by stoning (see Joshua 7:20-26). Later, Gehazi, the servant of Elisha, made the same mistake when he tried to deceive his master. Alas, he also suffered, for "he went out a leper as white as snow" (see 2 Kings 5:24-27). God had no delight in the death of these men, but by permitting it to happen, He effectively taught lessons which prophetical preaching failed to do. The Hebrews learned that it is extremely foolish to attempt to deceive the Almighty.

AN AMAZING APPRECIATION

And David lamented with this lamentation over Saul and over Jonathan his son. . . . The beauty of Israel is slain upon thy high places: how are the mighty fallen! (vv. 17 and 19).

David's Mournful Anthem

It was customary in Israel for grief to be expressed in song. Second Chronicles 35:25 relates that "Jeremiah lamented for Josiah; *and all the singing men and the singing women spake* of Josiah in their lamentations to this day, and made them an ordinance in Israel: and behold, they are written in the lamentations." Those musical efforts might be better described as dirges, for they expressed the grief of the singers. Many of the psalms of David were written or composed during times of great emotional stress. Psalm 51 is a notable example, for when Nathan, the prophet, denounced David's adultery with Bath-sheba and also the subsequent murder of her husband Uriah, the king was devastated. It was at that time that he wrote: "Have mercy upon me, O God, according to thy lovingkindness; according unto the multitude of thy tender mercies blot out my transgressions. . . . For I acknowledge my transgressions: and my sin is ever before me. Against thee, thee only, have I sinned, and done this evil in thy sight" (see Psalm 51:1-4).

David's Magnanimous Attitude

It is worthy of attention that David never permitted any bitterness to appear in his song. He could have recounted his experience of Saul as a ruthless, merciless enemy and stated that most of the unpleasantness he suffered had been caused by the king's inexcusable conduct. To his credit it must be recognized that David only remembered the nice things about his persecutor. He told no lies when he sang his mournful dirge, but made mention of everything that was charming and pleasant to repeat. For example, he said:

The beauty of Israel is slain upon thy high places: how are the mighty fallen! . . . Saul and Jonathan were lovely and pleasant in their lives, and in their death they were not divided: they were swifter than eagles, they were stronger than lions (vv. 19 and 23).

When a man meditates upon the unpleasant things of life and remembers the mistakes of other people, he adds to the poisonous thoughts already circulating in his mind. Paul was wise when he wrote to the Christians at Philippi, "Finally, brethren, whatsoever things are true . . . honest . . . just . . . pure . . . lovely . . . of good report; if there be any virtue, and if there be any praise, *think on these things*" (Philippians 4:8).

David's Meaningful Advice

> **Ye daughters of Israel, weep over Saul, who clothed you in scarlet, with other delights, who put on ornaments of gold upon your apparel (v. 24).**

David reminded the daughters of Israel to remember the good things about the deceased monarch. As they had sung "Saul hath slain his thousands, and David his ten thousands," they should now shed tears in memory of the king who had given them beautiful garments and whose protective arm saved them from the Philistines. David jealously guarded the good name of his people. He was afraid that the heathens would speak derogatively concerning their victim. He worried about the danger that girls in Gath might extol the triumph of the Philistine army. He desired that good things be said about the people of God, an attitude that should be an example to everybody. Lying tongues and exaggerated gossip do more harm to the cause of God than any other medium. Unfortunately, when a Christian falls from grace and when his indiscretions are revealed to the public, even his colleagues sometimes prolong the problems by their repetitious talk. David seemed to say, "Do not speak about the evil things; just mention the good things Saul did, and be grateful you were the recipients of his kindness."

David's Marvelous Affection

> **I am distressed for thee, my brother Jonathan: very pleasant hast thou been unto me: thy love to me was wonderful, passing the love of women (v. 26).**

David's life was unfortunately marred by his excessive love of women. He ruled a nation but never ruled himself. His inordinate desire to satisfy the lusts of his flesh was a quicksand into which he sank. Nevertheless, his love for Jonathan surpassed anything he had known. Their mutual affection was intense, warm, deep, and lasting; it never permitted jealousy nor envy to exist within their hearts. The slaying of his friend left a vacancy in David's life which was never filled. It is easy to believe that the love of God was "shed abroad in their hearts" (see Romans 5:5).

Episode 18

THEME: *David Becomes the King of Judah*

SCRIPTURE: 2 Samuel 2:1-11

KEY VERSES:

> And the men of Judah came, and there they anointed David king over the house of Judah. And they told David, saying, That the men of Jabesh-gilead were they that buried Saul. . . . And the time that David was king in Hebron over the house of Judah was seven years and six months (vv. 4 and 11).

OUTLINE:
   I.   Seeking Guidance (Verses 1-3)
   II. Sharing Glory (Verse 4a)
   III. Sincere Gratitude (Verses 4b-7)
   IV. Stubborn Guilt (Verses 8-11)

And it came to pass after this, that David inquired of the LORD, saying, Shall I go up into any of the cities of Judah? And the LORD said unto him, Go up. And David said, Whither shall I go up? And he said, Unto Hebron. So David went up thither, and his two wives also, Ahinoam the Jezreelitess, and Abigail Nabal's wife the Carmelite. And his men that were with him did David bring up, every man with his household: and they dwelt in the cities of Hebron (vv. 1-3).

Expository Notes on David's Desire to Pray

SEEKING GUIDANCE . . . David Seeks to Know the Will of God

David was a very strange and sometimes unreliable man. The Savior taught that men ought *always* to pray, but the soon-to-be king of Israel was unfortunately a man of moods; he only prayed when he needed something! Life had suddenly changed for the fugitive-prince. The death of Saul had terminated the search for the elusive captain, and it seemed he only had to march into Israel to claim what God had promised. He was loved throughout the nation, and his friends were waiting to welcome him. Yet, David was reluctant to move. Perhaps he had premonitions of the opposition to be expected from Saul's commanding officers. If the late king's followers opposed his coronation, their action could create grave problems. What could he do? He sent for the priest and the ephod and asked God for directions. He was evidently worried, for when the Lord's first answer seemed inconclusive, David asked again and was told to proceed to Hebron (see v. 1).

David had at least six hundred soldiers, and many were married with families. Approximately fourteen hundred people arrived in Hebron, but supplying accommodations for such a large influx of people presented no problem. The people of Judah were proud of David, and since their city had many suburbs, David's followers were given homes in nearby communities. That circumstance guaranteed to David all the assistance required if an emergency arose; it solved the immediate problems and set the stage for his coronation in Judah. At that time David was trusting implicitly in God and was careful to follow only His direction. As long as he continued in that fashion, he was perfectly safe. The mantle of divine protection fell upon him so that his future was assured. David had learned the lesson that "it pays to pray!"

And the men of Judah came, and there they anointed David king over the house of Judah (v. 4).

Expository Notes on an Incomplete Coronation

SHARING GLORY . . . David is Crowned King of Judah

The story of the incomplete coronation of David leaves many questions unanswered. Why did not all the tribes of Israel join in the celebrations? Did David ask that the coronation be confined to the tribe of Judah? Was he aware of the mounting opposition led by Abner, and did he wish to prevent a civil war in Israel? David was a Bethlehemite and was therefore one of the friendly people of Judah. The citizens were accepting a member of their own tribe and were proud of their kinsman. Abner had taken vows to be loyal to the house of Saul and felt obligated to elect Saul's son to be the king of Israel. It would be interesting to unravel the complicated details of those troublesome days. David seemed aware of what was taking place and, knowing the unity of the nation was threatened, was content to await the time when the entire nation would be his kingdom. He had come a long way since the terrifying days when he hid in the wilderness of Ziph and was able to write, "Bless the LORD O my soul: and all that is within me, bless his holy name" (see Psalm 103:1).

It is to be regretted that the rest of Israel viewed with suspicion the joyful event in Judah. Abner was probably very incensed and jealous that he had not been consulted concerning the choice of a king. His smoldering resentment increased daily. He probably recognized that Ish-bosheth, the son of Saul, was a very poor substitute for his father, but at least he was the heir to the throne. Abner believed that he was obligated to stand by the son of his former master. He never consulted the priest with the ephod because he believed that it was better to make his own decisions.

And they told David, saying, That the men of Jabesh-gilead were they that buried Saul. And David sent messengers unto the men of Jabesh-gilead, and said unto them, Blessed be ye of the LORD, that ye have shewed this kindness unto your lord, even unto Saul, and have buried him. And now the LORD shew kindness and truth unto you: and I also will requite you this kindness, because ye have done this thing (vv. 4-6).

Expository Notes on David's Message to Jabesh-gilead

SINCERE GRATITUDE . . . David Communicates With the Men of Jabesh-gilead

It is to be expected that when David took over the reins of government in Judah, his advisers would acquaint him with what had taken place during his absence from the country. Possibly, in the course of their conversations, he was informed of the courage of the men of Jabesh-gilead who had risked their lives to take the bodies of Saul and his sons from the walls of Beth-shan (for this account see 1 Samuel 31:7-13). David would have been particularly interested in the fate of Jonathan and, when told of the courageous exploit of the men of Jabesh-gilead, was overwhelmed with gratitude. He thanked the people from the southern city and expressed the hope that they would also be true to his own cause. He had been crowned king of Judah and would be honored to have such valiant men at his side. It is impossible to have too many friends, and words of appreciation can often change formidable foes into courageous allies (See the homily, The Men of Jabesh-gilead . . . Who Never Forgot," p. 163).

But Abner the son of Ner, captain of Saul's host took Ish-bosheth the son of Saul, and brought him over to Mahanaim; and made him king over Gilead, and over the Ashurites, and over Jezreel, and over Ephraim, and over Benjamin, and over all Israel. Ish-bosheth Saul's son was forty years old when he began to reign over Israel, and he reigned two years. But the house of Judah followed David. And the time that David was king in Hebron over the house of Judah was seven years and six months (vv. 8-11).

Expository Notes on Abner's Support for Ish-bosheth

STUBBORN GUILT . . . Abner's Refusal to Accept David

Abner, the commander in chief of Israel's army, was one of the greatest warriors in the nation. His rise to power was amazing; yet, when he died

David sorrowfully exclaimed, "Died Abner as a fool dieth" (see 2 Samuel 3:33). As will be seen in a later episode, David's assessment was correct. The great general was a proud man, and it was his foolishness which led to his downfall. This section of the story may be considered under three subheadings.

His Indisputable Greatness

The fact that Abner was able to gather all Israel to crown a new king should not be overlooked. David had countless friends in the nation— many influential men who would have preferred to accept David as their new leader. Yet, whatever they thought, they either admired or feared Abner to such an extent that they abandoned their desire to oppose the general. He had enjoyed the confidence of the late king Saul and had access to the monarch at all times. His advice had helped formulate policy, and with the single exception of Joab, there was no man who could challenge the authority of the great soldier. When he spoke, Israel listened; his commands were always obeyed. He was proud of his position, but David had so annoyed him that Abner never forgot what had been said.

His Iniquitous Grudge

When Saul marched with three thousand chosen men of Israel to overtake David in the wilderness, the fugitive approached the sleeping king and confiscated his spear and cruse of water. It was said that a deep sleep from the Lord came upon the company. Later when David escaped, he taunted Saul's general.

> **Then David went over to the other side, and stood on the top of an hill afar off; a great space being between them. And David cried to the people, and to Abner, the son of Ner, saying, Answerest thou not Abner? Then Abner answered and said, Who art thou that criest to the king? And David said to Abner, Art not thou a valiant man? and who is like to thee in Israel? wherefore then hast thou not kept thy lord the king? for there came one of the people in to destroy the king thy lord. This thing is not good that thou hast done. As the LORD liveth, ye are worthy to die, because ye have not kept your master, the LORD's anointed" (1 Samuel 26:13-16).**

Abner's pride was evidently hurt. His carelessness had been exposed before the entire army, and the old soldier resented David's remarks. His grudge became a cancer that destroyed his peace of mind. Abner believed that the upstart from Bethlehem should have been more considerate in his statements. If ever the opportunity occurred, he would make David regret his action! When Abner heard of the coronation in Hebron, the old warrior growled like a wounded bear and went out to make sure that the sedition did not spread. He should have known better; God had already revealed the identity of the next king, and even Saul had confessed this to David (1 Samuel 24:20). The general was very stubborn; neither God nor man would prevent what he intended to do.

His Inexcusable Gesture

"But Abner the son of Ner, captain of Saul's host, took Ish-bosheth the son of Saul, and brought him over to Mahanaim; and made him king . . . over all Israel" (2 Samuel 2:8-9). He had no thought of obeying the commandment of God, for he was determined to oppose David whatever the cost might be. As a result, he unfortunately destroyed himself! He divided the nation, an event which led to a battle in which Abner killed the brother of Joab. Abner was ultimately slain in the gateway to Hebron. He might have lived to be a very old man and could have received the highest accolade in Israel, but his pride and animosity ruined him. He lost everything. Any man who fights against God succeeds only in advertising his own stupidity.

HOMILIES FOR PREACHERS AND TEACHERS

Study No. 9

THE MEN OF JABESH-GILEAD . . . Who Never Forgot (1 Samuel 31:11-12)

It was night, and the flicker of the firelight alone disturbed the stillness of Israel's camp. The men sat around, but none desired conversation. They preferred to be alone with their memories, even though the memories were bitter. They would remember forever the nightmare experience when they had fled from a scene of horror. Their king was dead, their homes occupied by heathens, their loved ones were dead—they shuddered as they thought of other possibilities. Their future outlook was as bleak as the winds of winter, for it would be but a matter of time before these hateful conquerors, drunk with success and lusting for further conquests, would press forward into the country. And since the might of Israel had fallen, nothing remained to prevent the complete subjugation of the land. They stared moodily into the fire, and all around them the night was mysterious and still. An unannounced and unexpected diversion suddenly performed a miracle in the hearts of the despondent men.

We are not informed as to the identity of the messenger, and imagination alone seems able to supply the necessary details. A man staggered out of the eerie darkness, and as he approached the fire, watching men hurried to his assistance. Perhaps some of them recognized him and unthinkingly blurted out their questions, "Where have you been? How did you escape in the battle? We had given you up as dead." Slowly he shook his weary head and told of his escape from Beth-shan. He told of the mockery of their pagan conquerors and of the decapitation of Saul. There could be no mistake, for he had seen these terrors. He had been there. He sighed, and in the moments that followed a remarkable thing took place. Men approached from the shadows, and at the sound of their voices, the newcomer looked up. His tale was told again.

The men stood awhile considering; then finally their leader spoke. His voice was more like the growl of an angered beast. It was low and quiet and deadly. His eyes seemed to throw back the challenge of the firelight, and when he moved, his actions were those of a man who knew exactly what he intended to do. "Men, we are going to Beth-shan." The others immediately signified their approval, and to the bewilderment of the listening Israelites, within minutes they had commenced their journey.

In recording those illustrious moments, the historian wrote: "And when the inhabitants of Jabesh-gilead heard of that which the Philistines had done to Saul, all the valiant men arose, and went all night, and took the body of Saul, and the bodies of his sons from the wall of Beth-shan, and came to Jabesh, and burnt them there. And they took their bones and buried them under a tree at Jabesh, and fasted seven days." We can only ask why these men risked their lives in such an enterprise.

The answer is supplied in the earlier history of the city. Years before, an Ammonite invasion had taken place when Jabesh-gilead had been surrounded by merciless enemies. The heathen king Nahash, with conspicuous conceit, sat in his royal tent and waited. His captains were in command of the situation; his lines were unbroken. Jabesh-gilead would fall. He was satisfied. When emissaries sought peace terms, he replied: "On this condition will I make a covenant with you, that I may thrust out all your right eyes, and lay it for a reproach upon all Israel. And the elders of Jabesh said unto him, Give us seven days' respite, that we may send messengers unto all the coasts of Israel: and then, if there be no man to save us, we will come out to thee" (1 Sam. 11:2-3). Nahash indulgently agreed. He knew that the messengers would need to pass through his camp. He would be waiting for them. Yes, the respite was granted. Yet in spite of all his watchfulness, at least one young man penetrated the heathen lines and carried the news far into Israel. Saul, the son of Kish, heard of the plight of his brethren, "And the Spirit of God came upon Saul" (v. 6). He led his army to the battle, and the men of Jabesh were saved. They never forgot their savior. They loved him and could never rest while his body was being made an object of scorn. Their exploit is one of the most courageous recorded in history. Three shining words stand out in their record—gratitude, gallantry, glory. They did this for their dead savior. What would we do for the living Christ? (Reprinted from the author's book, *Bible Cameos*, pp. 35-36.)

Episode 19

THEME: *David's Covenant With Abner*

SCRIPTURE: 2 Samuel 3:1-21

KEY VERSES:

> And Abner had communication with the elders of Israel, saying, Ye sought for David in times past to be king over you: Now then do it: for the LORD hath spoken of David, saying, By the hand of my servant David I will save my people Israel out of the hand of the Philistines, and out of the hand of all their enemies (vv. 17-18).

OUTLINE:

I. A Forgotten Commandment (Verses 1-5)
II. A Foolish Charge (Verses 6-11)
III. A Friendly Commitment (Verses 12-13)
IV. A Frightening Condition (Verses 14-16)
V. A Fabulous Covenant (Verses 17-21)
VI. A Forgotten Commandment

Now there was long war between the house of Saul and the house of David: but David waxed stronger and stronger, and the house of Saul waxed weaker and weaker. And unto David were sons born in Hebron: and his first born was Amnon, of Ahinoam the Jezreelitess; and his second, Chileab, of Abigail the wife of Nabal the Carmelite; and the third, Absalom the son of Maachah the daughter of Talmai, king of Geshur; and the fourth, Adonijah the son of Haggith; and the fifth, Shephatiah the son of Abital; and the sixth, Ithream by Eglah David's wife. These were born to David in Hebron (vv. 1-5).

Expository Notes on David's Disobedience

A FORGOTTEN COMMANDMENT

David's inordinate desire for women was his "thorn in the flesh"; it ruined his happiness and spoiled his communion with the Lord. He either forgot or ignored a commandment of God, a sin that was an inexcusable error. Moses gave detailed instructions concerning the conduct of the kings of Israel, but David remained oblivious to that which was expected from him.

> **Thou shalt . . . set him king over thee, whom the LORD thy God shall choose: one from among thy brethren shalt thou set a king over thee: thou mayest not set a stranger over thee, which is not thy brother. But he shall not. . . . multiply wives to himself, that his heart turn not away: . . . And it shall be, when he sitteth upon the throne of his kingdom, that he shall write him a copy of this law in a book out of that which is before the priests the Levites: and he shall read therein all the days of his life: that he may learn to fear the LORD his God" (Deuteronomy 17:15-19).**

The psalmist in Psalm 119 wrote, "Thy word have I hid in my heart, that I might not sin against thee" (v. 11). This commandment was possibly in David's heart; but not in his head! He was a man with complex problems. Some days he was delightful, but at other times he was a terrible disappointment. He permitted carnal desires to have pre-eminence in his life. David was extremely foolish. His wives presented him with six sons in Hebron, but even that situation did not satisfy him. When Abner suggested that they make a covenant, David's prerequisite was that his first wife, Michal, should be returned to him. It was written later: "And David took him more concubines and wives out of Jerusalem, after he was come from Hebron, and there were yet sons and daughters born to David" (2 Sam. 5:13). The Bible supplies the names of seven additional children born to him in Jerusalem. Yet, in spite of the numerous marriages, the king desired more, and to obtain another woman, Bath-sheba, he murdered her husband (see 2 Samuel 11).

The attractive young shepherd boy from Bethlehem had become a sensuous man. In spite of the fact that God had issued strict instructions forbidding "the multiplicity of wives," David disregarded the commandment and did as he pleased. To repeat what has already been said, he ruled over Israel, but he never conquered himself. It might be beneficial to emphasize that healthy Christian living is based upon two facts—reading and remembering. "He shall write him a copy of this law in a book. . . . and he shall read therein all the days of his life that he may learn to fear the LORD his God . . . that his heart be not lifted up above his brethren . . . that he may prolong his days in his kingdom, he, and his children, in the midst of Israel" (Deuteronomy 17:18-20). A man who neglects reading the Word of God remains uninformed; a person who never remembers God's commandments can only be ignorant and displeasing in His sight. David was a sinful, lustful, arrogant man, and it remains a mystery why God continued to bless him.

A FOOLISH CHARGE

> **And it came to pass, while there was war between the house of Saul, and the house of David, that Abner made himself strong for the house of**

Saul. And Saul had a concubine, whose name was Rizpah, the daughter of Aiah: and Ish-bosheth said to Abner, Wherefore hast thou gone in unto my father's concubine? Then was Abner very wroth for the words of Ish-bosheth, and said, Am I a dog's head, which against Judah do shew kindness this day unto the house of Saul thy father, to his brethren, and to his friends, and have not delivered thee into the hand of David, that thou chargest me this day with a fault concerning this woman? So do God to Abner, and more also, except, as the LORD hath sworn to David, even so I do to him. To translate the kingdom from the house of Saul, and to set up the throne of David over Israel and over Judah, from Dan even to Beer-sheba. And he [Ish-bosheth] could not answer Abner a word again, because he feared him (vv. 6-11).

Expository Notes on Abner's Quarrel with His Master

Abner's altercation with his royal master did not belong primarily to the life of David, but it had a significant influence on his becoming king over Israel. If only for that reason, it must be mentioned in the study of David's life.

A Feeble Man . . . Unwanted

Nothing commendable was ever recorded concerning Ish-bosheth, a weak man who succeeded his father as king of Israel. It is significant that when Saul and Jonathan went to war against the Philistines, Ish-bosheth was left at home. It would be more interesting if authentic details of this incident were available. He was a weak, vacillating, jealous, suspicious man who was completely incompetent to rule over God's people. He seems to have been unreliable in times of danger and was a man upon whom his father could not depend. On the other hand, Saul may have decided to leave Ish-bosheth behind because he was incapable of conflict. It is not known if he was justified in accusing Abner of having had sexual relationships with his father's concubine. Abner's angry retaliation to the charge might suggest that Ish-bosheth was lying. On the other hand, Abner might have been angry because his indiscretion had been discovered! In view of a later incident with the same connotations, the charge was probably unjustified (see 2 Samuel 16:21).

A Foolish Man . . . Unwise

Abner was a warrior admired throughout Israel. Had he desired, he could have commanded the services of almost any woman in the nation. To accuse the old soldier of misconduct was an offense which could not be ignored. It was permissible for men to have concubines, but whether or not those women became the exclusive property of men is debatable. Saul was dead. Ish-bosheth might have inherited the throne, but that honor did not include his father's mistresses. If Rizpah had agreed to remain the exclusive property of Saul, that particular concubine could have severed her connection with the royal household. She possibly had no intention of doing this. Ish-bosheth was not only jealous, but he was also afraid that Abner was using the woman as a stepping-stone toward becoming king of Israel. In other words, he was taking Saul's place! There could be many ramifications to this ancient account, but when the king lost the services of that experienced warrior, he was without a friend.

A Fearful Man . . . Useless

"Then was Abner *very* wroth." His volcanic soul emitted loud and clear denunciations of his master. Yet, at the same time, he exposed his own iniquity. His statement was "*As the LORD hath sworn to David*, even so I do to him; to translate the kingdom from the house of Saul, and to set up the throne of David over Israel and over Judah, from Dan even to Beer-sheba" (vv. 9-10). If Abner were aware of God's covenant with David, he should not have opposed the fulfillment of that promise. He had been resisting the divine will, and perhaps his display of anger was a veiled indication that he desired to escape from captivating circumstances. He could have slain his accuser, but could not expect sympathy from David.

The king stared at the enraged, belligerent general and trembled. "He could not answer Abner a word again, because he feared him." He was a puppet, not a ruler, and was unworthy of kingship. Yet, it is remarkable that David refused to oppose Ish-bosheth's reign. He remembered his promise to Saul, who had said: "And now, behold, I know well that thou shalt surely be king, and that the kingdom of Israel shall be established in thine hand. Swear now therefore unto me by the LORD, *that thou wilt not cut off my seed after me, and that thou wilt not destroy my name out of my father's house.* And David sware unto Saul" (1 Samuel 24:20-22). Ish-bosheth never had a chance and did not deserve one!

A FRIENDLY COMMITMENT

And Abner sent messengers to David on his behalf, saying, Whose is the land? saying also, Make thy league with me, and, behold, my hand shall be with thee, to bring about all Israel unto thee. And he said, Well; I will make a league with thee (vv. 12-13).

Expository Notes on Abner's Offer to David

His Carefulness . . ."And Abner sent messengers"

Abner was apparently not certain of David's reactions. He could have gone personally to make a covenant with the king-elect. He had been a relentless enemy of the Bethlehemite. Did he have doubts about David's capacity to forgive and forget former indiscretions? Was he afraid his foe would order his execution? How would he be received by Joab, David's chief of staff? Evidently Abner was so impetuous that he never sought advice and made no attempt to discover what God's will might have been. He believed that "God helps those who help themselves." Perhaps he was afraid to consult the Lord because of his opposition to the man whom God had anointed. Abner had confusing problems and, in his need, decided to be careful. If David refused to cooperate, there would be time to flee or to organize resistance. As a crafty fox, Abner planned his strategy. If there were to be a display of vengeance, his men could die in his stead.

His Condition . . . "Make thy league with me"

His magnanimous offer of assistance was evidently conditional. If David decided to cooperate, then Abner would be his ally; he would betray his master and work hard to bring total disaster upon the house of Saul. If David were not interested in the proposal, Abner reserved the right to withdraw his offer. He never confessed guilt in that he had tried to slay David; apparently he felt no remorse. He was motivated only by his fierce anger and a determination to get even with his accuser. Had he knelt at David's feet to apologize for earlier conduct, he would have expressed sincerity in wishing to serve a new master. The old general was a self-centered soul, but his schemes failed; he never lived to see the fulfillment of his dream.

His Comparison . . . "Whose is the land?"

The question put to David is thought-provoking. Abner drew attention to the division of the nation and hinted that either of two claimants was eligible to become the king of Israel. His question was completely unnecessary; he knew what was taking place in the land. First Chronicles 12:18-22 says: "Then the spirit came upon Amasai, who was chief of the captains, and he said, Thine are we, David, and on thy side, thou son of Jesse: peace, peace be unto thee, and peace be to thine helpers; for thy God helpeth thee. Then David received them, and made them captains of the band. . . . And they helped David against the band of the rovers: for they were all mighty men of valor, and were captains in the host. For at that time, day by day there came to David to help him, until it was a great host, like the host of God." Abner was aware of current events. The ancient writer went on to write: "And these are the numbers of the bands that were ready armed to war, *and came to David to Hebron*, to turn the kingdom of Saul to him, according to the word of the Lord" (1 Chronicles 12:23). For details of the vast numbers of men who joined David's army, consult 1 Chronicles 12:24-40. No fewer than *3,822 soldiers* joined David's men, and many of them were experienced soldiers who brought "instruments of war." It is also said that David made for them a feast which lasted three days and for which he needed enormous supplies of provisions. The record says: "Moreover they that were nigh them even unto Issachar and Zebulun and Naphtali, brought bread on asses, and on camels, and on mules, and on oxen, and meat, meal, cakes of figs, and bunches of raisins, and wine, and oil, and oxen, and sheep abundantly: for there was joy in Israel" (see 1 Chronicles 12:40). This happened in Hebron *before* David became king over all the tribes of Israel. It may be safely assumed that Abner was well informed, and his motives for seeking an alliance with David could easily have been self-centered.

A FRIGHTENING CONDITION

And [David] said, Well; I will make a league with thee: but one thing I require of thee, that is, Thou shalt not see my face, except thou first bring Michal Saul's daughter, when thou comest to see my face. And David sent messengers to Ish-bosheth Saul's son, saying, Deliver me my wife Michal which I espoused to me for an hundred foreskins of the Philistines. And Ish-bosheth sent, and took her from her husband, even from Phaltiel the son of Laish. And her husband went with her along weeping behind her to Bahurim. Then said Abner unto him, Go, return. And he returned (vv. 13-16).

Expository Notes on David's Demand for His First Wife

It is to be expected that David would demand the return of his first wife, who had been given to another man. That dastardly deed had been unfair and illegal. Saul recognized no law but that of his own making. Michal became the spouse of a stranger, a fact which remained a thorn in David's flesh. It was anticipated that he would desire to reclaim that which was legally his own. Nevertheless, a study of Scripture creates doubts about his integrity.

Why Was He Insistent in His Plan?

David did not need another woman; he had too many already! There is no record of the intimate renewal of their wedding vows, and an unavoidable question arises as follows: "Did he intend to punish her and the man to whom she was given?" The fact that the husband sobbed bitterly when Michal was taken away had no effect either on Abner or David. Yet the king was adamant in his demands. Unless Michal was returned, his arrangement with Abner would be canceled, and Israel would be conquered by military power. David was evidently stubborn. He would have his way—or else!

Why Was He Insensitive to her Pain?

Michal had lived with Phaltiel for a number of years and had probably enjoyed a measure of happiness. The text to be considered in the next paragraph suggests that she knew the love of children and the safety of a home. Ruthlessly, without her consent, her safety was destroyed. The grief of her husband and any feelings of her own were ruthlessly ignored, and almost as a slave she was driven into a relationship she may not have desired. Had David loved her, he would have been more gentle. He could have asked what she desired and could have tempered his action with tenderness.

Was He Indecent in his Persecution?

Later, a problem arose concerning the Gibeonites, and when the offended tribesmen asked David for the heads of certain men, "the king took the two sons of Rizpah the daughter of Aiah, whom she bare unto Saul, Armoni and Mephibosheth; *and the five sons of Michal the daughter of Saul,* whom she brought up for Adriel the son of Barzillai the Meholathite" (see 2 Samuel 21:8). The translation is somewhat confusing because it is difficult to know whether Michal was the actual mother or the foster-mother of the five young men. Michal's sister may have been mentioned as the lady whose sons were deliberately sent to their execution. Either rendering is acceptable, but the final result remains unchanged. Michal, David's former wife, was related to the young men, and their death would have caused intense grief. Could David have found another way of satisfying the Gibeonites? Did he rejoice in seeing tears in Michal's eyes? Many other questions could be asked, but no answer could remove the stigma from David's name. An old proverb suggests "It is better to let sleeping dogs lie." When David remembered his wife Michal, he unfortunately awakened something in his conscience which accused him for the rest of his life.

A FABULOUS COVENANT

And Abner had communication with the elders of Israel, saying, Ye sought for David in times past to be king over you: Now then do it: for the LORD hath spoken of David, saying, By the hand of my servant David I will save my people Israel out of the hand of the Philistines, and out of the hand of all their enemies. . . . So Abner came to David to Hebron, and twenty men with him. And David made Abner and the men that were with him a feast. And Abner said unto David, I will arise and go, and will gather all Israel unto my lord the king, that they may make a league with thee, and that thou mayest reign over all that thine heart desireth. And David sent Abner away; and he went in peace (vv. 17-21).

Expository Notes on Abner's Last Meeting with David

A Strong Plea

"Ye sought for David in times past to be king over you: Now then, do it." As the commander in chief of the army, Abner had contacts with all the tribes of Israel. It was a simple matter to send communications to his friends throughout the nation. His influence was unequaled, so that when he spoke, everyone listened! Abner did not waste words; he said the time for action had arrived. Ish-bosheth was a friendless, useless figurehead. Israel needed a leader, and he, the general of the army, was recommending David, whom everyone knew had been appointed to rule the nation. The time to discuss possibilities was gone; the need for action was urgent! The tremendous response to Abner's appeal is recorded in 1 Chronicles 12:20-40.

A Special Presentation

It should be noticed that only the tribe of Benjamin received special attention. Abner sent messengers to the others, but felt it necessary to make a personal appearance before the Benjamites. Opposition might be forthcoming from those people as they had been attached to the house of Saul. The former king was a Benjamite (see 1 Samuel 9:1-2), and his tribesmen had been trusted helpers. They provided special bodyguards and many others to serve the royal house. The writer of Chronicles said: "And of the children of Benjamin, the kindred of Saul, three thousand: *for hitherto the greatest part of them had kept the ward of the house of Saul*" (1 Chronicles 12:29). Abner was convinced that there would be little if any opposition from the rest of Israel, but he had doubts about the reaction of Saul's kinsmen. He evidently convinced them so well that the Benjamites became David's enthusiastic supporters.

A Splendid Party

"And David made Abner and the men that were with him a feast." The commander was overjoyed; his happiness was boundless. He had been a ruthless enemy, yet, now he was riding on the crest of the wave of David's new popularity. He could reach the highest political position in the nation. He smiled as he envisaged future triumphs. He could trust his men, who were thrilled to be his associates. The nation would hear about this illustrious gathering. He would become David's commander in chief, and his future was bright with prospect and hope. If we may use modern words, he was "counting his chickens before they hatched!" Joab and his men were not at David's party because an old debt had to be paid. Abner did not realize his danger; he was skating on thin ice!

A Sacred Promise

"I will arise and go, and will gather all Israel unto my lord the king, that they may make a league with thee, and that thou mayest reign over all that thine heart desireth" (2 Sam. 3:21). Abner did his best to fulfill that promise. The records of history would have been dramatically changed if he had been wiser earlier in life. When it became obvious that David was the king-elect, Abner stubbornly arranged another coronation. Solomon said, "Whoso diggeth a pit shall fall therein" (Proverbs 26:27). Abner's earlier mistakes unfortunately had fatal consequences. Apart from the intervening grace of God, a man reaps what he sows, and Abner became a notable example of that indisputable fact.

Episode 20

THEME: *David's Grief Over Abner's Death*

SCRIPTURE: 2 Samuel 3:22-39

KEY VERSE:

And the king lamented over Abner, and said, Died Abner as a fool dieth? (v. 33).

OUTLINE:
    I. A Gallant Fighter Deceived (Verses 20-26)
    II. A Great Fool Destroyed (Verse 27)
    III. A Grand Funeral Described (Verses 31-39)

A GALLANT FIGHTER DECEIVED

Abner was either a trusting or a very forgetful man. He had slain the youngest brother of his rival and could have been reasonably sure that Joab would make an attempt to avenge that deed. That Abner tried to save the young man's life was of no consequence. The law said, "An eye for an eye; a tooth for a tooth; a life for a life." Had Abner been mentally alert, he would not have risked his life on an unreliable supposition. When he walked into David's city, was he trying to prove he was not afraid of Joab? Did he wish to ingratiate himself with David's soldiers? Was he so preoccupied with his project that he forgot everything else? Elated by the party which had been given in his honor, Abner was determined to persuade his army to join David's crusade. A wiser man would have moved more cautiously.

And when Joab was come out from David, he sent messengers after Abner, which brought him again from the well of Sirah: but David knew it not. And when Abner was returned to Hebron, Joab took him aside in the gate to speak with him quietly, and smote him there under the fifth rib, that he died, for the blood of Asahel his brother (vv. 26–27).

Expository Notes on Joab's Recall of Abner

The account of the death of Asahel reveals that he was an ambitious young man whose feet ran away with his brain! He might have lived to be an old man if he had been more sensible. In his imagination, he was already hearing the praises of fellow-officers if he either captured or killed the famous Abner. Ignoring the kindly, but desperate warning given, he determined to pursue the older soldier until the veteran either surrendered or died! Actually, it was not the fault of Abner that young Asahel was killed; the boy was slain by his own stupidity (read the complete account in 2 Samuel 2:17-23).

The older man appealed twice to the young pursuer, but his words only produced smiles on Asahel's face. Abner was a tired, aging man whom the young fellow believed would be compelled to stop running. He imagined the surprise on the faces of his comrades when Abner was led captive into David's city. He, Asahel, who was so young, would be hailed as one of Israel's greatest heroes. "And Abner said again to Asahel, Turn thee aside from following me: wherefore should I smite thee to the ground? how then should I hold up my face to Joab thy brother? Howbeit he refused to turn aside: wherefore Abner with the hinder end of the spear smote him under the fifth rib, that the spear came out behind him; and he fell down there, and died in the same place: and it came to pass, that as many as came to the place where Asahel fell down and died stood still" (2 Samuel 2:22-23).

The boy seemed to have Abner at his mercy, but a quick backward thrust of a spear brought pain and horror to Asahel's face. He staggered and fell; a victim to his own impetuosity. For a moment he writhed in agony and then lay motionless. It appeared that the saga had ended, but it had only just commenced! Joab, the eldest brother of the deceased, would never rest until Asahel's death was avenged.

When Joab heard of the visit recently concluded, his anger became intense, and losing all respect for the king, he stormed into the royal presence to express his rebellious thoughts. He accused David and affirmed that Abner was untrustworthy and that his reasons for promising help were false. David would have a snake in his bosom as long as he lived! David apparently made no response, and his indecision signed Abner's death warrant. The king could have commanded instant obedience, but no such edict was made with the result that the angry general went out to become an executioner.

"Abner, Abner." The elated general stopped and listened. Yes, someone was calling his name. He saw a man's waving arms and wondered what could have happened. Had an emergency arisen? He listened to the excuse given for the recall, and then, like an unsuspecting fly, walked into Joab's waiting web. As he approached the gate of Hebron he should have known something was wrong. His conscience surely warned him, but he was aware of watching people and, fearing gossiping tongues, permitted Joab to lead him aside. He was only a step from safety, but was too proud to take it (see the homily, Abner . . . Whose Pride Paralyzed His Feet!," p. 179).

A GREAT FOOL DESTROYED

And they buried Abner in Hebron: and the king lifted up his voice, and wept at the grave of Abner; and all the people wept. And the king lamented over Abner, and said, Died Abner as a fool dieth? (vv. 32-33).

Expository Notes on the Death of Abner

"And David sat between the two gates: and the watchman went up to the roof over the gate unto the wall, and lifted up his eyes, and looked, and behold a man running alone" (2 Samuel 18:24). This verse supplies an interesting explanation of the ease with which the assassination of Abner was accomplished. There were double doors, or gates, in the wall of Hebron, and built over them was a lookout place from which watchmen could view the approaches to the city. The gates were a double line of defense in case of an attack and also supplied a shadowy area in which Joab drew his sword without being seen. When Abner returned, he may or may not have been surprised to see Joab waiting for him. It may never be known whether Abner thought that he was there to offer a welcome or to avenge his brother's death. The act of taking Abner aside could have been necessary to discuss a secret project. A crafty man of Abner's caliber should have at least suspected treachery. Within the shadow-filled space between the gates, Abner was killed. When David heard the news he wept bitterly, "Died Abner as a fool dieth?" He was neither bound nor captured; he never struck a blow in his defense. He was tricked and caught off-guard. Had he given attention to details, he would not have been so easily deceived.

David's anger was intense; he not only wept bitterly, but also dismissed the murderer from his post of commander of the army. That position was never filled again until Joab seized an opportunity to reclaim what he had lost (see 1 Chronicles 11:6). To keep everything in perspective, it should be considered that Joab had reason to be angry with his master. David had made an agreement with an enemy, and Joab might have believed Abner was about to replace him. Maybe David planned to have two commanders by allowing Abner to lead his own people, while Joab would lead the tribe of Judah. That arrangement would have been disastrous and would have led to continued strife between the rival generals. It appeared that David had been secretive and underhanded in providing a poor reward for Joab, who had risked his life to protect his master. Viewed from any angle, David's covenant with Abner left much to be desired. Had he awaited Joab's return, the three men might have been able to discuss the details of uniting Israel, and the blood-feud could have ended. David's secretive

arrangements poured fuel on the fire of Joab's anger and led to the tragic
death of one of Israel's greatest heroes.

A GRAND FUNERAL DESCRIBED

**And the king lifted up his voice, and wept at the grave of Abner; and all
the people wept. . . . And when all the people came to cause David to eat
meat while it was yet day, David sware, saying, So do God to me, and
more also, if I taste bread, or ought else, till the sun be down. And all the
people took notice of it, and it pleased them: as whatsoever the king did
pleased all the people. . . . And the king said unto his servants, Know ye
not that there is a prince and a great man fallen this day in Israel? And I
am this day weak, though anointed king; and these men the sons of
Zeruiah be too hard for me: the Lord shall reward the doer of evil according to his wickedness (vv. 32-39).**

Expository Notes on David's Sorrow at the Grave of Abner

The custom of enjoying a meal after a funeral has long been practiced in
many countries. More often than not, this custom has met the need of
people who traveled long distances to be present at the graveside. Hebrew
writers, including Josephus, affirm that this custom was practiced in Israel
throughout the history of the nation. However, it became a time of disgusting revelry when the grief of a family was marred by the regrettable
conduct of thoughtless guests. People evidently gathered after Abner's
funeral to eat the customary meal, but when David refused to participate, it
became evident that his grief was genuine. He had lost a friend, and Israel
a valiant hero. This was one of his wisest acts. The people who had
followed Abner were incensed by the treachery of Joab as well as the
secretive manner in which David had conducted negotiations with their
commander. Had they believed that David was a collaborator in that execution, the unifying of Israel would have been impossible. When they heard
of David's grief, "all the people *and all Israel* understood that day it was
not of the king to slay Abner the son of Ner" (see v. 37).

The terrifying curse which David placed on the descendants of Joab was
uttered in great anger. The king envisaged the loss of the other tribes and
momentarily feared the future. His infuriating general could have ruined
the quest for the kingdom! Whether or not Joab was worried by the words
of David will never be known. If he had been forced to participate in the
national mourning, it may be safely assumed that his words and actions
were insincere. Joab never expressed regret for his deed or fear for his
future. It is interesting to note that in spite of the terrible curse placed upon
his family, he never deserted David. Time after time he exhibited outstanding bravery and proved himself to be the king's best friend. David
unfortunately carried animosity to his grave. Even on his deathbed he

remembered what had been done, and instructed Solomon to "let not his hoar head go down to the grave in peace" (see 1 Kings 2:5-6). It is to be regretted that the sweet psalmist of Israel ended his life on a discord!

HOMILIES FOR PREACHERS AND TEACHERS

Study No. 10

ABNER . . . Whose Pride Paralyzed His Feet! (2 Samuel 3:27)

If David had been invited to write the inscription for Abner's tombstone, his first attempt would probably have been something like the following: "In affectionate memory of a great man who threw away his life." And in that one tragic statement would lie one of the saddest of Old Testament stories. Poor Abner was a great fool.

How Serious his Danger

The battle was almost over, and with the bitterness of defeat beginning to overwhelm him, Abner ordered his men to retreat. The forces of David, led by General Joab, had gained the ascendancy, and not wishing to sacrifice his men needlessly, Abner mercifully ordered them to flee. It was a case of every man for himself. As Abner ran through the countryside, he realized that he was being followed by Asahel, Joab's youngest brother, and because he was unwilling to slay the young man, he cried a warning. "Then Abner looked behind him, and said, Art thou Asahel? And he answered, I am. And Abner said to him, Turn thee aside to thy right hand or to thy left, and lay thee hold on one of the young men. . . . But Asahel would not. . . . And Abner said again . . . Turn thee aside . . . wherefore should I smite thee to the ground? how then should I hold up my face to Joab thy brother? Howbeit [Asahel] refused" (2 Samuel 2:20-23). Abner killed the pursuing soldier, but from the moment Asahel fell, his slayer was in deadly danger. The law demanded "an eye for an eye" and "a tooth for a tooth," and Abner realized that once Joab heard of this unfortunate occurrence, he would vow vengeance. Abner's one hope was to flee to a city of refuge. God had made ample provision for such emergencies so that Abner had only to present himself before the priest to find safety.

How Stupid his Delay

His face was set in hard, grim lines. Wisdom urged obedience to the commands of God. Pride warned him that his flight would become known to all Israel. People might interpret this as an act of fear. Self-righteousness probably put up a praiseworthy argument. Why should he take the place of a guilty man? Had not his deed been committed in self-defense? Had he not warned the stupid boy whose impetuosity had overpowered his brain? No, Israel should never be given occasion to sneer. They should know that he was not afraid of Joab or any other man. He proudly followed his troops. Yet he was still in danger, for all his arguments would never alter the fact that Joab was entitled to his "eye for an eye." Abner was a silly man. He was a valiant warrior on every field of battle except the battlefield of his own soul.

How Sudden his Death

The scene has changed. Abner offered his services to David, and the offer was accepted. The magnificence of the royal reception overwhelmed the old general, and he returned to persuade his troops to support David's cause. Joab returned to camp and was told of Abner's visit. Hastily summoning young men, he sent them after his old enemy with commands to bring him back. Abner unwittingly returned to Hebron to find Joab waiting for him in the gateway. This was their first meeting since the death of Asahel, and as tension mounted, Abner permitted himself to be led aside. Because Hebron was one of the cities of refuge and since Abner was actually in the gateway, he was only a step from safety. Many onlookers were probably watching the proceedings, so that any insistence on Joab's coming into the city would betray nervous hesitance. Wisdom cried aloud for immediate action, but pride paralyzed his feet. His folly robbed him of life. "Joab . . . smote him there . . . for the blood of Asahel his brother."

How true-to-life is this ancient story. We are sinners also, but God has made provision for our safety. Within the city of Christ's eternal care, we can find security. Alas, many people who have heard and understood the gospel fail to respond. They know what they should do, but refuse to do it. Pride is a creeping paralysis. It begins in the heart and ends with the feet. (Homily reprinted from the author's book, *Bible Cameos*, pp. 37-38.)

Episode 21

THEME: *The Execution of Two Murderers*

SCRIPTURE: 2 Samuel 4:5-12

KEY VERSES:

> When one told me, saying, Behold Saul is dead, thinking to have brought good tidings, I took hold of him, and slew him in Ziklag, who thought that I would have given him a reward for his tidings. How much more, when wicked men have slain a righteous person in his own house upon his bed? shall I not therefore now require his blood of your hand, and take you away from the earth? (vv. 10-11).

OUTLINE:
  I.   A Profound Helplessness (Verse 1)
  II. A Passionate Hatred (Verses 6-8)
  III. A Pitiable Head (Verse 12)

A PROFOUND HELPLESSNESS

And when Saul's son heard that Abner was dead in Hebron, his hands were feeble, and all the Israelites were troubled (v. 1).

Expository Notes on a Lonely, Helpless Man

The situation in Israel was chaotic. Ish-bosheth was bewildered; the mainstay of his kingdom was dead, and to make matters worse, prior to his death, Abner was involved in treasonable negotiations. It was being said that the soldiers were restless and that they would have followed Abner's example. Israel's future was bleak. The princes of Israel suspected David of treachery, so that if he had attacked the ten tribes, he probably would have encountered resistance. When he refused to take advantage of the situation and did nothing, people began to ask questions. The news of his devastating sorrow intrigued the tribes. Then came the tidings that Joab, David's captain, had been relieved of his command, and with each passing day, the followers of Ish-bosheth increasingly approved of David's actions. Within the nation was widespread support for the king of Judah, and when

no outstanding leader arose to fight for Ish-bosheth, the situation deteriorated until "[the king's] hands were feeble and all the Israelites were
troubled." The forgotten, unpopular, and undesired ruler retired to his bedroom. He was within hours of his assassination.

Ish-bosheth could not seek comfort in the presence of a priest since his
father had murdered the representatives of the Lord. He had antagonized
his best friend and, accusing him of misconduct with a concubine, drove
the commander into the service of David. The king was alone and helpless.
Similarly, the Lord spoke of a very wealthy man who died a spiritual
pauper: "And in hell he lifted up his eyes, being in torments, and seeth
Abraham afar off, and Lazarus in his bosom. And he cried and said, Father
Abraham, have mercy on me, and send Lazarus, that he may dip the tip of
his finger in water, and cool my tongue; for I am tormented in this flame"
(see Luke 16:23-31). The man was alone in eternity; his only companions
were thoughts which reminded him of life's wasted opportunities.

The overconfident Simon Peter boasted that he would never betray his
Master, but he broke his promise and went out into the night to weep
bitterly. That was his loneliest moment. He had disappointed his Lord; the
disciples would be ashamed of him; he might as well be dead! The prodigal son, who exchanged his father's fellowship for a pigsty, felt very much
alone when he cried, "How many hired servants of my father's have bread
enough and to spare, and I perish with hunger?" (see Luke 15:17). Any
person who forgets God, ignores the claims of Christ, and lives in self-
indulgence feels lonely when the time comes to die. Only the people who
walk with God can say, "Yea, though I walk through the valley of the
shadow of death, I will fear no evil: for thou art with me; thy rod and thy
staff they comfort me" (Psalm 23:4).

A PASSIONATE HATRED

> **And Saul's son had two men that were captains of bands: the name of
> the one was Baanah, and the name of the other Rechab, the sons of
> Rimmon a Beerothite. . . . And they came thither into the midst of the
> house, as though they would have fetched wheat; and they smote [Ish-
> bosheth, the king] under the fifth rib. . . . they smote him, and slew him,
> and beheaded him, and took his head, and gat them away through the
> plain all night. And they brought the head of Ish-bosheth unto David to
> Hebron (vv. 2–8).**

Expository Notes on the Murder of Ish-bosheth

The account of the treachery of the two captains is intriguing, but it is
difficult to know what happened. The *Pulpit Commentary* says: "Not only
is the narrative confused, but the versions offer extraordinary varieties of

reading. The murder of Ish-bosheth is fully described in verse seven, and is there in its place, while it is out of place in verse six. And that the captains would themselves fetch wheat instead of having it carried from the granary by their men, and that they should go through the king's chamber to obtain it; are both improbable. The very act of going to get wheat at midday; when everybody was having a siesta, would itself be suspicious. . . . The Vulgate translation and LXX. lay the blame on the woman who kept the door; the narrative of the latter being as follows: 'They entered into the house of Ish-bosheth in the heat of the day and he was asleep in his midday chamber. And behold, the woman who kept the door of the house had been winnowing wheat, and she slumbered and slept. And the brothers Rechab and Baanah entered the house without being noticed and Ish-bosheth was asleep on his bed in his chamber, and they smote him'" (*The Pulpit Commentary*, vol. 4, p. 100).

The question might be asked why these captains committed a crime against the house of Saul. Their city, Beeroth, was one of four allocated to the tribe of Benjamin. They were originally Canaanite strongholds from which people came to deceive Joshua. It was only after he promised to spare them, that he discovered that their story was untrue and that in actual fact, they were people he was supposed to destroy (see Joshua 9:11-17). Saul violated Joshua's agreement and brutally attacked them (see 2 Samuel 21:1). Their homes were destroyed and their families slaughtered. The men who murdered Saul's son were perhaps avenging the death of their kinsfolk. They hated the house of Saul and believed that they would be rewarded for removing David's rival.

Their deed was a criminal offense, because if they had been more informed, they would not have expected David to reward their infamous act. He had promised to preserve the royal family. Saul had said: "And now, behold, I know well that thou shalt surely be king, and that the kingdom of Israel shall be established in thine hand. Swear now therefore unto me by the LORD, that thou wilt not cut off my seed after me, and that thou wilt not destroy my name out of my father's house. And David sware unto Saul" (see 1 Samuel 24:20-22). The assassins believed David would approve their act, but when they deposited the blood-stained head of the slain monarch, David frowned. An innocent man had been brutally murdered by two ambitious scoundrels. Israel did not need men of their caliber.

A PITIABLE HEAD

And David commanded his young men, and they slew them, and cut off their hands and their feet, and hanged them up over the pool in Hebron. But they took the head of Ish-bosheth, and buried it in the sepulcher of Abner in Hebron (v. 12).

Expository Notes on the Sight at Hebron's Pool

There are still places in the world where the hands of thieves are severed from their bodies as a warning to other people who may be tempted to commit similar crimes. Perhaps this custom has survived from biblical times. The severed hands and feet were displayed at the pool in Hebron so that all who drew water were warned of the inevitable consequences of evil. When the sepulcher of Abner was reopened to permit the burial of the king's head, the people surely recognized the sharp contrast between the time when a crown rested on that head and the present moment when the relic of a grizzly murder was gently laid to rest. It should be remembered that this happened when God was trying to teach the value of walking in the paths of righteousness. In these modern times, many would be horrified by such brutality, but the fact remains that if the laws of God were not made known to the nations, the world would still be a barbaric wilderness. Solomon wrote, "Good understanding giveth favor: but the way of transgressors is hard" (Proverbs 13:15). That statement represents the basic facts of life, and any person who seeks to change them is not a benefactor of society. Ish-bosheth apparently was never worthy of praise, so that it would have been difficult to write anything complimentary on his tombstone. "[Ish-bosheth] departed without being desired" (2 Chron. 21:20).

Episode 22

THEME: *David Becomes the King of Israel*

SCRIPTURE: 2 Samuel 5:1-12

KEY VERSE:

> And David went on, and grew great, and the LORD God of hosts was with him (v. 10).

OUTLINE:
      I.   A Belated Coronation (Verses 1-3)
     II.   A Big Conquest (Verses 4-8)
   III.   A Blessed Continuance (Verses 10-12)

A BELATED CORONATION

Then came all the tribes of Israel to David unto Hebron, and spake, saying, Behold, we are thy bone and thy flesh. Also in time past, when Saul was king over us, thou wast he that leddest out and broughtest in Israel: and the LORD said to thee, Thou shalt feed my people Israel, and thou shalt be a captain over Israel. So all the elders of Israel came to the king to Hebron; and king David made a league with them in Hebron before the LORD; and they anointed David king over Israel (vv. 1-3).

Expository Notes on David's New Coronation

The Bible relates how the coronations of David and Ish-bosheth took place at approximately the same time (see 2 Samuel 2:4 and 2 Samuel 2:8-9). It also says that Ish-bosheth reigned for two years and David for seven and one-half years. David remained the king of Judah for five and one-half years *after* the death of Ish-bosheth. Nothing has been recorded of this period; it is merely a matter of speculation what happened before the entire nation accepted David. It is evident that Judah prospered amazingly under the rule of their king, but the other tribes were divided by suspicion, intrigue, and infamy. The people who had been intensely loyal to Abner were angry because their leader had been murdered in David's camp. Everyone knew that Abner was negotiating a treaty between the two sections of the army, but many thought David was underhanded in his dealings. Some men accused him of planning the assassination of their general. Deep wounds do not heal overnight! Most of the people probably expected an attack in which David would try to force the ten tribes into subjection. When he remained inactive in Hebron and refused resolutely to take advantage of the adverse situation in Israel, many people changed their opinion. The fact that Joab had been punished for his deed and that David's grief had been intense increased their desire to share in Judah's prosperity. They had no military leader, and it could only be a matter of time before the Philistine armies would invade their country. The house of Saul had almost ceased to exist, their economy was in disarray, they needed a leader, and it was evident that David was their only prospect.

It was significant that *all* the elders of Israel came to meet David in Hebron; each tribe sent its elected representative. They had been prepared by the intercession of their former general. "And Abner had communication with the elders of Israel, saying, Ye sought for David in times past to be king over you: Now then do it" (see 2 Samuel 3:17-18). The verdict was unanimous as the entire nation became enthusiastic. As a result, the record states that nearly 349,000 soldiers came to Hebron to share and enjoy the national celebration. The most distant tribes sent the largest contingents; the nearest ones provided most of the food for the coronation (see 1 Chronicles 12:22-40). Everybody appreciated the glamorous and exciting occasion, and when the days of feasting expired, the nation was united. The captain of six hundred vagabonds and outlaws had been elevated to the throne of Israel. He who had been the rejected of men became the king of kings. Coming events were casting their shadows in advance!

A BIG CONQUEST

> **David was thirty years old when he began to reign, and he reigned forty years. . . . And the king and his men went to Jerusalem unto the Jebusites, the inhabitants of the land: which spake unto David, saying, Except thou take away the blind and the lame, thou shalt not come in hither: thinking, David cannot come in hither. . . . And David said on that day, Whosoever getteth up to the gutter, and smiteth the Jebusites, and the lame and the blind, that are hated of David's soul, he shall be chief and captain (vv. 4–8).**

Expository Notes on the Capture of Jerusalem

It is difficult for modern visitors to Israel to understand the type of Jerusalem that existed in the lifetime of David. Today there are roads along which taxis and tourist buses run; every part of the city is accessible in one way or another, and it is hard to believe that long ago this place was an impregnable fortress. There were no highways and no easy access; the city of the Jebusites stood behind awesome ravines, towering cliffs, and formidable defenses. David had often looked at the area and, perhaps during his wanderings in the wilderness, admired what he hoped would become his capital city. Later, when he wrote Psalm 48:2, he described Jerusalem as follows: "Beautiful for situation, the joy of the whole earth, is mount Zion, on the sides of the north, the city of the great King."

When David became king, his need for a center of administration became evident. He could not remain in Hebron, for that location was too far to the south. He would have encountered political opposition had he tried to merge the northern tribes with the tribe of Judah, and it was natural that David should turn his thoughts to the place he had often admired. The city had been conquered by Joshua (see Joshua 11:1-8 and Judges 1:8), but had been repossessed by its inhabitants who remained independent. "Jerusalem is situated on the edge of the precipitous wall which forms the western boundary of the valley of the Jordan; it occupies a promontory, on three sides of which are ravines so abrupt and steep that, were it not for their vast depth, they might seem to have been the work of men. On the north side only is it open to attack, but even there, when the besieger has obtained an entrance, he finds the city divided by another ravine" (*The Pulpit Commentary*, vol. 4, p. 114).

It must be remembered that since David advanced on the Jebusite city immediately after his coronation, he had enormous numbers of troops at his disposal. His army numbered almost 350,000 men, who had all the weapons of war available at that time. If David demanded the surrender of the citadel, his request was met with scorn. The words, "Except thou take away the blind and the lame, thou shalt not come in hither; thinking David cannot come in hither," has aroused the interest of theologians in all ages. Several interpretations have been given, but the most acceptable suggests that the inhabitants believed their city was impregnable and thus taunted David by saying, "The lame and blind can resist any attack, and David will be destroyed when the regular defenders of the city enter the conflict." David seemed to be attempting the impossible. His army was confronted by towering cliffs and steep ravines without bridges, and at all times his soldiers would be exposed to the archers, whose aim could be deadly.

And David said, "Whosoever smiteth the Jebusites first shall be chief and captain. So Joab the son of Zeruiah went first up, and was chief: and David dwelt in the castle; therefore they called it the city of David" (see 1 Chronicles 11:6-7).

David's statement "whosoever getteth up to the gutter" has been interpreted in several ways. It has been suggested that there existed a track up the steep precipice—a track like a gully. The most acceptable interpretation was made by Josephus who believed there was an underground tunnel or drain through the cliff. *The Pulpit Commentary,* quoting from Sir C. Warren's book, *Recovery of Jerusalem* (page 240) states: "At the northern end of the pool of Siloam he found an arched passage, gradually narrowing down from a considerable height till finally there was a passage of only fourteen inches, and as there was a depth of ten inches of water, there was left but four inches of space for breathing. Through this, his men struggled, and, at the end of four hours labor, reached the light of day at the spring called the Virgin's Fount. Beginning there on a subsequent day, they went along a passage sixty-seven feet in length, and came to a perpendicular shaft leading up through the solid stone of the hill, and having scaled this, they next came upon a sloping passage which finally conducted them to a spot on the hill of Ophel within the fortifications. Through this or some such tunnel, Joab and a few men may have worked their way, and so have effected an entrance into the city, which otherwise was impregnable. . . . and David's words mean: 'Whoever will undertake this dangerous enterprise, let him try this underground passage, and when he has entered the fortifications by its means, let him smite the lame and the blind that are hated of David's soul'" (R. Payne Smith. *The Pulpit Commentary*, vol. 4, p. 115). The same author continues to write: "It must be noticed that the K'tib, or the written text has '*who hate David's soul*,' and since this is what the Jewish Massorites found in the manuscripts, it has more authority than their correction." Evidently, Joab successfully entered the city through that underground passage and, having killed the sentries, proceeded to admit the waiting men. David decided to make Millo his official residence, which became known as "David's Castle."

> **And David dwelt in the castle; therefore they called it the city of David. And he built the city round about, even from Millo round about: and Joab repaired the rest of the city (1 Chronicles 11:7-8).**

It became evident to David that to accommodate his mighty men, it was necessary to erect additional buildings. Joab—now reinstated as the Commander in Chief—superintended the work and doubtless pleased his master. Thus, a measure of stability came to Israel, and with their armies based in such a stronghold, their enemies could only be disturbed by the presence of such a formidable neighbor.

A BLESSED CONTINUANCE

> **And David went on, and grew great, and the Lord God of hosts was with him. And Hiram king of Tyre sent messengers to David, and cedar trees, and carpenters, and masons: and they built David an house. And David perceived that the Lord had established him king over Israel, and that he had exalted his kingdom for his people Israel's sake (vv. 10-12).**

Expository Notes on the Establishing of David's Kingdom

This scripture may be summarized under three headings. David had (1) *a new home*; (2) *a new hope*; and (3) *a new happiness*. Finally, after years of trouble, when the ordinary privileges of life were denied, things began to improve for the new king.

A New Home

David had often coveted that imposing city of the Jebusites, for during his wilderness wanderings, the fortress in the hills seemed a very desirable place. It was different from the caves in which he was compelled to hide. Did he ever dream of happier days when he too would have that castle in the mountain? The conquest of the Jebusite city made it possible to forget the past, and with his mighty men encamped around him, the king believed that his problems had been solved. It has been said that Millo was the chief building, meeting house, or city hall of the former inhabitants. The new buildings were erected around that central location and extended outward toward the perimeter. When Hiram, king of Tyre, sent materials and workmen to assist in the construction of the new city, David believed that a new life was beginning. He and his kingdom had received official recognition from another potentate, an event which could be the commencement of an international relationship which would be of incalculable worth.

A New Hope

When Hiram supplied cedar wood and expert carpenters, he helped to overcome one of David's greatest difficulties. First Samuel 13:19-20 says, "Now there was no smith found throughout all the land of Israel: for the Philistines said, Lest the Hebrews make them swords and spears: But all the Israelites went down to the Philistines, to sharpen every man his share, and his coulter, and his axe and his mattock." Conditions were different when Israel left Egypt. At that time, the Hebrews were skilled and comparatively wealthy. The Bible quotes Moses as mentioning men "to devise curious works, to work in gold, and in silver, and in brass, and in the cutting of stones, to set them, and in carving of wood, to make any manner of cunning work" (see Exodus 35:30-33). The people were evidently skilled in many trades. The powerful Philistines had nevertheless so impoverished the Jewish people that at the time of David's coronation, the only tools possessed by the Israelites were those captured from adjacent nations. David had few if any skilled workmen, and the generosity of Hiram seemed as a gift from heaven. David was exceedingly pleased, for a strong friend would be invaluable if Israel ever needed assistance. Maybe wars would end, and David's kingdom would enjoy perpetual peace.

A New Happiness

"And David perceived that the LORD had established him king over Israel, and that he had exalted his kingdom *for his people Israel's sake.*" It is interesting to read that David perceived something! Had he been egotistical, he might have believed himself to be a very special person who was absolutely necessary for the establishing of God's kingdom. Maybe, he looked within himself and found very little of which to be proud; perhaps when he considered his mistakes, he remembered how God had been very displeased. Whether or not this observation is true is a matter of conjecture; it is certain, however, that the king realized Jehovah was determined to bless and honor His people. When people believe that they are indispensable to God, they are unfit for service. Blessed is the man who considers himself to be nothing. There was very little in David's life of which to boast; unfortunately, he was a far better lad than he was a man. When he went to meet Goliath he was an innocent boy with a pure mind and a complete trust in God; when as a man, he fought against a giant called Lust, he surrendered and laid his heart at the feet of concubines. Nevertheless, he realized that God was being faithful to promises made to Israel and that he, too, was a recipient of God's love. The next study reveals how David prayed about his problems, but played with his pleasures. He was a temperamental monarch. He could soar into heights of ecstasy, but then plunge into depths of lust to seek satisfaction for the baser instincts of his soul.

Episode 23

THEME: *David's Vices and Victories*

SCRIPTURE: 2 Samuel 5:13-25

KEY VERSE:

> And David inquired of the LORD, saying, Shall I go up to the Philistines? wilt thou deliver them into mine hand? And the LORD said unto David, Go up: for I will doubtless deliver the Philistines into thine hand (v. 19).

OUTLINE:
    I. David's Increasing Family (Verses 13-16)
    II. David's Infuriating Foes (Verses 17-25)
    III. David's Inspiring Fellowship (Verses 19 and 23)

DAVID'S INCREASING FAMILY

And David took him more concubines and wives out of Jerusalem, after he was come from Hebron: and there were yet sons and daughters born to David. And these be the names of those that were born unto him in Jerusalem; Shammua, and Shobab, and Nathan and Solomon, Ibhar also, and Elishua, and Nepheg, and Japhia, and Elishama, and Eliada, and Eliphalet (vv. 13-16).

Expository Notes on David's Continued Forgetfulness

The historian who wrote the parallel passage to these verses (1 Chronicles 2:5-9) mentioned David's additional children and others who remain nameless because they were the offspring of concubines. The king was unfortunately controlled by an intense yearning for sexual relationships, and although many suggestions have been made to justify his conduct, they have not been convincing. Nothing can change the fact that David disobeyed and dishonored his Lord; his disgraceful example was the greatest factor in the ruination of his son. The old saying "like father, like son" is exemplified in the foolishness and fall of Solomon, who at one time was said to be the wisest man who ever lived.

The Lord's Commandment

It becomes necessary, once again, to remember the instructions given by God.

> **When thou art come unto the land which the LORD thy God giveth thee. . . . Thou shalt . . . set him king over thee, whom the LORD thy God shall choose. . . . But he shall not. . . . multiply wives to himself, that his heart turn not away. . . . And it shall be, when he sitteth on the throne of his kingdom, that he shall write him a copy of this law in a book . . . and he shall read therein all the days of his life: that he may learn to fear the LORD his God" (Deuteronomy 17:14-19).**

That David violated the commandment of God cannot be denied. It remains an inscrutable mystery how God could tolerate such disobedience and continue to respond to David's requests for help. It is wise to remember that the Lord emphasized that He would honor His promises for "his people Israel's sake" (v. 12). God never abandons a righteous cause when one of its leaders becomes unreliable. When Moses forfeited the right to enter Canaan, Joshua was commissioned to lead Israel into the Promised Land. The sovereignty of God has never been challenged by the indiscretions of privileged people.

The Licentious Conduct

It is difficult to explain David's desire for increasing numbers of sexual partners. Was he trying to emulate the example of other kings? Had he become convinced that the importance of his family would be assessed by the number of his children? Did he disregard the feelings of his first wife when she was forgotten and replaced by other women? Even today sheikhs in Middle Eastern countries favor the multiplicity of wives, and Moslem laws permit men to possess several spouses. When the legal number has been obtained, they may enlarge their harems with unlimited numbers of concubines. African tribes also permit men to have as many wives as they can afford: the first wife favors the arrangement, for she becomes queen over the other women and is intensely proud of that honor. It is difficult to know whether such ideas influenced David's conduct. Nevertheless, it cannot be denied that he disobeyed, forgot, or ignored God's edict and permitted evil to dominate his thoughts. The lust of his eyes kindled unholy fires within his soul and aroused passionate desires. David believed that he had the authority to possess any woman within his kingdom, and when a husband presented problems, he was silenced and removed. The king decided all matters related to his sexual behavior, and opposition from God or man was inconsequential.

The Lost Cause

David was on a collision-course with disaster, and Solomon unfortunately emulated his father's example. The only commendable thing about David was his unfaltering faith in the one true God of Israel; he never worshiped idols. His son, who succeeded him on the throne of Israel, permitted innumerable wives to destroy his faith. Although he was given extraordinary wisdom, Solomon sacrificed that treasure on the altars of lust and idolatry. When he continually sought to satisfy the baser desires of his flesh, he lost the blessing of the Almighty and became a broken, disgraceful replica of the man who elevated Israel to heights of magnificence. If David had been a wiser father, Solomon might have been a more dedicated son.

And [Solomon] had seven hundred wives, princesses, and three hundred concubines: and his wives turned away his heart. For it came to pass, when Solomon was old, that his wives turned away his heart after other gods: and his heart was not perfect with the LORD his God, as was the heart of David his father. For Solomon went after Ashtoreth the goddess of the Zidonians, and after Milcom the abomination of the Ammonites. And Solomon did evil in the sight of the LORD, and went not fully after the LORD, as did David his father (1 Kings 11:3-6).

It was a major disaster when Solomon's son allowed Israel to degenerate, and ruthless enemies ultimately destroyed the nation. It was a long and sad journey from the glorious reign of David to the frightening days when Israel became slaves in Babylon. Another psalmist wrote: "By the rivers of Babylon, there we sat down, yea, we wept, when we remembered Zion. We hanged our harps upon the willows in the midst thereof. For there they that carried us away captive required of us a song; and they that wasted us required of us mirth, saying, Sing us one of the songs of Zion. How shall we sing the LORD's song in a strange land?" (Psalm 137:1-4).

Slavery in Babylon never supplied inspiration for the songs of the blessed, and all backsliders know that this fact is true.

DAVID'S INFURIATING FOES

But when the Philistines heard that they had anointed David king over Israel, all the Philistines came up to seek David; and David heard of it, and went down to the hold. . . . And David came to Baal-perazim, and David smote them there (vv. 17-20).

Expository Notes on David's Continuing Trouble With the Philistines

God's People Should Always Be Careful

The Bible teaches that periods of success are more dangerous than times of adversity. This truth is expressed in a strange text. "But Jeshurun waxed fat, and kicked . . . then he forsook God which made him, and lightly esteemed the Rock of his salvation" (Deuteronomy 32:15). When judges ruled Israel, the people prayed only when they were in trouble. They were apparently unable to cope with prosperity; success made them forget and forsake the ways of the Lord. When men achieve a significant victory, they need to exercise care, for success is often a time when temptation is near. David had been crowned as the king of Israel—it was his ultimate triumph—his dreams had come true. Then the Philistines decided to challenge the man they had formerly protected. When triumph makes people forget God, the victory becomes defeat. Christians are advised to wear the "whole armor of God" (see Ephesians 6:11-12) and be ready at all times to resist the devil.

God's People Should Always Be Consistent

It is significant that on two occasions "David inquired of the LORD" (vv. 19 and 23). He was not always as wise! The episodes of his life already considered in this book, reveal that each time he failed to seek the guidance of Jehovah, he made mistakes and his happiness was ruined. Self-confidence can be a great ally, but when it undermines dependence upon God, it destroys the soul. A person who believes he can do everything is often very weak! When Jesus said, "Men ought always to pray", He knew what He was talking about! David was wise when he refused to assume too much. His first prayer indicated a certain line of action; his second petition brought a different answer and redirected his thinking. God's methods are varied; He cannot be taken for granted! Sometimes He decides to work in a certain way, but that is not a guarantee that He will always move in an identical fashion. The knowledge that conditions can change in a moment should keep Christians in constant awareness. They should be able to say, "Moment by moment, I'm kept in His love; moment by moment, I've life from above."

God's People Should Always Be Confident

Christians should realize that the Lord is more anxious to help His people than they are to ask for assistance. When David sought the aid of the priest, he believed that his prayers would be answered. God has many ways by which to communicate His will, but although His replies may be delayed, He is never too late in supplying the needs of His children. It stimulates faith to remember that He sees the end from the beginning and knows the enemies intentions before those plans are formulated. Joshua was the undisputed leader of Israel's army only until a new Helper arrived. "And the captain of the LORD's host said unto Joshua, Loose thy shoe from off thy foot; for the place whereon thou standest is holy. And Joshua did so" (see Joshua 5:13-15). Thereafter, Joshua, with one exception, looked to the Lord for daily guidance; he nevertheless became over-confident at Ai and suffered a major defeat. God's people should never be too confident in their own ability. They should be confident in God. When David retained that quality, he remained invincible; when he forgot, his battles were lost before they commenced.

God's People Should Always Be Courageous

"The Philistines also came and spread themselves in the valley of Rephaim." David defeated the "spread-out" enemy, but they retired, regrouped, and launched a second offensive. It is significant that after their initial defeat, they abandoned their idols (see verse 21). The Philistines apparently carried images into the conflict hoping that the idols would help them win the battle. Their faith was shattered when Israel triumphed and when the man-made deities were suddenly cast away. Many of the Philistines unfortunately died before they learned that invaluable lesson. Other survivors failed to learn from their experience and lost far more than their lives. There is reason to believe that David's men went into battle completely confident that what God had commenced He would complete. Their bravery was never questioned. They triumphed gloriously, but probably their greatest victory came when they burned the images of the Philistines. Had they been foolish, they might have kept those idols as souvenirs of a great victory, and those objects could later have become snares. Idols should always be destroyed!

DAVID'S INSPIRING FELLOWSHIP

And David inquired of the Lord, saying, Shall I go up to the Philistines? (v. 19). And when David inquired of the Lord (v. 23).

Expository Notes on David's Fellowship with God

David's fervent belief in the power of prayer indicates three vital facts:

God Still Lives . . . He is Able

This truth is best understood when contrasted with the discarded idols of the Philistines. The heathens carried their gods into battle hoping that their assistance would help to win the war. Many prayers were doubtless offered, but the idols were unfortunately unable to respond. Their uselessness became apparent. David's prayer to Jehovah indicated his conviction that God was alive and able to answer prayer; He holds the world in His hand.

God Still Looks . . . He Is Aware of our Need

Images are inanimate objects without intelligence which can neither see nor help their worshipers. Jehovah is not only alive; He is "a very present help in time of trouble." God is not a remote being existing somewhere in space; He is aware of all that happens in the lives of His people. The psalmist wrote, "I will lift up mine eyes unto the hills, from whence cometh my help. My help cometh from the LORD, which made heaven and earth. He will not suffer thy foot to be moved: he that keepeth thee will not slumber. Behold, he that keepeth Israel shall neither slumber nor sleep" (see Psalm 121:1-4). Job rejoiced in the same truth for he said, "But he knoweth the way that I take: when he hath tried me, I shall come forth as gold" (Job 23:10).

God Still Loves . . . He is Approachable

To believe in the existence of a monarch is one thing, but to have access into his presence at all times is something else. David knew that it was almost impossible for people to enter into his own palace; yet, God's people had been encouraged to draw near to God's throne. The king was aware of the privilege of having a priest with an ephod and knew that God provided a high priest to intercede on behalf of the nation. Yet, superseding all was the knowledge that it was possible to pray to a prayer-answering God. In Psalm 34:18, David wrote, "The LORD is *nigh* unto them that are of a broken heart; and saveth such as be of a contrite spirit." Isaiah rejoiced in the same experience, for he wrote: "For thus saith the high and lofty One that inhabiteth eternity, whose name is Holy; I dwell in the high and holy place, and with him also that is of a contrite and humble spirit, to revive the spirit of the humble, and to revive the heart of the contrite ones" (Isaiah 57:15). God is gloriously accessible! The writer to the Hebrews was able to write: "Having therefore, brethren, boldness to enter into the holiest by the blood of Jesus, by a new and living way, which he hath consecrated for us, through the veil, that is to say, his flesh; and having an high priest over the house of God; *let us draw near with a true heart in full assurance of faith*" (Hebrews 10:19-22). IT PAYS TO PRAY!

Episode 24

THEME: *Bringing Back the Ark of God*

SCRIPTURE: 2 Samuel 6

KEY VERSES:

> So David would not remove the ark of the LORD unto him into the city of David: but David carried it aside into the house of Obed-edom the Gittite. And the ark of the LORD continued in the house of Obed-edom the Gittite three months: and the LORD blessed Obed-edom and all his household (vv. 10-11).

OUTLINE:

AN UNSUCCESSFUL ATTEMPT

And David arose, and went with all the people . . . to bring up from thence the ark of God. . . . And they set the ark of God upon a new cart, and brought it out of the house of Abinadab that was in Gibeah: and Uzzah and Ahio, the sons of Abinadab, drave the new cart. . . . And when they came to Nachon's threshingfloor, Uzzah put forth his hand to the ark of God, and took hold of it; for the oxen shook it. And the anger of the LORD was kindled against Uzzah; and God smote him there for his error [rashness] and there he died by the ark of God. And David was displeased, because the LORD had made a breach upon Uzzah. . . . And David was afraid of the LORD, that day, and said, How shall the ark of the LORD come to me? (vv. 2-9)

Expository Notes on David's Costly Forgetfulness

When David realized that the ark was missing from Jerusalem, he became restless. He had been concerned with many things, but the ark of God had been forgotten. He determined to bring it back, but unfortunately repeated an earlier mistake—he never consulted God. Thus, David's stupidity led to unprecedented tragedy. When confronted by Philistine armies, "[he] inquired of the Lord" what he should do. Yet, when he embarked upon this mission, he was self-reliant. He made a terrible mistake.

The ark had been captured by the Philistines and placed in the temple of Dagon. "And when they arose early on the morrow morning, behold, Dagon was fallen upon his face to the ground before the ark of the Lord; and the head of Dagon, and both the palms of his hands were cut off upon the threshold; only the stump of Dagon was left to him" (1 Sam. 5:4). That humiliating discovery dismayed everybody, and when it was followed by pestilences, the men of Ashdod said: "The ark of the God of Israel shall not abide with us" (see 1 Samuel 5:7). The lords of the Philistines thereupon placed it upon a new cart and sent it back to Israel. After a brief but tragic interlude at Beth-shemesh (see 1 Samuel 6:12-20), the ark was ultimately taken to Kirjath-jearim, where it remained for twenty years in the home of Abinadab (see 1 Samuel 7:1-2). David was aware of these details and joined the people as "all the house of Israel lamented after the Lord" (see 1 Samuel 7:2).

A Delightful Obsession . . . To Bring Back the Ark

David's desire was filled with merit; his motives were pure. That the sacred ark had been allowed to remain in the home of Abinadab, forgotten and abandoned, was unpardonable. Jerusalem was not only the city of David, but it was also God's city, and no temple would be complete without the symbol of the divine Presence. Its return was the first item of importance on the king's calendar of special events. It is significant that "Again David gathered together all the chosen men of Israel, thirty thousand; and David arose, and went with all the people that were with him from Baale of Judah, to bring up from thence the ark of God, whose name is called by the name of the Lord of hosts that dwelleth between the cherubims" (vv. 1-2). David intended to make this the most illustrious event in the history of the nation. The best people in the country would celebrate the homecoming since the music would be heavenly; the worship, sincere; the praise, overwhelming.

A Distressing Omission . . . David Did Not Seek God's Guidance

It is extremely difficult to understand David's stupidity. Among his followers was a priest with the ephod, and the king knew from personal experience that it was wise to pray. God had given explicit instructions regarding the moving of the ark, but it was problematical as to whether or not David was aware of God's commandments. If he knew the instructions, he either forgot or ignored them. Was he so exalted in his pride or overwhelmed by his enthusiasm that he thought it unnecessary to seek guidance from anyone? He apparently never considered the danger of doing the right thing in the wrong way!

And when the camp setteth forward, Aaron shall come, and his sons, and they shall take down the covering vail, and cover the ark of testimony with it: and shall put thereon the covering of badgers' skins, and shall spread over it a cloth wholly of blue, and shall put in the staves thereof.... But the sons of Kohath ... the service of the sanctuary belonging unto them was that they should bear upon their shoulders (Numbers 4:5-6, 15; 7:9).

"And they set the ark of God upon a new cart." The Philistines had done a similar thing when they returned the ark to the Hebrews (see 1 Samuel 6:7). David knew about their action and probably considered that if the heathen could honor the ark by supplying such transportation, he could do likewise. He should have been more enthusiastic about consulting the Lord. The heathens had little if any knowledge of Jehovah and therefore could hardly be punished for their actions. God's people had been explicitly told how to move the sacred symbol, and David's actions were contrary to the will of the Almighty. The king made his own plans and that was his undoing! It is better to please God than to do something for Him. I heard of a prostitute who tithed her earnings by giving to the church. Nevertheless, her sacrifice did not sanctify the donation nor her occupation. "And Samuel said, Hath the LORD as great delight in burnt offerings and sacrifices, as in obeying the voice of the LORD? Behold, *to obey is better than sacrifice*, and to hearken better than the fat of rams" (1 Samuel 15:22).

A Divine Objection . . . "The anger of the LORD was kindled"

The musicians filled the air with melody; the people were happy; David was elated. He was bringing home the ark of God! The procession was already moving. "And when they came to Nachon's threshingfloor, Uzzah put forth his hand to the ark of God, and took hold of it; for the oxen shook it. And the anger of the LORD was kindled against Uzzah; and God smote him there for his error; and there he died by the ark of God" (vv. 6-7). Within moments David's delight was shattered as the blue skies became somber, the music ceased, and the onlookers were sullen. God had killed a man who did something good! "And David was displeased" (v. 8)

Why did this happen? Uzzah, the son of Abinadab, was not responsible for David's mistake. Why should he be killed? Would it not have been more justifiable if David had been punished? At first glance, the casual reader might fail to appreciate the implications of this tragedy. God is neither harsh nor merciless. He who sees a sparrow falling to the ground is never a monster waiting to crush innocent people. There has to be a reason why God smote the man who tried to prevent the ark from falling from the cart (see the homily, "Obed-edom . . . Whose Parlor Became a Sanctuary," p. 205).

A Disappointing Outcome . . . "So David would not remove the ark"

The king was scowling; his eyes were filled with resentment. Jehovah had gone too far! The people were doing their utmost to please Him, but the death of Uzzah seemed to indicate that Jehovah had no pity! David's lips were moving; when the people listened, they heard, "How shall the ark of the LORD come to me? If God is that unappreciative, He can keep His ark!" The commands of the military leaders were crisp and definite. The soldiers began their return to Jerusalem. The crowd started to disperse. They were not interested when the ark was carried to the nearby house of Obed-edom, the Gittite. The sunshine had disappeared from the heavens and their hearts; it was a dark day in Israel. David blamed God, but had he been more thoughtful, he might have known that he was responsible for the tragedy. The nation knew many things concerning the power of God, but little about His holiness. They probably did not care as long as they were victorious in battle; they were satisfied. God is not only a very present help in time of trouble, but He is also holy. When He issued a command, it was Israel's duty to obey. God desired to reign both in Jerusalem and in their hearts.

AN UNCONDITIONED ACCEPTANCE

So David would not remove the ark of the LORD unto him into the city of David: but David carried it aside into the house of Obed-edom the Gittite. And the ark of the LORD continued in the house of Obed-edom the Gittite three months: and the LORD blessed Obed-edom, and all his household (vv. 10-11).

Expository Notes on Obed-edom the Gittite

Obed-edom was a remarkable man. Most of what is known about him refers to one incident in his life, but this reference, when compared with other passages, becomes entrancing. He, a Gittite, had been an inhabitant of Gath, a Philistine, and an enemy of Israel. Philistia was a small country where news traveled quickly. Every person was aware of the crushing, humiliating defeat inflicted on the god, Dagon. *All* the lords of the Philistines had made the decision to return the ark of the covenant to the Hebrews, but the people feared the consequences if it remained in their country. Obed-edom, contrary to expectation, was not afraid. The lords of the nation expelled the ark from their country, but Obed-edom welcomed it into his home.

Obed-edom Was a Changed Man

At some period in his life, the faith of Obed-edom had undergone a dramatic change. The citizens of Gath worshiped idols and believed Dagon to be the greatest of the gods. That explains why they placed the ark in the temple of Dagon; it was a trophy to honor their god (see 1 Samuel 5:2-4). Fear spread throughout the land when the people heard that their god had been mutilated and humiliated by a piece of inanimate furniture. It is amazing, therefore, to find among them a man of Obed-edom's caliber. He was not an ordinary citizen. He would not have welcomed the ark if idols had been in the dwelling. Since Dagon had been destroyed in his own temple, other idols would suffer the same fate. The Philistines saw the ark and trembled; Obed-edom saw it and rejoiced. There is no way of knowing whether the man was the wealthy owner of a magnificent mansion or the humble host in a mediocre cottage, but such as he possessed, he gave willingly. Obed-edom was evidently a believer who loved Jehovah. He was one of the first Gentiles to discover that divine love has no limitations; it embraces the world.

Obed-edom Was a Confident Man

"Obed-edom, you witnessed the tragedy on the roadside. Uzzah died when he tried to prevent the ark falling from the new cart. Jehovah, the God of Israel, is impossible! He appears to be a God of moods; His presence is a threat. What if He strikes you? You should think twice before permitting that God to enter your home." The owner of the house on the hill smiled and replied, "No, I am not afraid. There is never need to fear God if one's heart is clean. I am not worthy that Jehovah should dwell with me, but if He chooses to honor my simple abode, all I possess will be his."

So David . . . carried it aside into the house of Obed-edom the Gittite. And the ark of the Lord continued in the house of Obed-edom the Gittite three months: and the Lord blessed Obed-edom and all his household (vv. 10-11).

Obed-edom probably asked to be allowed to prepare a place to receive the sacred ark, and when all was in readiness, men carried it to the table or stand where it was to rest. When Obed-edom was alone, he reverently bowed and whispered, "Welcome to my home, O Lord." When he retired for the night, he probably said, "Good night, Lord," and when the sun rose, he exclaimed, "The Lord's mercies. . . . They are new every morning: great is thy faithfulness" (see Lamentations 3:22-23).

Obed-edom Was a Consecrated Man

The ark remained in his home for three months. This statement should be remembered by all the children of God. The Savior frequently visited a home in Bethany, but only stayed a few hours. During those short visits He made impressions which were never erased. Elijah visited a home in Zarephath and remained "many days" to assist a desperate woman. It was written, "And she went and did according to the saying of Elijah: and she, and he, and her house, did eat many days (see 1 Kings 17:15). The length of the prophet's stay is never revealed. The Bible says "many days", but the result of that sojourn became immortal. It would be interesting to know the normal occupation of that Gittite. Was he a farmer, builder, trader, or administrator? It is difficult to avoid the conclusion that whatever his ordinary duties might have been, they became unimportant for at least three months. Obed-edom resembled a priest, serving faithfully before the Lord. His house had become a sanctuary; even the walls seemed to be holy. Obed-edom never served a meal to his Guest; God fed him! He never offered a sacrifice except that of a very grateful soul, but Jehovah understood! (See the homily, "Obed-edom . . . Whose Parlor Became a Sanctuary," p. 205.)

AN UNQUESTIONED AUTHORITY

And it was told king David, saying, The Lord hath blessed the house of Obed-edom, and all that pertaineth unto him, because of the ark of God. So David went and brought up the ark of God from the house of Obed-edom into the city of David with gladness. And it was so, that when they that bare the ark of the Lord had gone six paces, he sacrificed oxen and fatlings. And David danced before the Lord with all his might; and David was girded with a linen ephod. . . . And they brought in the ark of the Lord, and set it in his place, in the midst of the tabernacle that David had pitched for it. . . . And as soon as David had made an end of offering burnt-offerings and peace offerings, he blessed the people in the name of the Lord of hosts. And he dealt among all the people . . . to the women as men, to every one a cake of bread, and a good piece of flesh, and a flagon of wine. So all the people departed every one to his house (vv. 12-19).

Expository Notes on David's Completed Project

Correcting a Mistake

David's impetuous decision to abandon the ark was followed by heart-searching. When his anger subsided, he wondered what happened to cause the death of Uzzah. Perhaps he consulted the priest to ask how or where he had displeased the Lord. He ultimately said, "None ought to carry the ark of God but the Levites: for them hath the Lord chosen to carry the ark of God, to minister unto him for ever" (see 1 Chronicles 15:2). It is possible that he consulted the law and refreshed his mind concerning the commandments of the Almighty. The news that Obed-edom had been blessed by the

Lord renewed David's desire to bring back the ark, and gathering all Israel, he prepared to complete what had been commenced. Mistakes should not be permitted to destroy good intentions; they should become stepping-stones to higher and greater achievements. Simon Peter vehemently assured the Savior of his determination to be faithful, but broke his promise and disowned the Lord. Yet, through the abounding grace of God, Peter benefited from his experience and climbed to heights of victory hitherto unknown.

Celebrating With Music

And David gathered all Israel together to Jerusalem, to bring up the ark of the LORD unto his place, which he had prepared for it. . . . And David called for Zadok and Abiathar the priests . . . and said unto them, Ye are the chief of the fathers of the Levites: sanctify yourselves, both ye and your brethren, that ye may bring up the ark of the LORD God of Israel unto the place that I have prepared for it. *For because ye did it not at the first, the LORD our God made a breach upon us,* **for that we sought him not after the due order (1 Chronicles 15:3-13).**

It became evident to Israel that it was impossible to honor God if His word were not obeyed. The same musicians evidently played their instruments, and the same Levites sang when David made his first attempt to bring the ark to Jerusalem. Identical crowds gathered to celebrate the occasion, but enthusiasm is not always evidence of obedient dedication. From the commencement of time, music was the medium by which people expressed joy. David wrote, "Make a joyful noise unto the LORD, all ye lands. Serve the LORD with gladness: come before his presence with singing" (Psalm 100:1-2). At funerals in Wales, men can be seen walking ahead of the casket, singing hymns. They believe the deceased is on his way to a heavenly home, and their music expresses faith and gladness. Perhaps David had similar thoughts. God was on His way home, and the singing of the Levitical choir announced that it was a time to be remembered.

David made special preparation for the homecoming. A tabernacle, or tent, was erected in Jerusalem, and there, with loving care, the Levites deposited the ark. They hoped and prayed that it would never be removed. "And they brought in the ark of the LORD, and set it in his place, in the midst of the tabernacle that David had pitched for it: and David offered burnt offerings and peace offerings before the LORD. And . . . David . . . blessed the people in the name of the LORD of hosts" (see 2 Samuel 6:17-18). Thus did God indicate what would happen when the TRUE ARK—His Son— was enthroned in the hearts of His people. Paul expressed this thought when he wrote about believers' "speaking . . . in psalms and hymns and spiritual songs, singing and making melody in your heart to the Lord" (Ephesians 5:19).

AN UNFORGIVEN ANGER

And as the ark of the LORD came into the city of David, Michal Saul's daughter looked through a window, and saw king David leaping and dancing before the LORD; and she despised him in her heart (v. 16).

Expository Notes on the Cause of Michal's Anger

An Unwarranted Criticism

The casual reader might believe that David's immodest conduct aroused the ire of his wife and that she resented his dancing naked before the crowd. David's dancing did not cause her anger. "And David danced before the LORD with all his might, And David was girded with a linen ephod." This ephod was the garment worn by a priest. David had lain aside his robes of royalty to be dressed as a priest. Another scripture supplies additional information. "And David was clothed *with a robe of fine linen*, and all the Levites that bare the ark, and the singers, and Chenaniah the master of the song with the singers: David also had upon him *an ephod of linen*" (1 Chronicles 15:27). This garment was not used exclusively by priests; it was worn by the child Samuel (see 1 Samuel 2:18). The linen ephod indicated its owner was engaged in special service for Jehovah. David wore a magnificent white robe instead of his royal uniform. He danced not as a monarch, but as an ordinary suppliant who welcomed God's return to Jerusalem. Michal's anger was caused, not by David's immodest clothing, but by the permanent animosity in her soul. She was the daughter of Saul and was becoming increasingly like her father so that she came to detest both David and his religion.

An Unholy Concern

Then David returned to bless his household. And Michal the daughter of Saul came out to meet David, and said, How glorious was the king of Israel to day, who uncovered himself to day in the eyes of the handmaids of his servants, as one of the vain fellows shamelessly uncovereth himself (v. 20).

Michal was evidently filled with envy; she hated the man who had taken the throne from her family. Her sarcasm irritated David, who tried in vain to explain the reason for his actions. Michal was unfortunately an embittered woman who refused to see any viewpoint except her own. To argue with her would have been a waste of time. She was only concerned with herself; she detested David for giving to Jehovah, the attention which should have been hers. Michal's outburst of jealous rage was hardly becoming since she had been with another man for years. To compare David with men guilty of indecent exposure was an injustice of the worst type. It is not a cause for amazement that God condemned her.

An Unfortunate Catastrophe

Therefore Michal the daughter of Saul had no child unto the day of her death (v. 23).

To be barren was a most feared catastrophe. During the lifetime of David, being childless was believed to be a punishment from the Almighty and a reproach upon women. "Now there was a certain man of Ramathaim-zophim, of mount Ephraim, and his name was Elkanah . . . and he had two wives; the name of the one was Hannah, and the name of the other Penninah: and Penninah had children, but Hannah had no children. . . . the LORD had shut up her womb" (see 1 Samuel 1:1-5). The continuation of the family name was considered to be one of the most important things in life, and even today, in countries of the Middle East, a man may divorce his wife if she fails to produce a son. Saul himself had been concerned over this problem and had made David promise not to cut off his name in Israel (see 1 Samuel 24:21). It should be remembered that Michal had been the wife of David, but was given by Saul to another husband. She had been presented with the opportunity of becoming pregnant on many occasions. That she remained childless suggests that she might have been incapable of conception. The historian concluded that her continued barrenness was a direct judgment from God. His deduction may have been correct, but readers should hesitate before assigning blame to God concerning their own suffering. It is easy to blame the Lord when our problems might be caused by other factors, some of which may be physical.

HOMILIES FOR PREACHERS AND TEACHERS

Study No. 11

OBED-EDOM . . . Whose Parlor Became a Sanctuary (2 Samuel 6:11)

And the LORD blessed Obed-edom and all his household (2 Samuel 6:11).

Obed-edom, I envy you a great deal. Not many people have the honor of a sanctuary in the parlor. Not every day does God go to live in a humble cottage. I would have liked to stand with you watching when King David came down into your district to take away the sacred ark of God. Were you excited when the thirty thousand fighting men paraded in the fields? Were you thrilled when the massed royal bands played on all manner of instruments, and did your heart nearly stop when they reverently carried the ark from the house of Abinadab? Were you shocked when the tragedy took place a few yards from your homestead?

THE MAN WHO DIED

I have been wondering a great deal about that event, for it seems so strange, Obed-edom, that God's hand of judgment should fall on a man apparently trying to do good. Oh yes, I know that the people had broken the law. The sacred furniture should have been carried on the shoulders of the priests, and not bumped on a wagon; but still, why should Uzzah suffer for the sins of others? It is very strange, Obed-edom. I wonder what you thought. Now, I may be wrong, but I'll tell you what I think: God hates hypocrisy. He is not pleased when men are two-faced. Obed-edom, did you ever hear of Ananias and Sapphira and that they died because they were hypocrites? I have wondered if Uzzah was like them. Did he hate the ark, considering it to be a nuisance taking up valuable room in the small cottage? Then, when the king came suddenly, he posed as its proud custodian. I cannot be sure, but perhaps, Obed-edom, you could give me a better idea?

THE MAN WHO DOUBTED

And poor King David! I think I am sorry for him, although he was a little stupid, don't you think? Of course, he had had a great shock, and his best plans were all wrecked, but surely he was silly to run off home like a spoiled schoolboy. I think it would have been wiser to try to discover the cause of the upset. There must have been some reason for it; but in this way, my brother, we humans are so strange. We like to have things our way and are upset when God interferes with our plans. I can almost see the shadows on David's face and hear his whispered mutterings of self-pity. Why are we so quick to believe the worst and slow to believe the best?

THE MAN WHO DECIDED

In thought I have often stood with you, Obed-edom, to watch the disappearing crowds. I have looked at the perplexed officer who stood alongside the new cart. I have tried to imagine what you said to him. Was it something like this?

"Officer, what are you going to do now? If you agree, I shall be so pleased to have the ark in my parlor.' And was he amazed? Did he ask, 'Sir, are you not afraid?' Did you reply, 'No one with a clean heart need fear God'? And so they carried it—Him—in. Of course, they gave you a breathing space in which to prepare, and then in a moment your parlor became a temple. Fortunate man, Obed-edom! But I'll let you into a secret, and I know you will be envious. You had the ark for three months, didn't you? I am more fortunate. He has come to live in my heart. One day I heard a voice saying, 'Behold, I stand at the door, and knock: if any man hear my voice, and open the door, I will come in to him, and will sup with him, and he with me.' When I opened the door, He came in. We have been together ever since. He's wonderful. Good-bye."

P.S.:

> I tell Him all my sorrows,
>   I tell Him all my joys;
> I tell Him all that pleases me,
>   I tell Him what annoys.
> He tells me what I ought to do,
>   He shows me how to try;
> And so we walk together,
>   My Lord and I.

(Homily reprinted from the author's book, *Bible Cameos*, pp. 39-40.)

Episode 25

THEME: *God's Covenant With David*

SCRIPTURE: 2 Samuel 7

KEY VERSE:

And thine house and thy kingdom shall be established for ever before thee: thy throne shall be established for ever (v. 16).

OUTLINE:
    I. An Expressed Desire . . . *A Meaningful Observation* (Verses 1–3)
    II. An Eternal Declaration . . . *A Memorable Objection* (Verses 4-17)
    III. An Ecstatic Devotion . . . *A Magnificent Outburst* (Verses 15-28)

AN EXPRESSED DESIRE . . . A Meaningful Observation

And it came to pass, when [David] sat in his house, and the LORD had given him rest round about from all his enemies; that the king said unto Nathan the prophet, See now, I dwell in an house of cedar, but the ark of God dwelleth within curtains. And Nathan said to the king, Go, do all that is in thine heart; for the LORD is with thee (vv. 1-3).

Expository Notes on David's Desire to Build a Temple

A Purpose Considered

Hiram of Tyre had completed the palace, and David had moved into his new residence. Warfare had temporarily ceased so that Israel's leader was able to relax. His enforced inactivity was a blessing in disguise, since he wrote later, "While I was musing the fire burned" (see Psalm 39:3). His continuing meditation doubtless related to the law of God, and his thoughts probably centered on a specific commandment: "But when ye go over Jordan, and dwell in the land which the LORD your God giveth you. . . . Then there shall be a place which the LORD your God shall choose to cause his name to dwell there; thither shall ye bring all that I command you" (Deuteronomy 12:10-11). When David either remembered or read that statement, he became agitated. He was ashamed that while he dwelt in luxury, Jehovah lived in a tent! This was not right in his estimation, and as he continued to consider the situation, the fire of desire burned within his soul. He would build a magnificent temple for God. When he confided in the prophet, Nathan concurred with his royal master, and even Jehovah seemed to be pleased with David's plan. The king was unfortunately making his decision based on false assumptions. He did not consult the priest with the ephod and failed to seek divine guidance. David was an impetuous man who acted in haste and repented at leisure! He probably thought that it was unnecessary to ask God's permission to do something good! David evidently learned his lesson, for he wrote: "Who shall ascend into the hill of the LORD? or who shall stand in his holy place? He that hath clean hands, and a pure heart; who hath not lifted up his soul unto vanity, nor sworn deceitfully" (see Psalm 24:3-4).

A Plan Conceived

When David decided to proceed with his project, he could hardly wait for the morning when the builders and architects could be commissioned. Poor David—there was so much he needed to learn. His idea was excellent, but his hands were dirty! His vision was filled with merit, but his soul was impoverished. He was probably encouraged by the enthusiasm of Nathan, but even prophets were human. There were occasions when, inspired by the Holy Spirit, they spoke as the oracles of God, but they were not sinless. At other times they were capable of making mistakes. When Nathan agreed with David, he was not speaking for the Lord, but listening to one of his friends. He assumed that there was no need to ask permission to do good! The king should have known better. He was undoubtedly doing good when he tried to bring the ark to Jerusalem, but to please God it is necessary to do the right thing in the right way! Sacred acts can only be performed by sanctified hands. Acceptable songs of praise can only be sung by dedicated lips and consecrated singers. An apparently glorious deed can be ruined by impure motives. A gift of a million dollars to the continuing work of the Lord can be defiled if that money is made illegitimately. To express that truth in modern terminology, gamblers will never please God by building churches, and unclean people can never buy an entrance into the kingdom of God. Simon tried to do this kind of thing and was told, "Thy money perish with thee" (see Acts 8:20).

A Prophet's Consent

It may be assumed that David and Nathan were such close friends that they shared each other's confidence. The king believed that the nation needed a temple which would be a habitation for Jehovah and a rallying place for the tribes. The late Prime Minister Ben-Gurion, one of the leaders of modern Israel, expressed identical convictions when he said, "We need our temple to bind us all together." The prophet Nathan, who was an ardent patriot, believed that David's idea was excellent and said, "Do all that is in thine heart, for the LORD is with thee. And it came to pass that night, that the word of the LORD came unto Nathan, saying, Go and tell my servant David . . . Shalt thou build an house for me to dwell in?" (2 Sam. 7:3-5). At first glance, it seemed that God approved of David's plan, but preferred that the building be erected by David's son. Another scripture supplies additional information.

> And David said to Solomon, My son, as for me, it was in my mind to build an house unto the name of the LORD my God: but the word of the LORD came to me, saying, Thou hast shed blood abundantly, and hast made great wars: thou shalt not build an house unto my name, because thou hast shed much blood upon the earth in my sight. Behold, a son shall be born to thee. . . . He shall build an house for my name (1 Chronicles 22:7-10).

It was never revealed whether this revelation was given to Nathan after he encouraged David to proceed with the erection of the temple. If it were, then the prophet corrected his mistake when he met David the following day.

AN ETERNAL DECLARATION . . . A Memorable Objection

> Moreover I will appoint a place for my people, and will plant them, that they may dwell in a place of their own, and move no more. . . . And when thy days be fulfilled . . . I will set up thy seed after thee. . . . He shall build an house for my name, and I will establish the throne of his kingdom for ever (vv. 10-13).

Expository Notes on God's Covenant with David

If David were disappointed by God's rejection of his request to erect a temple, his sorrow was quickly banished by the magnificence of a divine covenant. There are eight "for evers" in this chapter. Three of them were uttered by the Lord; the other five appeared in David's response to the promises of the Almighty. God indicated that David's family, throne, and kingdom would continue indefinitely. The king wished to build a house for God; the Lord replied by promising to build a different kind of house for His servant.

The far-reaching effects of this covenant became obvious. It was said that Israel "may dwell in a place of their own, and move no more; neither shall the children of wickedness afflict them any more, as beforetime." At a later date, God's people were taken into captivity in Babylon and remained there for seventy years. Therefore, it is difficult to avoid the conclusion

that the Davidic covenant extended to ages beyond Old Testament generations. The tragic history of the Jews brought unprecedented suffering; they
had no homeland until the modern state of Israel was founded in Palestine.
Even now, the nation does not possess the eternal rest promised to their
famous ancestor. The only logical interpretation of these promises is that
God will yet perform all that was predicted. The Lord was referring to the
days of which Micah wrote: "And they shall beat their swords into plow-
shares, and their spears into pruning hooks: nation shall not lift up a sword
against nation, neither shall they learn war any more. But they shall sit
every man under his vine and under his fig tree; and none shall make them
afraid: for the mouth of the LORD of hosts hath spoken it" (Micah 4:3-4).

AN ECSTATIC DEVOTION . . . A Magnificent Outburst

**Then went king David in, and sat before the LORD and he said, Who am
I, O LORD God? and what is my house, that thou hast brought me hitherto? . . . thou hast spoken also of thy servant's house for a great while to
come. . . . For thou hast confirmed to thyself thy people Israel to be a
people unto thee for ever: and thou, LORD, art become their God. . . . with
thy blessing let the house of thy servant be blessed for ever (vv. 18-29).**

Expository Notes on David's Prayer of Thanksgiving

"Then went king David in and sat before the LORD." The king had already prepared a tent in which the ark of Jehovah rested. To this sacred
shrine, David went to sit in the presence of his God. He was unafraid
because his conscience was clear (compare with 2 Samuel 6:8-9). It was
natural for a worshiper to sit during his meditation. Moslems continue to
do so when they pray. They sit cross-legged upon the ground with their
bodies resting upon their heels. David's utterance was not a prayer, but a
spontaneous outburst of deep gratitude. He contrasted the simplicity and
unimportance of his family with the expanding greatness and kindness of
God. He had been elevated from obscurity to become the king of God's
great nation. That fact filled his soul with praise, but when David continued to think about the extent of the covenant which had been made, it
became difficult to express what he felt. That his throne, family, and name
would continue eternally was beyond comprehension. God had used the
term "for ever" on three different occasions, but the king used it five times
(see vv. 24, 25, 26, and 29). God was eternal and as a result foresaw
everything beyond time. David would have appreciated the hymn which
says:

> O God our Help in ages past;
>   Our hope for years to come.
> Our shelter from the stormy blast,
>   And our ETERNAL home.

David's exclamation of praise was threefold. (1.) *God is Gracious.* "For thy word's sake, and according to thine own heart, hast thou done all these great things, to make thy servant know them" (v. 21); (2.) *God is Great.* "Wherefore thou art great, O LORD God: for there is none like thee, neither is there any God beside thee, according to all that we have heard with our ears" (v. 22); and (3.) *God is Glorious.* "And now, O Lord GOD thou art that God, and thy words be true, and thou hast promised this goodness unto thy servant: Therefore now let it please thee to bless the house of thy servant, that it may continue for ever before thee: for thou O LORD God, hast spoken it: and with thy blessing let the house of thy servant be blessed for ever" (vv. 28-29). Micah asked a very pertinent question, "Who is a God like unto thee, that pardoneth iniquity, and passeth by the transgression of the remnant of his heritage? he retaineth not his anger for ever, because he delighteth in mercy" (Micah 7:18).

Episode 26

THEME: *The Extension of David's Kingdom*

SCRIPTURE: 2 Samuel 8

KEY VERSE:

And the LORD preserved David whithersoever he went (vv. 6, 14).

OUTLINE:
    I. David's Conquests . . . *Devastating* (Verses 1-13)
   II. David's Compassion . . . *Discernible* (Verse 2)
  III. David's Collectibles . . . *Dedicated* (Verse 11)
  IV. David's Companions . . . *Devoted* (Verses 16-18)

DAVID'S CONQUESTS

And after this it came to pass, that David smote the Philistines, and subdued them: and David took Metheg-ammah, out of the hand of the Philistines (v. 1).

Expository Notes on David's Continuing Victories

The peaceful period in which the king was able to give attention to the commandments of God had ended. Threats from adjacent nations possibly made it imperative that Israel's armies defend their territory, but there could have been another reason for Hebrew aggression. David had planned to erect a magnificent temple, but his people were unable to provide the gold, silver, and other precious metals to adorn the structure. Successive invasions by numerous enemies had impoverished the land, and if the dream of David would become reality, it was necessary to obtain supplies of the valuable commodities from foreign sources. It was significant that after each battle, the Hebrew people captured much spoil, most of which was dedicated to the service of Jehovah. The king evidently believed that by going to war, he would be killing "two birds with one stone."

It may or may not be significant that he first attacked Metheg-ammah, another name for Gath (1 Chronicles 18:1), the greatest of five Philistine cities. The name means: "The bridle of the mother city." Gath had become the greatest place in Philistia and had earned its name; it was the force which "bridled" or controlled warlike neighbors. When David became the conqueror of Gath, he asserted his authority over the entire Philistine nation. Verse twelve explains the extent of David's influence. He seized the spoils of war from "all the nations which he subdued; of Syria and of Moab, and of the children of Ammon, and of the Philistines, and of Amalek, and of the spoil of Hadadezer, son of Rehob, king of Zobah" (2 Samuel 8:11-12). The continuing triumphs of David emphasized the important fact that no man could outgive God. When the king was totally surrendered to the Almighty, he was invincible with the result that God delivered all his enemies into his hand. David's history endorsed all that Christ announced many years later. Jesus said, "But seek ye first the kingdom of God, and his righteousness; and all these things shall be added unto you" (Matthew 6:33).

DAVID'S COMPASSION

And he smote Moab, and measured them with a line, casting them down to the ground; even with two lines measured he to put to death, and with one full line to keep alive. And so the Moabites became David's servants, and brought gifts (v. 2).

Expository Notes on David's Strange Actions

Brutality is a word which should never be associated with the Lord. It is necessary, therefore, to remember that the customs of David and of the age in which he lived can hardly be compared with the customs practiced within the Christian church. Sensitive souls may be horrified by David's treatment of prisoners of war. The historian described how the Moabites were thrown to the ground where they lay to be measured with lines. That action decided who would be spared and who would be executed. It should be remembered that these people had ravaged the land of Israel and massacred complete communities. Had David killed all his enemies, he would have emulated the example of his foes, who never extended mercy to prisoners. There appear to be two interpretations of this perplexing text.

The famous commentators Jamieson, Fausset, and Brown write: "This refers to a well-known practice of Eastern kings, to command their prisoners of war, particularly those, who, notorious for the atrocity of their crimes . . . had greatly incensed the victors, to lie down on the ground. Then a certain portion of them, which was determined by lot, but most commonly by a measuring line, were put to death. Our version suggests he put two-thirds to death, and spare one third. The *Septuagint* and *Vulgate* make one-half. This war usage was not, perhaps, usually practiced by the people of God, but Jewish writers assert the cause of this particular severity against the people, was their having massacred David's parents and family, whom he had, during his exile, committed to the king of Moab" (*The Bethany Parallel Commentary on the Old Testament*, p. 589).

The other suggestion comes from Dr. Adam Clarke, who wrote: "It has generally been conjectured that David, after he had conquered Moab, consigned two-thirds of the inhabitants to the sword; but I think the text will bear a meaning much more reputable to that king. The first clause of the verse seems to determine the sense, *he measured them with a line, casting them down to the ground*—to put to death, and with one line to keep alive. Death seems here to be referred to the cities by way of metaphor, and from this view of the subject, we may conclude that two-thirds of the cities, that is, the strong places of Moab were erased. The text adds: *"So the Moabites became David's servants, and brought gifts,* i.e. were obliged to pay tribute." (*The Bethany Parallel Commentary on the Old Testament*, p. 589). There appears to be some significance in the fact that David used *a full long line* when he measured those to be spared. Had he permitted all the Moabites to return to their homes, he might have been protecting a nest of hornets! His act might have been interpreted as a sign of weakness, and his own position would have been undermined. Even in moments of supreme triumph, David remembered to be gracious. The world should applaud his kindness.

DAVID'S COLLECTIBLES

David smote also Hadadezer. . . . And David took from him a thousand chariots, and seven hundred horsemen, and twenty thousand footmen: and David houghed all the chariot horses, but reserved of them for an hundred chariots. . . . And Joram brought with him vessels of silver, and vessels of gold, and vessels of brass: which also king David dedicated unto the LORD, with the silver and gold that he had dedicated of all nations which he subdued (vv. 3-4, 10-11).

Expository Notes on David's Preparation to Build the Temple

The parallel passage in 1 Chronicles 18, adds an interesting detail. "And David took the shields of gold that were on the servants of Hadarezer, and brought them to Jerusalem. Likewise from Tibhath, and from Chun, cities of Hadarezer, brought David very much brass, wherewith Solomon made the brasen sea, and pillars and the vessels of brass" (1 Chron. 18:7-8). To repeat an earlier statement, David went to war to "kill two birds with one stone!" It might be wise to consider David's faithfulness. When God refused permission to build the temple, the king could have reacted in several ways.

1. *He Could Have Been Angry*, thus abandoning the project. Had selfishness dominated his life, David could have bequeathed the task to

Solomon. Why should he do all the preparation when another man would inherit the glory of completing what David had planned? Men of lesser stature would have accepted that alternative as an escape from increasing responsibility.

2. *He Could Have Been Avaricious* and as a result become increasingly wealthy. When gold, silver, and brass began to reach Israel, the king could have retained the wealth for himself. Within a year he would have been the richest man in the world. The fact that he dedicated the captured treasure to the work of God spoke of the purity of his motives.

3. *He Could Have Been Ambitious* by commencing another project. He might have erected hospitals, homes for the aged, schools, and colleges, each one bearing his name. David could have bequeathed to posterity memorials to his own grandeur and filled the land with everlasting monuments to the splendor of his reign. That he chose to exalt the Lord indicates that he was the friend of God.

DAVID'S COMPANIONS

> **And David reigned over all Israel; and David executed judgment and justice unto all his people. And Joab . . . was over the host; and Jehoshaphat . . . was recorder; . . . and Zadok . . . and Ahimelech . . . were the priests; and Seraiah was the scribe; and Benaiah . . . was over both the Cherethites and the Pelethites; and David's sons were chief rulers (vv. 15-18).**

Expository Notes on David's Excellent Administration

David is remembered, not only for his excellence as a warrior, but also because he was the first man to attempt to make an organized nation out of a multitude of people. Moses began this task when he led a host of men and women out of Egypt. At first, he was the only judge in the nation, but later, at the suggestion of his father-in-law, he divided that responsibility among chosen men (see Exodus 18:14-27). Samuel provided some organization for the people and annually went to chosen cities to consider the complaints of the people. Throughout the reign of Saul, there was little if any attempt made to place Israel on a reliable legal foundation. The people were divided into twelve disorganized tribes, and apart from religious activities, each was responsible for its own legislative process. David was the first man to recognize that if the Jews were to survive, gifted men had to become responsible for important things within the nation. He, therefore, selected talented people and made them heads of the various departments of government. Each man probably had his trained staff of employees, and since the financial resources of the land were overwhelming, there was never danger of a national deficit. It might be beneficial to consider David's administrative officials.

The Department of Defense

"And Joab the son of Zeruiah was over the host." Joab had lost his position as the commander in chief of Israel's army, but had regained it when he captured the city of the Jebusites (see 1 Chronicles 11:6). Thereafter, Joab made himself indispensable to his royal master. There were times when David detested his general and possibly would have dismissed him, had he dared. As will be considered in subsequent studies, Joab frequently criticized David, and more often than not, the objections were justified. The king made unfortunate mistakes which led to increasing troubles within the tribes. Joab alone had the courage to question the decisions of the king. If David could have found another capable man he would have unquestionably dismissed his old friend.

Joab was an outstanding warrior, a brilliant strategist, and a constant protector of the affairs of Israel. Although wars had temporarily ceased, there was no guarantee the enemies had been vanquished for ever. It was to be expected that the Philistines would renew their attacks, and the armies of Israel had to be ready to withstand efforts to reduce the people to slavery. Significant victories had been won, but David's conquests had made tremendous changes in the defensive capabilities of the nation. Israel now possessed chariots and specially trained horses. Such equipment, as was known in those times, belonged to David, and it was Joab's task to oversee the training of men capable of making the most of the new acquisitions. Earlier, Abner had possessed identical qualifications, but his death left Joab as the only man able to do what had to be done. He was a fearless man of exceptional ability who never hesitated to express his thoughts. The general was a man to be trusted, but, alas, even David resented his influence and later ordered his execution (see 1 Kings 2:5-6).

The Department of Information

"And Jehoshaphat the son of Ahilud was recorder [—the remembrancer]." The tasks given to this man were probably varied. He was the king's private secretary, who committed to writing the decrees issued by David. These manuscripts were later read to the king, who signed them into law. There was no elected body of officials. David was the sole ruler of his country, and his decisions were final so that there was never a court of appeal. The recorder—or remembrancer—was responsible for enforcing David's commands, and later, when everything was satisfactory, the details of what transpired were written into the "books of remembrance." Jehoshaphat was the first elected historian. David valued the survival of ancient records and marveled how they had endured through centuries of time and testing. He was an author in his own right and desired his writings to be preserved for posterity. There is reason to believe that this little-known official was responsible for the preservation of David's psalms and the proverbs of Solomon. During those ancient periods, information was preserved on clay tablets, a process which demanded time and skill. Je-hoshaphat was one of the busiest and most important people in Israel.

The Department of Religion

"And Zadok the son of Ahitub, and Ahimelech the son of Abiathar were the priests." Had David been able to foresee the times in which we live, he would either have been amused or confounded by our continued arguments over the separation of church and state. Modern religious leaders sometimes become aggressive in demanding that never, for any reason, should the state be permitted to interfere with the church. Believing themselves to be the supreme custodians of the affairs of God, they assert their own importance by neither accepting help nor permitting interference from politicians. At least, that is what they would like the world to believe. David had no knowledge of organized religion, but he fervently desired God to be preeminent within the land. Qualified men should be in charge of everything spiritual; it was their task to ensure that Jehovah would be pleased with all matters pertaining to the temple: the ritual, the singing of the Levitical choir, and the upkeep of the sanctuary. There would have normally been one priest, but David was aware of the peculiar circumstances in his country.

Prior to the capture of Jerusalem, the center of religious activity had been at Nob. After the massacre of the priests, the sole survivor, Abiathar, fled to David to become his priest. When David decided that Jerusalem should be the center of his religious organization, the son of Ahitub became the official high priest of the sanctuary. Thereafter, until disaster overwhelmed the country, there were two official priests in Israel. One might have been a junior priest in Jerusalem, but one of the two was probably the high priest in one of the cities of refuge, six of which existed in Israel. A comparison can perhaps be made between Israel's priests and the great ecclesiastical leaders of the Church of England. The Archbishops of York and Canterbury both serve the same cause, but only the Archbishop of Canterbury resides near the reigning monarch. York is the administrative center of the same church and governs matters relative to the church in the northern section of Great Britain. There was no religious discord in Israel; both priests were loyal to God and David. Perhaps the most important by-product of that arrangement was that in Israel no detail, however insignificant, was overlooked.

The Department of Border Control

"And Benaiah the son of Jehoiada was over both the Cherethites and the Pelethites." These people might have been two insignificant tribes of Philistines who inhabited the southern borders of Palestine. David probably made their acquaintance when he resided at Ziklag, and when the conquest of the land was completed, he preserved their friendship by offering employment under the supervision of Benaiah. Two ideas about this arrangement have been expressed by theologians. Since these people lived at the extremity of David's kingdom, a territory not easily defended, they could have been appointed as controllers of the border country in order to keep out unwanted people and to repel invaders until help arrived from northern cities. On the other hand, some teachers believe that they were the personal bodyguards of David.

All visitors to the Vatican City are aware of the Swiss Guards who protect the sacred places of the Catholic Church. The guards at Buckingham Palace in London are known throughout the world. Their colorful tunics and bearskin helmets provide unending delight to all tourists. David's guards perhaps came from the southern tribes, and the training and oversight of these men were the responsibility of Benaiah, one of David's most trusted captains. Adam Clarke, the noted commentator, wrote an interesting paragraph concerning these men. "[Benaiah was] the chief of the second class of David's worthies . . . *The Cherethites and the Pelethites*! The former supposed to be those who accompanied David when he fled from Saul; the latter, those who came to him at Ziklag. But the Targum translates these two names thus: 'The archers and the slingers', and this is by far, the most likely" (*The Bethany Parallel Commentary on the Old Testament*, p. 590).

The Department of the King's Household

"Seraiah was the scribe . . . and David's sons were chief rulers." David was now the ruler of a vast territory, many nations were paying tribute, and numerous letters had to be written and dispatched. It is likely that the king employed his own private secretary, whose salary was paid from state funds. This man was responsible for the operation of the royal office. Some teachers believe that he was the secretary of state, David's direct contact with all foreign countries. He was not only the head of the legal department, but the official stand-in for David when circumstances prevented his attendance at royal functions. That David gave special appointments to two of his sons was very thought-provoking. First Chronicles provides an interesting footnote to an earlier statement as follows: "and the sons of David were chief about the king" (1 Chronicles 18:17). Various suggestions can be made concerning this position. They could have been private chaplains, personal advisers, interceptors who prevented unauthorized entry into David's presence, or even minor judges who handled complaints thought to be unworthy of the king's attention.

To revert to the introduction to this episode, David was attempting to provide an administration within his kingdom; the best available people were placed in strategic positions to guarantee that affairs within Israel would be managed efficiently. After David's decease, Solomon continued this work until Israel became famous for its magnificence so that even the Queen of Sheba was able to say, "It was a true report that I heard in mine own land of thy acts and of thy wisdom. Howbeit I believed not the words, until I came, and mine eyes had seen it: and, behold, the half was not told me: thy wisdom and prosperity exceedeth the fame which I heard" (see 1 Kings 10:6-7).

Episode 27

THEME: *David's Kindness to Mephibosheth*

SCRIPTURE: 2 Samuel 9

KEY VERSE:

> And David said unto him, Fear not: for I will surely shew thee kindness for Jonathan thy father's sake, and will restore thee all the land of Saul thy father; and thou shalt eat bread at my table continually (v. 7).

OUTLINE:
    I. A Remembered Promise (Verse 1)
    II. A Receptive Prince (Verses 2-6)
    III. A Remarkable Provision (Verses 7-10)
    IV. A Royal Protector (Verses 11-13)

A REMEMBERED PROMISE

And David said, Is there yet any that is left of the house of Saul, that I may shew him kindness for Jonathan's sake? (v. 1).

Expository Notes on David's Remembered Covenant

King Saul had four sons, but after the turbulent times through which David passed, those boys had almost been forgotten. "And Saul begat Jonathan and Malchi-shua, and Abinadab, and Esh-baal" (1 Chronicles 8:33). The name of Jonathan has become immortal, but what happened to the others? The historian informs us that Saul and his sons died together on Mount Gilboa. Esh-baal was another name for Ish-bosheth, whom Abner crowned king of Israel. That David had to ask if any descendants of the house of Saul still survived indicates that he was uninformed concerning events which transpired during his wandering in the wilderness. His inquiry led to the discovery of an interesting section of Hebrew history.

David had promised Saul to be kind to the king's children. The text reads: "Swear now therefore unto me by the LORD, that thou wilt not cut off my seed after me, and that thou wilt not destroy my name out of my father's house. And David sware unto Saul" (1 Samuel 24:21–22). David had apparently forgotten that promise until he began to reminisce during his relaxation. At the same time, he evidently remembered another promise made to Jonathan, "And thou shalt not only while yet I live shew me the kindness of the LORD, that I die not: but also thou shalt not cut off thy kindness from my house for ever: no, not when the LORD hath cut off the enemies of David every one from the face of the earth" (1 Samuel 20:14-15). When David remembered his obligations, he set in motion inquiries which led him to Ziba, an employee of the royal household, who was able to supply the necessary information since he had always been the steward of the late king's estate.

A RECEPTIVE PRINCE

And the king said, Is there not yet any of the house of Saul, that I may shew the kindness of God unto him? And Ziba said unto the king, Jonathan hath yet a son, which is lame on his feet. And the king said unto him, Where is he? And Ziba said unto the king, Behold, he is in the house of Machir, the son of Ammiel, in Lo-debar. Then king David sent and fetched him out of the house of Machir, the son of Ammiel, from Lode-bar (vv. 2-5).

Expository Notes on Mephibosheth the Crippled Son of Jonathan

This wonderful story about Mephibosheth (also named Merib-baal in 1 Chronicles 8:34) can be progressively studied under seven informative headings.

His Persistent Problem

"And Jonathan, Saul's son, had a son who was lame on his feet. He was five years old when the tidings came of Saul and Jonathan out of Jezreel, and his nurse took him up, and fled: and it came to pass, as she made haste to flee, that he fell, and became lame. And his name was Mephibosheth" (2 Samuel 4:4). Josephus, the Jewish historian, wrote, "She snatched him up, and fled away, and let him fall from her shoulders, and his feet were lame" (*The Antiquities of the Jews*. Book 7. Chapter 5. Paragraph 5).

Evidently the child suffered permanent damage to his legs and feet and remained a cripple throughout the rest of his life. Second Samuel 19:24 suggests that his feet needed constant attention. As a result, there were wounds which perhaps would not heal; his feet might have needed to be "dressed" every day.

His Protective Parents

The unnamed nurse evidently considered the boy's life to be threatened;

her effort to protect him occasioned his infirmity. It is not known how the child went to live with a wealthy family from Lo-debar, but the possibility exists that when he heard of the child's helplessness, the foster father decided to welcome the lad into his family. A great amount of discussion has centered around the name of that desert city; there are at least three localities which scholars assert might be its original site. The name means "pastureless", and that clue is the most reliable guide to its location. It has been claimed the city was on the eastern side of the river Jordan close to Mahanaim. It was definitely situated near a wilderness or desert.

Second Samuel 17:27-29 states that Machir, the son of Ammiel, was a very wealthy man who, along with others of his type, brought many gifts to David and his hungry soldiers. Questions raised include: (1.) Had Ammiel and his son, Machir, found springs in the desert and become successful farmers in that area? or (2.) Had they made their money elsewhere and, after adopting the orphaned Mephibosheth, gone as far as possible from Jerusalem to keep the new king from threatening the life of their little boy? It is not possible to supply irrefutable answers to these questions. They evidently loved their adopted child. Eventually after many years, the lad became an adult, was married, and had a son whom he named Micah (v. 12). The descendants of Mephibosheth became numerous, for Micah eventually married and had several sons who became leading citizens in the tribe of Benjamin (see 1 Chronicles 8:35-40).

His Predominant Problem

When Ziba, the emissary of David, explained the reason for his unexpected visit to Lo-debar, Mephibosheth was confronted by his greatest problem. He was told that David had remembered a promise made to Jonathan and now desired to become his friend and savior. Ziba's visit as a special messenger compares with those who explain the eternal covenant made between God and His Son so that eternal salvation has come within the reach of sinners (see the homily, "Mephibosheth . . . and His Glorious Wretchedness," at the end of this episode). It could not have been a simple matter for the listener to believe what was being said. As a member of the household of Saul, Mephibosheth belonged to the enemies of David. Could this offer then be a trick? Was it true that David was offering friendship, or was this a trap into which the king was trying to lure another victim? It should not be too difficult to comprehend that situation, for the same question continues to be asked by unbelievers who debate whether or not to believe the gospel.

His Positive Perception

Mephibosheth listened to Ziba's account and considered his options. If the message were false, he would die, but his condition suggested that he was almost dead already! What did he have to lose? If, on the other hand, the king's offer was genuine, Mephibosheth had everything to gain. This was something which could be tested. It would be inexcusable to reject that which could lead to a transformation of his life. That crippled man had to decide whether or not to believe his good news.

A REMARKABLE PROVISION

Now when Mephibosheth, the son of Jonathan . . . was come unto David, he fell on his face, and did reverence. And David said, Mephibosheth. And he answered, Behold thy servant! And David said unto him, Fear not: for I will surely shew thee kindness for Jonathan thy father's sake, and will restore thee all the land of Saul thy father; and thou shalt eat bread at my table continually. And he bowed himself, and said, What is thy servant, that thou shouldest look upon such a dead dog as I am? (vv. 6-8).

Expository Notes on David's Promises to Mephibosheth

His Plentiful Provision

The property which David planned to return to Mephibosheth included the land which Saul owned in Gibeah, but there was also the family inheritance from Kish and his ancestors. Ziba had retained possession of the land since he had been the steward of the late king Saul. It is extremely important to remember that he alone knew of the existence of Jonathan's son; yet, he did nothing to aid the child. He probably hoped that the lad's whereabouts would never be discovered and that he could retain the land for himself. He was in an awkward predicament when David began to ask questions. The appearance of Jonathan's son in Jerusalem and the king's promise to restore Saul's property to Saul's grandchild produced unexpected problems. Ziba had possibly helped himself to the profit made during the years. He had become the head of his own important household and had "fifteen sons and twenty [slaves]." David's edict meant that Ziba had to revert, with his sons, to "tilling the field" and working hard to support a man he never desired to see. Such an arrangement was common practice in the Middle East. The land remained the property of the owner, but one half of the profit was given to the steward as compensation for his labor. Ziba apparently responded with alacrity, but a later episode in the life of David revealed the treachery which filled the steward's soul.

A ROYAL PROTECTOR

As for Mephibosheth, said the king, he shall eat at my table, as one of the king's sons (v. 11).

Expository Notes on Sitting at the King's Table

His Perfect Peace

There were days when the cripple wondered if he were dreaming. It was inconceivable that a person like him should have found favor in the eyes of the king. He was now wealthy and had workmen appointed by David to attend to his extensive property; his income was assured. The barren wastes of his former surroundings belonged to the past; his immediate future was bright with prospect and hope. His own increasing family necessitated a home near the palace, but he was assured of a seat at the royal table at every royal function. His presence among the princes was of more value than his property and accumulating wealth. David was his benefactor. There was never need to worry about anything; his desires would always be granted. His life had changed dramatically when he accepted the offer of salvation. He was no longer lonely, harassed, or despondent. His life was in the hand of his wonderful benefactor. Faith banished doubts; joy replaced sadness; smiles removed frowns. He possessed a peace almost beyond comprehension.

His Powerful Protector

Mephibosheth had been introduced to a glorious fellowship. The king who had given him a new life was close at hand. They could converse at any time of the day or night; problems could be shared; the way into the royal presence would never be closed. David's strength would be made perfect in his protege's weakness. If at any time danger threatened, around him would be the everlasting arms of royal patronage. Mephibosheth was safer in his chair than other men were in their chariots. He possessed a peace beyond the purchasing power of rubies. It is possible to see in the life of this fortunate man the gospel of the grace of God. The Lord, who saw the end from the beginning, wrote on the pages of a human life, the greatest story ever told.

HOMILIES FOR PREACHERS AND TEACHERS

Study No. 12

MEPHIBOSHETH . . . and His Glorious Wretchedness (2 Samuel 19:24)

"And Mephibosheth the son of Saul came down to meet the king, and had neither dressed his feet, nor trimmed his beard, nor washed his clothes, from the day the king departed until the day he came again in peace." And this marked the highlight of David's homecoming. It is exceedingly interesting to know that this unlovely sight is perhaps the most charming picture seen in the experiences of King David. The story of Mephibosheth falls into two sections and is best appreciated that way.

THE SALVATION OF A SINNER

It had been a poignant scene when Jonathan, the prince, revealed to David his knowledge of the identity of Israel's future king. God had chosen David and by so doing had rejected the house of Saul. Jonathan, whose love for David had grown intensely, rejoiced in the favor shown to his friend and one day asked David to remember him in the day of his ultimate triumph by showing kindness to his children. But many years had passed before David said, "Is there not yet any that is left of the house of Saul, that I may shew him the kindness of God unto him? And Ziba said unto the king, Jonathan hath yet a son, which is lame on his feet. . . . Then king David sent and fetched him out of the house of Machir, the son of Ammiel, from Lo-debar" (2 Sam. 9:3-5). It is easy to visualize the coming of the royal servant to the house in the wilderness and to understand the suspicion with which he was received. Mephibosheth belonged to the house of Saul and expected hatred from David's line. But all his fears were subdued when the great offer of salvation was made known. He was made to understand that he could never merit this gift of David made entirely for Jonathan's sake. The crippled fellow could hardly believe his good fortune, but sweeping aside all his doubts, he gladly accepted the offered mercy and was lifted out of his wilderness home and brought to the palace. The Old Testament picture seems to have been painted with New Testament colors. God offers salvation to the sinner. Man can neither deserve nor earn this treasure, and no works of righteousness can ever merit it. It is the supreme gift of the love of God, because One who is greatly beloved has died. "God for Christ's sake has forgiven you," said the apostle Paul, and in every presentation of the gospel message, we have the fulfillment of the veiled foreshadowings enshrined in the story of the ancient cripple. Alas, many people seem to be less intelligent than he since they prefer a home in the wilderness.

THE FAITHFULNESS OF A SAINT

The scene has greatly changed, for rebellion has broken out in the city of Jerusalem. Fleeing from the murderous intentions of Absalom, David has escaped into the countryside, where he is met by Ziba, the servant of Mephibosheth. "And the king said, And where is thy master's son? And Ziba said unto the king, Behold, he abideth at Jerusalem: for he said, Today shall the house of Israel restore me the kingdom of my father. Then said the king to Ziba, Behold, thine are all that pertained unto Mephibosheth"

(2 Samuel 16:3-4). Alas, the convert upon whom so much grace had been showered was now seen to be unreliable—or so it seemed. Later, when the battle for the kingdom had been won, David returned to find Mephibosheth awaiting his coming. The king asked, "Wherefore wentest not thou with me, Mephibosheth?" And in reply he heard of the treachery of Ziba. The servant had slandered his master in the hope of obtaining royal favor. We can almost hear Mephibosheth's whispered appeal, "Master, if you have any doubt, just look at me." And David's eyes grew strangely misty when he beheld the utter wretchedness of the cripple. His wounds had not been cleansed, the bandages remained unchanged, and his entire appearance suggested pain and neglect. Realizing that he had been slandered before his royal savior, Mephibosheth persistently refused to flirt with the usurper prince and remained an object of scorn throughout Absalom's stay in the city.

This Old Testament scene wonderfully illustrates the whole theme of the gospel. In this present day our Savior is the despised and rejected One, for the prince of this world is attempting to steal the kingdom. Yet, the ultimate triumph will soon be won, and He will return. Have we been loyal to Him during his absence? (Homily reprinted from the author's book, *Bible Cameos*, pp. 43-44.)

Episode 28

THEME: *The Abusing of David's Ambassadors*

SCRIPTURE: 2 Samuel 10

KEY VERSE:

> Be of good courage, and let us play the men for our people, and for the cities of our God: and the LORD do that which seemeth him good (v. 12).

OUTLINE:

     I.   David's Sympathetic Message (Verses 1-2)

    II.   David's Shamed Messengers (Verses 3-5)

  III.   David's Strong Man (Verses 6-12)

  IV.   David's Stupendous Mission (Verses 13-19)

DAVID'S SYMPATHETIC MESSAGE

And it came to pass after this, that the king of the children of Ammon died, and Hanun his son reigned in his stead. Then said David, I will shew kindness unto Hanun the son of Nahash, as his father shewed kindness unto me. And David sent to comfort him by the hand of his servants for his father. And David's servants came into the land of the children of Ammon (vv. 1-2).

Expository Notes on David's Message of Good Will

A Forgotten Message

This was one of the most disconcerting episodes in the life of David; it revealed his ever-increasing capacity for getting into trouble. How could a man who had often been reproved for his mistakes continue to make the same error? How could a mature soul be so foolish? At one time in his life, David wrote, "Thy word have I hid in mine heart, that I might not sin against thee" (see Psalm 119:11). It is difficult to avoid the conclusion that he hid it so effectively that sometimes he forgot it!

Nahash, the king of the Ammonites, was a ruthless enemy of the Lord whose practices were detestable. When his army surrounded the city of Jabesh-gilead, his conditions for peace were appalling. He demanded that every male within the city consent to the removal of his right eye. Nahash was a merciless bigot who never exercised mercy. Had not the Lord used a ploughman named Saul, Israel would have been subjected to infamous indignity. God was fully aware of the atrocities of the Ammonites, and His word was very explicit. "An Ammonite or Moabite shall not enter into the congregation of the LORD; even to their tenth generation shall they not enter into the congregation of the LORD for ever: Because they met you not with bread and with water in the way, when ye came forth out of Egypt; and because they hired against thee Balaam . . . to curse thee. . . . *Thou shalt not seek their peace nor their prosperity all thy days for ever*" (Deuteronomy 23:3-6). David's mission was a violation of God's commandment. A prophet named Jehu, who spoke to king Jehoshaphat, asked a very pertinent question, "Shouldest thou help the ungodly, and love them that hate the LORD?" (2 Chronicles 19:2).

A Favored Memory

At some time during David's flight from Saul, he had been befriended by Nahash the Ammonite. No other mention was made of this incident; what it was and where it happened were never revealed. Yet, even David might have known that Nahash had no love for the Hebrews. He probably helped David because Saul hated him. The king of the Ammonites had neither forgotten nor forgiven Saul for the devastating defeat at Jabesh-gilead. He would have helped anybody who was detested by the king of Israel. When David was a fugitive, he was too self-centered to recognize the impure motives of a pagan monarch. Had he possessed clearer vision, he would have known it was better to be protected by Jehovah, than to be assisted by a thousand heathens. Compromise could only lead to calamity.

When news reached David that his former benefactor had died, sadness filled his soul as he said: "I will shew kindness unto Hanun the son of Nahash, as his father shewed kindness unto me" (v. 2). Once again, he never sought the assistance of the priest with the ephod; did he think it unnecessary to ask permission to do something which he considered to be virtuous? He remembered the incident when Nahash exhibited kindness and decided that he would return the favor by offering solace to the son of the deceased ruler. If a metaphor may be used, David was beginning to pet a venomous serpent!

A Foolish Mistake

Unfortunately, the life of David was marred by events of this nature. He was an impulsive king whose enthusiasm sometimes ran away with his brain! It will be seen in a later episode that David planned to conduct a census within his nation. Joab warned him of the consequences of his impulsive act, but the king was stubborn and proceeded with his untimely and foolish plan. This brought upon the nation a terrible tragedy in which innocent people died. That irresponsible monarch ignored all danger signs throughout his career. When God erects warning signals on life's highway, He is not trying to beautify the scenery, but is making a supreme effort to prevent eternal tragedies. Our gracious Lord knows the problems confronting human beings, and because His love is changeless and enduring, He does His utmost to help travelers. The writer to the Hebrews must have had this thought in his mind when he wrote: "How shall we escape, if we neglect so great salvation" (see Hebrews 2:3). Signposts can never prevent accidents if travelers ignore them.

DAVID'S SHAMED MESSENGERS

And the princes of the children of Ammon said unto Hanun their lord, Thinkest thou that David doth honor thy father, that he hath sent comforters unto thee? hath not David rather sent his servants unto thee, to search the city, and to spy it out, and to overthrow it? Wherefore Hanun took David's servants, and shaved off the one half of their beards, and cut off their garments in the middle, even to their buttocks, and sent them away (vv. 3-4).

Expository Notes on the Humiliation of David's Ambassadors

To understand the insulting nature of Hanun's act, it is almost necessary to be a citizen of an eastern country. Among people of the western world, the growing of a beard is a matter of personal choice; to the majority of people, it is insignificant. Among Arabs and Jews, this is not the case.

Dr. John Kitto wrote: "To shave off one side of the beard only was even more ignominious than to remove it altogether, although *that*, among the ancient and modern Eastern nations that cultivate the beard, was an offense not to be named without horror. It is very difficult for us to realize the intense appreciation of, and respect for, the beard which is entertained among Persians, Arabians and other bearded nations. They treat their own beards with respect, suffering no defilement to come near them, and handling them with deliberate care. They bury with solicitude any stray hairs that come from the beard; and to lose it by accident, was worse than the loss of the head itself, which would, in their esteem, become ridiculous and useless without this essential appendage. For any one else to touch a man's beard irreverently, to speak of it lightly, to cast a reproach upon it, was an offense never to be forgotten nor forgiven; but to cut or remove it by violence or stealth, was an affront, a disgrace, a horror, which scarcely the heart's blood of the offender could expiate. All these notions respecting the beard doubtless had their origin in its being the grand mark of distinction between the male and the female face, whence it became the symbol of manly dignity and strength, and the want of it, the sign of weakness and effeminacy" (*Kitto's Daily Bible Illustrations*, vol. 1, p. 763).

It should be remembered that men in the Arab world wore no undergarments. The priests did so in accordance with sacerdotal laws, but ordinary citizens wore a long, flowing robe which covered their entire bodies. This custom still prevails in lands where the weather is uncomfortably hot. The robes help to offset the unpleasantness of heavier clothing. When Hanun cut off the garments of David's ambassadors "even to their buttocks," he made the men the objects of shame and derision. The lower and intimate parts of their bodies were exposed, and although some makeshift covering could have been made from leaves, the fact remained they became objects of shame. David had probably chosen some of his most distinguished friends to be emissaries to the king of Ammon. They were honorable men, but their reception and treatment by that heathen king was deplorable; he gave them the appearance of slaves. This was as insulting as if he had spat in David's face.

DAVID'S STRONG MAN

When they told it unto David, he sent to meet them, because the men were greatly ashamed: and the king said, Tarry at Jericho until your beards be grown, and then return. And when the children of Ammon saw that they stank before David, the children of Ammon sent and hired the Syrians of Beth-rehob, and the Syrians of Zoba, twenty thousand footmen, and of king Maacah a thousand men, and of Ish-tob twelve thousand men. And when David heard of it, he sent Joab, and all the host of the mighty men (vv. 5-7).

Expository Notes on the Value of David's Commander in Chief

The parallel account in 1 Chronicles 19:7 tells that the pagan forces gathered at a place called Medeba. The narrative also suggests that Joab was just in time to prevent the merging of the armies of the Ammonites and the Syrians. He probably realized the combined strength of his enemies might have been too great to overcome; "Joab saw that the front of the battle was against him before and behind" (v. 9). He was caught between the hammer and the anvil, or as Americans would say, "between a rock and a hard place." His experience and strategic excellence stood him in good stead; he never panicked. He calmly assessed the situation and divided his forces. Knowing that the Syrians were the more formidable foe, he took his greatest warriors and instructed them to oppose the enemy from the north. The other soldiers were given to his younger brother Abishai, who was asked to oppose the Ammonites. Joab's final words of exhortation were destined to become immortal. "And he said, If the Syrians be too strong for me, then thou shalt help me: but if the children of Ammon be too strong for thee, then I will come and help thee. *Be of good courage, and let us play the men for our people, and for the cities of our God: and the LORD do that which seemeth him good*" (v. 11, 12). The text may be summarized thus: (1) *His campaign was strategic,* (2) *His confidence was strong,* and (3) *His conquest was superb.*

Joab was not over-confident and did not assume his cause to be pleasing in the sight of God. He was facing a very difficult experience since the odds were against him, but whether he succeeded or failed, he was determined to do his best. If the Lord were pleased to grant victory, he would be profoundly and eternally grateful. If the Lord decided otherwise, he would bow before Jehovah's throne and not complain. "The LORD do that which seemeth him good" (v. 12). Simply expressed, Joab said: "May the will of God be done, for that is all that matters." He was determined to do his best, leave the rest to God, and never worry! All spiritual warriors should remember Joab's words. Worry is sometimes the greatest foe. Christians should always ask, "If the Lord is for us, who can be against us?"

DAVID'S STUPENDOUS MISSION

And when the Syrians saw that they were smitten before Israel, they gathered themselves together. And Hadarezer sent, and brought out the Syrians that were beyond the river: and they came to Helam; and Shobach the captain of the host of Hadarezer went before them. And when it was told David, he gathered all Israel together, and passed over Jordan, and came to Helam. . . . And the Syrians fled before Israel. . . . And when all the kings that were servants to Hadarezer saw that they were smitten before Israel, they made peace with Israel, and served them. So the Syrians feared to help the children of Ammon any more (vv. 15-19).

Expository Notes on David's Conquest of the Syrians

The foolishness of Hanun, the king of the Ammonites, became increasingly evident when many thousands of innocent people died in the battles which followed the abusing of David's ambassadors. When he employed Syrian mercenaries, he stepped into quicksands which ultimately engulfed him. It should be remembered that God's people had little experience in international wars, their neighbors treated them with disdain and insult, and it became necessary for God to teach those pagans an important lesson. When they oppressed the Hebrews, they were challenging the might of Jehovah. Sometimes only a rod of chastening can teach foolish people the error of their ways.

It became evident to David that the Syrian force had been reorganized and strengthened. Powerful allies had joined the army from the north, and under the command of the general, Shobach, the combined armies were planning to renew their offensive. That David decided to lead his own soldiers was not a reflection upon the capabilities of Joab. It was customary for a monarch to assume charge in all conflicts as important as the forthcoming battle at Helam. The fact that David had left the safety of his palace to share dangers and hardships on the field of battle, was a great encouragement for his men. Had there been any deserting soldiers, their presence at home would have indicated treachery, and they would have been shunned for the rest of their lives. If some of the men had grown weary with the conflict, the knowledge of the king's presence restored their desire to "play the men for our people, and for the cities of our God" (v. 12). Everyone knew this would be a battle to the death. If David died, the future of the nation would be in jeopardy, prosperity would terminate, freedom would vanish, and slavery would return. David was wise to accept the Syrian challenge. Had he remained at home, criticism would have nullified the strength of his army.

Episode 29

THEME: *David's Desire for Bath-sheba*

SCRIPTURE: 2 Samuel 11

KEY VERSE:

> And when the mourning was past, David sent and fetched her to his house, and she became his wife, and bare him a son. But the thing that David had done displeased the LORD (v. 27).

OUTLINE:
    I.   David Is Tempted (Verses 1-5)
   II.   David Is Thwarted (Verses 6-13)
  III.   David Is Treacherous (Verses 14-25)
  IV.   David Is Tarnished (Verses 26-27)

DAVID IS TEMPTED

And it came to pass in an eveningtide, that David arose from off his bed, and walked upon the roof of the king's house: and from the roof he saw a woman washing herself; and the woman was very beautiful to look upon. And David sent and enquired after the woman. And one said, Is not this Bath-sheba, the daughter of Eliam, the wife of Uriah the Hittite? And David sent messengers and took her; and she came in unto him, and he lay with her; for she was purified from her uncleanness: and she returned unto her house (vv. 2-4).

Expository Notes on David's Desire for Bath-sheba

It was late in the afternoon when David, arising from his bed, walked on the roof of his palace, where the gentle breezes offered relief from the oppressive heat of the eastern midday. He suddenly paused and stared as "he saw a woman washing herself; and the woman was very beautiful to look upon." That moment introduced the saddest incident in the life of King David, a calamity from which he never recovered. It was significant that there was thereafter no mention of any outstanding exploit; David's usefulness ended long before he died! He reached the height of his career, but afterward difficulties of every kind beset him. His family was torn by several discordant events: the rape of Tamar, the insurrection of Absalom, the deaths of Amnon and Adonijah—all of which were heartaches for which he was indirectly responsible. The terrible example set before his family disrupted his own life and ruined the happiness of his home. David became infamous for his excessive desire for sexual partners, and permissiveness finally led to his downfall. God's grace forgave his sin, but the historian could find nothing of merit to include in the remaining part of the royal biography. David sacrificed usefulness upon the altar of lust.

The king was surrounded by women, but was never satisfied. He had the ability to do many things, but he unfortunately never denied himself. All eastern men carefully guarded their wives, but it probably never occurred to Uriah and Bath-sheba that the private apartments of their home could be seen from the roof of the nearby palace.

When David looked upon the unsuspecting woman, an unholy fire commenced to burn within his soul. Had he denied his carnal instincts and turned away, he would have prevented the greatest tragedy of his career. He unfortunately remained motionless until the flames of desire had consumed his intelligence. "And David sent messengers and took her." It is difficult to interpret the statement "and took her." Was she taken by force or was she persuaded to accept David's summons and obey his command? Did she object to what was done? What was thought to be the "Divine Right of Kings" was seldom challenged, but if Bath-sheba resisted David's amorous advances, the king's guilt increased immeasurably. Years later, Solomon asked very important questions. "Can a man take fire in his bosom, and his clothes not be burned? Can one go upon hot coals, and his feet not be burned? So he that goeth in to his neighbor's wife; whosoever toucheth her shall not be innocent" (Proverbs 6:27-29). Solomon was given wisdom by God, but the question might be asked: "Did he learn some of his insights from his father's experience?" David allowed fire to burn within his soul until his entire life was singed; he trod upon hot coals of destructive passion until his walk with God was seriously hindered.

DAVID IS THWARTED

And David sent to Joab, saying, Send me Uriah the Hittite. And Joab sent Uriah to David. . . . And David said to Uriah, Go down to thine house and wash thy feet. . . . But Uriah slept at the door of the king's house with all the servants of his lord, and went not down to his house. And when they had told David, saying, Uriah went not down unto his house, David said unto Uriah, Camest thou not from thy journey? why then didst thou not go down unto thine house? And Uriah said unto David, The ark, and Israel, and Judah, abide in tents; and my lord Joab, and the servants of my lord, are encamped in the open fields; shall I then go down to my house, to eat and to drink, and to lie with my wife? as

thou livest, and as thy soul liveth, I will not do this thing. . . . and [David] made him drunk (vv. 6-13).

Expository Notes on David's Repeated Frustration

The news that Bath-sheba was an expectant mother filled David with dismay. Her husband was one of the nation's heroes; he was one of the king's "mighty men" (see 2 Samuel 23:39). It would be disastrous for public relations if news of Bath-sheba's conception became known. David considered his problem and smiled; there was a way by which his adultery could be hidden. Uriah should be given leave of absence from the army to enjoy time with his wife. If this were done quickly, Bath-sheba's neighbors would assume that her husband fathered her child. David exhibited no remorse; he probably believed that he was clever in being able to hide his transgression. Had he succeeded in carrying out his plan, he would have seized every opportunity to repeat his immorality.

A better translation of the statement "for she was purified from her uncleanness" would be "and when she had purified herself from her uncleanness." This supplies an insight into the woman's faith and character. Evidently, Bath-sheba was aware of the Mosaic commandments which said: "The woman also with whom man shall lie with seed of copulation, they shall both bathe themselves in water, and be unclean until the even" (Leviticus 15:18). Uriah's wife evidently knew she had become unclean, but scrupulously fulfilled the legal requirements. Her body was cleansed, but her soul remained contaminated. Perhaps she was afraid, for her action was punishable by death (see Leviticus 20:10). Had her crime been revealed, the consequences in Israel could have been revolutionary. Strictly speaking, both David and Bath-sheba deserved death by stoning. David could have pardoned himself and the woman, but had this happened, it would have been a serious violation of the law. When Uriah refused to do as David suggested, the guilty couple became frightened because their predicament was serious. Therefore, something had to be done quickly.

DAVID IS TREACHEROUS

And it came to pass in the morning, that David wrote a letter to Joab, and sent it by the hand of Uriah. And he wrote in the letter, saying, Set ye Uriah in the forefront of the hottest battle, and retire ye from him, that he may be smitten, and die (vv. 14-15).

Expository Notes on David's Complicity in the Murder of Uriah

The direction given by David to Joab was nothing short of premeditated murder. The Ammonites had retired into their city and were prepared to withstand a seige. Joab, a skilled commander, knew where their greatest warriors were stationed, but it was recorded for posterity that "the men of the city went out, and fought with Joab: and there fell some of the people of the servants of David; and Uriah the Hittite died also" (v. 17). Joab obeyed his orders as a man in his position was expected to do. He was aware that the Hittite had fallen out of the king's favor, but whether or not he knew the reason for the execution is not revealed. Maybe he was aware of David's misconduct, for the men who had identified the beautiful woman would not preserve the king's secret. Twelve months later after the birth of the child, David apparently had no remorse within his soul. It was only after the prophet Nathan had denounced the insensitive monarch that David admitted his guilt. The king repented of his sin and expressed sorrow in writing Psalm 51. Nevertheless, neither the writing of a psalm nor tears upon his face could bring back an innocent man whom he had murdered. When Uriah fell outside the walls of the Ammonite city, David also began to die, but his death was long and very painful. He was compelled to live with a conscience which never slept!

DAVID IS TARNISHED

And when the wife of Uriah heard that Uriah her husband was dead, she mourned for her husband. And when the mourning was past, David sent and fetched her to his house, and she became his wife, and bare him a son. But the thing that David had done displeased the LORD (vv. 26-27).

Expository Notes on David's Ruined Testimony

David was the proud owner of everything—except honor. His possessions were enormous, many of his friends remained faithful, and God eventually gave to him a son whom he named Solomon. Yet, the serenity which superseded all material treasures had disappeared. He wrote many beautiful psalms, but his nightmare would not go away; it haunted him through the rest of his life. Had he been able to relive the past, he might have avoided the pitfall into which he fell. Even when he tried to pray, the memory of his detestable deed filled his thoughts. If another man had committed the same sin, David would have ordered his execution. Alas, he had wandered so far from God, he knew no remorse. When Nathan delivered his startling parable, the king failed even then to recognize its implications. Cataracts of lust had ruined his vision, destroyed his influence, and banished his serenity.

Once again the question arises: What had happened to the innocent lad who fearlessly accepted the challenge of the Philistine giant? David was a much better child than he ever was a man. He ceased looking into the face of Jehovah because it was more desirable to watch beautiful women. His failures should be warnings to every servant of God. It is difficult to understand how a man of whom it was written, "And the Lord preserved David whithersoever he went" (2 Sam. 8:6, 14), could be so foolish.

HOMILIES FOR PREACHERS AND TEACHERS

Study No. 13

THE WEAKNESSES OF GOD'S GREAT MEN

With the exception of Joseph and Elisha, God's great servants, in one way or another, exhibited weakness. Often the men who climbed to the highest heights of moral and spiritual excellence, fell into the deepest depths of shameful degradation. Yet, in some mysterious way, God with His untiring patience used those disappointing people to perform the impossible. The Bible supplies numerous examples of this truth.

MOSES . . . The Meekest of All Men Who Lost His Temper

"Now the man Moses was very meek, above all the men which were upon the face of the earth" (Numbers 12:3). Nevertheless, beneath his serenity lay a volcanic soul which was capable of erupting with blazing anger. The patriarch was exasperated; his people vexed his soul. They were ungrateful and critical. God had brought them from Egypt and had supplied their needs. Yet, as the days passed, they seized every opportunity to find fault with what had been accomplished. They were thirsty; they demanded that Moses supply water to quench their thirst; their faces were scowling. Moses had reached the end of his patience. Then God instructed him *to speak to a rock* from which water would flow. But Moses was greatly disturbed, and his anger suddenly became evident. He took his rod and *smote the rock twice*, "and the water came out abundantly, and the congregation drank, and their beasts also" (see Numbers 20:10-12). That solitary mistake prevented his entry into the promised land.

Afterward, as generation succeeded generation, God used the act of disobedience to enrich and teach His people. When Hebrew mothers told stories to their children, they spoke of the man to whom the nation owed everything. Boys and girls were enthralled when they heard that Moses defied Pharaoh and delivered the captives, but the mothers always said: "But he never came into this land. He disobeyed the Lord." Thus did God succeed in teaching His people, "To obey is better than sacrifice" (see 1 Samuel 15:22).

ELIJAH . . . The Bravest Man, Who Became a Coward

He stood alone against a king, a nation, and hundreds of men who desired his death. Yet, he never flinched; he was a man of steel who feared Jehovah and nobody else! During a long period of three and a half years he had been the most wanted man in Israel. He had predicted an approaching drought, but embittered people now blamed him for the calamity which had devastated the nation. Elijah stood calmly before the assembled host. His eyes flashed as defiant tones awed his listeners. He was God's man, and he meant business! When life-giving rain began to fall, the people prostrated themselves, but the dauntless prophet had not completed what he desired to say. Those false prophets, the real enemies of the nation, deserved to die. "And Elijah said . . . Take the prophets of Baal; let not one of them escape. And they took them: and Elijah brought them down to the brook Kishon, and slew them there" (1 Kings 18:40). "Then Jezebel sent a messenger unto Elijah, saying, So let the gods do to me, and more also, if I make not thy life as the life of one of them by to morrow about this time. And when he saw that, he arose, and went for his life" (see 1 Kings 19:2-3). Poor Elijah! The queen's threat ruined his faith in God, and demoralized, he fled. That terrible mistake terminated his ministry; his preaching had ended. Had he tried again to exhort Israel, the scoffers would have asked, "Why did you not practice your own preaching?" Elijah's ministry went up in flames!

DAVID . . . *Who Failed to Kill a Giant*

The king of Israel was a great warrior; his training in schools of combat had made him an expert protagonist. He began showing his fighting skill when he was a lad by killing Goliath, but his subsequent successes made him notorious. His invasion of adjacent countries filled neighbors with dread.

Yet, that famous soldier was his own greatest enemy. There existed within his heart a foe called lust who was clever, ruthless, and untiring. The famous psalmist of Israel, who wrote, "One thing have I desired of the LORD, that will I seek after; that I may dwell in the house of the LORD all the days of my life, to behold the beauty of the LORD, and to enquire in his temple" (Psalm 27:4), suddenly produced music of another kind. Turning his back on the sanctuary "he saw a woman washing herself; and the woman was very beautiful to look upon" (2 Samuel 11:2). David was soon fighting for his life; with fingers of steel, a giant had gripped his soul. The battle was unfortunately lost before it commenced. David had no desire to struggle because he had already been mesmerized by a woman's body. Soon his soul was stained with the blood of murder, his happiness disappeared, and his future became exceedingly bleak. Emulating the act of an ancient ancestor, he sold his birthright for a mess of pottage (see Genesis 25:29-34).

The scriptures supply other examples of the same type. Simon Peter, the over-confident man, disowned his Lord. Paul, the determined missionary, allowed his personal desires to overrule God's instructions (see Acts 21:4). The prophet Jonah refused to obey God's command. It would be easy to condemn these fallen giants, but they remind people that the higher a man climbs, the greater may be his fall (see 1 Corinthians 10:12).

Episode 30

THEME: *David's Confrontation With Nathan, the Prophet*

SCRIPTURE: 2 Samuel 12:1-25

KEY VERSE:

> And David said unto Nathan, I have sinned against the LORD. And Nathan said unto David, The LORD also hath put away thy sin; thou shalt not die (v. 13).

OUTLINE:
- I. A Prophet's Parable (Verses 1-6)
- II. A Publicized Punishment (Verses 7-12)
- III. A Pitiful Plea (Verses 13-19)
- IV. A Painful Practicality (Verses 20-23)
- V. A Personal Pleasure (Verses 24-25)

A PROPHET'S PARABLE

And the LORD sent Nathan unto David. And he came unto him, and said unto him, There were two men in one city; the one rich, and the other poor. The rich man had exceeding many flocks and herds: but the poor man had nothing, save one little ewe lamb. . . . And there came a traveler unto the rich man, and he spared to take of his own flock . . . but took the poor man's lamb, and dressed it for the man that was come to him. And David's anger was greatly kindled against the man; and he said to Nathan, As the LORD liveth, the man that hath done this thing shall surely die (vv. 1-5).

Expository Notes on Nathan's Message to David

Almost a year had passed since David made his fatal mistake. Bathsheba had given birth to her child, and the king had reflected upon his deed. Yet, there was unfortunately neither any indication of his repentance nor any sign of remorse in anything he did or said. Matthew Henry wrote of this period, "It seems to have been a great while after David had committed adultery with Bath-sheba before he was brought to repentance. For, when Nathan was sent to him, the child was born. What shall we think of David's state all this while? We may well suppose his comforts and the exercises of his graces were suspended and his communion with God interrupted. During all that time . . . he penned no psalms; his harp was out of tune, and his soul like a tree in winter, had life in the root only" (*Matthew Henry's Commentary*, vol. 2, pp. 499-500).

"And the Lᴏʀᴅ sent Nathan unto David." Seldom, if ever, does a lost sheep search for a shepherd. That God sent a prophet to speak with David indicates the indestructibility of divine compassion. Paul was correct when he wrote, "For I am persuaded, that neither death, nor life, nor angels, nor principalities, nor powers, nor things present, nor things to come, nor height, nor depth, nor any other creature, shall be able to separate us from the love of God, which is in Christ Jesus our Lord" (Romans 8:38-39). Nathan was a worthy representative of Jehovah. There were three outstanding characteristics in his ministry.

His Faithfulness

He was commissioned by God to perform a special task. Nathan was David's friend, but it was obvious that he was nearer to God than to the ruler of Israel. The prophet only visited David, but he lived with God! The presence of the Almighty was his natural habitat. He existed to serve Jehovah, and all his commissions were accepted gladly and gratefully. True prophets are alike. The success of their missions suggests that they listen to the voice of the Lord before they meet their congregations. It was said of the Lord's forerunner, "There was a man sent from God, whose name was John" (see John 1:6). Every preacher of the gospel should be able to claim that distinction.

His Fearlessness

The preacher who fears God should never fear anyone else. It should be remembered that David was both judge and jury in Israel. His word was authoritative since he held in his hands the power of life and death. The king had sinned, but apparently had never been disturbed by guilt. Almost a year had passed since he committed adultery with Bath-sheba, but he had done nothing to demonstrate any repentance for murdering her husband. If David had become indifferent to the commandments of Jehovah, he could have fiercely resented interference from a preacher. David was capable of great anger, and his impulsive decisions frequently brought suffering to his people. Had Nathan considered the consequences of his denouncing the king, he would have recognized the possibility of an imminent execution. Nathan was unafraid because his life was in the hands of the Almighty, and with that assurance, he went to fulfill his mission. When a preacher becomes afraid of offending an influential man in his audience, he ceases to be a prophet.

His Friendliness

Solomon wrote, "Faithful are the wounds of a friend; but the kisses of an enemy are deceitful" (Proverbs 27:6). If David ever informed his son about the visit of Nathan, Solomon probably recalled the incident when he remembered that Nathan said, "Thou art the man." God's servant was not vindictive when he confronted his royal master. True friends never gloat over the failures of other people. If they are obliged to criticize their comrades, they do so with a sob in their voice. If they find it necessary to chastise a friend, the hand that holds the rod is controlled by tenderness. Nathan detested the king's sin, but he loved David.

Similarly, there was a compelling charm about the Savior. His hearers knew that He loved everybody; His face, eyes, hands, and words were vehicles by which compassion reached out to everybody. To follow that glorious example is the greatest privilege ever bestowed upon men and women.

Nathan's illustration was easily understood. Throughout the western world, families care for a dog or a cat, but since dogs are considered unclean in the Middle East, many Bedouins rear a lamb, which becomes a beloved member of the family. The prophet's description of the stingy landowner aroused David's anger to such an extent that he denounced the offender as a criminal. It is written: "And David's anger was greatly kindled against the man; and he said to Nathan, As the LORD liveth, the man that hath done this thing, shall surely die: And he shall restore the lamb fourfold, because he did this thing, and because he had no pity" (vv. 5-6). David was referring to the law which said: "If a man shall steal an ox, or a sheep, and kill it, or sell it; he shall restore five oxen for an ox, and four sheep for a sheep" (Exodus 22:1). Had the man been executed, he would have been unable to make restitution for his crime. A better translation of David's statement would be: "He is worthy of death; he is a beast who should die."

When Nathan calmly said, "Thou art the man" (v. 7), the king was appalled. Perhaps that was the first time he became aware of his guilt. It remains incomprehensible that David could listen to Nathan's parable and be ignorant of its veiled insinuations. Had twelve months of indifference bred callousness? Had he become so accustomed to his situation that it no longer troubled him? The prophet's denunciation was the touch of a surgeon's scalpel which released poisonous pus from an infected soul.

A PUBLICIZED PUNISHMENT

Wherefore hast thou despised the commandment of the LORD, to do evil in his sight? thou hast killed Uriah the Hittite with the sword, and hast taken his wife to be thy wife, and hast slain him with the sword of the children of Ammon. Now therefore the sword shall never depart from thine house. . . . and I will take thy wives before thine eyes, and give

them unto thy neighbor, and he shall lie with thy wives in the sight of this sun. For thou didst it secretly: but I will do this thing before all Israel, and before the sun (vv. 9-12).

Expository Notes on God's Predicted Punishment of David

It should be remembered that at the time of Nathan's confrontation with David, Israel was a stage upon which a great drama was being viewed by a national audience. One of the charges made against the king was as follows: "Thou hast given great occasion to the enemies of the LORD to blaspheme" (v. 14). There was more at stake than David's survival. The law stated, "And the man that committeth adultery with another man's wife, even he that committeth adultery with his neighbor's wife, the adulterer and the adultcress *shall surely be put to death*" (Leviticus 20:10). If the king escaped while others guilty of a similar offense died, people could have complained of unfairness. It is true that Jehovah is above all law and that He is the supreme Judge, but even He has to honor His commandments. It is safe to assume that every family in Israel watched closely as the problem in the palace was resolved by God's representative.

Insurmountable Suffering

"Thou hast . . . slain [Uriah] with the sword of the children of Ammon. Now therefore the sword shall never depart from thine house; because thou hast despised me, and taken the wife of Uriah the Hittite to be thy wife" (vv. 9,10). If an illustration may be used, David had disturbed a colony of wild bees and as a consequence was to be stung throughout the rest of his life. Henceforth he would not defend his country against heathen nations, but would be besieged by enemies of a different type. The first of God's judgments indicated that as a sword had destroyed Uriah's home, so it would cause endless suffering within David's family. To paraphrase a modern proverb, his own chicken would return home to roost. David was destined to remember that terrible prediction. The rape of the beautiful Tamar by her half-brother Amnon, his subsequent slaying by Absalom, the rebellion of Absalom and the problems which arose from his insurrection, and the heartaches which accompanied Adonijah's desire to be king supply indisputable evidence that David's error had far-reaching effects. He was responsible for continuing disasters.

Indescribable Shame

"Thus saith the LORD . . . I will take thy wives before thine eyes, and give them unto thy neighbor, *and he shall lie with thy wives in the sight of this sun* [—*openly, publicly, for all men to see*]. For thou didst it secretly, but I will do this thing before all Israel, and before the sun" (vv. 11-12).

Later a counselor named Ahithophel gave the following advice to Absalom: "Go in unto thy father's concubines, which he hath left to keep the house; and all Israel shall hear that thou art abhorred of thy father: then shall the hands of all that are with thee be strong. So they spread Absalom a tent upon the top of the house; and Absalom went in unto his father's concubines in the sight of all Israel" (2 Samuel 16:21-22). It may never be known how great was David's shame and anger when he heard of the events in Jerusalem. Gossip traveled fast, and soon all the Hebrews discussed Absalom's defiance. Many people doubtless laughed, but others felt pity for the fugitive monarch who had lost everything. The wheels of God grind slowly, but they grind exceeding small.

Inescapable Sorrow

"The child also that is born unto thee shall surely die" (v. 14). Perhaps this became the heaviest of all David's burdens. When the king confessed his guilt, the prophet replied, "The LORD also hath put away thy sin; thou shalt not die" (v. 13). Dr. Adam Clarke suggested that there might have been a very remarkable revelation in Nathan's statement. He translated this scripture thus: "And Jehovah hath caused thy sin to pass over, or transferred thy sin, thou shalt not die. And this . . . is the very point on which the prophet gives him the most direct information. 'The child that is born unto you shall surely die—dying, he shall die'" (*The Bethany Parallel Commentary on the Old Testament*, p. 596).

There may be value in that suggestion. The belief that guilt could be transferred was accepted in Israel. On the Day of Atonement, the sin of the nation was thought to be "passed over" to a scapegoat, which was then led into the wilderness. No scapegoat was ever found again, and in that way God taught His people the necessity for an offering for sin. If the Lord placed David's guilt upon the child, that transfer, at least would have been considered a just decision and would have been interpreted as forgiveness for a man who was genuinely repentant. When David grieved for his ailing child, he was reminded of the sadness his crime had brought to Jehovah.

A PITIFUL PLEA

David therefore besought God for the child; and David fasted, and went in, and lay all night upon the earth. . . . And it came to pass on the seventh day, that the child died. And the servants of David feared to tell him that the child was dead. . . . But when David saw that his servants whispered, David perceived that the child was dead: therefore David said unto his servants, Is the child dead? And they said, He is dead (vv. 16-19).

Expository Notes on God's Refusal to Grant David's Request

It was at this time that David wrote: "For I acknowledge my transgres-

sions: and my sin is ever before me" (Psalm 51:3). It was probably during
the same period that he wrote: "For mine iniquities are gone over my head:
as an heavy burden they are too heavy for me. My wounds stink and are
corrupt because of my foolishness. I am troubled; I am bowed down
greatly; I go mourning all the day long. For my loins are filled with a
loathsome disease: and there is no soundness in my flesh" (Psalm 38:4-7).

It is strange that David prayed for the recovery of his child when God
had specifically stated the boy would die. There are three reasons why God
could not grant his request.

God Cannot Condone Sin

The fact that David was the king of Israel could not obliterate his guilt.
God was not a respecter of persons. The king had deliberately violated
God's law, and divine justice demanded the punishment of the offender.
Neither wealth nor fame can guarantee forgiveness. Even though God's
love for David remained unchanged, His righteousness demanded retribu-
tion.

God Cannot Give Peace to an Unrepentant Sinner

The Creator installed within every human being a self-monitoring system called conscience. It was destined to be a warning device to protect
and preserve man from evil. The by-product of that mental machinery is
conviction, which is a voice which cannot be silenced and a critic to
destroy complacency. It reveals God's way of reminding man of things he
would like to forget. David had committed murder and had perhaps tried to
banish the incident from his thoughts. He had probably known sleepless
days and nights when he preferred death to life. Nothing could silence the
accusing voice, and even God could not prevent the king's misery.

God Cannot Break His Promises

The Word of God is not only given as a guide to sinful men; it is also
the standard by which Jehovah is to be known. If the Almighty violates
His commandments, He can hardly expect obedience from His subjects.
The writer to the Hebrews stated: "Wherein God, willing more abundantly
to shew unto the heirs of promise the immutability of his counsel, confirmed
it by an oath: that by two immutable things, in which it was impossible for
God to lie, we might have a strong consolation, who have fled for refuge to
lay hold upon the hope set before us" (Hebrews 6:17-18). God is rich in
mercy, but repentance and faith are the twin keys which open the door of
His treasure house. Without them, man's efforts are vain.

A PAINFUL PRACTICALITY

Then David arose from the earth, and washed, and anointed himself, and changed his apparel, and came into the house of the LORD, and worshipped: then he came to his own house; and when he required, they set bread before him, and he did eat. Then said his servants unto him, What thing is this that thou hast done? thou didst fast and weep for the child, while it was alive; but when the child was dead, thou didst rise and eat bread. And he said, While the child was yet alive, I fasted and wept: for I said, Who can tell whether God will be gracious to me, that the child may live? But now he is dead, wherefore should I fast? can I bring him back again? I shall go to him, but he shall not return to me (vv. 20-23).

Expository Notes on David's Change of Attitude

It seems strange that David should change so suddenly. His servants and friends were amazed when he went from grief to intense gratitude and joy. Dr. R. Payne Smith supplies an excellent summary of the reasons for David's behavior. "If David's grief had been occasioned by love for the child, then its death, and the consciousness that, while his guilt had caused its sickness, his prayers had not availed to save it would have aggravated his anguish. There was much personal regard for the child, which had been made the more precious by these events. But David's sorrow was . . . that of penitence and not that of natural affection. *When, therefore, the threatened penalty had been paid by the death of the child* [emphasis mine], David felt it to be his duty to shew his resignation, and, therefore, he went into the sanctuary and worshipped in proof that he acknowledged the justice of God's dealings, and was content to bear the punishment as his righteous desert." (*The Pulpit Commentary*, vol. 4, p. 289).

David's statement supplies an insight into his faith. He believed in the immortality of the soul and expressed confidence that he and his child would meet again beyond the grave. It should be remembered that the New Testament revelation had not been given and that there was no convincing teaching regarding survival. Job expressed the normal belief of the people when he described death as the end of all trouble when he said: "Why died I not from the womb? . . . for now should I have lain still and been quiet . . . then had I been at rest. . . . *There the wicked cease from troubling; and there the weary be at rest*" (see Job 3:11-17). Job expressed the belief that death was a termination—the end of life's road. Yet, through the experiences which overwhelmed him, he discovered a greater fact. Later he exclaimed confidently: "For I know that my redeemer liveth, and that he shall stand at the latter day upon the earth: *and though . . . worms destroy this body, yet in my flesh shall I see God*" (see Job 19:25-26). Both Job and David evidently discovered the same truth. The grave was a tunnel to another world! Centuries before Paul wrote his epistles, the patriarchs could have said, "O death, where is thy sting? O grave, where is thy victory?" (see 1 Corinthians 15:55).

A PERSONAL PLEASURE

And David comforted Bath-sheba his wife, and went in unto her, and lay with her: and she bare a son, and he called his name Solomon: and the Lord loved him. And he sent by the hand of Nathan the prophet; and he called his name Jedidiah, because of the Lord (vv. 24-25).

Expository Notes on the Birth of Solomon

It is thought-provoking that the ancient historian made no mention of the lapse of time between the death of the unnamed child and the birth of Solomon. At first glance it might be assumed that the comfort offered by David included the birth of Solomon, which happened within a year of the loss of their first baby. This supposition is not possible. Bath-sheba gave birth to four additional children, and Solomon was her last child (see 1 Chronicles 3:5). Why her fourth son should be chosen to succeed David remains an inscrutable mystery. The possibility exists that during the intervening years, suffering and meditation prepared both parents for the time when into their lives would come a child specially acceptable to God. There may or may not be significance in the fact that David and Bath-sheba decided to call the new arrival Solomon, a word which means "peacefulness". Perhaps this indicates that David had found a peace which had been elusive for several years. On the other hand, it might have expressed the fact that an era of tranquillity had commenced for the nation.

It was written that "the Lord loved him." God, who had witnessed the birth of every child, saw something special in the baby who enriched David's life. When the Lord saw the tiny fingers and toes; the chubby legs; the wide, staring eyes; and perhaps some hair on his head, God's heart was stirred. Maybe that baby reminded Him of earlier days when David had been young and innocent. When the prophet arrived to give the child another name, the proud parents surely asked why Solomon should be called Jedidiah. The servant of God might have replied, "He is beloved of the Lord." Even the angels might have smiled approvingly if they were permitted to see the new baby cradled in the arms of his adoring mother.

Episode 31

THEME: David Completes the Capture of Rabbah

SCRIPTURE: 2 Samuel 12:26-31

KEY VERSE:

> Now therefore gather the rest of the people together, and encamp against the city, and take it: lest I take the city, and it be called after my name (v. 28).

OUTLINE:
    I.   The Conquest of the City (Verse 26)
    II. The Concern of the Captain (Verses 27-28)
    III. The Capture of the Crown (Verses 29-30)
    IV. The Condemnation of the Captives (Verse 31)

THE CONQUEST OF THE CITY

And Joab fought against Rabbah of the children of Ammon, and took the royal city (v. 26).

Expository Notes on the Conquest of Rabbah

This episode in the life of David should be examined carefully. For example, the battle against the Ammonite city may have taken place before Nathan's visit to David. Most theologians believe that the historian, having commenced his story of the indiscretion of the king, decided to complete his account before reverting to other historical events. Between the fall of David and his being rebuked by Nathan were approximately twelve months in which many things could have taken place. The murder of Uriah did not end the siege of Rabbah; that campaign evidently continued, so that what is about to be considered may have happened during the time David was in Jerusalem. The ongoing siege of the Ammonites continued until the royal city was captured. The pagan stronghold had two sections: a lower area known as "the city of waters" and the citadel, which was famous for its fortifications. The palace of the heathen king and the pagan temple in which was the idol Milcom, the god of the Ammonites, were both in the upper area. The lower section was built around the river Jabbok and was known as "the water city" because it supplied the entire district with water. Joab had evidently cut off the supplies of water, and it was only a matter of time before the defenders would be compelled to surrender.

THE CONCERN OF THE CAPTAIN

> **And Joab sent messengers to David, and said, I have fought against Rabbah, and have taken the city of waters. Now therefore gather the rest of the people together, and encamp against the city, and take it: lest I take the city, and it be called after my name (vv. 27-28).**

Expository Notes on Joab's Request to David

Joab's message to David is thought-provoking. If the king were troubled by his conscience, the request from his commander in chief provided a welcome distraction; it gave him something else about which to think and an opportunity to quiet his thoughts with aggressive action against his enemies. Josephus wrote: "But Joab sorely distressed the Ammonites in the seige by cutting off their waters, and depriving them of the means of subsistence, till they were in the greatest want of meat and drink, for they depended only on one small well of water, and this they durst not drink of too freely, lest the fountain should entirely fail them." (*See The Antiquities of the Jews*. Book 7, Chapter 7, Paragraph 5.) The citadel was evidently supplied with water from the lower area, and when Joab severed that lifeline, its defenders encountered insurmountable obstacles. Joab knew this fact and, believing that the end of his campaign was imminent, sent for David. Perhaps the final assault needed additional soldiers, and David was requested to bring reinforcements. Joab suspected that his popularity with the king had been undermined and also knew that David feared and distrusted him. The monarch had earlier dismissed his commander, and Joab only regained his rank by capturing the city of Jerusalem. Their friendship had been deteriorating, and this might have been an attempt, by a very shrewd man, to increase his influence in the palace. If this observation is true, the scheme only brought temporary relief. Neither David nor Joab trusted each other, so that, although many of the warnings issued by Joab were sincere and justified, the king unfortunately resented everything his general suggested. The result was that David ultimately arranged his commander's execution.

THE CAPTURE OF THE CROWN

> **And David gathered all the people together, and went to Rabbah, and fought against it, and took it. And he took their king's crown from off his head, the weight whereof was a talent of gold with the precious stones: and it was set on David's head. And he brought forth the spoil of the city in great abundance (vv. 29-30).**

Expository Notes About the Crown of the Ammonite King

The British Museum displays a two-talent weight from Lagash which weighs 133 1/2 pounds. According to this, a calculation of almost sixty-seven pounds for the crown would have made it too heavy to wear. It has been suggested that since the city of Rabbah contained the temple of the heathen god, this crown was suspended above the head of the idol. Others think that it was suspended above the head of the king and that it was ultimately transferred, at least for a short time, to the head of David. The commentators Jamieson, Fausset, and Brown wrote: "Its great weight makes it probable that it was like many ancient crowns, not worn, but suspended over the head, or fixed on a canopy at the top of the throne." Another commentator Adam Clarke believed that the talent signified a weight of approximately seven pounds and that the crown was literally worn by the monarch. It had an insert of precious stones, which was removed and placed permanently into the crown of David. It is significant that although David permitted his men to share in the spoils of war, he retained for himself the crown as an indication that he had become the supreme ruler of the region.

THE CONDEMNATION OF THE CAPTIVES

And he brought forth the people that were therein, and put them under saws, and under harrows of iron, and under axes of iron, and made them pass through the brickkiln: and thus did he unto all the cities of the children of Ammon. So David and all the people returned unto Jerusalem (v. 31).

Expository Notes on the Fate of the Ammonite Prisoners

The parallel passage in 1 Chronicles 20:3 says: "And he brought out the people that were in it, *and cut them with saws, and with harrows of iron, and with axes.*" If this statement is literally accurate, then it would appear that David had become an enraged monster who was venting his frustration and guilt on the prisoners captured at Rabbah. Another explanation deserves consideration. The statement "he put them under saws" can be interpreted as "he put them to work" under saws and axes. The *Amplified Bible* translates the passage as follows: "He brought forth the people that were there, *and put them to work with saws and iron threshing-sledges, and axes, and made them labor at the brickkiln.*" Josephus, however, expressed the other view by writing, "After David had tortured them, he put them to death." David probably subjugated the Ammonites and consigned them to labor in what had become an extension of his kingdom. Had he annihilated the entire population, there would have been no material gain in his conquest. A precedent had been provided by Joshua, for when the Gibeonites tricked him into the making of a covenant, Joshua said, "Now therefore ye are cursed, and there shall none of you be freed from being bondmen, and hewers of wood and drawers of water for the house of my God" (Joshua 9:23). It is difficult to be dogmatic about the details of David's treatment of prisoners, but to say the least, it would be refreshing to believe that the king of Israel manifested the kindness and mercy about which he wrote so eloquently in his psalms.

Episode 32

THEME: David's Weakness in Dealing With Amnon

SCRIPTURE: 2 Samuel 13

KEY VERSE:

But when king David heard of all these things, he was very wroth (v. 21).

OUTLINE:
  I.   A Deceptive Prince (Verses 1-7)
  II. A Devastated Princess (Verses 8-19)
  III. A Deadly Purpose (Verses 20-29)
  IV. A Disturbed Parent (Verses 30-39)

A DECEPTIVE PRINCE

And it came to pass after this, that Absalom the son of David had a fair sister, whose name was Tamar; and Amnon the son of David loved her. And Amnon was so vexed, that he fell sick for his sister Tamar; for she was a virgin. . . . But Amnon had a friend whose name was Jonadab. . . . And Jonadab said unto him, Lay thee down on thy bed, and make thyself sick. . . . So Amnon lay down, and made himself sick: and when the king was come to see him, Amnon said unto the king, I pray thee, let Tamar my sister come, and make me a couple of cakes in my sight, that I may eat at her hand. Then David sent home to Tamar, saying, Go now to thy brother Amnon's house, and dress him meat (vv. 1-7).

Expository Notes on Amnon's Deception

This story, one of the saddest episodes in the life of David, began the fulfillment of God's prediction that "the sword shall never depart from thine house" (see 2 Samuel 12:10). The tragedy might have been avoided, but David's guilt impaired his wisdom.

Prince Amnon was the heir to the throne and the first-born in David's family. His mother's name was Ahinoam, a Jezreelitess (see 2 Samuel 3:2). This young man had become obsessed with a passionate desire for his half-sister Tamar, the daughter of Maacah, whom David married in Hebron.

This very attractive princess was probably about sixteen or seventeen years of age and exceedingly charming. Her brother Absalom was very protective of his younger sister and evidently was aware of the danger which could beset a woman of her rank and charm. Absalom was possibly jealous of his half-brother Amnon, who apparently would become the next king of Israel. Unmarried princesses wore garments of bright colors, a custom which signified their eminence. No males were permitted to visit the women's apartments unless by special permission, and they always had to be accompanied by chaperons. These laws were known throughout Israel, and any man who violated them was considered to be a fool (see v. 13).

When lustful desires began to dominate Amnon, his physical condition deteriorated, and a friend named Jonadab, recognizing the symptoms, suggested a plan by which the prince could be satisfied. The scheme was disgusting and abominable, for no consideration was given to the gravity of the crime or to the anguish that would result. Amnon unfortunately had no conscience since he was acquainted with the moral laxity of his father and saw no harm in emulating David's example. Had David been a better father, his sons probably would not have caused so many heartaches.

A DEVASTATED PRINCESS

> So Tamar went to her brother Amnon's house; and he was laid down. And she took flour and kneeded it, and made cakes in his sight. . . . And she took a pan, and poured them out before him. . . . he took hold of her, and said unto her, Come lie with me, my sister. And she answered him, Nay, my brother, do not force me; for no such thing ought to be done in Israel. . . . Howbeit he would not hearken unto her voice: but, being stronger than she, forced her, and lay with her. Then Amnon hated her exceedingly. . . . Then he called his servant that ministered unto him, and said, Put now this woman out from me, and bolt the door after her. . . . And Tamar put ashes on her head, and rent her garment of divers colors that was on her, and laid her hand on her head, and went on crying (vv. 8-19).

Expository Notes on the Rape of Tamar

Since the Bible already supplies a very graphic account of that terrible scene in Amnon's house, there is no need to repeat its sordid details. Yet, some things must be considered. When the guilty man refused to permit the young woman to stay in his home until darkness hid her appearance, he exhibited a deplorable facet of his character. He probably hoped that her expulsion from the house would be interpreted as an attempt to get rid of a prostitute. People would see her torn dress and the ashes upon her head, and the gossiping folk in the street would believe that Amnon had resisted her solicitations. Women of the street were hardly worth mentioning, but a royal prostitute might add fervor to their conversation. Amnon was a detestable man who fully deserved the fate which awaited him.

Women of the East wore veils over their faces, and the fact that Tamar placed her hand upon her head indicates that she had left her covering in the home of her half-brother. She perhaps removed it to proceed unhindered with her baking. Overwhelmed by shame, Tamar ran away crying. She had become the victim of terrible circumstances; her life seemed at an end! When Absalom saw her dejected figure, torn garments, and tear-stained face, he knew instantly what had transpired. To his credit let it be emphasized that he offered her his heart and home. He did nothing immediately to avenge his sister's tragedy; he might have possibly waited to see what David would do with the offender. Moses had issued explicit instructions concerning such crimes. David did become angry, but unfortunately did nothing. The historian wrote: "But when king David heard of all these things, he was very wroth" (see v. 21). His inexcusable inactivity increased his problems.

The sin committed by Amnon was punishable by death (see Leviticus 20:17). David had also committed crimes for which death was the punishment, and his problem seems to be the difficulty of punishing his son for a similar offense. He was obliged to make a choice between obedience to the law of God and love for a favored son. David was an impulsive man dominated by emotions. He seldom, if ever, denied himself. When Nathan spoke of a wealthy man who stole a pet lamb from a neighbor, the king vehemently exclaimed, "As the LORD liveth, the man that hath done this thing shall surely die" (2 Sam. 12:5). Yet, when he was accused of being the perpetrator of such villainy, he knelt to pray! His repentance was very commendable, but when a judge enforces the law upon other people and excuses himself, his conduct is despicable. He made a great mistake when he refused to take action against the heir to the throne. Describing the situation, Josephus wrote: "When David the father knew this, he was grieved at the actions of Amnon, *but he had an extraordinary affection for him, for he was his eldest son, and was compelled not to afflict him*" (Josephus, *The Antiquities of the Jews.* Book 7, Chapter 8, Paragraph 2), an opinion that was also expressed in the Septuagint Version of the Scriptures.

A DEADLY PURPOSE

And Absalom her brother said unto her, Hath Amnon thy brother been with thee? but hold thou thy peace, my sister: he is thy brother. . . . So Tamar remained desolate in her brother Absalom's house. . . . And it came to pass after two full years, that Absalom had sheep shearers in Baal-hazor. . . . Then said Absalom [to David] . . . Let my brother Amnon go with us. And the king said unto him, Why should he go with thee? But Absalom pressed him, that he let Amnon and all the king's

sons go with him. Now Absalom had commanded his servants, saying, Mark ye now when Amnon's heart is merry with wine, and when I say unto you, Smite Amnon; then kill him, fear not: have not I commanded you? be courageous, and be valiant. And the servants of Absalom did unto Amnon as Absalom had commanded. Then all the king's sons arose, and every man gat him up upon his mule, and fled (vv. 20-29).

Expository Notes on the Slaying of Amnon

There remains no doubt that Absalom planned the murder of his half-brother when he saw his grief-stricken sister. Nevertheless, the question remains, Why did he wait two years? During that interval, at least two—and possibly three—sheepshearers' banquets could have been celebrated. The natural response from an enraged man would have been immediate action. Had Absalom rushed instantly to assassinate the rapist, only a few men in Israel would have condemned the action. Yet, he remained apparently unconcerned until people believed that the incident had been forgotten.

Was He Considerate?

His young sister had been mercilessly raped so that she was embarrassed and humiliated. If he killed the offender, he would only publicize her shame. Was Absalom so protective of the young woman that he restrained himself to prevent national gossip for her sake? Was he content to await for a more opportune moment to exact vengeance on his despicable half-brother?

Was He Cautious?

Did he wait to see what his father would do to Amnon? If David would have obeyed the commandment of Moses, there would be no need to kill the offensive man; the king would do that work for him. The nation would accept Absalom as a man of great restraint and Tamar as an innocent young lady, worthy of her family and friends. Absalom was not a fool. He was a very shrewd man who was never impulsive. He planned his actions carefully and never moved until he knew what he intended to do.

Was He Clever?

Absalom was David's third son (see 2 Samuel 3:3). Amnon was first in line for the throne; Chileab was the second, but of him nothing is known. Was Absalom already planning to succeed his father as the king of Israel? Later, he made a supreme attempt to steal the kingdom and succeeded in forcing David into exile. He evidently had no love for his father, and if David executed Amnon, then the third son would legally be closer to his coronation. Absalom patiently wove a web in which to trap his victims. Throughout the two years he watched and waited, and it was only when it became obvious that David was protecting his errant son that he decided to take action against his rapist brother. He was thorough in his plans so that, although David was suspicious when Amnon was invited to the feast, Absalom's persistency overcame his father's reluctance. The servants at the feast were told what to do, and excessive drinking quietened Amnon's fear. The fact that the festivities were held in Baal-hazor gave Absalom a considerable advantage when he began his journey to Gesher. It is significant that he was the son of Maachah, the daughter of Talmai, who was king of Geshur (see 2 Samuel 3:3 and 1 Chronicles 3:2). Absalom evidently believed that he would be protected by his grandfather, and his faith was justified. He remained in Geshur for three years. The place where the sheepshearers met apparently about eight miles north of Jerusalem, and Absalom was therefore reasonably sure that if David organized a pursuing party of soldiers, he would be far ahead of his pursuers.

A DISTURBED PARENT

And it came to pass, while they were in the way, that tidings came to David, saying, Absalom hath slain all the king's sons, and there is not one of them left. Then the king arose and tare his garments, and lay on the earth; and all his servants stood by with their clothes rent. And Jonadab . . . answered and said . . . Amnon only is dead: for by the appointment of Absalom this hath been determined from the day that he forced his sister Tamar. . . . Absalom fled, and went to Geshur, and was there three years. And the soul of king David longed to go forth unto Absalom: for he was comforted concerning Amnon, seeing he was dead (vv. 30-39).

Expository Notes on David's Restlessness

It is difficult to avoid the conclusion that these unfortunate events were only the beginning of David's problems; he was destined to be haunted by many unhappy memories. The situation was best summarized by Dr. R. Payne Smith, who wrote: "[David] would think of the words of his sentence, that 'the sword shall never depart from thy house.' It had claimed one victim, and who could now stop the outburst of angry passions in a family which, previously, had dwelt in kindly friendship. Probably he reproached himself for not punishing Amnon. Had he done so with sufficient severity to have satisfied Absalom, he would have saved the life of his first-born, and not have driven his third son into terrible crime. He had not done so because his own sins had tied his hands. Yes, David had good reason for weeping sore" (*The Pulpit Commentary*, vol. 4, pp. 327-328).

An old proverb states that *absence makes the heart grow fonder*, a true observation in David's relationship with Absalom. David was perhaps beginning to blame himself for what had transpired and came to the conclusion that it would be best to permit the fugitive's return. The Revised Version reads, "He was consumed to go forth unto Absalom," and yet, when reconciliation became possible, David's pride refused to yield. He had a dual personality. When his soul communed with God, the king was a delightful person whose psalms charmed innumerable people. When he permitted carnal desires to dominate his life, he became disgusting. The manner in which God tolerated His disappointing servant provides a monument to the magnitude of His divine grace.

Episode 33

THEME: David Meets an Actress From Tekoah

SCRIPTURE: 2 Samuel 14

KEY VERSE:

> For we must needs die, and are as water spilt on the ground, which cannot be gathered up again; neither doth God respect any person: yet doth he devise means, that his banished be not expelled from him (v. 14).

OUTLINE:
  I. The Definite Plan (Verses 1-3)
  II. The Delightful Performance (Verses 4-11)
  III. The Direct Preaching (Verses 12-17)
  IV. The Discreet Plea (Verses 18-20)
  V. The Dangerous Pride (Verses 21-24)
  VI. The Distinguished Prince (Verses 25-28)
  VII. The Difficult Problem (Verses 29-33)

THE DEFINITE PLAN

Now Joab the son of Zeruiah perceived that the king's heart was toward Absalom. And Joab sent to Tekoah and fetched thence a wise woman, and said unto her, I pray thee, feign thyself to be a mourner, and put on now mourning apparel, and anoint not thyself with oil, but be as a woman that had a long time mourned for the dead: and come to the king, and speak on this manner unto him. So Joab put the words in her mouth (vv. 1-3).

Expository Notes on Joab's Desire to Help David

An Astute Assessment

"Now Joab . . . perceived that the king's heart was toward Absalom." It has always been difficult to determine the true meaning of the words "toward Absalom." For example, *The Pulpit Commentary* says that the preposition translated "toward" usually meant "against" and was so translated in verse 13. David could not forget the crime of Absalom so that he carried resentment within his soul. Even when Joab brought the fugitive prince from exile, the king's forgiveness was incomplete. He refused to welcome his erring son and ordered Absalom to live a secluded life on the outskirts of Jerusalem. The theologians who share this viewpoint believe that Joab was politically motivated. The wise general knew that it was harmful to the nation that the royal prince should be in exile and desired to end the animosity between David and his son. Others who disagree with that conclusion believe that David was secretly grieving over the loss of Absalom, that his health was being undermined, and that Joab, his very loyal friend, was trying to circumvent the king's pride.

An Accomplished Actress

"And Joab sent to Tekoah and fetched thence a wise woman." Tekoah was a small town twelve miles south of Jerusalem and six miles south of Bethlehem. Tekoah was near enough for Joab to be acquainted with the woman's fame as well as sufficiently distant that she would not be recognized by David and his friends. She was an accomplished actress, but how Joab discovered her is never revealed. The captain carefully planned the details of his scheme, and the danger of recognition was possibly offset by her skill as a make-up artist. She knew how to disguise her features, and since women in those days covered their faces, the chances of her being recognized were minimal. It may be safely assumed that Joab's preparations, including his sending for this woman, were veiled in secrecy. David was an impulsive, easily offended man, and if the intent of the actress would be discovered, he could easily order her punishment. She was to perform before an audience of one while her life was in jeopardy. If she succeeded, her reward would be great; if she failed, she would never act again!

An Accepted Appointment

The messengers secretly brought her to Joab, before whom she bowed respectfully. What could he desire of her? She looked through questioning eyes and waited for an explanation. Then Joab outlined his plan and in some mysterious way—either by eloquence or threats—persuaded her to accept the assignment. Whether or not the crafty general told a fictitious story of a family feud which threatened the happiness of a mother—or whether this account was actually based on a local event—is never revealed. The actress was asked to risk her life and reputation, and her survival depended upon her skill. It was known by all people that David was susceptible to the charms of young women, but whether or not an elderly, harassed, miserable woman could influence him was open to conjecture. One error could bring upon her head the wrath of a merciless monarch.

Most women would have refused the assignment, and it would be interesting to discover the secret of Joab's success. Did he offer protection and wealth? Did he threaten to annihilate her family or confiscate her estate? Joab was the second most powerful man in Israel and could make things very difficult for any person who refused to cooperate. The lady actually had no alternative; had she refused to help, she might have been signing her death warrant.

THE DELIGHTFUL PERFORMANCE

And when the woman of Tekoah spake to the king, she fell on her face to the ground, and did obeisance, and said, Help, O king. And the king said unto her, What aileth thee? And she answered, I am indeed a widow woman, and mine husband is dead. And thy handmaid had two sons, and they two strove together in the field, and there was none to part them, but the one smote the other, and slew him. And, behold, the whole family is risen against thine handmaid, and they said, Deliver him that smote his brother, that we may kill him, for the life of his brother whom he slew (vv. 4-7).

Expository Notes on the Performance of the Actress

Joab evidently told her what to say to the king, but the method of her approach was the product of her experience. "She was a wise woman," a fact that became evident in her three-fold appeal to David.

She Prayed . . . David's Friendliness

There were courts of appeal in every district of Israel to which every Hebrew had access. Only in very extreme cases were complaints taken to David, who was the highest court in the land! She described personal tragedy in which one son had killed another. The plaintiff understood the right of the family to demand an eye for an eye and a tooth for a tooth. This woman never questioned the justice of the law, but challenged its wisdom as it applied to her desperate situation. To become childless without the possibility of extending her lineage was one of the greatest tragedies recognized throughout the land. David listened to her petition, and promised to speak to the judge in her area to arrange leniency in her case. That might have been sufficient for most women, but it fell short of what was necessary. What if David forgot to honor his promise?

She Persisted . . . David's Forcefulness

She appeared to be a woman completely overwhelmed by fear and sorrow. With ashes upon her hair and garments of mourning, she was not attractive. Her copious tears and cries of anguish appealed to David's sympathy so that it became difficult to dismiss the suppliant. When she offered to bear the guilt for the regrettable slaying of her son, David became very protective and said, "Whosoever saith ought unto thee, bring him to me, and he shall not touch thee any more" (v. 10). Beneath her mask of sorrow the actress suppressed a smile; she was winning her case. Now the king could hardly forget his promise, for he had authorized access into his presence at any time. She could bring any accuser and David would personally deal with that person. Yet, there remained a weakness in the arrangement. What if David should change his mind or discover her deception? The woman was very shrewd; she required a commitment from which there could be no escape. She had evidently prepared for this eventuality.

She Persevered . . . David's Faithfulness

The king was perhaps irritated when she continued to seek assistance. He had given his word. Why did she continue to pester him? His patience seemed at an end when he exclaimed, "*As the LORD liveth*, there shall not one hair of thy son fall to the earth" (v. 11). The eyes of the actress suddenly gleamed. The king had sworn by the name of the Lord; he could not abrogate that vow. She seemed to have discovered a New Testament truth long before it was enunciated. The Savior urged His followers to pray as follows: "Ask, and it shall be given you; seek, and ye shall find; knock, and it shall be opened unto you" (Matthew 7:7). The woman of Tekoah asked for David's help, persisted until he made a deeper commitment, and persevered until her case was won. When the ancient writer described her as "a wise woman;" he was correct in his assessment.

THE DIRECT PREACHING

Then the woman said, Let thine handmaid, I pray thee, speak one word unto my lord the king. And he said, Say on. And the woman said, Wherefore then hast thou thought such a thing against the people of God? for the king doth speak this thing as one which is faulty, in that the king doth not fetch home again his banished. For we must needs die, and are as water spilt on the ground, which cannot be gathered up again; neither doth God respect any person: *yet doth he devise means, that his banished be not expelled from him* (vv. 12-14).

Expository Notes on the Application of the Woman's Message

At that moment the life of the actress from Tekoah was in jeopardy; it hung, as it were, from a thread. David knew that he had been tricked by a stranger. His anger was perhaps offset by admiration for her performance. He knew that her argument was irrefutable, but he detested being proved wrong in his treatment of Absalom. What could he do? He had made a vow before Jehovah. He could not forget her statement that even God made provision whereby His banished ones were not expelled. Absalom had gone to a distant country, but he had not been eternally expelled from his own land. To be banished was one thing, but to be expelled was another. Jehovah recognized this truth when, through the blood of sacrifice, He made it possible for sinners to draw near to His throne. David reminisced. Yes, he had often wandered from the Lord, but God had permitted his return. How then could he deny to his offending son what Jehovah had given him freely and often?

She was suddenly speaking again: "The word of my lord the king shall now be comfortable [restful; peaceful]: for as an angel of God, so is my lord the king to discern good and bad: therefore the LORD thy God will be with thee" (v. 17). Her wisdom and flattery captivated the listening monarch. She was an accomplished actress, but could a woman be so clever? David's eyes narrowed; he was debating a possibility. The entire performance left an unanswered question. Yes, he would grant the woman's desire, but not until he asked one important question. (See the homily, "The Woman of Tekoah . . . Israel's Famous Actress," p. 256.)

THE DISCREET PLEA

Then the king answered and said unto the woman, Hide not from me, I pray thee, the thing that I shall ask thee. And the woman said, Let my lord the king now speak. And the king said, Is not the hand of Joab with thee in all this? And the woman answered and said, As thy soul liveth . . . none can turn to the right hand or to the left from ought that my lord the king hath spoken: for thy servant Joab, he bade me, and he put all these words in the mouth of thine handmaid (vv. 18-19).

Expository Notes on David's Question Concerning Joab

David was a man of conflicting emotions. He was glad that his fugitive son would return home, but he disliked the way in which this had been arranged. Certain details seemed to point to Joab's ingenuity. At first it seemed the woman was only concerned with her personal problem, but when she challenged the king's conduct, David realized that there were undisclosed reasons which brought the actress into his presence. Many commentators believe that Joab had often interceded on behalf of Absalom and that his entreaties had been rejected. Both David and his commander in chief were stubborn men who disliked losing any kind of battle. Joab's inability to restore Absalom to royal favor presented a new challenge. If David had to be ensnared into granting a wish, then such a way had to be found. David thought of these possibilities and directly asked the woman if his suspicions were justified. Her reply was cleverly phrased; her flattery prevented the deepening of any anger. Someone has said, "It is sometimes easier to go around a rock than to tunnel through it." Joab was very wise, but David unfortunately did not always appreciate the thoughtfulness of his friend.

THE DANGEROUS PRIDE

And the king said unto Joab, Behold now, I have done this thing: go therefore, bring the young man Absalom again. . . . So Joab arose and went to Geshur, and brought Absalom to Jerusalem. And the king said, Let him turn to his own house, and let him not see my face. So Absalom returned to his own house, and saw not the king's face. . . . So Absalom dwelt two full years in Jerusalem, and saw not the king's face (vv. 21-24 and v. 28).

Expository Notes on David's Disappointing Reception of Absalom

It appears that David's forgiveness of Absalom was partial and insincere. Although he had yearned to be with his son, when the opportunity came to embrace the returning prince, David adamantly refused to welcome the prodigal. After all that had happened, the king's action was as inexcusable as it was unexpected. Surely there had to be a reason for David's unfriendliness.

Did His Conscience Condemn Him?

David had broken the law of God. Moses commanded: "So ye shall not pollute the land wherein ye are: for blood it defileth the land: and *the land cannot be cleansed of the blood that is shed therein, but by the blood of him that shed it*" (Numbers 35:33). According to the words of Moses, David not only defiled his soul, but his actions also polluted the nation. Absalom should have been executed for his crime. If an appeal were possible, it should have been presented. The crime of murder had been unpunished and uncondemned. How could David pass sentence on other offenders when he condoned the slaying of Amnon? Was his conscience beginning to trouble him? Was David afraid of the people's opposition to his exonerating a criminal?

Did His Counselors Criticize Him?

David had friends who were concerned about the moral standards of the nation. They may not have agreed with Joab, but rather expressed their belief that to welcome Absalom to the palace would have been another violation of God's law. Did these honorable men urge the king not to accept the advice of the commander in chief? Was this a by-product of a power struggle within the nation?

Did His Confidence Change?

Absalom was admired throughout Israel and had supporters in every city. His commanding appearance, his beautiful hair, and even his slaying of Amnon seem to be admired by many thousands of Hebrews. Was David apprehensive concerning the return of a man who might become the next king? The prince ultimately attempted to steal the kingdom. David was forced to flee from Jerusalem, and the usurper prince almost achieved his purpose. Did David have premonitions of what was to happen? Did he regret calling Absalom home?

Did His Captain Concern Him?

David was not pleased with the subterfuge by which the actress from Tekoah obtained his assistance. It hurt his pride when he was deceived. Joab was responsible for that scheme, and the more the king thought about her deception, the more irritated he became. Joab seemed to be having things all his own way—at David's expense. Did this trouble the king? Did he prevent Absalom's return to the palace in order to spoil Joab's satisfaction? Viewed from any angle, what David did was wrong. He fed the fires of resentment in the soul of the prince and created problems which could have been avoided.

THE DISTINGUISHED PRINCE

But in all Israel there was none to be so much praised as Absalom for his beauty: from the sole of his foot even to the crown of his head there was no blemish in him. And when he polled his head . . . he weighed the hair of his head at two hundred shekels after the king's weight. And unto Absalom there were born three sons, and one daughter, whose name was Tamar: she was a woman of a fair countenance. So Absalom dwelt two full years in Jerusalem, and saw not the king's face (vv. 25-28).

Expository Notes on the Popularity of Absalom

That David contributed to his eventual downfall, no one can deny. Coming events were casting their shadows, and every thoughtful person in Israel must have been aware of storm clouds on the national horizon. Arthur W. Pink in *The Life of David* wrote: "Absalom was not esteemed for his moral worth, for he was utterly lacking in piety, wisdom and justice. His handsome physique appealed to the people, his abominable wickedness was ignored, but his person was admired—which only increased his arrogance, ending in utter ruin. Allowing his luxuriant hair to grow to such a length, and then afterward weighing it, showed his pride and effeminacy. His three sons evidently died at an early age" (see 2 Samuel 18:18). Absalom's daughter was named Tamar, after her mother. She is called Maachah in 1 Kings 15:2.

It is generally believed that the weight of the prince's hair was between two and four pounds. Josephus wrote: "Now his beauty was not impaired, even by the grief he had been under, or by the want of such care, as was proper to be taken of a king's son; he still surpassed and excelled all men in the tallness of his body, and was more eminent in a fine appearance than those that dieted the most luxuriously. Such was the thickness of his hair that it was with difficulty he was polled every eighth day; his hair weighed two hundred shekels, which are five pounds" (Josephus, *Antiquities of the Jews*. Book 7, Chapter 8, Paragraph 5). Theologians believe the discrepancy regarding the weight of Absalom's hair was occasioned by a difference between the weight of the common shekel and the king's shekel. There can be no doubt that during the two years in which the prince lived in seclusion, Absalom carefully made his plans to steal the kingdom. That he ostentatiously welcomed all visitors to the city was a part of his scheme. His smiling face was a mask that hid the evil intentions of his soul.

THE DIFFICULT PROBLEM

> **Therefore Absalom sent for Joab, to have sent him to the king; but he would not come to him: and when he sent again the second time, he would not come. Therefore he said unto his servants, See, Joab's field is near mine, and he hath barley there; go and set it on fire. And Absalom's servants set the field on fire. . . . Then Joab arose, and came to Absalom unto his house, and said unto him, Wherefore have thy servants set my field on fire? . . . So Joab came to the king, and told him: and when he had called for Absalom, he came to the king, and bowed himself on his face to the ground before the king: and the king kissed Absalom (vv. 29-33).**

Expository Notes on the Burning of Joab's Field

A Repeated Frustration . . . Disturbing

It would be impossible to underestimate Absalom's disappointment when he discovered that he was placed under house arrest. He was not permitted to leave his home, but only allowed to speak with his family and servants. He was a proud man who believed that his forgiveness was only a pretense; he was still considered to be a criminal and had exchanged the freedom of Geshur for captivity in Jerusalem. The turmoil within his soul constantly increased, and on two occasions he sought interviews with Joab. It is significant that he could not visit the man who had brought him from

Geshur. Joab possibly had no desire to listen to Absalom's complaints. He had brought the prince home for the welfare of David and the country. His task had been well performed; there was no need for further conversations with a murderer. When Joab's attitude became apparent, Absalom's rage deepened so much that he conceived a method of obtaining a response from the indifferent commander.

A Raging Fire . . . Destroying

When Joab heard that his field of barley was burning and that his property was being destroyed with the result that there would be no harvest, he was incensed. He knew that Absalom was responsible for the carnage, and in the ensuing interview sought reasons for the willful destruction. Joab's anger was possibly suppressed, for he had ignored Absalom's repeated requests. The prince appeared to be justified when he complained of unfair treatment. He possibly said to Joab, "If I am still considered to be a criminal, then kill me." Joab reluctantly appealed once again to David, and his solicitations were successful. After five years, Absalom was taken to the royal palace, where he bowed before David. The raging fire in Joab's field was unfortunately nothing when compared with the smoldering fire in Absalom's soul. The one was easily extinguished; the other fire of resentment became a devastating inferno which almost destroyed the nation.

A Restored Fellowship . . . Deceiving

"Absalom . . . came to the king, . . . and the king kissed him." The reconciliation was doubtlessly preceded by a long conversation, but what was said is never revealed. Neither man trusted the other. The prince already anticipated the day when he would become king of Israel. David listened to his son and wondered what lay ahead. It is significant that during all of these proceedings, David never sought the guidance of God. He intended to pardon Absalom so that it was of no consequence what God might desire. David—whether he knew it or not—was now compelled to live with a serpent in his bosom. The next four years were a nightmare. Some of David's psalms reveal the pitiable plight of a sick monarch, the intrigues within the land, and, above all, the national uprising in which the usurper prince threatened the life of his father. The fact that David had little, if any, fellowship with Jehovah ruined that period in his life. With God, he had everything; without Him, he had nothing.

HOMILIES FOR PREACHERS AND TEACHERS

Study No. 14

THE WOMAN OF TEKOAH ... Israel's Famous Actress (2 Samuel 14:1-23)

"Now Joab the son of Zeruiah perceived that the king's heart was toward Absalom" (v. 1), and the matter caused grave concern. Joab sighed as he remembered the tragic events of former years. Absalom's favorite sister had been seduced by her evil step-brother, and the proud prince had ruthlessly planned to exterminate Amnon. His schemes had succeeded, and fleeing before justice, Absalom had gone to a distant land. All these details were well known throughout the nation; but Joab, the most intimate of the king's friends, knew that David was grieving. "And Joab sent to Tekoah, and fetched thence a wise woman, and said unto her, I pray thee, feign thyself to be a mourner, and put on mourning apparel, and anoint not thyself with oil, but be as a woman that had a long time mourned for the dead: and come to the king, and speak on this manner unto him. So Joab put the words in her mouth" (2 Samuel 14:2,3).

HOW GREAT SORROW

She was a great actress. Only those with similar gifts will understand how she succeeded in deceiving her royal master, for as King David listened to her pitiful cry, his heart melted. "What aileth thee?" he asked; and she replied, "I am indeed a widow woman, and mine husband is dead" (v. 5). Then she told the heart-rending account of her two boys fighting in the field, and how one had been slain. She described the fact that the rest of her family now demanded the slayer's execution and that she was in danger of losing her second boy. Her body shook with suppressed sobbing as she unfolded her sad story. When she lifted a tear-stained face to look at King David, he saw her anguish and said, "Go to thine house, and I will give charge concerning thee" (v. 8). Still she persisted in pleading until the king, irritated by her persistence, exclaimed, "As the LORD liveth, there shall not one hair of thy son fall to the earth" (v. 11). As he watched, a transformation then took place before him, until he became speechless with wonder.

HOW GREAT SERMON

She slowly shook the dust from her dress and threw back her cloak, and immediately David perceived a change in her demeanor. Her eyes filled with accusations as she said, "The king doth speak this thing as one which is faulty, in that the king doth not fetch home again his banished" (v. 13). King David, you swear that my boy shall be protected. Why, then, do you not protect your own son who occupies a similar position? "For we must needs die, and are as water spilt on the ground . . . neither doth God respect any person: yet doth he devise means, that his banished be not expelled from him" (v. 14). King David, you believe in the law and the prophets and regularly offer the sacrifices. Why is this so? Is it not because God has made provision whereby His sinful children may draw near to His footstool? Although through the folly of sin we may be banished from His presence, God's grace does not expel us forever. We may bring our offerings, confess our sins, and at the altar of mercy receive pardon. If God can do such things, should you not follow His example?

HER GREAT SUCCESS

Against the wiles of this talented actress, David had no defense. He ultimately asked, "Is not the hand of Joab with thee in all this?" (v. 19). Then the king was told the complete story, and he finally sent for his trusted servant and said, "Behold now, I have done this thing: go therefore, bring the young man Absalom again" (v. 21). The woman bowed in the dust while her eyes were twinkling. She had played to the smallest audience of her career, but had given her greatest performance. In spite of the fact that her theological outlook was limited to a tabernacle, the laws of Moses, and the daily offerings, she presented an outstanding case before the royal judge and won the verdict. We can only imagine what she might have said if she had been able to speak of the love of God in Christ, the reconciliation made through the cross, and the glorious gospel of saving grace. In very deed and truth, "he doth devise means that his banished be not expelled from him" (v. 14). Dear lady, we salute you! What a pity you are unable to stand in our pulpits. Our churches would be packed to capacity if you were the preacher. (Homily reprinted from the author's book, *Bible Pinnacles*, pp. 43-44.)

Episode 34

THEME: *The Insurrection of Absalom*

SCRIPTURE: 2 Samuel 15

KEY VERSES:

> And the king said unto Zadok, Carry back the ark of God into the city: if I shall find favor in the eyes of the LORD, he will bring me again, and shew me both it, and his habitation: But if he thus say, I have no delight in thee; behold, here am I, let him do to me as seemeth good unto him (vv. 25-26).

OUTLINE:

    I. David's Sickness Revealing (Psalms 41 and 55)
   II. David's Son Rebelling (Verses 1-12)
  III. David's Servants Remaining (Verses 13-24)
  IV. David's Strategy Resisting (Verses 25-37)

A NECESSARY INTRODUCTION

Expository Notes on a Four-Year Interlude

It is necessary to understand that there is a copyist's mistake in this verse (v. 7). Absalom was born in Hebron after the coronation of David, who reigned for forty years and six months. It would have been impossible for forty years to separate Absalom's homecoming from his insurrection. Adam Clarke wrote: "There is no doubt that the reading is corrupt, though supported by the commonly printed Vulgate, the Septuagint, and the Chaldee. But the Syriac has 'four years,' the Arabic the same, and Josephus has the same; so also the Sistine edition of the Vulgate and several mss. of the same version. Theodoret also reads 'four,' not 'forty,' and most learned men are of the opinion that *arbaim*, 'forty,' is an error for *arba*, 'four'; yet this reading is not supported by any Hebrew manuscript yet discovered" (*The Bethany Parallel Commentary on the Old Testament*, p. 604).

It is a safe assumption that during the four years which followed David's reunion with his son, Absalom perfected his plans to annex the kingdom. Life in David's palace was fertile soil in which seeds of rebellion germinated.

DAVID'S SICKNESS REVEALING

The historian, for reasons best known to himself, refrained from mentioning the four years which vexed the soul of David. The only obtainable information comes from psalms which David wrote during his time of distress. David's compositions provided grim pictures of his problems.

Mine enemies speak evil of me, When shall he die and his name perish? And if he come to see me, he speaketh vanity: his heart gathereth iniquity to itself; when he goeth abroad, he telleth it. All that hate me whisper together against me: against me do they devise my hurt. An evil disease, say they, cleaveth fast unto him: and now that he lieth he shall rise up no more. Yea, mine own familiar friend, in whom I trusted, which did eat of my bread, hath lifted up his heel against me (Psalm 41:5-9). For it was not an enemy that reproached me; then I could have borne it: neither was it he that hated me that did magnify himself against me; then would I have hid myself from him: But it was thou, a man mine equal, my guide, and mine acquaintance. We took sweet counsel together, and walked into the house of God in company (Psalm 55:12-14).

Expository Notes on David's Sickness and Sadness

It is necessary to read carefully David's psalms to understand the depression he endured for four apparently endless years. He said, "The terrors of death are fallen upon me" (Psalm 55:4). That was far removed from the confidence expressed in another psalm, where he wrote: "Yea, though I walk through the valley of the shadow of death, I will fear no evil: for thou art with me" (Psalm 23:4). The king was evidently dangerously ill, so that men believed he was dying. Some people said, "An evil disease . . . cleaveth fast unto him: now that he lieth he shall rise up no more" (Psalm 41:8) Some enemies were delighted to say that his crimes had overtaken him. They whispered that his loins were stricken and insinuated that his lustful behavior had produced an incurable illness. If those people lived in the twentieth century, they would probably be more definitive in their statements. Lawlessness had spread through Jerusalem, and conditions within the nation were chaotic, but David's grief was occasioned by the treacherous behavior of one of his closest associates. Someone in whom he had implicit trust, who ate at the royal table, and who accompanied the king to the sanctuary had betrayed him. When David was seriously ill, the traitor circulated all kinds of rumors throughout the city, and plans were made to replace David with a successor. David might have been referring to Absalom or Ahithophel; the traitor had been a close associate of the king.

It is not difficult to visualize the word-picture behind these psalms. David was bedridden, his physical problems appeared to be insurmountable, and since he was unable to rule the kingdom efficiently, ambitious men were hoping he would die and make way for a successor. When the king's health improved, Absalom decided the time for action had arrived.

DAVID'S SON REBELLING

And it came to pass after this, that Absalom prepared him chariots and horses, and fifty men to run before him. And Absalom rose up early, and stood beside the way of the gate: and it was so, that when any man that had a controversy came to the king for judgment, then Absalom called unto him, and said, Of what city art thou? And he said, Thy servant is of one of the tribes of Israel. And Absalom said unto him, See, thy matters are good and right; but there is no man deputed of the king to hear thee. Absalom said moreover, Oh that I were made judge in the land, that every man which hath any suit or cause might come unto me, and I would do him justice! And it was so, that when any man came nigh to him to do him obeisance, he put forth his hand, and took him, and kissed him. . . . so Absalom stole the hearts of the men of Israel (vv. 1-6).

Expository Notes on Absalom's Efforts to Steal the Kingdom

If the friends of the bedridden David informed him of the actions of Absalom, his psalms written at that time are easily understood. The prince was a traitor within the palace, and an obvious threat to David's safety and authority. The opening statement in 2 Samuel 15 states, "And it came to pass after this. . . . " There was no specific mention of time, but—as was previously mentioned—after four years, Absalom was ready to become king of Israel. The fact that men ran before his chariot indicates his aspiration (see 1 Samuel 8:11).

The illness of the king had apparently thrown everything into disarray; the judicial system did not function, there was a backlog of cases waiting to be heard, and people throughout the nation criticized the delays in having their complaints heard by a judge. Absalom met these disgruntled people as they entered the city. When he rose early in the morning to go down to the customary place of judgment, he said to the visitors: "There is no man deputed of the king to hear thee. . . . Oh that I were made judge in the land, that every man . . . might come unto me, and I would do him justice!" That he said this to every man indicates that he had no love for justice; he desired power, not integrity, in administering the law.

All visitors to Buckingham Palace in London, England, would be thrilled if a prince went down to the gate to speak with tourists. Recipients of the royal favor would always remember being kissed and encouraged by a member of the royal family. Returning to their homes, they would never cease talking about the moment when a prince held their hand. That was precisely the situation in Israel.

And it came to pass after [four] years, that Absalom said unto the king, I pray thee, let me go and pay my vow, which I have vowed unto the LORD, in Hebron. . . . And the king said unto him, Go in peace. . . . But Absalom sent spies throughout all the tribes of Israel, saying, As soon as ye hear the sound of the trumpet, then ye shall say, Absalom reigneth in Hebron. . . . And Absalom sent for Ahithophel the Gilonite, David's counselor, from his city, even from Giloh, while he offered sacrifices. And the conspiracy was strong; for the people increased continually with Absalom (vv. 7-12).

Expository Notes on Absalom's Nefarious Schemes

Absalom believed that the moment for his long-planned coup had arrived. Israel had been prepared for insurrection, so that there existed in every city a group of rebels awaiting the call to arms. When the decision was made that Hebron should be the rallying place for the insurgents, spies were dispatched with their orders, and Absalom went to await the arrival of his supporters. David apparently did not expect an uprising against him at that time and granted the prince leave of absence to honor a vow in Hebron.

"And Absalom sent for Ahithophel . . . David's counselor." This man had been David's adviser on all matters of state importance. It was said: "And the counsel of Ahithophel, which he counseled in those days, was as if a man had inquired at the oracle of God: so was the counsel of Ahithophel both with David and with Absalom" (2 Samuel 16:23). He had given invaluable service to David and was numbered among the king's most intimate friends, but then David committed adultery with Bath-sheba and, to cover his transgression, arranged the murder of her husband. That crime might have been overlooked had not Bath-sheba been Ahithophel's granddaughter. When he heard of her disgrace and the death of his son-in-law, Ahithophel became incensed and disgusted. His mind was dominated by bitterness; he detested the king and everything associated with him. When his services were requested by Absalom, the old man joyfully seized the opportunity to destroy his former friend (see the homily, "Ahithophel . . . the Man Who Could Not Forgive," p. 280).

DAVID'S SERVANTS REMAINING

And there came a messenger to David, saying, The hearts of the men of Israel are after Absalom. And David said unto all his servants that were with him at Jerusalem, Arise, and let us flee. . . . And the king's servants said unto the king, Behold, thy servants are ready to do whatsoever my lord the king shall appoint. . . . And the king left ten women, which were concubines, to keep the house. . . . And Ittai the Gittite passed over, and all his men, and all the little ones that were with him. . . . And lo Zadok also, and all the Levites were with him, bearing the ark of the covenant

of God . . . and Abiathar went up, until all the people had done passing out of the city (vv. 13-24).

Expository Notes on the Faithfulness of David's Friends

It is significant that among the people who accompanied David were Ittai and his six hundred soldiers. That select band of men was mentioned in 1 Samuel 27:2 and 1 Samuel 30:9. They had followed David from the days when he had been a fugitive in Gath and had become trusted servants of the king. Some theologians believe that Ittai was the son of the king of Gath and that his allegiance to David led to banishment from his country. Six hundred of his chosen men followed him into Israel, where they renounced their idols and became converts of the Hebrew faith. Their love for David was never questioned; their commitment to their king was constant. With them were the Cherethites and Pelethites, people who also came from the southern extremities of the land. This fact is a cause for increasing amazement, for during crises the "foreigners" were more trustworthy than the Hebrews. When David suggested their return to Jerusalem, Ittai rejected the advice, saying, "As the LORD liveth, and as my lord the king liveth, surely in what place my lord the king shall be, whether in death or life, *even there also will thy servant be*" (v. 21). Ruth used similar words when she refused to leave Naomi to return to her own land (see Ruth 1:16-17). Her love for her mother-in-law resembled the love of Ittai for David. Those ancient characters should be an example for all who serve the King of kings. Absolute love for Christ should lead to total dedication to His service.

When the Levites carefully carried the ark of the covenant of God to the Kidron valley, David surely remembered an earlier occasion when the priests of God were murdered because they helped him; now their successors were willing to risk their lives to accompany the king into exile. They did not worry what Absalom might do if he became the king of Israel. They were willing to be "faithful unto death."

"And they set down the ark of God; and Abiathar went up, *until all the people had done passing out of the city*" (v. 24). Absalom's arrival in Jerusalem would soon be a reality, and there was need for David to get as far away as possible. Yet, he lingered until his friends were out of the city. "And Abiathar went up." Some teachers believe that he went ahead and offered sacrifices which were always associated with the removal of the ark. It is difficult to accept that interpretation, for the sacrificing of animals would necessitate time, and David was in a hurry! It might be easier to believe that somewhere in the Kidron Valley, David paused to ascertain the safety of his friends. The high priest accompanying the ark of God was told to "go up"—return up—the hill to see if any people had been left behind and, if there were, to hasten their march. When everyone was present, David and his faithful friends continued their journey toward the wilderness east of the Jordan River.

DAVID'S STRATEGY RESISTING

And the king said unto Zadok, Carry back the ark of God into the city: If I shall find favor in the eyes of the Lᴏʀᴅ, he will bring me again, and shew me both it, and his habitation: But if he thus say, I have no delight in thee; behold, here am I, let him do to me as seemeth good unto him. The king said also unto Zadok the priest, Art not thou a seer? return into the city in peace, and your two sons with you. . . . I will tarry in the plain of the wilderness, until there come word from you to certify me. . . . And it came to pass, that when David was come to the top of the mount . . . he worshipped God (vv. 25-32).

Expository Notes on the Beginning of David's Resistance

The mental fog was slowly beginning to clear from David's mind; there appeared a light at the end of his tunnel. He knew that indiscretions had occasioned his misfortunes, and the memory of God's prediction that the sword would never depart from his household haunted him. He decided to return the ark of God to the sanctuary. If Jehovah occupied His rightful place in the affections of Israel, other things would fall into place. He believed that the priests should be with the ark, for they alone were commissioned to attend to its welfare. When he looked at the two sons of Zadok, his eyes narrowed; it became evident that he was thinking clearly again. How could he act wisely if he remained uninformed? Zadok could be his spy within the city, and his sons could be trusted messengers. If God desired to restore his throne, it would be necessary to cooperate with Him. If the Lord had forsaken him, nothing could be done to change the Almighty's opinion. But who could tell what lay ahead? David was down, but not out; defeated, but not destroyed. His night of anguish was exceedingly dark, but if God permitted the dawn of a new day, he would be ready to meet its challenge. When David worshiped, the onlookers knew that it was better to praise God than to grumble and to begin climbing again, instead of remaining disconsolately in the valley of bewilderment.

Behold, Hushai the Archite came to meet him with his coat rent, and earth upon his head: unto whom David said, If thou passest on with me, then thou shalt be a burden unto me: But if thou return to the city . . . then mayest thou for me defeat the counsel of Ahithophel. . . . what thing soever thou shalt hear out of the king's house, thou shalt tell it to Zadok and Abiathar the priests. . . . So Hushai David's friend came into the city, and Absalom came into Jerusalem (vv. 32-37).

This event is one of the most intriguing episodes in the life of David; it reveals the system by which his agents worked and was the Old Testament equivalent of "having saints in Caesar's household!" The story of Hushai may be considered under three headings.

A Devoted Counselor

Hushai the Archite belonged to the territory west of Bethel (see Joshua 16:1-2). He became the king's friend and confidant as well as possibly one of the chief advisors in every matter of policy. He was not a soldier, but his wisdom often turned defeats into victories. He was a friend in whom David had perfect confidence. When he heard of Absalom's insurrection, Hushai rent his clothes and covered his head with dust. As quickly as possible, he joined his friend and confessed his unshaken loyalty to the crown. People overwhelmed by despondency would have welcomed the outpouring of affection, but David was beginning to resist adversity.

Hushai was probably an elderly man who was completely unable to fight. His presence would have been a nuisance, for David would be compelled to assume responsibility for his safety. The king considered the possibility of asking his friend to undertake a hazardous mission.

A Dangerous Commission

If the elderly statesman returned to Jerusalem to pretend to be a supporter of the new regime, his expertise could be of incalculable worth. David had the utmost confidence in his friend, but the job would be dangerous. If the usurper-prince discovered the deception, Hushai's life would be forfeited. Nevertheless, it was imperative to have an informant in the palace, and since the two sons of the priest were waiting to carry information, this plan would be more likely to succeed if an experienced man took charge of the operation. Hushai recognized that his friend had something important to say and that he was connected with whatever the king was planning. When David explained his need for espionage, Hushai offered his services. If success attended his mission, David would resume his monarchy. If it did not, at least he would have done his best for David and would be content. To die for his king was better than to live without him! It would be preferable to die with honor than to live in shame.

A Delightful Consent

"So Hushai David's friend came into the city, and Absalom came into Jerusalem." Some theologians condemn David's complicity in deception, intrigue, and lying; but it must be remembered that he lived in desperate times when a mistake could have been fatal and when the future of Israel hung, as it were, by a thread. It would be easy to condemn the king, but at that time prophets were silent! Something had to be done immediately, and whether he was justified in relying upon his own ingenuity cannot easily be ascertained. Doubtless, David did what he thought was best for himself, for the nation, and for the cause of God. Hushai's readiness to help reveals the integrity of his soul. The king was a fortunate man who had reliable friends. It has been said that a faithful friend is one of heaven's best gifts. Hushai's loyalty endorses that statement.

HOMILIES FOR PASTORS AND TEACHERS

Study No. 15

AHITHOPHEL . . . the Man Who Could Not Forgive (2 Samuel 17:23)

The cause of God is always greater than the man who represents it, and no one can ever be justified in leaving his place of service because he has discovered sin in high places of responsibility. Ahithophel was one of the greatest men of his time, but he allowed memories of injustice to color his entire horizon.

AHITHOPHEL'S GREATNESS

This eminent man occupied one of the stately homes of Israel, for he was not only a great man in his own right but he was also the bosom friend and honored counsellor of the king. When he gave counsel, he spoke as the "oracle of God" (2 Sam. 16:23), and on innumerable occasions the king had cause to thank God for the presence of his old and trusted friend. Ahithophel had a son whose name was Eliam (see 2 Samuel 23:34), a distinguished captain in David's army. He was very proud of his boy and perhaps even more proud of his beautiful grandchild Bath-sheba (2 Samuel 11:3). He watched her and wistfully thought of the future. When Uriah the Hittite, another valiant captain, fell in love with this charming girl, both her father and grandfather joyously consented to their marriage. And then came tragedy!

AHITHOPHEL'S GRIEF

"And it came to pass in an eveningtide, that David arose from off his bed, and walked upon the roof of the king's house: and from the roof he saw a woman washing herself and the woman was very beautiful to look upon. And David sent and enquired after the woman. And one said, Is not this Bath-sheba, the daughter of Eliam, the wife of Uriah the Hittite? And David sent messengers and took her" (11:2-4). Poor Bath-sheba; she was just a helpless woman in an eastern land and could hardly be expected to resist the attentions of an irresponsible passionate monarch. The weeks and months which followed were dark with apprehension and dread. Fearful suspense tortured her mind, and even David regretted the madness of former days. The threat of discovery constantly hung over his head, and, as a last resort, he ordered the execution of the faithful young husband. Bathsheba bowed in sorrow and mourned for her lover, but her grandfather Ahithophel knew no such restraint. This act of David was despicable to the extreme—it was murder! Incensed, the great counsellor saddled his ass and went home to Giloh. Uriah was in the grave; his lovely Bath-sheba had been seduced. The old man was furious.

AHITHOPHEL'S GUILT

The subsequent story of David's bitter repentance only hardened Ahithophel's heart. Could tears bring back the dead Uriah? Could tears remove the stain from the soul of a seduced girl? Bah! When Absalom's treachery threatened the safety of King David, Ahithophel heard the news and smiled. Had not David forfeited his right to reign? "And Absalom sent for Ahithophel. . . . And the conspiracy was strong. . . . Then said Absalom to Ahithophel, Give counsel among you what we shall do. And Ahithophel said unto Absalom, Go in unto thy father's concubines . . . and all Israel shall hear that thou art abhorred of thy father: then shall the hands of all that are with thee be strong. . . . And the counsel of Ahithophel, which he counseled in those days was as if a man had inquired at the oracle of God" (2 Samuel 15:12; 16:20-23). Poor man, bitterness had blinded his eyes to the fact that the cause of God is always greater than the man who represents it.

AHITHOPHEL'S GRAVE

The dramatic story of Hushai's opposition to the counsel of Ahithophel makes good reading. Driven by increasing animosity, David's former friend would have pursued the weary king to slay him. Yet, doubt was implanted in Absalom's mind, and ultimately Ahithophel was rejected. "And when Ahithophel saw that his counsel was not followed, he saddled his ass, and arose, and gat him home to his house, to his city, and put his household in order, and hanged himself, and died, and was buried in the sepulcher of his father" (2 Samuel 17:23). Did David ever visit the grave of his old friend? Did he weep as he read the epitaph, "Here lies Ahithophel—the man who could not forgive"? (Homily reprinted from the author's book, *Bible Cameos*, pp. 43-44).

Episode 35

THEME: *The Events Which Followed the Departure of David*

SCRIPTURE: 2 Samuel 16

KEY VERSES:

> And David said to Abishai, and to all his servants, Behold, my son, which came forth of my bowels seeketh my life: how much more now may this Benjamite do it? let him alone, and let him curse; for the LORD hath bidden him. It may be that the LORD will look on mine affliction, and that the LORD will requite me good for his cursing this day (vv. 11-12).

OUTLINE:
   I. Ziba's Covetousness (Verses 1-4)
   II. Shimei's Cursing (Verses 5-14)
   III. Hushai's Caution (Verses 15-19)
   IV. Ahithophel's Counsel (Verses 20-23)

ZIBA'S COVETOUSNESS

And when David was a little past the top of the hill, behold, Ziba the servant of Mephibosheth met him, with a couple of asses saddled, and upon them two hundred loaves of bread, and a hundred bunches of raisins, and an hundred of summer fruits, and a of bottle wine. . . . And the king said, And where is thy master's son? And Ziba said unto the king, Behold, he abideth at Jerusalem: for he said, To day shall the house of Israel restore me the kingdom of my father. Then said the king to Ziba, Behold, thine are all that pertained unto Mephibosheth. And Ziba said, I humbly beseech thee that I may find grace in thy sight, my lord, O king (vv. 1-4).

Expository Notes on Ziba's Untruthful Report to David

David's death seemed to be imminent because the human vultures were gathering. Among the disgusting people hoping to gain from the overthrow of the king were Ziba, Shimei, Absalom, and other people who planned to take advantage of the situation. A few had no desire for financial success but, motivated by hatred, were determined to deepen the king's misery.

Shimei cursed and threw stones at the fleeing monarch. Ahithophel, who in all probability was a wealthy man, dedicated his talents to the humiliation and overthrow of his former friend. The outlook was exceedingly bleak, but, amid the darkness, one star began to shine. Hushai, the head of David's secret service agents, had reached the palace and confronted Absalom. He was probably one of the bravest men in Israel.

It should be remembered that Ziba, the chief steward of Saul's estate, had been commissioned to find the crippled son of Jonathan. David had arranged for the young man to receive his inheritance, and Ziba and his family were commanded to manage his estate. Although they obeyed David's command, they resented having to work for their new master. They legally received a sizable proportion of the income gained, but they begrudged every moment of the labor considered to be servitude.

When Ziba heard of David's flight, he saw the possibility of obtaining what he most desired. He evidently believed that the fleeing king would return, but was sure that Absalom would execute David's friend Mephibosheth. If he died, there would be no claimant to his property, and Ziba would at least be able to claim a part, if not all, of his land. He did not have much time to decide what to do, for David was already leaving Jerusalem. His plans were perhaps already made and he was ready to act.

Knowing that the king's escape would be attended by many problems, Ziba gathered a considerable amount of supplies and hurried to intercept the desolate fugitive. Anticipating David's question regarding Mephibosheth, Ziba knew what to say in response to the royal enquiry. His lies concerning Mephibosheth were not only defamatory, but they also presented a false picture of the integrity of his crippled master. David was disturbed and disappointed and was not thinking clearly when he said to Ziba, "Behold, thine are all that pertained unto Mephibosheth" (v. 4). The king did not seek the guidance of God, and apparently never thought of corroborating Ziba's story. Activated by impulse, he made a wrong decision which unfortunately was never rescinded (see 2 Samuel 19:29). David was now "paddling his own canoe." Alas, he sailed into troubled waters which almost capsized his boat!

It is unwise to listen to gossip and always dangerous to be influenced by criticism. Irreparable damage was done by the lies of Mephibosheth's servant, and David was partly responsible, for he made no effort to verify what was reported. If Solomon heard of Ziba's untruthfulness, the knowledge probably influenced him when he wrote, "The getting of treasures by a lying tongue is a vanity tossed to and fro of them that seek death" (Proverbs 21:6).

SHIMEI'S CURSING

And when king David came to Bahurim, behold, thence came out a man of the family of the house of Saul, whose name was Shimei, and son of

Gera: he came forth and cursed still as he came. And he cast stones at David, and at all the servants of king David: and all the people and all the mighty men, were on his right hand and on his left. And thus said Shimei when he cursed, Come out, come out, thou bloody man, and thou man of Belial: The LORD hath returned upon thee all the blood of the house of Saul, in whose stead thou hast reigned; and the LORD hath delivered the kingdom into the hand of Absalom thy son: and, behold, thou art taken in thy mischief, because thou art a bloody man (vv. 5-8).

Expository Notes on the Foolishness of Shimei

Bahurim was a small town about four miles from Jerusalem. It was the place to which the husband of Michal had followed when David had demanded the return of his first wife (see 2 Samuel 3:16). It will be remembered that Saul had given his daughter to another man. As David traveled, the road was evidently on the side of a hill. A man suddenly emerged from the nearby town and ran along the hill where David and his friends marched. The man was named Shimei, a member of the family of the late king who was evidently exceedingly angry. He had allowed bitterness to dominate his thinking, and the fires of resentment within him suddenly burst forth as a volcanic eruption. He seemed to be like a demented maniac as he shouted curses at the despondent king and threw stones at the travelers. When he abused David and his friends, the anger of a captain was aroused.

Shimei's Accusation Was Untrue

The despicable stranger implied that David had been responsible for the slaying of Saul's family. Yet, the facts show that the king had done his utmost to spare Saul and assist his descendants. The misguided man claimed that God had given the kingdom to Absalom and that by divine appointment the right to rule had been transferred to the murderous prince. The fellow was evidently beside himself with rage, and this unpardonable outburst arose from his personal conviction that he, as kinsman of the late king, should have received an inheritance from Saul's estate. He was a contemptuous, selfish man who thought only of himself. The ferocity of his attack on David expressed the anger within his embittered soul.

Shimei's Action Was Unholy

God gave instructions concerning the respect to be shown to a king. "Thou shalt not revile the gods [judges], nor curse the ruler of thy people" (Exodus 22:28). This law was neither abandoned nor forgotten. Solomon wrote: "Curse not the king, no *not in thy thought*" (Ecclesiastes 10:20). Shimei's actions were unforgivable. From his place on the hill, he looked down at the travelers and, disregarding consequences, commenced his diatribe. His violation of the laws of God was worthy of death. David never forgot that terrible experience and years later commissioned Solomon to destroy the detestable man who had stoned him during the flight from Absalom (see 1 Kings 2:8-9 and the homily, "Shimei . . . and the Ghost That Killed Him," p. 312).

Shimei's Anger Was Unrestrained

It would appear as if Shimei were completely demented, for even when the captains desired to kill him, he continued to shout insults. The historian wrote, "And as David and his men went by the way, Shimei went along on the hill's side over against him, and cursed as he went, and threw stones at him, and cast dust" (v. 13). The man was very angry and cared nothing for his own survival. When a man becomes that incensed, he is less than that which upset him. Anger should never be dominant in the life of a child of God. Paul was correct when he wrote, "[Love] doth not behave itself unseemly, seeketh not her own, *is not easily provoked*, thinketh no evil . . . beareth all things, believeth all things . . . endureth all things" (1 Corinthians 13:5, 7).

HUSHAI'S CAUTION

And it came to pass, when Hushai the Archite, David's friend, was come unto Absalom, that Hushai said unto Absalom, God save the king, God save the king. And Absalom said unto Hushai, Is this thy kindness to thy friend? why wentest thou not with thy friend? And Hushai said unto Absalom, Nay; but whom the Lord, and this people, and all the men of Israel, choose, his will I be, and with him will I abide. And again, whom should I serve? should I not serve in the presence of his son? as I have served in thy father's presence, so will I be in thy presence (vv. 16-19).

Expository Notes on the Ambiguity of Hushai's Testimony

Some people believe that the testimony of Hushai was filled with lies, but that conclusion may be misleading. David's friend was in great danger; one mistake would have been fatal. That agent basically uttered no falsehoods. When he exclaimed, "God save the king," evidently he was thinking of David. When he spoke of serving the man whom the people would choose, he believed that it would only be a matter of time before David returned to his throne. His remarks concerning serving in the presence of Absalom did not imply treachery. Hushai had served faithfully in the court of David; he would continue to do so even in the presence of enemies. The would-be king was mistaken, but Hushai told no lies. He evidently tried to deceive Absalom, but his actions and speech only endorsed the historian's statement that he was a wise man. David's life was threatened; Hushai was playing an important role in trying to prevent that disaster. The king was protected by wonderful friends.

AHITHOPHEL'S COUNSEL

Then said Absalom to Ahithophel, Give counsel among you what we shall do. And Ahithophel said unto Absalom, Go in unto thy father's concubines, which he hath left to keep the house; and all Israel shall hear that thou art abhorred of thy father: then shall the hands of all that are with thee be strong. So they spread Absalom a tent upon the top of the house; and Absalom went in unto his father's concubines in the sight of all Israel. And the counsel of Ahithophel . . . was as if a man had inquired at the oracle of God: so was all the counsel of Ahithophel both with David and with Absalom (vv. 20-23).

This incident did not directly apply to David, but it must be included in this study because it was the link which joined two episodes of his life together. It can be considered under three headings.

Ahithophel's Unique Position

The fact that Absalom asked Ahithophel for advice suggests that the usurper-prince was not over-confident. He had impulsively stolen the throne, but—to use a modern statement—"he had bitten off more than he could chew!" Many problems were already confronting the new regime so that there existed the possibility that his popularity might wane, but as long as David remained alive, he would be a threat. The future appeared to be ominous. What could be done to safeguard his position? Ahithophel was an astute politician, whose guidance could be invaluable.

Ahithophel's Unholy Plan

It was said that his advice was as "if a man had inquired at the oracle of God." His wisdom was so obvious that it seemed as if he were using the Urim and Thummim in seeking and receiving from Jehovah irrefutable wisdom. Matthew Henry wrote, "It would have been more appropriate if it had been said 'he enquired at the oracle of Satan.'" The advice given to Absalom was corrupt and inexcusable, but perfect for his strategy to gain his own ends. The men of his generation guarded harems more than their riches. To intrude upon the privacy of that part of the household was an unpardonable sin which was punishable by death.

David had left ten of his concubines to attend to the house and to manage the property until his return. Ahithophel looked at the roof of David's palace and probably remembered that it was from that vantage point that the king watched Bath-sheba bathing. The old man had not forgiven David for committing such a heinous crime and with deliberation suggested that the same roof should be used for Absalom's infamy. The royal tent was set up, the ten concubines were summoned, and "Absalom went in unto his father's concubines in the sight of all Israel." The crafty adviser knew that David could never forgive that public insult and that there would never be a reconciliation between the king and his rebellious son. Ahithophel not only perpetuated the bitterness between David and Absalom, but he also made sure his new master could never disown him. He was exceedingly foolish, for he ignored God and forgot that any person who opposes the Lord's anointed endangers himself.

Ahithophel's Uncanny Power

The counselor's ability to solve problems and overcome adversity was sensational. With some people that instinct may be hereditary; with others it is God-given, as was the case with Solomon. It would be interesting to know the source of the knowledge which made Ahithophel famous. The next episode describes his rejection and subsequent suicide. Alas, he was dead before he died! It is strange that such a wise man could become so foolish.

Episode 36

THEME: *The Faithfulness of David's Friends*

SCRIPTURE: 2 Samuel 17

KEY VERSE:

> And Absalom and all the men of Israel said, The counsel of Hushai the Archite is better than the counsel of Ahithophel. For the LORD had appointed to defeat the good counsel of Ahithophel, to the intent that the LORD might bring evil upon Absalom (v. 14).

OUTLINE:

    I.   The Faithful Witnesses ... *Conflicting* (Verses 1-14)

    II. The Friendly Women ... *Cooperating* (Verses 15-22)

    III. The Famous Wise Man ... *Collapsing* (Verse 23)

    IV. The Fervent Workers ... *Collecting* (Verses 25-29)

THE FAITHFUL WITNESSES ... CONFLICTING

Moreover Ahithophel said unto Absalom, Let me now choose out twelve thousand men, and I will arise and pursue after David this night. . . . Then said Absalom, Call now Hushai the Archite also, and let us hear likewise what he saith. . . . And Hushai said unto Absalom, The counsel that Ahithophel hath given is not good at this time. . . . Therefore I counsel that all Israel be gathered unto thee . . . and that thou go to battle in thine own person. . . . And Absalom and all the men of Israel said, The counsel of Hushai the Archite is better than the counsel of Ahithophel. For the LORD had appointed to defeat the good counsel of Ahithophel, to the intent that the LORD might bring evil upon Absalom (vv. 1-14).

Expository Notes on Absalom's Choice of Counselors

It can never be denied that David was in very great danger when Ahithophel gave advice to Absalom. He was weary after his hurried departure from Jerusalem, his followers were few, and his capabilities for battle were inconsequential. When Ahithophel assessed the pros and cons of the situation, his deductions were flawless. Had he attacked David's camp, his twelve thousand soldiers would have overcome all opposition, killed David, and changed the history of Israel. The alternate suggestion made by Hushai was brilliant and inspired. Three facts become obvious.

The Committed Friends of God

True friends are never more loyal than in time of need. This story speaks of a counselor, two priests, two messengers, two faithful women, and an unknown number of soldiers who refused to desert their king when his death seemed imminent. Adversity is the testing ground of loyalty. It has been claimed that "fair-weather" friends are unworthy of trust. David's helpers were stars in a very dark sky.

The Constant Faithfulness of God

David was unable to see and hear Hushai's performance before Absalom, but he knew his counselor would not be disappointing in the hour of need. It remains problematical whether or not the king's faith in God remained strong. Did he worry about possible eventualities or did he smile, knowing that the Lord's help was assured? David had not been an exemplary character, since there was little about his conduct which merited praise. Yet, God had never forsaken him. This realization possibly inspired Jeremiah to write: "It is of the LORD's mercies that we are not consumed, because his compassions fail not. They are new every morning: great is thy faithfulness" (Lamentations 3:22-23). The faithfulness of God cannot be changed by the inconsistencies of His people. Even when David was a despondent man in the wilderness, God continued to protect him.

The Confounded Foes of God

The Lord used the talent of an inconspicuous man to defeat the advice of the wisest counselor in Israel. Hushai's words were carefully and shrewdly spoken, but his courage and confident demeanor were remarkable. He was a spy in enemy territory, but he never flinched from his duty because he was never scared by possibilities of disaster. He was willing to die for his master, but believed that it was better to live and faithfully serve him. His brilliant efforts were of incalculable worth. No one was aware of the importance of that moment except Ahithophel, whose counsel was rejected. "And when Ahithophel saw that his counsel was not followed, he saddled his ass, and arose, and gat him home to his house, to his city, and put his household in order, and hanged himself, and died, and was buried in the sepulchre of his father" (v. 23). The dejected man had nothing left for which to live.

THE FRIENDLY WOMEN . . . COOPERATING

Then said Hushai unto Zadok and to Abiathar the priests. . . . Send quickly, and tell David, saying, Lodge not this night in the plains of the wilderness. . . . Now Jonathan and Ahimaaz stayed by Enrogel . . . and a wench went and told them; and they went and told king David. Nevertheless a lad saw them, and told Absalom: but they went both of them away quickly, and came to a man's house in Bahurim, which had a well in his court; whither they went down. And the woman took and spread a covering over the well's mouth, and spread ground corn thereon; and the thing was not known (vv. 15-19).

Expository Notes on the Courage of Two Women

This little-known episode in the life of David supplies one of the most dramatic stories in the Bible; it has all the elements of a modern novel. When Zadok and Abiathar returned to Jerusalem, they made arrangements by which communication could be maintained with the fugitive king. Many obstacles had to be overcome, and every detail of their plans was veiled in secrecy. Absalom knew the direction in which David had fled, and as soon as he could gather an army, he intended to follow him. Meanwhile, every gate was carefully watched. It was to be expected that some of David's friends might try to join the king's followers; therefore, no person was allowed to leave Jerusalem without permission. That difficulty was easily overcome. Outside of the city was Enrogel—"the place of waters." Explaining the word, Adam Clarke wrote: "Enrogel means the 'Fuller's Well'—the place where they were accustomed to tread the clothes with their feet; hence *ein*—a well, and *regel*—the foot. *And a wench went and told them.* The word *wench* occurs nowhere else in the Holy Scriptures, and indeed, has no business here. The Hebrew word should have been translated "girl, maid, or maidservant."

It is easy to visualize the ancient scene. The two young priests who were to be messengers stayed at Enrogel. The young woman who rendezvoused with them would be permitted to leave the city, either under pretense of having to wash clothes or to obtain water. The city guards would neither suspect her departure nor prevent her re-entrance into the city. When her message had been delivered, she proceeded with her task, and the young men went on their appointed errand. One of the guards unfortunately saw the priests and informed Absalom. The delay enabled the messengers to get ahead of the pursuers, but the situation was becoming desperate when the couriers reached Bahurim, east of the Mount of Olives.

The Bible describes how they came to a home where the owner "had a well in his court." This "well" was probably a cistern in which rainwater was caught and stored. At that time it was dry and provided an excellent hiding place for the hunted men. The farmer's wife, having heard of the approaching danger, hurriedly asked the men to descend into the cistern, covered the opening, and then placed drying corn on the cover. Her action was—and still is—a common practice in the Middle East. When the pursuing enemies arrived, she misinformed the soldiers, who left hurriedly in a vain attempt to overtake the fleeing priests. That woman would have been killed had her deception been discovered. When the men delivered their message to David, the king and his company hurriedly continued their journey to a safer area. It has been said that friends are worth their weight in gold! If that opinion is correct, David was the wealthiest man in the world! This dramatic story of ancient espionage suggests certain thought-provoking truths.

God's Insignificant People

Even "little people" are essential for the fulfillment of God's purposes. Two unnamed women were leading figures in the clandestine operation. The maidservant was never mentioned again, and the woman who hid the young men in her well passed immediately out of the story. They were "little cogs in God's machinery," but without their assistance, the operation would have failed. The servant was evidently known to Zadok and Abiathar, but the farmer's wife apparently came into the story unexpectedly. Even though their names were never mentioned, their deeds became immortal. Scripture supplies other illustrations of "little-big people"! A maid from Israel was instrumental in saving the life of a Syrian captain (see 2 Kings 5:2). A Negro from Ethiopia rescued Jeremiah from the well into which enemies had placed the prophet (see Jeremiah 38:7-10). An unnamed lad supplied a lunch with which Christ fed a multitude of people (see John 6:9). A young relative supplied information to a Roman soldier and thereby saved the life of his Uncle Paul (see Acts 23:16-19). David knew the value of small things, for he chose five small pebbles from a brook to slay a giant. Someone said that even God knows the value of ordinary people—He made so many of them!

God's Indisputable Presence

Faithfulness to God is always rewarded by fellowship with Him. Was it by chance that the young messengers reached a home in Bahurim when a woman was working in her garden? Was it a coincidence that her rain-cistern was dry? Was it strange that she should be willing to risk her life by hiding fugitives? It may be impossible to know all the facts relevant to this account, but would it not be wise to ask if God arranged these details? Did He go ahead of the priests to make sure everything would be in readiness for their arrival? When the travelers hid in the darkness of the water cistern, did they realize that the Lord had taken the water *out* so that they could get *in*? Did they believe that God was in the well with them? He was never far from His faithful servants.

God's Indestructible Purposes

To see God fulfilling His purposes in the affairs of men is probably the greatest thrill ever known by human beings. Circumstances and people may appear to hinder the purposes of the Lord, but the final word always rests with Him. The poet wrote:

> God is working His purpose out
> As year succeeds to year.
> God is working His purpose out,
> And the time is drawing near.
> Nearer and nearer draws the time,
> The time that shall surely be.
> When the earth shall be filled with the glory of God
> As the waters cover the sea.

The psalms that were written by David indicate that he sometimes became despondent; he feared that his enemies might prevail against him. Yet, it became increasingly evident to him that the Lord was in charge of all that happened. God is never surprised or worried about the future, for He sees the end from the beginning. Job said, "But he knoweth the way that I take; when he hath tried me, I shall come forth as gold" (see Job 23:10). If David had trusted more, he would have worried less!

THE FAMOUS WISE MAN . . . COLLAPSING

And when Ahithophel saw that his counsel was not followed, he saddled his ass, and arose, and gat him home to his house, to his city, and put his household in order, and hanged himself, and died, and was buried in the sepulcher of his father (v. 23).

Expository Notes on the Death of Ahithophel

The suicide of Ahithophel terminated a brilliant career. The man whose abilities were unlimited, whose wisdom was seldom questioned, and who enjoyed a place of eminence among the aristocracy of his land, became petulant, unforgiving, and angry—and was discovered hanging by a rope. He had become enraged by David's lustful deeds. He never spoke with his friend about the terrible incident, and it became a spreading cancer within his soul. He could think of nothing else; bitterness enslaved him, and nothing mattered except to get even with the murderer who had been his royal friend (see 2 Samuel 11). The molehill of anger became a mountain of evil intent, and his outlook finally became so dark that he was unable to see beyond his disappointment.

An ancient tradition says that Ahithophel died of a *quinsy* and that the word might be translated "he was strangled or choked". That interpretation cannot be substantiated. Such commentators suggest that he was already suffering from a terrible throat infection and that when he recognized that retribution was imminent, he finally decided to commit suicide. Ahithophel was not mentally deranged, for, he attended with great care to the affairs of his estate—"he put his household in order." His life and death were tragedies. It could be said of him: "He might have been, but was not!" He might have become one of the greatest men in Hebrew history, but he unfortunately faded into insignificance. His tragedy could have been avoided—had he known how to forgive! (See the homily, "Ahithophel . . . the Man Who Could Not Forgive," p. 280).

THE FERVENT WORKERS . . . COLLECTING

And Absalom made Amasa captain of the host instead of Joab. . . . So Israel and Absalom pitched in the land of Gilead. And it came to pass, when David was come to Mahanaim, that Shobi . . . and Machir . . . and Barzillai . . . brought beds, and basons, and earthen vessels, and wheat, and barley, and flour, and parched corn, and beans, and lentiles, and parched pulse, and honey, and butter, and sheep, and cheese of kine, for David, and for the people that were with him, to eat: for they said, The people is hungry, and weary, and thirsty, in the wilderness (vv. 25-29).

Expository Notes on the Offerings of Three Great Men

Stars always appear to shine more brightly on dark nights! This observation is exemplified in the most gloomy experiences of David's life. When he was driven from his city and when everything appeared to be disastrous, the thoughtful provision of three wonderful men was overwhelming. Those illustrious people deserve investigation.

Shobi . . . The Gracious Man

To some degree this man was the most interesting of the three. His father, Nahash, the king of the Ammonites, had been infamous; his demand made to the men of Jabesh-Gilead had been inhuman and merciless (see 1 Samuel 11). His brother, Hanun, abused the messengers of David, and as a result, the king declared war on the pagans (see 2 Samuel 10). The atrocities perpetrated by his brother infuriated Shobi, who decided to become an ally of David. Not much was recorded about this delightful man; some think he was given land in Israel and became a minor chief. He probably embraced the monotheistic religion of the Hebrews, for idol worship would have been unpopular during the reign of David. Shobi was a very gracious man, for he gave up everything to become the friend of David. During the remaining part of his life, he was a true convert and never disappointed his master. He set an example which all Christians should emulate. When adversity overwhelmed the king, this delightful man hastily gathered supplies that David needed and hurried to Mahanaim to present his love-offerings.

Machir . . . The Grateful Man

Machir had been the foster-parent of Mephibosheth. Hearing about the injured son of Jonathan, he protected the helpless boy until the day David sent Ziba to bring the young man to Jerusalem. Machir loved his son and evidently never forgot the king's kindness. His child had been given a home in Jerusalem; his inheritance had been restored; his son was safe! The old man remembered the kindness shown to the crippled Mephibosheth, but he could not have anticipated what was to happen. When Absalom rebelled and David was forced to flee, Machir heard the sad news and decided the time had arrived to repay his debt of love. He had received so much that it was now time to give! He gathered provisions and began his journey to Mahanaim.

Barzillai . . . The Godly Man

Most of what is known of this wonderful man was described in a later episode of David's life. He was an exceedingly wealthy eighty-year-old man who preferred to remain in the country. He was a quiet, devoted soul who disliked the noise and glamour of the city; he loved the stillness where he could clearly hear the whispers of God. Material pleasures did not attract him; popularity did not appeal to him; he loved God and His servants. Had he been an ordinary man, he would have been content to let David fight his own battles and attend to his own destiny. Why should he forsake his home and accompany a fugitive into the wilderness? It would appear that his two associates delivered their love-offerings and departed for home. Barzillai had time to spare, and David needed encouragement. The old man smiled and refused to leave his king. His later testimony indicates that he was deaf, partially blind, and insensitive to taste. He lived in the seclusion of his own world, at the center of which was God. When he sat in David's tent, his calm expression announced that he had come to stay. He had no intentions of leaving, and David knew it was useless to argue with him. The king was glad because it would be impossible to be lonely when such a friend was near.

David looked at the abundance of provisions and, temporarily forgetting the threat of tomorrow, arranged a banquet beneath the stars. It would be difficult to decide who possessed greater happiness—the men who gave or David who received!

Episode 37

THEME: *The Death of Absalom*

SCRIPTURE: 2 Samuel 18

KEY VERSE:

> But the people answered, Thou shalt not go forth: for if we flee away, they will not care for us; neither if half of us die, will they care for us: but now, thou art worth ten thousand of us: therefore now it is better that thou succor us out of the city (v. 3).

OUTLINE:
    I.   A Definite Desire (Verses 3-4)
    II. A Deserved Death (Verses 14-15)
    III. A Disputed Denial (Verses 19-23)
    IV. A Devastated David (Verses 32-33)

A DEFINITE DESIRE

And the king said unto the people, I will surely go forth with you myself also. But the people answered, Thou shalt not go forth: for if we flee away, they will not care for us; neither if half of us die, will they care for us: but now thou art worth ten thousand of us: therefore now it is better that thou succor us out out of the city. And the king said unto them, What seemeth you best I will do. And the king stood by the gate side, and all the people came out by hundreds and by thousands (vv. 2-4).

Expository Notes on the Decision of David's Army

"And David numbered the people that were with him, and set captains of thousands and captains of hundreds over them" (18:1). The number of soldiers accompanying David when he left Jerusalem was very small, but as news of the insurrection spread through the land, men rallied to the aid of the king. Josephus wrote: "But when David had numbered his followers, and found them to be about four thousand, he resolved not to tarry till Absalom attacked him, but set over his men captains" (*Antiquities of the Jews*, Book 7, Chapter 10, Paragraph 1). Most of these untrained men probably came from Gilead and brought such weapons as were available.

David, an experienced warrior, divided his army into three sections. The main force was to be flanked on the right and the left sides by supporting troops. One section was placed under the command of Abishai, Joab led the chief section, and the third was led by Ittai, a Philistine from Gath who had become David's friend and was commander of his own special troops. While Absalom gathered his army, David's generals quickly but expertly organized their divisions and prepared to launch their attack against the usurper prince.

The king's emotions were stirred as he looked at the men who were willing to die for him, but when he proudly offered to lead them into battle, the commanders and men resolutely rejected the idea. They said, "Master, if we die, what would that matter? but, if you were slain, what would be left in Israel? Thou art worth ten thousand of us." A more accurate reading would be as follows: "There are thousands of us, but no one is like you." They suggested that David would help more by "succoring them out of the city." The center column would engage the enemy, while the divisions on the right and left flanks would support Joab. David, with a specially chosen company, would wait in the city, and if any of the three columns needed help, his group would assist wherever they were needed. Perhaps that idea helped David accept the suggestion that he should refrain from leading the army. The king would recognize the wisdom of the arrangement and at the same time feel proud he was being trusted with a key role in the military operation. This explanation shows how he could "succor his troops" by remaining within the city of Mahanaim.

A DESERVED DEATH

It must have been a solemn and emotional time when the elderly king stood on the wall of Mahanaim to survey his departing soldiers. They were ready to fight, and the three commanders were anxious to begin the battle. Then, David lifted his hand to command attention. He had a final command for his men. "And the king commanded Joab and Abishai and Ittai, saying, Deal gently for my sake with the young man, even with Absalom. And all the people heard when the king gave all the captains charge concerning Absalom" (v. 5). It would have been interesting to know the thoughts of the listening soldiers. They were ready to die for David, and yet he apparently thought more of his renegade son than he did of his friends. Their thoughts remain unrevealed, but Joab's eyes narrowed, and his countenance set resolutely. He knew precisely how he would handle the young prince if Absalom became his prisoner. Joab decided that if David were unable to make a just decision, perhaps he needed assistance. The general was prepared for that ominous moment.

So the people went out into the field against Israel: and the battle was in the wood of Ephraim; Where the people of Israel were slain before the

servants of David, and there was there a great slaughter that day of twenty thousand men. For the battle was there scattered over the face of all the country: and the wood devoured more people that day than the sword devoured.... And Absalom rode upon a mule, and the mule went under the thick boughs of a great oak, and his head caught hold of the oak, and he was taken up between the heaven and the earth; and the mule that was under him went away.... And [Joab] took three darts in his hand, and thrust them through the heart of Absalom, while he was yet alive in the midst of the oak. And ten young men that bare Joab's armor compassed about, and smote Absalom, and slew him (vv. 6-15).

Expository Notes on the Death of Absalom

Absalom not only deserved to die, but he had already been sentenced to death by the laws of God. Moses said, "If a man have a stubborn and rebellious son, which will not obey the voice of his father, or the voice of his mother, and that, when they have chastened him, will not hearken unto them: then shall his father and mother lay hold on him, and bring him out unto the elders of his city, and unto the gate of his place. . . . And all the men of his city shall stone him with stones, that he die" (Deut. 21:18, 21). David's love for his rebellious son may be understood by all parents, but the fact remains that the king's excessive love for Absalom and his intense desire to spare his life brought about a violation of the commandment of God and an unpardonable failure in administering justice. God said, "So shalt thou put away evil from among you; and all Israel shall hear, and fear" (Deut. 21:21). David had difficulty obeying God because he desired to preserve one whom the Lord had sentenced to death.

When the battle commenced, "the wood devoured more people that day than the sword devoured." The battlefield formed a dense mass with its swamps and tangled growth of terebinth and other trees. Also, some areas had precipices which jutted up from the Dead Sea. The terebinth grows to a height of thirty-five feet; its foliage is thick so that its shade was able to provide excellent concealment for the idolatrous sacrifices offered during some periods of Jewish history. The Hebrew text suggests that "the battle was a scattering." Joab's columns effectively divided and routed the army of Absalom, and the men of Israel fled in disarray. Some soldiers stumbled into swamps and others fell down precipices, while others lost their way and became easy prey for the relentless servants of David.

Throughout the centuries it has been assumed that Absalom's long and beautiful hair became entangled in branches, and he was left hanging from a tree. This has no verification in the Word of God. Others believe that the onrushing mule passed beneath the trees so that Absalom's head became wedged between two branches. When Absalom released his hold on the reins, the animal moved away, thus leaving its helpless rider suspended in the air. His head was firmly wedged between the branches, and although he tried to extricate himself, he remained helpless.

When Joab arrived on the scene, he took three darts which probably were pieces of wood sharpened at one end. These darts he drove into Absalom's body and the young men who were the bodyguards of their leader completed what Joab commenced. The soldier who refused to take advantage of Absalom's helplessness thus showed his intense desire to please David. The reward suggested by Joab meant promotion in the army. A girdle was a sash, a sign of rank and authority, and the insignia of a commission. The man was probably correct when he said: "Thou thyself wouldest have set thyself against me." When Absalom's body was thrown into a ditch and covered with stones, the place became a memorial to the folly of a prince and a reminder of the advice: "Put not your trust in princes, nor in the son of man, in whom there is no help" (Psalm 146:3).

A DISPUTED DENIAL

> **Then said Joab to Cushi, Go tell the king what thou hast seen. . . . And Joab said [to Ahimaaz], Wherefore wilt thou run, my son, seeing thou hast no tidings ready? But howsoever, said he, Let me run. And he said unto him, Run. Then Ahimaaz ran by the way of the plain, and overran Cushi. . . . And the king said, Is the young man Absalom safe? And Ahimaaz answered, When Joab sent the king's servant, and me thy servant, I saw a great tumult, but I knew not what it was. And the king said unto him, Turn aside, and stand here. . . . And the king said unto Cushi, Is the young man Absalom safe? And Cushi answered, The enemies of my lord the king . . . be as that young man is (vv. 21-32).**

Expository Notes on the Conflicting Reports of Two Messengers

It seems incongruous that Joab should be reluctant to dispatch Ahimaaz and yet be willing to send Cushi. Later, the general yielded to persuasion and allowed the son of the priest to do as he desired. There is an explanation of the problem. One messenger was Cushi, who was possibly an Ethiopian—a black man. The other was the son of the high priest and was considered by Joab to be "his son." He was one of the two men who hid in the water cistern at Bahurim. Later, when a watchman said to David, "Methinketh the running of the foremost is like the running of Ahimaaz the son of Zadok," the king replied, "He is a good man." Maybe Joab remembered that when an Amalekite carried news of Saul's death to David, the messenger was executed! These details suggest that since his messenger would be a bearer of sad news, David impulsively might inflict a similar punishment upon the courier. That would explain his readiness to send Cushi, the Ethiopian who was possibly a slave, instead of the "son" who had won an abiding place in the general's affections. Afterward, believing the first messenger would have prepared David for the arrival of Ahimaaz, he permitted the son of Zadok to proceed on his mission. Joab did not know that by taking a short cut, Ahimaaz would overtake the first runner and be the first to tell the king about the battle. The ancient historian described the two runners and their conflicting reports.

George Adam Clarke believed that Ahimaaz was unaware of the execution of Absalom (*The Bethany Parallel Commentary on the Old Testament*, p. 612) and therefore could not inform David about his death. That suggestion is difficult to accept. Cushi, who was first dispatched, knew about the demise of Absalom, so the people present at the time evidently had already heard the news when Cushi commenced his journey. Ahimaaz was with Joab even before Cushi was told to leave; therefore, he surely knew about the execution in the wood. It was his decision not to tell David the details of Absalom's death. His report was partial, but considerate. Cushi was blunt, but truthful. That comparison evokes a provocative question. Which of the messengers was the more reliable? If it is permissible to superimpose that scene upon the modern world, the question might be asked: Which of today's preachers would be more acceptable to God—the kind speaker who says nothing to hurt or offend anyone or the preacher who speaks the truth even though listeners may be upset by unpleasant facts? Popularity won through compromise is always superficial and temporal and never brings peace to the soul.

A DEVASTATED DAVID

And the king was much moved [trembled], and went up to the chamber over the gate, and wept: and as he went, thus he said, O my son Absalom, my son, my son Absalom! would God I had died for thee, O Absalom, my son, my son (v. 33).

Expository Notes on David's Lament Over the Death of Absalom

David evidently sat in a special chamber above and between the gates of the city. When the runners arrived carrying tidings of the conflict, he descended to hear their reports, and that fact explains why, after hearing of the death of his son, "[he] went up to the chamber over the gate." He was very sad because of the death of Absalom, but it is difficult to avoid the conclusion that his grief was intense because he was responsible for the misfortune which had overtaken his family. After the murder of Bathsheba's husband, God pronounced judgment upon David by saying, "Now therefore the sword shall never depart from thine house; because thou hast despised me, and hast taken the wife of Uriah the Hittite to be thy wife. Thus saith the LORD, Behold, I will raise up evil against thee *out of thine own house*, and I will take thy wives before thine eyes, and give them unto thy neighbor, and he shall lie with thy wives in the sight of this sun" (2 Samuel 12:10-11).

Is it so far from thee,
  Thou canst no longer see
In the chamber over the gate
  That old man desolate,
Weeping and wailing sore,
  For his son who is no more?
O Absalom my son!

Somewhere at every hour
  The watchman on the tower
Looks forth to see the fleet
  Approach of hurrying feet
Of messengers that bear
  The tidings of despair.
O Absalom my son.

That 'tis a common grief
  Bringeth but slight relief;
Ours in the bitterest loss,
  Ours is the heaviest cross;
And forever the cry will be,
  "Would God I had died for thee
O Absalom my son!"

—Lord Alfred Tennyson, 1809-1892

Episode 38

THEME: *David's Return to Jerusalem*

SCRIPTURE: 2 Samuel 19

KEY VERSE:

And [David] bowed the heart of all the men of Judah, even as the heart of one man; so that they sent this word unto the king, Return thou, and all thy servants (v. 14).

OUTLINE:
   I.   A Solemn Rebuke (Verses 1-8)
   II. A Senseless Remark (Verses 9-14)
   III. A Spoiled Return (Verse 15)
   IV. A Sincere Remorse (Verses 16-23)
   V.   A Splendid Revelation (Verses 24-30)
   VI. A Sublime Refusal (Verses 31-39)
   VII. A Shameful Reaction (Verses 40-43)

A SOLEMN REBUKE

And it was told Joab, Behold, the king weepeth and mourneth for Absalom. . . . And Joab came into the house to the king, and said, Thou hast shamed this day the faces of all thy servants. . . . in that thou lovest thine enemies, and hatest thy friends. . . . I perceive, that if Absalom had lived, and all we had died this day, then it had pleased thee well. Now therefore arise, go forth, and speak comfortably unto thy servants; for I swear by the LORD, if thou go not forth, there will not tarry one with thee this night, and that will be worse unto thee than all the evil that befell thee from thy youth until now. Then the king arose and sat in the gate (vv. 1-8).

Expository Notes on Joab's Condemnation of David

The battle in the wood was over, the enemy had been put to flight, and Joab's victorious army was returning to Mahanaim. The men were exultant, the young women would be dancing and singing, and the sound of the trumpets would be exhilarating. The men could already feel the enthusiasm of the victory celebrations. Then the outlook suddenly changed. The city was wrapped in silence, the welcoming crowds were absent, and the place was filled with gloom. When the astonished soldiers asked what had happened, they were informed of the king's reaction to the news of Absalom's death. David was weeping and wishing he also had been slain. The men slowly broke rank and went into the city. They were ashamed, their joy was turned to sorrow, "and the people gat them by stealth that day into the city, as people being ashamed steal away when they flee in battle" (v. 3). Joab, the victorious general, was annoyed; his face was set in firm resolute lines as he angrily went in search of his disappointing master.

David heard the ominous footsteps on the stairs and looked through tear-filled eyes at the intruder. The relationship between them had gradually deteriorated since the day when Joab killed Abner, and it had become evident that they detested each other. David had dismissed his leader from the post of commander in chief of the army and had only restored this position after the capture of Jerusalem. Had the king been able to manage the affairs of state without him, he would have done so. It appears that Joab served because he desired to be a man of importance in the nation, but his respect for the king had diminished to such an extent that on this occasion he was gruff and rude. Both men merely tolerated each other.

The irate commander looked at the weeping David, and his indictment was scathing: "Thou hast shamed this day the faces of all thy servants, which this day have saved thy life, and the lives of thy sons, and of thy daughters, and the lives of thy wives, and the lives of thy concubines . . . thou lovest thine enemies, and hatest thy friends." Joab's tirade was scornful, harsh, and devoid of the respect customarily shown to a king. His manner might have been deplorable, but he spoke the truth. David's excessive sorrow had ruined what should have been a day of rejoicing. His attitude shamed the brave men who fought for him. The king was thoughtless and revolting! Joab's anger was unrestrained, and his criticism justified.

When the people said, "And Absalom, whom we anointed over us is dead," they remembered a coronation in Hebron. Absalom had not only tried to steal the kingdom, but his insurrection had also been supported by multitudes of Hebrews, and a ceremony had been officially held. The death of the usurper and the subsequent flight of his army did not change the two facts that David had been rejected in favor of Absalom and that the enemies who approved this action still existed in Israel. Joab was aware that his victory in the wood of Ephraim could be negated by the stupidity of an old king. David should have been rallying his forces for a march on Jerusalem. If his enemies insisted on his abdication, they had to be confronted either with powerful objections or by military force. Even if the battle had been won, the future remained in jeopardy. If Joab's manner lacked prudence, he was justified in making his remarks. That David immediately responded to the advice of his general indicates that he recognized the wisdom of what was spoken. Unfortunately, it soon became evident that the king resented what he considered to be intolerable interference from a man who should have attended to his own business!

A SENSELESS REMARK

And king David sent to Zadok and to Abiathar the priests, saying, Speak unto the elders of Judah, saying, Why are ye the last to bring the king back to his house? . . . And say ye to Amasa, Art thou not of my bone, and of my flesh? God do so to me, and more also, if thou be not captain of the host before me continually in the room of Joab (vv. 11-13).

Expository Notes on the Foolishness of David

At that period in his life, David was out of touch with God. He never called for the priest with the ephod, he never consulted a prophet, and his actions were self-centered. His intention to replace Joab with the leader of Absalom's followers was a crime in itself, and Joab would have been less than human had he not resented David's plan. Some teachers believe that the king's act was wise in that his winning of Amasa ended his animosity toward David and assured the king of a favorable reaction to his request to be recalled to Jerusalem. Honor gained through treachery breeds disgrace; as a result, David permitted his hatred of Joab to dominate his thoughts.

Amasa was the son of David's sister (see 1 Chronicles 2:17), and with the departure of Joab, Absalom appointed him as the new commander in chief of Israel's army, even though his superior forces had been defeated and in spite of the evidence that Amasa was less skilled then Joab. David's actions may be compared with a modern situation. World War II was won by the Allied Forces, of which Great Britain was a part. If the British government had invited Adolf Hitler to replace Winston Churchill as its leader, the free world would have been angry. Yet, it was a similar action that David planned to do in Israel. To succeed with his plans it would be necessary to remove Joab. If he were assassinated, Abishai would avenge his death. David's treachery and the selfishness by which his plans were formulated were among the basest features of the king's life.

There were three kinds of people in Israel: many who were faithful to David, a far greater number who had vowed allegiance to Absalom, and a third group which had no interest in either David or a successor. The death of Absalom had created problems for his friends. If David were restored to the throne of Israel, would he execute his enemies? The elders in Jerusalem had been among the insurgents and had assisted the usurper prince. If they invited David to resume his leadership, would he punish them for their indiscretion? Maybe such a fear explains their delay in recalling the exiled monarch. David's intention to replace Joab with Amasa might have been reassurance to everybody that he had no ill feelings against anyone. Amnesty would be granted to all offenders, and as that news spread through the land, "[David] bowed the heart of all the men of Judah, even as the heart of one man; so that they sent this word unto the king, Return thou and all thy servants."

A SPOILED RETURN

So the king returned, and came to Jordan. And Judah came to Gilgal, to go to meet the king, to conduct the king over Jordan (v. 15).

It is to be regretted that most of David's decisions at this time were unwise. He had embarked upon a course of self-destruction, but was unaware of the consequences of his foolish decisions. His appeal to the tribe of Judah and his neglect of the other tribes aroused fierce resentment, and his return home was ruined. The northern tribes became infuriated, and David, who never sought advice from anyone, created circumstances which almost proved to be fatal. This dangerous situation was accentuated by the fact that a thousand Benjamites had welcomed the returning exile (see the notes under the section, "A Sublime Refusal," p. 310).

A SINCERE REMORSE

And Shimei the son of Gera, a Benjamite which was of Bahurim, hasted and came down with the men of Judah to meet king David. And there were a thousand men of Benjamin with him. . . . And Shimei . . . fell down before the king . . . and said unto the king, Let not my lord impute iniquity unto me, neither do thou remember that which thy servant did perversely the day that my lord the king went out of Jerusalem. For thy servant doth know that I have sinned. . . . But Abishai . . . said . . . Shall not Shimei be put to death for this, because he cursed the LORD's anointed? And David said. . . . Shall there any man be put to death this day in Israel? Therefore the king said unto Shimei, Thou shalt not die. And the king sware unto him (vv. 16-23).

Expository Notes on David's Reception of Shimei

The story of Shimei may be considered under four headings.

His Sinful Rebellion

The fact that he brought one thousand men to meet David suggests that he was a chief with considerable influence. He was also a member of the household of Saul, a fact that might conceivably have accounted for his jealousy toward David. He possibly believed that he had stronger claims to the throne, a belief that explains his rash action when he cursed and stoned the departing monarch (see 2 Samuel 16:5-6). His stupidity could have been fatal, but the despondent king refused to slay the offending Benjamite. Nevertheless, it was evident that Shimei loathed David and would have killed him had that been possible.

His Sober Reflection

Theologians have been divided in their opinion concerning the change in Shimei's attitude. When David returned, the man who had cursed him apologized for his former behavior. Was his repentance genuine, or was he motivated by fear of an impending execution? The fact that he was accompanied by such a large number of men might have been a promise that his friends would support David in his attempt to regain the throne of Israel. He said: "For thy servant doth know that I have sinned; therefore, behold, I am come the first this day of all the house of Joseph to go down to meet my lord the king." Abishai was not impressed, either by Shimei's confession or by his large group of followers, and asked permission to slay the offender. The king was wise not to ruin his homecoming by committing murder. Shimei reflected on his actions and knew that he needed forgiveness.

His Sincere Remorse

It is interesting that Shimei claimed to belong to "the house of Joseph." The prophet Amos (5:6) spoke of that same house and implied that he was addressing *all* the northern tribes! Shimei indirectly claimed affiliation with the greater section of the nation and, by so doing, enhanced his appeal for clemency. His confession of guilt and his prostration at the feet of David indicated that he was truly repentant and was appealing for undeserved forgiveness. Maybe he had learned genuine repentance within the sanctuary of Jehovah. If God could pardon the guilty, perhaps David might be willing to follow His example.

His Sublime Relief

"Therefore the king said unto Shimei, Thou shalt not die. And the king sware unto him." Relief filled the soul of the guilty man when David vowed to protect him. David's word was reliable; it was inconceivable that it would ever be violated. The forgiven man rose to his feet; he was free to return to his home. That morning, he came to the Jordan with a cloud of apprehension on his mind, but suddenly his burdens were removed since he was a free man. David unfortunately was unlike Jehovah. When God forgave sin, He also forgot it (see Jeremiah 31:34). Years later, Shimei learned that his sin had never been forgotten. His indiscretions were resurrected, and he was executed (see the homily, "Shimei . . . and the Ghost That Killed Him," p. 312).

A SPLENDID REVELATION

And Mephibosheth the son of Saul came down to meet the king, and had neither dressed his feet, nor trimmed his beard, nor washed his clothes, from the day the king departed until the day he came again in peace. And it came to pass . . . the king said unto him, Wherefore wentest not thou with me, Mephibosheth? And he answered, My lord, O king, my servant deceived me: for thy servant said, I will saddle me an ass, that I may ride thereon, and go to the king; because thy servant is lame. . . . And the king said unto him, Why speakest thou any more of thy matters? I have said, Thou and Ziba divide the land. And Mephibosheth said unto the king, Yea, let him take all, forasmuch as my lord the king is come again in peace unto his own house (vv. 24-30).

Expository Notes on the Faithfulness of Mephibosheth

This event was one of the most delightful in the life of David; it was a resplendent sunrise seen against the blackness of adversity. The account may be summarized under four headings.

The Inescapable Problem

Mephibosheth, the crippled son of Jonathan, had been brought to Jerusalem by Ziba. David had restored his inheritance, and Ziba and his fifteen sons were commissioned to attend to the estate and to share the profits with their master. The news that Absalom was attempting to steal the kingdom devastated David's friends, but Mephibosheth was the most helpless of them all. Others were able to leave their homes and follow the king into exile, but the cripple was a victim of circumstances. Although handicapped by infirmity, he did what was possible and commanded his servant to make preparation to accompany David. Ziba unfortunately refused to obey his orders. He carried provisions to David and slandered his master. When that servant did not return, Mephibosheth was confronted by his greatest problem. The king would believe he had been unappreciated and would seek an explanation if David ever returned to Jerusalem. Ziba's story would be repeated, and it would be his word against the testimony of Mephibosheth.

His Illustrious Profession

When Absalom saw the cripple, his scorn was unmistakable. Mephibosheth had decided not to attend to his wounds, wash his clothes nor trim his beard. The story implies that the feet of the handicapped man needed daily attention, but when his needs were neglected, the consequences became obnoxious. As the stench accentuated, people detected its source. Mephibosheth resolutely refused to trim his beard, an unpardonable action since a beard was the pride and joy of every man. If Absalom asked why he had allowed himself to become an object of derision, Mephibosheth explained that he had no desire to live in comfort while David was a fugitive. If the king died, then he also desired to die. David had supplied him with happiness beyond his wildest dreams, and Mephibosheth would always remain true to his friend. Absalom and his followers could make life miserable, but nothing would destroy the cripple's love for the deposed king. He intended to be loyal to David even though the king may never know Mephibosheth's self-sacrifice.

The Indisputable Proof

When David returned to Jerusalem, he asked for an explanation, and the younger man in so many words said: "Master, I know that you were misinformed by the lies of my servant, but actually I asked him to saddle an ass so that I could ride with you. Unfortunately, he never returned, and I was helpless. But David, look at me! If you cannot believe your ears, perhaps you can trust your eyes!" "And the king saw he had neither dressed his feet, nor trimmed his beard, nor washed his clothes from the day the king departed, until the day he came again in peace." Mephibosheth had been faithful all the time David had been the "despised and rejected of men" (isa. 53:3), a faithfulness that should be an example for all Christians.

His Infinite Pleasure

Perhaps David was a little embarrassed as he looked at his friend; he had been too quick to condemn and had not sought corroboration of Ziba's report. His friend watched as the king considered what action to take. "And the king said unto him, Why speakest thou any more of thy matters? I have said, Thou and Ziba divide the land." It is hard to avoid the conclusion that David's decision left much to be desired. He did not condemn the lies of Ziba, and there was no punishment for the deliberate falsehoods. Yet, the king could not remove Ziba and his family from the service of Mephibosheth, for without their assistance, the man would have been helpless. The dividing of the land was normal procedure. Ziba was returned to his former position, and although the land remained the possession of Mephibosheth, the profits were equally divided between the master and his workmen. Joy shining in the eyes of Mephibosheth expressed the happiness surging within his soul. Material possessions had lost their attractiveness because the safe return of David supplied all that his faithful friend required (see the homily, "Mephibosheth . . . and His Glorious Wretchedness," p. 227).

A SUBLIME REFUSAL

And Barzillai the Gileadite came down from Rogelim, and went over Jordan with the king, to conduct him over Jordan. Now Barzillai was a very aged man, even fourscore years old: and he had provided the king of sustenance while he lay at Mahanaim; for he was a very great man. And the king said unto Barzillai, Come thou over with me, and I will feed thee with me in Jerusalem. And Barzillai said unto the king, How long have I to live, that I should go up with the king unto Jerusalem? I am this day fourscore years old. . . . wherefore then should thy servant be yet a burden unto my lord the king? . . . Let thy servant, I pray thee, turn back again, that I may die in mine own city, and be buried by the grave of my father and of my mother. . . . And all the people went over Jordan. And when the king was come over, the king kissed Barzillai, and blessed him; and he returned unto his own place (vv. 31-39).

Expository Notes on the Wisdom of Barzillai

Barzillai was one of the few people described in the Bible as being "a very great man." What was recorded of him may be summarized under three headings.

His Wealth Was Shared

My friend the late Dr. Frank Boreham often said: "If you possess anything without which you cannot live, give it away." Some people work hard to acquire wealth, but are reluctant to give any of it to others. Barzillai lived for eighty years and was one of the richest men in the nation, but he was also wealthy in spiritual values. When he heard that the anointed of God had been driven into exile, he hastily gathered a great amount of food and went to Mahanaim to sustain David and his army. He was richer because of his generosity. Barzillai had learned a New Testament truth long before Jesus taught it. "Give, and it shall be given unto you; good measure, pressed down, and shaken together, and running over, shall men give into your bosom. For with the same measure that ye mete, withal it shall be measured to you again" (Luke 6:38).

His Wisdom Was Shown

Barzillai's wisdom increased with his age. His health had unfortunately deteriorated, since his eyesight was poor; his hearing impaired; and his sense of taste, non-existent. The entertainment in David's palace was unattractive because the old man loved stillness. When he sat in his garden, he looked into the hereafter, which, was infinitely better in his sight than sitting in David's palace watching artists perform. On his eightieth birthday, he asked a very potent question, "How long have I to live?" The aged man knew that only a limited number of days or weeks remained, and to waste precious moments seeking the pleasures of earth would be foolish. He would soon be journeying to another palace—one which was eternal in the heavens.

His Wish Was Special

Gratefully, but firmly, he declined David's magnanimous offer, but said that he would appreciate any kindness which might be extended to his son Chimham. If showing kindness brought happiness to David, then by all means the boy should go to Jerusalem. The king consented, and it appears from the sacred record that he gave to the son of Barzillai some of his personal estate close to Bethlehem. The prophet Jeremiah wrote, "And they departed, and dwelt in the habitation of Chimham, which is by Bethlehem, to go to enter into Egypt" (Jeremiah 41:17). It is significant that David never forgot the kindness of Barzillai. When the king was dying, he said to Solomon, "But shew kindness unto the sons of Barzillai the Gileadite, and let them be of those that eat of thy table: for so they came to me when I fled because of Absalom thy brother" (1 Kings 2:7). Barzillai bequeathed to humanity an additional beatitude—"Blessed are they who think kindly of others." (See the homily, "Barzillai . . . Who Went Home to Wait for God," p. 314.)

A SHAMEFUL REACTION

And, behold, all the men of Israel came to the king, and said unto the king, Why have our brethren the men of Judah stolen thee away? . . . And all the men of Judah answered . . . Because the king is near of kin to us. . . . And the men of Israel answered . . . and said, We have ten parts in the king, and we have also more right to David than ye: why then did ye despise us? . . . And the words of the men of Judah were fiercer than the words of the men of Israel. And . . . a man of Belial, whose name was Sheba . . . blew a trumpet, and said, We have no part in David . . . every man to his tents, O Israel. So every man of Israel went up from after David, and followed Sheba . . . but the men of Judah clave unto their king, from Jordan even to Jerusalem (vv. 19:41—20:2).

Expository Notes on the Villainy of Sheba

David was always capable of "falling out of the frying pan into the fire"! His return to Jerusalem was ruined by either thoughtlessness or selfishness. The men of Judah deliberately, or by an oversight, forgot to share their privileges with the rest of the nation, an omission that caused strife. The other tribes resented their exclusion, and their anger was exploited by a man called Sheba, who blew a trumpet and shouted, "We have no part in David, neither have we inheritance in the son of Jesse: every man to his tents, O Israel." That rebellious act turned rejoicing into dismay. The depravity of human nature was never seen more clearly than in the catastrophic division of Israel, when fierce pride and provocative arguments confronted the jealousy and anger of the opposition. The bitter quarreling between the two sections of Israel revealed superlative need. Humanity requires a new nature, not an improvement of the old one. The Savior said, "That which is born of the flesh is flesh; and that which is born of the Spirit is spirit" (John 3:6). Human beings are always experts at getting into trouble! They need help from someone capable of turning disasters into deliverance, shamefulness into success, and vices into victories. David reaped what he had sown. What happened in Jerusalem is evidence to substantiate the words of the poet who said: "Oh, what a tangled web we weave, when first we practice to deceive." David's sin led him into quicksands from which escape seemed impossible. The harder the king struggled, the lower he sank. Sheba caused havoc in Israel, but David's problems could have been avoided had he exercised more care. A fence on the top of a cliff is better than an ambulance at the bottom!

HOMILIES FOR PREACHERS AND TEACHERS

Study No. 16

SHIMEI . . . and the Ghost That Killed Him
(2 Samuel 16:5-8; 1 Kings 2:8-9)

It has been said that a policeman can always be recognized by his feet! The same is true of a saint, for the Christian's walk is indicative of his character. Alas, many people are like Nebuchadnezzar's image—they have a head of gold and feet of clay. I sorrowfully confess that one of my biblical idols proved to be of this type. David, the sweet singer of Israel, ended his life in discord. He whose songs of praise had reached highest heaven failed to hold his note, and the harmony of a lifetime was shattered.

A GUILTY MAN

Treachery in the city had forced David to flee. The incoming of Absalom and his evil associates had threatened murder, and David, with a few of his faithful friends, had slipped away into the country. Then, suddenly, a man came running across the fields. "And when king David came to Bahurim, behold, thence came out a man of the family of the house of

Saul, whose name was Shimei, the son of Gera: he came forth, and cursed still as he came. And he cast stones at David. . . . And thus said . . . Come out . . . thou bloody man. . . . The LORD hath returned upon thee all the blood of the house of Saul. . . . Then said Abishai . . . unto the king, Why should this dead dog curse my lord the king? let me go over, I pray thee, and take off his head. . . . And the king said. . . . let him curse" (2 Sam. 16:5-10). Thus a very guilty man was spared. He deserved death, but David forbade his execution.

A GRACIOUS MONARCH

The scene has changed. The deciding battle has been fought and won, and the king returned to his palace. "So the king returned. . . . And Shimei . . . came down with the men of Judah to meet king David. . . . But Abishai . . . said, Shall not Shimei be put to death for this, because he cursed the LORD's anointed? Therefore the king said unto Shimei, Thou shalt not die. And the king sware unto him" (2 Samuel 19:15-23). David's actions at this time have won the admiration of many people. Shimei had great cause for gratitude. Forgiveness is a wonderful thing—when it is forgiveness. David seemed to be a giant among virtuous men—but, alas, his feet were of clay! Thirty years later, "the days of David drew nigh that he should die; and he charged Solomon his son, saying, I go the way of all the earth: be thou strong therefore, and shew thyself a man. . . . And, behold, thou hast with thee Shimei . . . which cursed me with a grievous curse. . . . Now therefore hold him not guiltless . . . his hoar head bring thou down to the grave with blood" (1 Kings 2:1-9). What a tragedy! Surely our psalmist was out of tune!

A GHASTLY MURDER

This final request of King David was among the most disappointing actions of biblical history. He had apparently forgiven the offender, but had retained his bitter memories. He had forgiven, but had not forgotten Shimei's sin. The subsequent story of murder has been told for us in 1 Kings 2:36-46. Some may attach blame to Shimei for disobeying Solomon, but nothing will ever alter David's last request. Even Solomon was condemned by the fact that the man whose execution he ordered had been one of his faithful servants during the insurrection of Adonijah (1 Kings 1:8). Those were days when personal loyalty and genuine gratitude were sacrificed on the altar of passion. How refreshing it is to turn to the words of God in Jeremiah 31:34: "I will forgive their iniquity, *and I will remember their sin no more.*" When God forgives, He forgets, a fact which gives us security and peace. The precious blood of Jesus washed our sins away forever. The ghost of Shimei's past returned after thirty years. His arrival was inopportune and tragic. I am so glad that I met Christ. I don't believe in ghosts—now.

> Gone, Gone, Gone, Gone, Yes, my sins are gone:
> Now my soul is free, And in my heart's a song.
> Buried in the deepest sea, Yes, that's good enough for me:
> I shall live eternally; Praise God, my sins are gone.

(Homily reprinted from the author's book, *Bible Cameos*, pp. 41-42.)

HOMILIES FOR PREACHERS AND TEACHERS

Study No. 17

BARZILLAI ... Who Went Home to Wait for God (2 Samuel 19:33-37)

Dear Barzillai,

You are one of the not-so-well-known characters of the ancient writings, for your story is hidden in history—but we have found you out! You did not like a lot of publicity, and perhaps even now you will shrink from being brought into the limelight. Accept our apologies, noble sir, and if our actions seem to offend, grant an indulgence. We like you—we like you a lot—for in that wise old head of yours you possess much wisdom. Again and again we have read the brief record of your exploits, and it seems to us that you passed through four definite phases. Forgive us if we seem to be chopping up your story; but, dear friend, we are preachers. I suppose that proves one thing or another. I don't know which!

YOUR PERSONAL REGARD

We have been told that when David fled from the rebellion of Absalom, you with others "brought beds, and basons, and earthen vessels, and wheat, and barley, and flour, and parched corn, and beans, and lentiles, and parched pulse, and honey, and butter, and sheep, and cheese of kine, for David, and for the people that were with him, to eat: for they said, The people is hungry, and weary, and thirsty, in the wilderness" (2 Samuel 17:28-29). Nice work, Barzillai! You thought of everything in that hour of emergency. In these modern days people would have taken a collection of canned goods and would have forgotten the can opener! We have often considered your liking for David. You surely thought a great deal of your master, for at the time of your allegiance, the outlook was gloomy. We admire loyalty and faithfulness, and your glorious deed has become an immortal example. Well done, old man. We are proud of you.

YOUR PERSISTENT REFUSAL

How we would have loved to see David's face when you disappointed him. Oh, Barzillai! He had planned to give you the time of your life. What a present for your eightieth birthday—a royal present, too —and you refused it. How long did David try to persuade you to change your mind? Old friend, we know many people who would have jumped at the chance to accompany David to the palace in order to live in the lap of luxury. The soft lights and sweet music of the royal household would ravish their hearts, and no consideration would make them refuse a king's offer. We can still hear David saying, "Come thou over with me, and I will feed thee with me in Jerusalem" (v. 19:33)—and you shook your head.

YOUR POTENT REALIZATION

"I am this day fourscore years old: and can I discern between good and evil? can thy servant taste what I eat or what I drink? can I hear any more the voice of singing men and singing women? wherefore then should thy servant be yet a burden unto my lord the king? . . . Let thy servant I pray thee, turn back again, that I may die in mine own city, and be buried by the grave of my father and of my mother" (vv. 19:35, 37). You crafty old man—you were an expert diplomat. Even David could not have been offended at the refusal, for your arguments were unassailable. You could not hear nor taste—quite right, Barzillai—but you could see, and there was a great deal to be seen in David's presence. But you were looking elsewhere, your eyes were on eternity. "How long have I to live?" you asked, and at the same time you could have supplied an approximate answer. "A few weeks, a few months, but at most a few years. Should I waste my precious moments on the frivolities of the earth when I shall soon commence the important journey into the hereafter? No, David, I am going home to attend to the most important business in life."

YOUR PEACEFUL READINESS

Old friend, we would like to ask a question. How long did you have to wait before the call came? We see you sitting peacefully at home; we appreciate the deep content filling your soul. Your lifetime of ready service was a source of constant satisfaction; your opportunities had not been lost. The unknown road ahead did not fill you with misgivings. Your people had gone that way, and their Guide would soon be coming to lead their aged son. Of course, you could not tell us about your funeral; but we believe that it was a procession of quiet dignity. It was not a funeral, but a home-going and a reunion. You were ready for the eternal call, and God was pleased to welcome you. Fortunate man! How we wish that all men would learn from your story. We struggle and scheme—we save and plan—and often forget that a similar call could come to us at any moment. Oh, Barzillai, we are all mixed up. We say, "A bird in the hand is worth two in the bush," a saying that is not always true. A mansion in Immanuel's land would be worth a city in this land. Barzillai, we have much to learn! (Homily reprinted from the author's book, *Bible Treasures*, pp. 29-30.)

Episode 39

THEME: *David and His Rival Commanders*

SCRIPTURE: 2 Samuel 20:3-10

KEY VERSE:

> When they were at the great stone which is in Gibeon, Amasa went before them. And Joab's garment that he had put on was girded unto him, and upon it a girdle with a sword fastened upon his loins in the sheath thereof; and as he went forth it fell out (v. 8).

OUTLINE:
  I.   The King's Concubines . . . *Outcasts* (Verse 3)
  II. The King's Command . . . *Obeyed* (Verses 5-7)
  III. The King's Captain . . . *Outraged* (Verses 8-10)

THE KING'S CONCUBINES . . . Outcasts

And David came to his house at Jerusalem; and the king took the ten women his concubines, whom he had left to keep the house, and put them in ward, and fed them, but went not in unto them. So they were shut up unto the day of their death, living in widowhood (v. 3).

Expository Notes on the Fate of David's Concubines

It will be remembered that Absalom entered into a tent erected on the roof of David's palace and, in the sight of all Israel, engaged in illicit intercourse with the king's concubines. That was a public insult to David, but he was a fugitive escaping from Absalom and had no authority in Jerusalem. It must be emphasized that the concubines were helpless and at the mercy of the demanding prince. Royal wives and concubines were never allowed to remarry; they remained widows, with an allowance granted from the estate of their late husband. *The Pulpit Commentary* explains: "We are not to conclude that all widows had to live in seclusion, but only that those women who belonged to the royal harem, and had been taken by another, were not allowed to return to it, but condemned to a sort of imprisonment. This is explained by the Chaldee as lasting only during

David's life; its rendering being 'in widowhood while their husband was alive.'" Jamieson, Fausset, and Brown, the famous theologians, wrote, "Nor was their confinement to a sequestered life a very heavy doom in a region where women have never been accustomed to go much abroad." Adam Clarke adds, "Therefore he shut them up, and *fed them*—made them quite comfortable, and they continued as widows to their death" (*The Bethany Parallel Commentary on the Old Testament*, p. 616).

THE KING'S COMMAND . . . Obeyed

Then said the king to Amasa, Assemble me the men of Judah within three days, and be thou here present. And Amasa went to assemble the men of Judah: but he tarried longer than the set time which he had appointed him. And David said to Abishai, Now shall Sheba the son of Bichri do us more harm than did Absalom: Take thou thy lord's servants, and pursue after him, lest he get him fenced cities, and escape us (vv. 4-6).

Expository Notes on David's Determination to Remove Joab

The king's animosity toward his former commander in chief was relentless. His mind was warped by bitterness and resentment which became evident in all his actions. David could neither forget nor forgive the intrusion of Joab into private matters of royal life, and the king would have welcomed his general's death. When he communicated with the elders of Israel, he instructed them to say to Amasa, "God do so to me, and more also, if thou be not captain of the host before me continually in the room of Joab" (2 Samuel 19:13). David never forgot his vow and, as soon as it became possible, instructed Amasa to gather an army to pursue after the rebellious Sheba. Such a commission was unpardonable and might explain why Amasa had difficulty raising an army within the stipulated time of three days. The men of Judah knew that he had been the head of Absalom's forces and would have readily killed David. It is inconceivable that the faithful Joab should be dismissed in favor of a traitor. When they considered the issue, they wondered if David was so biased in his hatred of Joab that he had become unfit to rule the kingdom. Judah did not cover a large territory, but the men evidently refused to respond because they did not trust either David or Amasa. At that time David was an unattractive bigot, determined to humiliate his old friend. This became evident when Amasa failed to return within the allotted time. Impatient with the unforeseen delay, David again ignored Joab and gave a new commission to the commander's younger brother, Abishai. The monarch had become an egomaniac whose judgments were questionable.

And there went out after him Joab's men . . . to pursue after Sheba the son of Bichri. When they were at the great stone which is in Gibeon, Amasa went before them. And Joab's garment that he had put on was girded unto him, and upon it a girdle with a sword fastened upon his loins in the sheath thereof; and as he went forth it fell out. And Joab said to Amasa, Art thou in health, my brother? And Joab took Amasa by the beard with the right hand to kiss him. But Amasa took no heed to the sword that was in Joab's hand: so he smote him therewith in the fifth rib, and shed out his bowels to the ground, and struck him not again; and he died. So Joab and Abishai his brother pursued after Sheba the son of Bichri (vv. 7-10).

Expository Notes on the Slaying of Amasa

It is significant that although Abishai became the new commander of the army, Joab accompanied the soldiers in their pursuit of the renegade Sheba. The two brothers evidently shared a common affection, and even though Abishai had replaced Joab, the older man was unwilling to oppose the brother whom he loved and admired. Nevertheless, during those difficult days, Joab was the real leader of Israel's armies. The reference made to "Joab's men" indicates that the historian was aware of that fact. Abishai was intent on overtaking Sheba, while Joab thought only of slaying Amasa.

"The great stone which was in Gibeon" must have been a well-known landmark in the mountains to the northwest of Jerusalem. It was the appointed meeting place for all men rallying to the cause of David. The statement "Amasa went before them" provides a problem of interpretation. Did Amasa arrive ahead of Abishai, or did Abishai surrender his command to David's original appointee? Both parties were probably united under one command, and the approach of Joab was interpreted as an act of respect when he went to congratulate his successor. Had Amasa been a better judge of character, he might have lived longer!

The details given by the historian are extremely interesting. The statement that "the sword fell out of its sheath" invites investigation. Ordinarily, this could not happen, for swords were held in position by a small safety strap. Josephus believed that the falling of the weapon was arranged and that the slaying of Amasa was premeditated murder! "Now Joab was girded with a sword, and his breastplate on; and when Amasa came near to salute him, *he took particular care that his sword should fall out, as it were, of its own accord*; so he took it up from the ground, and while he approached Amasa, who was then near him, as though he would kiss him, he took hold of Amasa's beard with his other hand, and he smote him in his belly, when he did not foresee it, and slew him. This impious and altogether profane action, Joab did to a good young man, and his kinsman, and none that had done him injury, and this out of jealousy, that he would obtain the chief command of the army" (Josephus, *Antiquities of the Jews, Book 7*. Chapter 11, Paragraph 7).

Joab planned his murderous mission very carefully. His smiles effectively hid the hatred within his soul. As he deliberately stumbled, his sword slipped out of its sheath, and he probably picked it up with his left hand. Amasa was so overwhelmed with the unexpected affection that he was preparing to return the kiss of congratulation when Joab's sword entered his abdomen so that the career of the commander in chief came to an abrupt end. The sordid details of what followed were carefully recorded by the ancient author, but the story of the wise woman who prevented the destruction of her city was only indirectly associated with David and is not included in this commentary.

Episode 40

THEME: *The Execution of the Seven Descendants of Saul*

SCRIPTURE: 2 Samuel 21

KEY VERSE:

> Then there was a famine in the days of David three years, year after year; and David inquired of the LORD" (v. 1).

OUTLINE:
  I.   A Promise . . . *Broken* (Verse 1)
  II. A Problem . . . *Bothering* (Verses 2-6)
  III. A Punishment . . . *Bidden* (Verses 7-9)
  IV. A Parent . . . *Bemoaning* (Verses 10-14)
  V.   A Participation . . . *Berated* (Verses 15-22)

A PROMISE . . . Broken

Then there was a famine in the days of David, three years, year after year; and David inquired of the LORD. And the LORD answered, It is for Saul, and for his bloody house, because he slew the Gibeonites (v. 1).

Expository Notes on the Prolonged Drought in Israel

The execution of the seven descendents of King Saul provides one of the most controversial events in the life of David. The Bible speaks about a devastating drought which brought economic disaster to Israel. Troubled by circumstances beyond his control, the king asked God why this catastrophe had been permitted and was told that it had been occasioned by the brutality of Saul toward the Gibeonites. He had broken a sacred promise made by Joshua, an action which had displeased the Almighty, who then withheld rain (see Joshua 9). At first glance the story appears to be self-explanatory, but an examination of the scripture provokes some questions. Most scholars agree that this account is not in its proper chronological setting. An entire generation had passed between Saul's crime and its denunciation by the Almighty. A question becomes unavoidable—Why did God wait so long before expressing His disapproval? The evidence seems to place this event earlier in the reign of David, but for some inscrutable reason, the historian decided—almost as an after-thought—to place the story where it is located now. King Saul had taunted the tribe of Benjamin by saying, "Hear now, ye Benjamites; will the son of Jesse give every one of you fields and vineyards, and make you all captains of thousands, and captains of hundreds?" (1 Samuel 22:7). The king was evidently referring to large areas of land, for he implied that he was giving fields and vineyards to all his supporters in Benjamin. How did he obtain so much cultivated property?

It is safe to assume that after the massacre of the Gibeonites, he confiscated their land and divided it among his friends. There is no record that any survivors complained; they were probably afraid of additional reprisals. It cannot authoritatively be stated when this prolonged drought occurred in Israel, but it had to be earlier than would be supposed by a casual reading of this chapter. It would have been inconceivable that God would wait thirty or forty years before denouncing the crime of a man who, in the interval, had died.

A PROBLEM . . . Bothering

(Now the Gibeonites were not of the children of Israel, but of the remnant of the Amorites; and the children of Israel had sworn unto them: and Saul sought to slay them in his zeal to the children of Israel and Judah.) Wherefore David said unto the Gibeonites, What shall I do for you? and wherewith shall I make the atonement, that ye may bless the inheritance of the LORD? And the Gibeonites said unto him, We will have no silver nor gold of Saul, nor of his house; neither for us shalt thou kill any man in Israel. And he said, What ye shall say, that will I do for you. And they answered. . . . let seven men of [Saul's] sons be delivered unto us, and we will hang them up unto the LORD in Gibeah of Saul, whom the LORD did choose. And the king said, I will give them (vv. 2-6).

Expository Notes on the Request of the Gibeonites

It is interesting that, although these people had belonged to a race of idolatrous people, they now conversed freely about the Lord. Their prolonged stay in Israel had changed their faith, and although they were foreigners, they worshiped Jehovah. The request made to David was thought-provoking. The king recognized that an injustice had been suffered by these people, and he was morally indebted to grant any request they made. They could have sought release from the curse of bondage. Joshua had sentenced their ancestors to a life of servitude as drawers of water and hewers of timber; as a result, they were to be the slaves of the Hebrews forever. The yoke of bondage could have been lifted had they so desired.

That they never asked for financial compensation suggests that these people were not poor. There was no need for David to kill anyone; they would be responsible for the execution of the sons of Saul. The Gibeonites had no ill-feelings toward the Israelites, but their request might prevent the recurrence of their problem.

Because they had become the servants of the Hebrews, it may be assumed, therefore, that they lived among all the tribes also and suffered the adverse effects of the prolonged drought. Their crops were being destroyed and their cattle were dying. They needed relief from God, and perhaps their need was their true motivation when they desired that God be appeased and His anger cease. Let it be emphasized that they were not antagonized by the fact they were second-class citizens. They were slaves of their neighbors, but were not resentful. If Jehovah sent rain, everybody would benefit. Some aspects of this story suggest that the slaves were superior to the people they served.

A PUNISHMENT . . . Bidden

But the king spared Mephibosheth, the son of Jonathan, the son of Saul, because of the LORD's oath that was between them, between David and Jonathan the son of Saul. But the king took the two sons of Rizpah the daughter of Aiah, whom she bare unto Saul . . . and the five sons of Michal . . . whom she brought up for Adriel the son of Barzillai the Meholathite; And he delivered them into the hands of the Gibeonites, and they hanged them in the hill before the LORD; and they fell all seven together, and were put to death in the days of the harvest, in the first days, in the beginning of barley harvest (vv. 7-9).

Expository Notes on the Execution of Seven Descendents of Saul

The fact that David spared the life of Mephibosheth helps in deciding when this event took place. It could not have been *before* Ziba brought the crippled son of Jonathan to Jerusalem, for at that time David had no knowledge of the man's existence. This event, therefore, happened near the time when the king met Bath-sheba and subsequently murdered her husband.

David's associations with the daughters of Saul had been frustrating and disappointing, an experience that perhaps reflected in the fact that he chose seven of their offspring to die, regardless of the pain which would devastate their families. Rizpah was one of the king's concubines with whom Abner was accused of associating by Ish-bosheth, the new king of Israel (see 2 Samuel 3:7). Michal was never married to Adriel. Another daughter of Saul named Merab, who should have become David's wife, was given to Adriel, the Meholathite. She bore his children, who were apparently later adopted by Michal.

It was a terrible event when those seven men were dragged from their homes to be executed in Saul's city. Nothing was ever revealed about their spiritual and moral standards, but it is incomprehensible that they were condemned for something of which they were innocent. It is difficult for modern people to appreciate all that happened in the days of Israel's immaturity, but this story from a bygone age enhances the transformation produced by the gospel of Christ. Today, men are innocent until they are proved guilty; long ago, they were considered guilty even when they were innocent.

A PARENT . . . Bemoaning

And Rizpah the daughter of Aiah took sackcloth, and spread it for her upon the rock, from the beginning of harvest until water dropped upon them out of heaven, and suffered neither the birds of the air to rest on them by day, nor the beasts of the field by night. And it was told David what Rizpah the daughter of Aiah, the concubine of Saul, had done (vv. 10-11).

Expository Notes on the Long Vigil of Rizpah

Her Sorrowful Resignation

Rizpah was one of Saul's concubines, a woman who either by choice or compulsion became a member of the royal harem. Her assignment deprived her of the dignity of marriage; she existed only to satisfy her master's desire for sexual entertainment. After Saul's death, his successor accused Abner of illicit intercourse with the king's concubine, a charge fiercely resented by the general (see 2 Samuel 3:7-8). Rizpah gave birth to two of Saul's sons, and there is every reason to believe that she loved her children immensely. Yet, she was helpless and angry when David's officials took her sons away to be publicly executed on a hill at Gibeah. According to Mosaic law, Rizpah was entitled to remove the bodies at sunset on the day of their death, but for reasons of her own, she refrained from exercising that privilege (see Deut. 21:22-23).

Her Strong Resolution

The tragic story of this bereaved mother is extraordinary. When she saw the bodies of her sons, she resolved that their death would not be in vain. If—as was said throughout the land—the death of the seven men was a sacrificial offering to Jehovah, then even He would be reminded of the anguish within her soul. She took sackcloth and probably fastened it to the rock to make a lean-to covering in which she lived throughout her ordeal. The woman vowed to complete her task, however long it would take. It was recorded that she "took sackcloth, and spread it for her upon the rock, from the beginning of harvest until water dropped upon them out of heaven" (v. 10). The barley was ready for harvesting about the middle of April (see Deut. 16:9), and the rainy season began in October. Therefore, Rizpah continued her lonely vigil for six months. During that time the bodies were decaying, but vultures were prevented from eating the flesh, and prairie dogs and other scavengers were not permitted to approach the corpses. Rizpah seldom slept during that period, but when she did, servants or friends guarded the site. What that pathetic woman saw day after day was revolting, but evidently she was determined that others would share her grief. Doubtless, the events at Gibeah were discussed throughout the nation, and David ultimately decided to terminate the prolonged suffering of the vigilant mother.

Her Surprising Reward

And David went and took the bones of Saul and the bones of Jonathan his son from the men of Jabesh-Gilead . . . and they gathered the bones of them that were hanged. And the bones of Saul and Jonathan his son buried they in the country of Benjamin in Zelah, in the sepulchre of Kish his father. . . . And after that God was entreated for the land (vv. 12-14).

Rizpah's sons died ignominiously while being indirectly responsible for the massacre of the Gibeonites and for the resultant distress in Israel. By contrast, they were buried magnificently with their ancestors in the family sepulchre at Zelah. This achievement may seem unimportant to people of the modern world, but to the mother who kept vigil for six months, it was an outstanding triumph. Furthermore, when the rain fell on the parched fields, Rizpah was assured that God had looked favorably upon her action and that all Israel would be indebted to her. These details from a bygone age suggest a question, how can this account benefit readers today? Certain details are worthy of consideration: (1) God desired to help His people, but something hindered the outpouring of His blessing. (2) There was need in Israel to identify and remove that hindrance. (3) God did and still can meet the need of His people. We ask Him for assistance, but He waits for our complete dedication to the extension of His kingdom. It was not an easy task for Rizpah to maintain her vigil for six months; neither is it easy for Christians to do what is necessary to bring Pentecostal showers from heaven. The price to be paid for the fullness of God's blessing is always high, but never beyond the reach of sincere souls.

A PARTICIPATION . . . Berated

Moreover the Philistines had yet war again with Israel; and David went down, and his servants with him, and fought against the Philistines: and David waxed faint. And Ishbi-benob . . . girded with a new sword, thought

to have slain David, But Abishai the son of Zeruiah succored him, and smote the Philistine, and killed him. Then the men of David sware unto him, saying, Thou shalt go no more out with us to battle, that thou quench not the light of Israel (vv. 15-17).

Expository Notes on David's Inability to Lead His Army

Blessed is the man who grows old gracefully! Since the commencement of time, the aging process has been man's greatest enemy. Its victory over human beings may be delayed, but inevitably, the end is never in doubt. Increasing age is always accompanied by diminishing capabilities. Some servants of God recognize this truth, but never submit to it. They continue to attempt what has become impossible and, more often than not, become embarrassed by failure. David apparently was saved from that experience by the wisdom of his friends. It has always been difficult for strong men to admit that they cannot do what they did once. David challenged the might of Goliath, but from the family of the giants arose another man with whom the aged David could not cope. Abishai came to the king's rescue and prevented a tragedy on the battlefield. The leaders of Israel agreed that David's combat days were over, and their request to the king could not be denied. That they considered him to be the "light of Israel" was an eloquent testimony of their affection for their leader. Blessed are they who know how to offer excellent advice, and more blessed are they who know how to accept it!

The recurring battles against the Philistines were to be expected, for as long as they were led by giants, the Philistines were determined to vanquish Israel. Matthew Henry sums up these incidents in a very effective paragraph. He wrote: "These giants were probably the remains of the sons of Anak, who, though long feared, fell at last. It is folly for the strong man to glory in his strength. David's servants were no bigger nor stronger than other men, yet thus, by divine assistance, they mastered one giant after another. The most powerful enemies are often reserved for the last conflict. David began his glory with the conquest of one giant, and here concludes it with the conquest of four. Death is the Christian's last enemy, and a son of Anak. But through Him who triumphed for us, we hope to be more than conquerors, even over that enemy." For special notes on David's administrative officials (2 Sam. 20:23-26), see the exposition in Episode 26, p. 218).

Episode 41

THEME: *David's Synopsis of His Songs*

SCRIPTURE: 2 Samuel 22

KEY VERSES:

And he said, the LORD is my rock, and my fortress, and my deliverer; the God of my rock; in him will I trust: he is my shield, and the horn of my salvation, my high tower, and my refuge, my savior; thou savest me from violence (vv. 2-3).

OUTLINE:
   I.   David's Unfailing Strength . . . *My Rock* (Verses 1-2)
   II. David's Uncommon Shelter . . . *My Refuge* (Verse 3)
   III. David's Unlimited Support . . . *My Deliverer* (Verses 2-3)
   IV. David's Unique Song . . . *My Lamp* (Verses 1, 49-50)
   V.   David's Unsurpassed Savior . . . *My Savior* (Verses 3, 51)

DAVID'S UNFAILING STRENGTH . . . My Rock

And David spake unto the LORD the words of this song in the day that the LORD had delivered him out of the hand of all his enemies, and out of the hand of Saul: and he said, The LORD is my rock, and my fortress, and my deliverer (vv. 1-2).

Expository Notes on the Reminiscences of David

David was rapidly approaching the end of his life. His experiences had been varied, and he seemed like a pugilist who had fought a grueling fight. Yet, the long and exacting contest had had its intervals in which the warrior had reflected on what had happened. He was not only a courageous opponent, but he was also a mystic, a seer, a poet. In moments of rest, between his struggles, David expressed the deepest feelings of his soul. Whenever it became possible, the king sang his lyrics to the accompaniment of his harp. Those poems became known as the "psalms of David," which were destined to enrich people of all generations.

David composed many songs, but none of them surpassed the one now being considered. For example, Psalm 23 described his immortal love for the Good Shepherd; Psalm 46 spoke of his refuge in storms; Psalm 91 expressed amazing confidence in the Almighty. But Psalm 18 said everything! There is no way by which the date of its composition can be ascertained. The historian who collected David's writings was content to say that this psalm was written "in the day that the LORD had delivered him out of the hand of all his enemies, and out of the hand of Saul" (2 Samuel 22:1). Perhaps it was written in the latter part of the king's reign, for its language expresses the faith of a mature soul. David had acquired an amazing conception of his heavenly Father that was clearly revealed in the names or illustrations associated with the Almighty.

JEHOVAH—MY ROCK

The rocky crags of the Sinai peninsula were well known to the Hebrews, for the nation wandered among them for forty years. They contrasted with the shifting sands blown by the desert storms. The Israelites usually lived in tents, but when permanent buildings were erected, slabs of stone offered solid foundations. The rock spoke of strength and reliability and of something upon which to depend. The limestone had been a source of sustenance, for when Moses smote a rock in the wilderness, water came forth to quench the thirst of the complaining people. It was natural, therefore, for David to refer to God as *his* Rock. Through the changing vicissitudes of his life, God had never failed him; Jehovah had been his most dependable Friend. He had been the unfailing source of living water which satisfied the king's soul. If another text can be used, then it could be said that God's strength was made perfect in David's weakness, a truth that had been the reason for his success as a warrior, statesman, and monarch. The "Rock" was one of David's favorite words; he used it three times in the eighteenth psalm.

DAVID'S UNCOMMON SHELTER . . . My Refuge

The God of my rock; in him will I trust . . . and my refuge (v. 3).

In the thoughts of David *the rock* and *the refuge* were synonymous; they belonged together. When Saul became antagonistic, the fugitive sought refuge among the rocks of Sinai. The Mosaic law directed that six cities of refuge be provided in Israel so that fugitives would have a place of safety in times of danger. The gates of those cities were never closed. David had often been attacked by enemies, and there were occasions when he felt desolate. Yet, God had never refused to listen when he prayed, the gates of the heavenly city had never been closed, and David possibly remembered that fact when he wrote this psalm. He would have appreciated the words of William O. Cushing:

O safe to the Rock that is higher than I;
My soul in its conflicts and sorrows would fly.
So sinful, so weary, Thine, Thine would I be,
Thou blest Rock of Ages, I'm hiding in Thee.

DAVID'S UNLIMITED SUPPORT . . . My Deliverer

The LORD is . . . my deliverer . . . and the horn of my salvation, my high tower (vv. 2-3).

David was an old man, but as he reflected upon his career, he remembered that God had delivered him from many enemies. As a lad he fought with a lion and a bear and had triumphed over both adversaries. The same kind of assistance had been given when Saul and his army surrounded the hillside on which David and his men were hiding. The illustrations used in this psalm are exceedingly informative. When he referred to "the high tower," he might have been thinking of the citadel in the mountains from which he commanded an excellent view. There, he was able to see the approach of enemies and had sufficient warning to arrange an escape. He could have been thinking of the towers in vineyards where watchmen lived during their periods of labor. A tower was a place of vigilance, a refuge, and a resting place when the heat of the day became oppressive. When David reminisced, he remembered that Jehovah had provided all of these amenities for weary souls. God had been his Deliverer from all kinds of difficulties and dangers. The king would have appreciated the words in the hymn by Robert Robinson: "Oh, to grace, how great a debtor, daily I'm constrained to be." The horn to which he referred was probably the ram's horn used to make special announcements from the sanctuary. The faithfulness of the Lord deserved long and loud testimony that God never failed His servants. David was a fortunate man; the hand that held the universe held him!

DAVID'S UNIQUE SONG . . . My Lamp

And David spake unto the LORD the words of this song in the day that the LORD had delivered him. . . . thou hast delivered me from the violent man. Therefore I will give thanks unto thee, O LORD, among the heathen, and I will sing praises unto thy name (vv. 1, 49-50).

A lamp shone in the darkness; as an illumination made possible by a supply of oil. Within the tabernacle the lamp burned continually, for Moses commanded that it should never go out (see Leviticus 6:12). The fact that David "sang in the dark" testifies to the flow of God's grace which never diminishes. His testimony, as a light from his soul, penetrates the darkness, and even heathens hear of the faithfulness of God. When songs emanated from the king's soul, they proved that in all the vicissitudes of human experience, he had an infallible source of assistance. This turned sorrow into singing, tragedy into triumph, and problems into praise. David gave thanks—he was grateful—and secondly, he sang that others might hear of the magnificent kindness of the Almighty. David wrote many songs and thereby indicated that this was not an isolated event, but an experience known at intervals throughout his lifetime.

DAVID'S UNSURPASSED SAVIOR . . . My Savior

My savior (v. 3). . . . He is the tower of salvation for his king: and sheweth mercy to his anointed (v. 51).

The delivering power of God can be seen in the names used by David in this psalm. There are also three word-pictures which summarize the king's message.

The Sanctuary in the Hills

The five names mentioned in verse three are all meaningful: the "Shield", the means of defense; the "Horn", the way of proclamation; the "high Tower", the place of vision; the "Refuge", the place of safety; and the "Savior", the object of worship. David was aware of the existence of a national sanctuary, but he had discovered a greater truth. An eminent shrine could be an empty shell, an ornate and expensive building, and a center of ritualistic ceremony unrelated to the presence of God. The Lord had promised to be near those who had a contrite heart, a truth that applied even in the rocky fastness of the wilderness. Many times during his adversity, David bowed reverently before God and within moments, had been aware of the encircling arms of his heavenly Father's tenderness. Perhaps it was then that he wrote, "I will lift up mine eyes unto the hills, from whence cometh my help" (Psalm 121:1). Jehovah had promised to abide with His people; therefore, if a man's soul were responsive to the divine Presence, he could stand in a field and at the same moment be kneeling before the throne of grace. David said: "In my distress I called upon the LORD, and cried to my God: and he did hear my voice out of his temple, and my cry did enter into his ears" (v. 7). The king was a devout worshiper in his cathedral in the hills.

The Storm in the Heavens

There were occasions when David prayed desperately and when God's answers were extremely spectacular. Perhaps he sat in the mouth of a mountain cave to witness a spectacle in the heavens. David's descriptions were not only poetic, they were also sensational in describing the majesty of a mountain storm. "He bowed the heavens also, and came down; and darkness was under his feet. And he rode upon a cherub, and did fly: and he was seen upon the wings of the wind. . . . The LORD thundered from heaven, and the most High uttered his voice. And he sent out arrows, and scattered them; lightning, and discomfited them" (vv. 10-15). When the royal poet listened to the rolling thunder and saw the flashes of lightning piercing the darkness of the heavens, he saw them not only as evidence of a storm, but also as the weapons of the Almighty. Jehovah was able to shake mountains with earthquakes and divide continents with oceans. It aroused David's praise when that power helped the fugitive from Bethlehem. He wrote:

He sent from above, he took me; and drew me out of many waters; He delivered me from my strong enemy, and from them that hated me: for they were too strong for me. They prevented me in the day of my calamity: but the LORD was my stay. He brought me forth also into a large place: he delivered me, because he delighted in me (vv. 17-20).

The Song in the Heart

David would have appreciated the words uttered by the Savior. "I tell you that, if these [people] should hold their peace, *the stones would immediately cry out*" (Luke 19:40). To witness the power of God in the universe was amazing, but to experience it within the soul was beyond comprehension. When David wandered from the Lord, he saw only clouds of despondency; when he bowed in the presence of the Almighty, the clouds dispersed, and the suppliant saw again the blue heavens of God's unfailing kindness. He wrote, "The heavens declare the glory of God; and the firmament sheweth his handiwork. Day unto day uttereth speech, and night unto night sheweth knowledge. There is no speech nor language, where their voice is not heard" (Psalm 19:1-3). Praise is an outpouring of love from grateful hearts.

> The birds upon the tree-top sing their song.
> The angels chant their praises all day long;
> The flowers in the garden blend their hue,
> Then why shouldn't I; why shouldn't I praise God too?

Episode 42

THEME: *David's Roll of Honor*

SCRIPTURE: 2 Samuel 23

KEY VERSE:

> Although my house be not so with God; yet he hath made with me an everlasting covenant, ordered in all things, and sure: for this is all my salvation, and all my desire, although he make it not to grow (v. 5).

OUTLINE:
　　I.　David's Final Words (Verses 1-7)
　　II.　David's Famous Warriors (Verses 8-23)
　　III.　David's Faithful Workers (Verses 24-39)

DAVID'S FINAL WORDS

Now these be the last words of David. David the son of Jesse said, and the man who was raised up on high, the anointed of the God of Jacob, and the sweet psalmist of Israel, said, The Spirit of the Lord spake by me, and his word was in my tongue. The God of Israel said, the Rock of Israel spake to me. He that ruleth over men must be just, ruling in the fear of God. . . . But the sons of Belial. . . . shall be utterly burned with fire in the same place (vv. 1-7).

Expository Notes on One of David's Final Utterances

It would seem that the facts recorded in 2 Samuel 23 were an author's interpolation into an ancient manuscript. David's life was rapidly terminating, and the historian, who had already described the major portion of the king's life, suddenly decided to inject into his story events concerning the royal autobiography. Here and in the parallel account in 1 Chronicles 11, he included incidents not mentioned elsewhere. Some were exciting and spectacular; others were strange and provocative. The section may be summarized under three headings.

A Pertinent Problem

The chapter opens with the statement: "Now these be the last words of

David." The statement is difficult to explain since they quite obviously were not the final words of the king. As will be seen in the closing episodes of David's life, he had more to say, and some of his statements would have been better left unspoken. The best interpretation of the apparent discrepancy is possibly that these were the final *inspired* words of David. He said: "The Spirit of the LORD spake by me, and his word was in my tongue." If the historian were thinking of the better side of the king's life, his statement was appropriate. Perhaps he was trying to say, "These words are the last meritorious action which can be reported concerning the ailing king. Thereafter, I can only record his stubbornness in taking an unwise census and his disappointing words when he commissioned Solomon to murder disliked people."

A Prolonged Pause

At first glance it appears that the opening verses of chapter 23 were meant to be a continuation of the preceding chapter. David mentioned the "Rock" in both places, and the sequence of thought is obvious. The general consensus of the commentators is that the king repeated an earlier message, that a considerable period of time had elapsed; and that in the interval he had reflected upon various subjects. As David approached the end of his life, he remembered being raised from obscurity to prominence, from the remote fields of Bethlehem to become the reigning monarch in Israel. Certain episodes in his career inspired psalms, but most of his compositions came when his mind was liberated from the responsibility of ruling a turbulent nation. David knew that he was a spokesman for the Almighty and that the Holy Spirit had enabled him to be a prophet of the Highest. His household had been unworthy of such honors, but in spite of repeated failure, he had entered into an everlasting relationship with God in an immutable covenant. Knowing this to be true, the historian believed that this was the last time when David was truly inspired.

A Preserved Peace

Perhaps this section of David's life related to another commandment: "Be still, and know that I am God" (Psa. 46:10). When the king was involved with national and domestic problems, his mind was preoccupied. When peace reigned within the nation, David reflected on the kindness of Jehovah by writing, "Yet, he hath made with me an everlasting covenant, ordered in all things, and sure: for this is all my salvation, and all my desire" (v. 5). The psalmist seems to be concerned with three ideas.

Careful Planning

The covenant made with God had been arranged in heaven; it began with Jehovah. The king was able to arrange treaties with other nations, but he was completely dependent upon a higher Ruler. He could not dictate policy with the Lord, but remained a suppliant. The Almighty had devised an everlasting covenant and had graciously allowed David to participate. Its details had been meticulously arranged so that the end result would never be in doubt—it was sure!

Constant Protection

David could never trust himself! He knew the truth of Paul's statement, "For what I would, that do I not; but what I hate, that do I" (Romans 7:15). David dreamed of moral and spiritual perfection, but indiscretions ruined his happiness so that his noblest ambitions were never realized. Nevertheless, when he considered his covenant with God, he knew that it was neither subject to nor conditioned by time. It was eternal. He who commenced the operation would complete it. David made many mistakes, but the Lord overruled all of them so that they would work together for the well-being of His servant. The covenant was sure; the participant, safe.

Constant Pleasure

David contemplated the greatness of salvation and exclaimed, "This is . . . all my desire." At another time, he wrote, "One thing have I desired of the LORD, that will I seek after; that I may dwell in the house of the LORD all the days of my life, to behold the beauty of the LORD, and to inquire in his temple" (Psalm 27:4). When he considered spiritual realities, he saw the throne of God's grace and desired to live in its shadow. David was aware of an acute hunger and thirst within his soul. What he required could only be obtained by intimate communion with God, and that realization explains why he wrote: "As the hart panteth after the water brooks, so panteth my soul after thee, O God. My soul thirsteth for God, for the living God" (Psalm 42:1-2). As a lad he had watched antelope drinking at a mountain stream and had been fascinated by those graceful animals. Later, he thought of himself as drinking the living water which came from the throne of God and rejoiced that Jehovah could satisfy the inherent longings of the human soul. The Lord's everlasting covenant promised that the encircling arms of divine tenderness would never be withdrawn.

DAVID'S FAMOUS WARRIORS

These be the names of the mighty men whom David had. . . . Adino the Eznite. . . . Eleazar the son of Dodo. . . . Shammah the son of Agee (see vv. 8-11).

Since this is not a detailed commentary on the Second Book of Samuel, it is unnecessary to comment on all the followers of David. Within this chapter the historian presented a list of the mighty men in David's army. Their numerous exploits make captivating reading, but their accomplishments were unrelated to the experiences of the king. The ancient writer compiled a list of David's illustrious warriors, whose eminence was decided by the magnitude of their exploits.

Dr. R. Payne Smith summarized the chapter admirably by writing: "Those admitted to the list were evidently the outlaws who had been with David in his wanderings and at Ziklag. They were now receiving their reward, and became, moreover, the stay of David's throne. It was their past history which accounts for the strange composition of the list. A large number came from Judah and especially from Bethlehem. Several are David's relatives. Seven towns or families furnish sixteen out of the whole list. We find a father and his son, and pairs of brothers. There are, moreover, numerous foreigners. There are Hittites, Ammonites, Moabites, a Syrian from Zobah, and Gibeonites descended from the original aboriginal inhabitants of the land. Such a list would have been sorely resented had it not been formed out of men who had earned it by their past services, and their fidelity to David" (*The Pulpit Commentary*, vol. 4, p. 569).

> **And three of the thirty chief went down, and came to David in the harvest time unto the cave of Adullam: and the troop of the Philistines pitched in the valley of Rephaim. And David was then in an hold. . . . And David longed, and said, Oh that one would give me drink of the water of the well of Bethlehem, which is by the gate! And the three mighty men brake through the host of the Philistines, and drew water out of the well of Bethlehem, that was by the gate, and took it, and brought it to David: nevertheless he would not drink thereof, but poured it out unto the LORD. And he said, Be it far from me, O LORD, that I should do this: is not this the blood of the men who went in jeopardy of their lives? therefore he would not drink it. These things did these three mighty men (vv. 13-17).**

Expository Notes on the Exploits at the Well of Bethlehem

This episode is an informative throw-back to the perilous days when David was a fugitive hiding in the cave of Adullam. When cataloguing David's great warriors, the ancient writer supplied historical details unmentioned elsewhere. The account of the bravery of three men is prominent among the items of the list. David's action in refusing to drink the water reveals an interesting facet of his character. It deserves careful consideration.

An Intense Desire

It was harvest time, and the air was filled with dust. Farmers were threshing and winnowing their crops. Workmen were throwing grain into the air, thus enabling the gentle winds to blow away the chaff. From his vantage point in the mountains, David saw the haze which almost obliterated the beauty of the countryside. His men were coughing and sneezing, and water seemed to be the most valuable commodity in the world. David sighed and remembered how he had often quenched his thirst at the well in Bethlehem. He suddenly exclaimed, "Oh that one would give me drink of the water of the well of Bethlehem, which is by the gate." He was thinking aloud! Three unnamed captains heard their leader's sigh and instantly decided that his wish should be granted. They desired to please the one who had done so much for them. The Lord Jesus reminded His followers that it was better to give than to receive. Unfortunately, many people are content to receive, but unwilling to give. The courage of the men who risked their lives to please David should be an example for all Christians.

An Invincible Determination

"And the three mighty men brake through the host of the Philistines, and drew water out of the well of Bethlehem . . . and took it, and brought it to David" (v. 16). The details of their accomplishment were never disclosed. Water was always scarce in Palestine, and it would appear that the Philistines in Bethlehem maintained a strict supervision over the distribution of supplies. The well had permanent guards who were asleep, tricked into leaving their posts, or slain while attempting to resist invaders. The parallel account in 1 Chronicles 11:15-19 states that the men "put their lives in jeopardy" to obtain water for David.

A troop of soldiers was encamped nearby, but perhaps the invaders arrived during the night when most people, including the guards, were asleep. The verb "brake" suggests conflict, but it remains an inscrutable mystery how these warriors accomplished their feat. They were not requested to embark on the dangerous mission, but their endeavor was the evidence of personal loyalty to David. They loved their captain and believed that it was a privilege to please him. Similar sentiments were expressed by John when he wrote of the early evangelists, "For his name's sake they went forth, taking nothing of the Gentiles" (3 John 7). Genuine affection leads to faithful service.

An Illustrious Decision

"Nevertheless [David] would not drink thereof, but poured it out unto the LORD" (v. 16). This action could have been interpreted as a waste of precious refreshment and an affront to the men whose efforts were nullified. The soldiers' reaction to the deed would have been governed by their spiritual perception. If they recognized that David had made their gift an offering unto God, they knew that their exploit had become "a sweet smelling savor" unto Jehovah. Inasmuch as they had done this for David, they had done it unto Him (compare Matthew 25:40). If the men had truly desired to please their leader, what he did with the water was immaterial. Perhaps the men understood that as they endeavored to quench David's thirst, he was attempting to please God, who was thirsting for the unsullied devotion of His people.

A careful examination and a comparison of texts might identify the men who performed this act, but at first glance it appears that the heroes were unnamed. The greatest exploits for God are not performed exclusively by the publicized leaders of God's people. Picturesque mountains often have their foundations in inauspicious plains. Great rivers have small beginnings and become important only when tributaries contribute to the magnificence of the waterway.

DAVID'S FAITHFUL WORKERS

Asahel the brother of Joab was one of the thirty. . . . Uriah the Hittite: thirty and seven in all (vv. 24-39).

Expository Notes on David's Ordinary Soldiers

The lists of David's mighty men provide startling contrasts. Among the dominant personalities were people who might be classified as "his little men." They were seldom if ever mentioned in royal bulletins, but they were never late arriving at their places of duty. The famous warriors did spectacular things. "Adino the Eznite, lifted up his spear against eight hundred [soldiers], whom he slew at one time (v. 8). Eleazar smote the Philistines until "his hand clave unto the sword" (v. 10). Shammah saw Israel fleeing before the enemy, "but he stood in the midst of the ground, and defended it, and slew the Philistines, and the LORD wrought a great victory" (v. 12). The historian described the exploits of David's magnificent soldiers and then proceeded to mention others for whom no outstanding achievement could apparently be claimed. The list of names supplied in 1 Chronicles mentions additional people, and others could probably have been included. The king's "little men" appeared to be insignificant, but the army could not have functioned successfully without them.

The modern church has its popular leaders who possess special gifts. Nevertheless, the strength of the church and every other movement is always found in the grass-roots of the organization, where ordinary volunteers faithfully perform their unsung ministry. It should never be forgotten that God still has His army of "little people," and one of the greatest privileges in life is to serve among them.

Episode 43

THEME: *The Consequences of David's Census*

SCRIPTURE: 2 Samuel 24

KEY VERSE:

And David said unto Gad, I am in a great strait: let us fall now into the hand of the LORD; for his mercies are great: and let me not fall into the hand of man (v. 14).

OUTLINE:
  I.   David Plans a Census (Verses 1-2)
  II. David Perplexes His Critics (Verses 3-9)
  III. David Provided a Choice (Verses 10-14)
  IV. David Prevents a Catastrophe (Verses 15-25)

DAVID PLANS A CENSUS

And the anger of the LORD was kindled against Israel, and he moved David against them to say, Go, number Israel and Judah. For the king said to Joab the captain of the host, which was with him, Go now through all the tribes of Israel, from Dan even to Beer-sheba, and number ye the people, that I may know the number of the people (vv. 1-2).

Expository Notes on David's Desire for a Census

This passage is a difficult one to expound. A great sin had evidently been committed, but it is hard to decide what it was. That seventy thousand men perished indicates the gravity of the situation. If the ancient historian had supplied more facts, many of the problems of interpretation would have been avoided. It is said that the Lord influenced David to act as he did. Therefore, the inference seems to suggest that Jehovah was responsible for the catastrophe which overwhelmed the nation. Yet, in 1 Chronicles 21, it is said, "And Satan stood up against Israel, and provoked David to number Israel" (v. 1). There is no problem in these verses, for it becomes evident that a difference must be discussed between the *perfect* and *permissive* will of God. The Lord cannot be accused of promoting evil, but "whom the Lord loveth he chasteneth" (Heb. 12:6). What happened in

Israel was not the perfect will of the Almighty; the Lord allowed Satan to act as he did because flaws in the moral and spiritual life of the nation needed to be exposed and removed.

God was evidently displeased with David's census, but there was a precedent for the king's action. God commanded Moses, "Take the sum of all the congregation. . . of Israel, from twenty years old and upward, throughout their fathers' house, all that are able to go to war in Israel" (see Numbers 26:2). Nevertheless, David's methods were different from those used by Moses. The divinely authorized census taken earlier was conducted by Eleazer the priest. Furthermore, it had religious connotations, for every man was assessed half a shekel as a ransom for his soul, money that was devoted to the service of the sanctuary (see Exodus 30:13).

God did not authorize David's action, and the officials responsible for the task were not priests. Furthermore, God had limited the numbering of the fighting men to those over twenty years of age. This stipulation was apparently ignored by the king's representatives, and there was no mention of a tax being received from the people. If money was gathered, it did not go to the ecclesiastical authorities. Some commentators express the belief that money might have been collected, but that David took it for his own use and thus displeased the Lord. This interpretation has no biblical support, and even if it were founded on fact, it could not explain why seventy thousand men died because of a sin they did not commit.

This census was not commenced without the convening of the King's council. Joab and the captains of the host opposed David and endeavored to thwart his intentions. They evidently discerned that the king's motives were self-centered and impure, but their objections were overruled. The king had decided to number his fighting men and vetoed all objections to his plan. David was temporarily beginning to trust in his abilities rather than in God, who had made him the king of Israel. Was he already contemplating new military action? When a man becomes great in his own estimation, his future is threatened!

DAVID PERPLEXES HIS CRITICS

And Joab said unto the king, Now the Lord thy God add unto the people, how many soever they be, an hundredfold, and that the eyes of my lord the king may see it: but why doth my lord the king delight in this thing? Notwithstanding the king's word prevailed against Joab, and against the captains of the host. And Joab and the captains of the host went out from the presence of the king, to number the people of Israel. . . and there were in Israel eight hundred thousand valiant men that drew the sword; and the men of Judah were five hundred thousand men (vv. 3-9).

Expository Notes on Joab's Opposition to David's Plan

For a little while, David became a self-made god who worshiped at his own shrine. This fact perplexed Joab and the captains, who recognized that their leader had embarked upon a course of self-destruction. It was unfortunate that Joab had become unpopular at the royal court. Had he enjoyed the favor of the king, his recommendations might have been acceptable. The animosity in David's heart guaranteed that any suggestion made by the general would be disregarded. The fact that Joab was argumentative only increased the king's determination to promote what Joab disapproved. This stubbornness was to be regretted, for the nation was destined to suffer more than the two antagonists.

The king eventually saw the error of his ways. "David's heart smote him after that he had numbered the people. And David said unto the LORD, I have sinned greatly in that I have done" (v. 10). Yet, there is no record of his apologizing to Joab and he apparently made no attempt to remove the misunderstanding which had ruined their fellowship. David's animosity deepened, and finally he commissioned Solomon to slay the old soldier (see 1 Kings 2:5-6). The historian wrote, "David's heart smote him after that he had numbered the people." It is interesting that Joab quit his task before the census was completed. "And Joab gave the sum of the number of the people unto David. . . . *But Levi and Benjamin counted he not among them: for the king's word was abominable to Joab*" (see 1 Chronicles 21:5-6).

The king resented interference, and the soldier probably despised David because of the brutal murder of Bath-sheba's husband. Neither man forgave his neighbor. They were stubborn men convinced that they had done no wrong. If they had sat down together to discuss frankly their problems and if they had wept upon each other's shoulder, a new era might have dawned for Israel. It would have been interesting to assess the effect of Paul's message if he had been able to speak with those disappointing men. The apostle wrote: "Let all bitterness, and wrath, and anger, and clamor, and evil speaking, be put away from you, with all malice: and be ye kind one to another, tenderhearted, forgiving one another, even as God for Christ's sake hath forgiven you" (see Ephesians 4:31-32).

DAVID PROVIDED A CHOICE

And David said unto the LORD, I have sinned greatly. . . . when David was up in the morning, the word of the LORD came unto the prophet Gad, David's seer, saying, Go and say unto David, Thus saith the LORD, I offer thee three things; choose thee one of them. . . . Shall seven years of famine come unto thee in thy land? or wilt thou flee three months before thine enemies, while they pursue thee? or that there be three days pestilence in thy land?. . . And David said unto Gad, I am in a great strait: let

us fall now into the hand of the Lord; for his mercies are great: and let me not fall into the hand of man (vv. 10-14).

Expository Notes on the Consequences of David's Error

Many theologians have considered a perplexing question. Since this episode in the life of David only involved the king, why should the people of Israel be permitted to become the objects of divine wrath? They neither suggested the idea to David nor willingly participated in what was done. At first glance it appears that they were innocent victims of royal indiscretions. Unless a legitimate reason is found to explain the tragic events of the pestilence, the decease of seventy thousand valiant men is horrendous.

Earlier in this commentary, mention was made of the three classes of people in Israel. There were a small number who followed David into exile, a very large number who participated in the coronation of Absalom, and many others who remained uninterested in whatever happened. Those who assisted in the rebellion of the usurper prince were guilty before God, and the indifferent citizens were equally guilty in that they did nothing to support the Lord's anointed. David forgave their insurrection, but there had never been any spontaneous repentance. In addition, whatever God felt about the matter was ignored. "Whom the Lord loveth he chasteneth" (Heb. 12:6), and His chastening hand is sometimes heavy! People forget that the laws of God apply both in heaven and upon earth. God could not ignore the sins of His people, for that would be contrary to His commandments. To condone evil would be to encourage its repetition. The judgment poured upon the guilty nation was just; yet, the mercy of God postponed that terrible day as long as possible.

The Messenger of God. . . Unafraid

God never delays in answering the prayer of a repentant sinner. David's remorse became evident even before the completion of the census. "And David said unto the Lord, I have sinned greatly in that I have done: and now, I beseech thee, O Lord, take away the iniquity of thy servant; for I have done very foolishly" (v. 10). "It appears also that the displeasure of God was manifesting itself before David repented (1 Chronicles 21:7, and 1 Chronicles 27:24). Some sign of this, either in public trouble, or in the brooding of the pestilential miasma over the land, brought home to David's mind the conviction of sin; and he at once humbled himself before God, for the vanity. . . which had engendered in him a wicked lust after martial glory, and thirst for bloodshed" (*The Pulpit Commentary*, vol. 4, p. 598). When the king asked for forgiveness, God immediately instructed the prophet Gad to take a message to the royal palace. The early-morning confrontation with David revealed the confidence of the fearless messenger. It was never easy to accuse a monarch in whose hands lay the power of life and death. A true prophet fears none but God and never dilutes his message.

The Majesty of God... Unsurpassed

David was offered a choice of three judgments, all of which troubled his soul. Seven years of famine would devastate the land, impoverish the nation, and starve the people. To be invaded and defeated by heathen nations would hurt the king's pride, cause problems among the tribes, and be a threat to the stability of the nation. Many people would be slain, and others carried into captivity. To endure a plague would disturb the serenity of all households. It would remind the king that his stupidity had caused grief throughout the land. What could he do? Did he realize that behind the three possibilities was the majesty of the Almighty? God was able to perform any or all of the three suggestions. He controlled the weather, the future, and the existence of the nation. What He decreed would surely happen; He was Lord of the universe.

The Mercy of God... Unmistakable

"And David said unto Gad, I am in a great strait; let us fall now into the hand of the LORD; for his mercies are great: and let me not fall into the hand of man" (v. 14). The king knew that God was infinitely kinder than human beings. If the Philistines overran the nation, their insatiable thirst for conquest would probably extend to a longer period of subjugation. If famine ruined the crops, the catastrophe would continue for several years. If disease swept through the land, it would be impossible to assess the resultant loss of life. David realized that it would be wiser to trust in the mercy of God than in his own understanding. His choice was wise. There was reason to believe that the terrible plague was caused by those whose shameful support of Absalom had violated the laws of God. It was a belated punishment upon sins which should not have been committed.

> So the Lord sent a pestilence upon Israel from the morning even to the time appointed; and there died of the people from Dan even to Beer-sheba seventy thousand men. And when the angel stretched out his hand upon Jerusalem to destroy it, the Lord repented him of the evil, and said to the angel that destroyed the people, It is enough: stay now thine hand. And the angel of the Lord was by the threshingplace of Araunah the Jebusite (vv. 15-16).

It has been said that "every cloud has a silver lining," and that was true when God unexpectedly terminated the punishment of Israel. The Lord saw the anguish of His afflicted people and was filled with compassion. Paul was thinking of that same love when he wrote: "There hath no temptation taken you but such as is common to man: but God is faithful, who will not suffer you to be tempted above that ye are able; but will, with the temptation also MAKE A WAY TO ESCAPE, that ye may be able to bear it" (1 Corinthians 10:13). God's mercy resembles an ocean—it becomes deeper and deeper until it is unfathomable. Perhaps it was at this time that David wrote Psalm 136. The poem provides a masterpiece in the questionable art of reiteration. It contains twenty-six verses, and in every one the writer wrote: "for his mercy endureth for ever." He was surely trying to say something! The writer to the Hebrews stated that "it is a fearful thing to fall into the hands of the living God" (see Hebrews 10:31). That can hardly be true when God is your Heavenly Father!

DAVID PREVENTS A CATASTROPHE

And David spake unto the Lord when he saw the angel that smote the people, and said, Lo, I have sinned, and I have done wickedly; but these sheep, what have they done?. . . And Gad came that day to David, and said unto him, Go up, rear an altar unto the Lord in the threshingfloor of Araunah the Jebusite. . . . And Araunah looked. . . and. . . said, Wherefore is my lord the king come to his servant? And David said, To buy the threshingfloor of thee, to build an altar unto the Lord that the plague may be stayed from the people. And Araunah said unto David, Let my lord the king take and offer up what seemeth good unto him. . . . And the king said unto Araunah, Nay; but I will surely buy it of thee at a price: neither will I offer burnt offerings unto the Lord my God of that which cost me nothing. . . . And David built there an altar unto the Lord. . . . and the plague was stayed from Israel (vv. 17-25).

Expository Notes on the Purchase of Araunah's Threshingfloor

The parallel account of this event as given in 1 Chronicles 21:16-30 is very informative. Araunah or Ornan was a Jebusite, an original inhabitant of Jerusalem. After the fall of the rocky fortress, he evidently decided to remain among the Hebrews, and his threshingfloor in the hills was destined to become famous. Whether or not he embraced the faith of the Israelites is open to conjecture, but his willingness to cooperate with David indicates that he was aware of the gravity of the situation. If the devastating plague reached the city, his life would be threatened and his family ruined. Three outstanding features regarding his story invite investigation.

A Magnificent Offer

Araunah's threshingfloor probably occupied one of the best places for threshing grain. Workmen customarily threw grain into the air, thus enabling gentle winds to blow away the chaff. The site in the hills guaranteed that more often than not, the winds would help the farmer. The fact that Araunah offered oxen and instruments of wood to David indicates that he owned valuable equipment and that his estate was something to be desired. It was reported, "All these things did Araunah *as a king, give* unto the king." (v. 23). Some theologians have expressed the belief that the man was a descendent of the ancient kings of the Jebusites and that, figuratively at least, he acted with regal authority. There may or may not be evidence to support this assertion, but it is evident that he acted with the dignity of a monarch by offering to David the best of his possessions. He knew that the need was urgent; the opportunity, unique; and his privilege, immense. He was neither stingy nor reluctant, and his magnanimous spirit set an example for all Israel.

A Memorable Objection

David's response is thought-provoking! He had been offered a cheap way to solve his problem, but he replied, "Nay; but I will surely buy it of thee at a price: neither will I offer burnt offerings unto the LORD my God of that which doth cost me nothing" (v. 24). It would have been easy to give away the property of another man. True giving is measured by sacrifice. Someone has said that no gift is adequate unless it hurts to give. David was determined that Araunah should not be impoverished by his devotion. "So David bought the threshingfloor and the oxen for fifty shekels of silver."

There is no contradiction in the additional account found in 1 Chronicles 21:25, where it was reported that "David gave to Ornan for the place six hundred shekels of gold." There were probably two sales. The initial need was for a small portion of land upon which a temporary altar could be erected. David knew that a sacrifice had to be offered to prevent the terrifying plague from reaching Jerusalem. He hurriedly paid fifty shekels of silver to solve that problem. Later, when he decided this would be an ideal place for the temple, he bought the entire estate for six hundred shekels of gold. The king was a wealthy man, and the purchase of this property would not have been a financial embarrassment. David could have bought a very much larger site and would not have missed the money! A far greater principle was at stake. He was not prepared for a stranger to pay for the repair of the damage for which he himself was responsible.

A Marvelous Outcome

"Then Solomon began to build the house of the LORD at Jerusalem in mount Moriah, where the LORD appeared unto David his father, in the place that David had prepared *in the threshingfloor of Ornan the Jebusite*" (2 Chronicles 3:1). It is interesting that Mount Moriah, where the offering of a ram brought deliverance to Isaac; the threshingfloor of Araunah, where a sacrifice prevented the destruction of Jerusalem; and the site of the temple should be linked together. The temple, which had yet to be erected, would be the center of Israel's worship, where the High Priest would intercede for the nation. God was beginning to teach that communion could only be based upon redemption.

Although David was not permitted to erect the sacred house, he saw the possibilities of that property in the hills and was permitted to prepare materials to be used in its construction. The king had not led an exemplary life, but he was allowed to participate in one of the greatest projects ever entrusted to mankind. He provided materials at an immense cost; on the other hand, centuries later, a widow known to Christ brought "two mites, which make a farthing" (see Mark 12:42-44). It would be interesting to know who brought the greater gift—the king or the widow! (See the following homily, "David . . . Who Refused a Magnificent Gift.")

HOMILIES FOR PREACHERS AND TEACHERS

Study No. 18

DAVID . . . Who Refused a Magnificent Gift (2 Samuel 24:24)

There was great trouble in Israel; a plague was destroying the people. The king had acted unwisely and was seeking forgiveness. "And David said unto the LORD, I have sinned greatly in that I have done: and now, I beseech thee, O LORD, take away the iniquity of thy servant; for I have done very foolishly" (2 Samuel 24:10). His cry of anguish reached the heart of God, and the prophet Gad was sent to reveal a way of escape. "And Gad came that day to David, and said unto him, Go up, rear an altar unto the LORD in the threshingfloor of Araunah the Jebusite. And David. . . went up as the LORD commanded" (vv. 18-19).

A PRESENT REFUSED

The farmer was startled when he saw the royal procession coming toward him, and "[he] bowed himself before the king on his face upon the ground. And Araunah said, Wherefore is my lord the king come to his servant? And David said, To buy the threshingfloor of thee, to build an altar unto the LORD , that the plague may be stayed from the people" (vv. 20, 21). Then the man stood and graciously offered to give everything needed for the carrying out of David's plans. He fully realized that the tide of evil had reached his own property, and soon he and his family would become its victims. "Master," he cried, "You can have it all. I want no money. Take whatsoever you desire and the Lord thy God accept thee."

David's eyes probably became misty as he listened to the words of his subject; yet, he slowly shook his head and answered, "Nay; but I will surely buy it of thee at a price: neither will I offer burnt offerings unto the Lord my God of that which doth cost me nothing" (v. 24). Many people are eager to give away other people's possessions because their giving then costs nothing. David refused to belong to this category. He had hurt God; therefore, his atonement must hurt him.

A PRICE PAID

"So David bought the threshingfloor and the oxen for fifty shekels of silver. And David built there an altar unto the Lord" (vv. 24-25). All true giving to God costs something, and our Lord Jesus Christ provides the greatest example of this fact. He also saw a plague sweeping through the world. The erection of that altar was not easily accomplished. (1) *He yearned until He wept.* When He saw men as sheep without a shepherd and when He saw a city without hope, nothing could prevent His tears of sorrow. (2) *He prayed until He bled.* The garden conflict broke His heart, and "his sweat was as it were great drops of blood falling down to the ground." (3) *He gave until He died.* The triumph of Calvary reveals how great was the price He paid for our salvation. Eternal love is sacrificial love. Is it not a cause for amazement that some who profess His name can offer to their Lord something which costs nothing?

A PLAGUE REMOVED

"So the Lord was entreated for the land, and the plague was stayed from Israel" (v. 25). And from that day, the people gratefully remembered the threshingfloor of Araunah. The altar and its sacrifice had robbed a plague of power. And Araunah himself had the greatest cause for rejoicing; he might have been dead had not salvation come to his house. Thus, even in the twilight ages preceding the coming of Christ, God endeavored to prepare His people for the glorious gospel of His salvation. Man's happiness would be eternally linked with an altar, for there the power of sin would be defeated, his own safety would be assured, and songs of praise would instinctively arise from his heart. When the news of David's altar spread through the land, suffering people obtained new hope, and it was more than likely that many of them left their homes in search of healing. And if such a search took place, it foreshadowed a large group of people who, in the fullness of time, have sought shelter in the shadow of Calvary's cross.

> I take, O Cross, thy shadow
> For my abiding place;
> I ask no other sunshine than
> The sunshine of His face;

Content to let the world go by,
    To know no gain nor loss;
My sinful self my only shame,
    My glory all the Cross.

(Homily reprinted from the author's book, *Bible Pinnacles*, pp. 47-48.)

Episode 44

THEME: *The Last Days of David*

SCRIPTURE: 1 Kings 1

KEY VERSES:

> And the king sware, and said, As the LORD liveth, that hath redeemed my soul out of all distress. Even as I sware unto thee by the LORD God of Israel, saying, Assuredly Solomon thy son shall reign after me, and he shall sit upon my throne in my stead; even so will I certainly do this day (vv. 29, 30).

OUTLINE:
- I.   A Special Servant (Verses 1-4)
- II. A Sinful Son (Verses 5-10)
- III. A Startled Spouse (Verses 11-31)
- IV. A Saintly Successor (Verses 32-40)
- V.   A Safe Sanctuary (Verses 41-53)

A SPECIAL SERVANT

> **Now king David was old and stricken in years; and they covered him with clothes, but he gat no heat. . . . So they sought for a fair damsel throughout all the coasts of Israel, and found Abishag a Shunammite, and brought her to the king. And the damsel was very fair, and cherished the king, and ministered to him: but the king knew her not (vv. 1-4).**

Expository Notes on Abishag, David's Beautiful Nurse

This occasion is another problematical event in the life of David. His physical condition had evidently deteriorated, and death was quickly approaching. The doctors had determined that his blood circulation was poor, and it was consequently almost impossible to prevent chills from spreading throughout his body. The historian wrote that "he gat no heat." Water bottles and heating blankets were evidently unknown, and maintaining heat in David's body became of primary concern. Then someone suggested the need for a young virgin to "stand before the king. . . cherish him, and let her lie in thy bosom that my lord the king may get heat." The suggestion was accepted, and a search began throughout all Israel to find a suitable maiden. The plan is straightforward and easy to understand, but the narrative leaves many unanswered questions. Why should search be made for an attractive woman when the king already had wives and a harem? Bath-sheba, the mother of Solomon was there, and unless they had either died or been released from their obligations, numerous concubines resided in or near the palace. Were these women no longer attractive to the aging monarch? The need was explained to David that "a young virgin" should become his constant companion, and the king approved of the plan. The concubines had no influence in the decision, but Bath-sheba could have vetoed the plan since another woman was to lie beside her husband. Did she object and was the objection overruled? Did the queen refuse to sleep with David because she had become disenchanted with him and no longer cared what happened? It would have been informative if the ancient historian had supplied additional information regarding the intriguing decision to bring a beautiful young woman into David's palace.

Somewhere in Israel the searchers found a charming young lady named Abishag, who consented to become the king's nurse. Her decision was destined to have far-reaching repercussions. Her appearance in the palace sent ripples of excitement through the entire household, and prince Adonijah soon sought her hand in marriage (see 1 Kings 2:17). Solomon was also charmed with her and refused to give his consent to Adonijah's proposal, saying "God do so to me, and more also, if Adonijah have not spoken this word against his own life. Now therefore. . . Adonijah shall be put to death this day" (see 1 Kings 2:23-24).

When Abishag consented to help the ailing monarch, she left her home and family and went to the royal palace. Some teachers believe that she left an ardent shepherd who eventually went to Jerusalem to search for his sweetheart (see the author's book, *Bible Cameos*, pp. 75-76). There is reason to believe that God was overruling the affairs of men. He was the Master Artist, who, seeing the end from the beginning, paints on human canvas things yet to be.

A SINFUL SON

> **Then Adonijah the son of Haggith exalted himself, saying, I will be king: and he prepared him chariots and horsemen, and fifty men to run before him. . . . And he conferred with Joab. . . and with Abiathar the priest: and they following Adonijah helped him. . . . But Nathan the prophet, and Benaiah,. . . and the mighty men, and Solomon his brother, he called not (vv. 5-10).**

Expository Notes on the Insurrection of Adonijah

The First Book of Chronicles relates that four sons were born to David in Hebron, that in Jerusalem another thirteen were born, and that an un-specified number were the children of David's concubines. He probably fathered between twenty and thirty boys, but the number could have been higher. His first four sons were born in Hebron, where David reigned seven and a half years. Among these princes, Adonijah was the fourth in line to succeed David on the throne of Israel. The first son, Amnon, had been slain by Absalom for the rape of Tamar. The second is thought to have died early in life, and the third son, Absalom, had been killed by Joab after his insurrection. Adonijah, the only remaining son of David's first four children, appeared to be the legal heir to the throne. Later, when David became the ruler of all Israel, he made Jerusalem his capital city, and his wives bore thirteen additional sons. Bath-sheba, the former wife of Uriah, bore four sons of whom Solomon was the last. The concubines presented him with many more. It must be recognized that Solomon was legally far down the list of potential heirs to the throne and had little if any chance of succeeding his ailing father. That he was chosen by God to become the king of Israel indicates that Jehovah was not bound by tradi-tion; His appointee was chosen not because of individual virtue, but because of ability to do what needed to be done. God can never be limited by circumstance. The Bible says that "the letter [of the law] killeth; but the spirit giveth life" (see 2 Corinthians 3:6).

Perhaps Adonijah suspected that David favored Solomon and unwisely decided to fight for what he believed belonged to him. It is significant that, although Joab and many illustrious leaders assisted in the rebellion, others, including the priests and Nathan the prophet, refused to be associated with the premeditated insurrection. Joab, who had been David's trusted captain, apparently resented the attitude of his king and decided that he could no longer tolerate the capricious moods of his master. After a lifetime of meritorious service, he left his high command to be affiliated with a move-ment which had no chance of success (see the homily at the end of this section). It has already been explained that there were two high priests in Israel, and it is a cause for regret that their unity was destroyed when Adonijah attempted to steal the kingdom. One priest followed the usurper-prince, hoping to win acclaim, while the other priest faithfully served Jehovah and refused to leave the Lord's anointed. Nathan, the prophet, resembled an immovable rock. As God's spokesman, he resolutely refused to follow anybody unless he was directed from heaven. A man's ears can be lines of communication! It is better to wait and listen than to act hastily and repent leisurely. Adonijah was in a great hurry to get nowhere, and he reached his destination! His exaggerated enthusiasm inflated a bubble of success which burst in his face (see the homily, "Joab. . . Who Lacked Staying Power," which follows).

HOMILIES FOR PREACHERS AND TEACHERS

Study No. 19

JOAB . . . Who Lacked Staying Power (1 Kings 1:7)

Joab was one of the greatest of David's servants, and it will ever be a source of regret that this fine man failed in the end. There are details which suggest that provocation forced the valiant warrior into error; but whether or not this is true, he who had run his race so well failed near the winning line! There are many instances of this man's chivalrous conduct so that the following quotations will provide a most suggestive study.

HIS GREAT FAME

"And David reigned over all Israel; and David executed judgment and justice unto all his people. And Joab the son of Zeruiah was over the host" (2 Samuel 8:15-16). We are not conversant with all the details concerning the promotion of this intrepid warrior, but it may safely be assumed that his acts of bravery, his ability to lead men, and his unwavering courage brought him to prominence. David recognized his greatness and conferred upon him the honor which every Israelite coveted—the position of commander in chief. Joab's subsequent record vindicated David's decision.

HIS GREAT FRIENDSHIP

Joab knew the details concerning the flight of Prince Absalom, but prudently minded his own business. Yet, as the years passed, he recognized that "the soul of king David longed to go forth unto Absalom: for he was comforted concerning the death of Amnon, seeing he was dead" (2 Samuel 13:39). The wise and friendly commander watched his royal master daily and ultimately decided to arrange a reconciliation. His commission to the wise woman of Tekoah has been previously studied (see the author's book, *Bible Pinnacles*, p. 43). It is sufficient now to remember that through the kindly intervention of this thoughtful man, David's sadness was banished. The king did not act very graciously in the matter of Absalom's return, but at least Joab had done his best.

HIS GREAT FAITHFULNESS

Utterly unselfish and unquestionably loyal, Joab proceeded to do his duty and on one notable occasion refused to press home his victorious attack on an enemy stronghold until his master had arrived to be credited with the success of the campaign. This exercise of patience would probably rank as his greatest act of self-denial. Joab desired David to have the pre-eminence in all things. A runner was dispatched with news of the impending victory, and the king was urged to come immediately to receive the praises of his people (2 Samuel 12:26-31). This act of self-effacement deserved the greatest honor in the kingdom.

HIS GREAT FEARLESSNESS

It is not true to say that love is blind. This man adored his master, but he was able to see the faults in David's attitude. It probably required far more courage to rebuke the king than it did to advance against an invading army. The wounds of a friend are faithful, and on several occasions the brave general quietly rebuked his monarch. David resented these admonitions, but subsequent events proved Joab to be right. After the death of Absalom, David's sorrow grieved the people, and it was Joab's advice which prevented serious repercussions. Later, the king stupidly embarked upon a course of action displeasing to God. It was suicidal, but only Joab had the courage to oppose the royal command. His objections were overruled, and seventy thousand people perished as a result. The king's stupidity was unimaginable, but alas, David had wandered far from God.

HIS GREAT FOLLY

Let us not be too severe in our condemnation of this weakening soldier. The increasing folly of the aged king and the people's whispering that Solomon had been commissioned to execute the great general (1 Kings 2:3-6), were sufficient to disillusion any man. Mistrust and intrigue affected the frustrated leader so much that the renegade Adonijah found him to be fertile soil in which to plant seeds of rebellion (1 Kings 1:7). Joab was like a wonderful racehorse whose stout heart and untiring legs had brought it to within inches of the winning line. What a shame! It would have been better had he retired from the political scene before he blemished his record of service. We should learn from the story and be determined to "run with patience the race that is set before us, looking unto Jesus the author and finisher of our faith" (see Hebrews 12:1-2). (Homily reprinted from the author's book, *Bible Treasures*, pp. 31-32.)

A STARTLED SPOUSE

Wherefore Nathan spake unto Bath-sheba the mother of Solomon, saying, Hast thou not heard that Adonijah the son of Haggith doth reign?. . . Now therefore come, let me, I pray thee, give thee counsel. . . . Go and get thee in unto king David, and say unto him, Didst not thou, my lord, O king, swear unto thine handmaid, saying, Assuredly Solomon thy son

**shall reign after me. . . . why then doth Adonijah reign?. . . I also will
come in after thee, and confirm thy words. And Bath-sheba went in unto
the king. . . . And, lo, while she yet talked with the king, Nathan the
prophet also came in (vv. 11-22).**

Expository Notes on Bath-sheba's Message to David

Bath-sheba, David's wife, might have been a very inscrutable woman,
and for that reason it could have been difficult to know her thoughts.
Another beautiful lady had been commissioned to sleep with David, and
although the two were never intimate, the queen might have secretly resented
the strange arrangement. Yet, she never opposed what had been recommended. She apparently had little interest in the proceedings until
circumstances threatened Solomon. David was dying, and the future depended upon her son for whom she would have done anything. At an
earlier date David had evidently made a promise that Solomon would
become the next king of Israel, and the queen was determined that he
would not forget his promise.

When Nathan mentioned Adonijah's insurrection, the placid Bath-sheba
became an aggressive antagonist who, instructed by the prophet, accomplished the impossible. Sick and old as David was, his wife made him
listen to her complaint. She and her mentor Nathan became accomplices in
a private conspiracy from which the king had no escape. Bath-sheba had
never been denied access to the royal bedroom, so it was easy to reach her
husband. As she made her statement, Nathan, who was listening at the
door, awaited the opportune moment and then entered to make his dramatic
statement of events within the city. David was suddenly overwhelmed with
consternation and remembered his obligation both to God and Bath-sheba.
He remembered that he had said: "My son, as for me, it was in my mind to
build a house unto the name of the LORD my God: but the word of the LORD
came to me, saying. . . . Behold, a son shall be born to thee, who shall be a
man of rest. . . his name shall be Solomon. . . . He shall build a house for
my name; and he shall be my son, and I will be his father; and I will
establish the throne of his kingdom over Israel for ever" (1 Chronicles
22:7-10). The prophet and the queen awaited the king's response, and
David was obliged to take action against the renegade prince. That Adonijah
had a legal right to succession seemed to be meaningless. God had elected
Solomon, and David was determined to do what Jehovah had decreed.
Nathan listened carefully to the royal command to convene an assembly,
but even his facial immobility failed to hide the gleam in his eyes. Bath-
sheba, who had left the room, was asked to return, and when she heard
what David commanded, she bowed reverently and gratefully. A true prophet
of God is more than a talking human parrot! He uses every part of his

being to further the cause he represents. Nathan had a brain which was in constant use.

A SAINTLY SUCCESSOR

> So Zadoc the priest, and Nathan the prophet. . . and the Cherethites, and the Pelethites, went down, and caused Solomon to ride upon king David's mule, and brought him to Gihon. And Zadok the priest took an horn of oil from the tabernacle, and anointed Solomon. And they blew the trumpet; and all the people said, God save king Solomon. And all the people came up after him, and the people piped with pipes, and rejoiced with great joy, so that the earth rent with the sound of them (vv. 38-40).

Expository Notes on the Coronation of Solomon

The coronation of Solomon was an event never to be forgotten in Israel. The people who thronged the streets of Jerusalem shouted their acclaim until the noise could be heard in every suburb. When the historian tried to describe the scene, he seemed at a loss for words and could only write, "The earth rent with the sound of them." Nevertheless, against the blue skies of the national happiness, dark clouds on the horizon were the harbingers of the approaching storm. Solomon had been the replacement-child after the death of Bath-sheba's first son. That tragic loss had reminded both David and Bath-sheba of the event which led to the murder of Uriah. At that time God had said: "Now therefore the sword shall never depart from thine house; because thou hast despised me, and hast taken the wife of Uriah the Hittite to be thy wife. Thus saith the LORD, Behold, I will raise up evil against thee out of thine own house, and I will take thy wives before thine eyes, and give them unto thy neighbor, and he shall lie with thy wives in the sight of this sun. For thou didst it secretly: but I will do this thing before all Israel, and before the sun" (2 Samuel 12:10-12).

Nevertheless, when Solomon was born, "the LORD loved him" (see 2 Samuel 12:24) and later promised that the boy would become king in Israel. God honored that promise, but the new king unfortunately proved to be unworthy of his exalted position. The amazing wisdom which God gave to him was sacrificed upon an altar of lust. Solomon in all his glory faded into insignificance. It was written: "But king Solomon loved many strange women. . . . he had seven hundred wives, princesses, and three hundred concubines: and his wives turned away his heart. For it came to pass, when Solomon was old, that his wives turned away his heart after other gods: and his heart was not perfect with the LORD his God, as was the heart of David his father. For Solomon went after Ashtoreth the goddess of the Zidonians, and after Milcom the abomination of the Ammonites. And Solomon did evil in the sight of the LORD, and went not fully after the LORD, as did David his father" (1 Kings 11:1-6). It is difficult to reconcile some of the preceding statements with the disappointing conduct of David. The king committed many errors, but he never worshiped idols. In that area he was perfect in all of his ways and followed fully after the Lord. God could never be blamed for Solomon's folly. He gave wisdom to David's son, but this gift was unfortunately dissipated by foolishness. The Lord was accurate when He said to David, "The sword shall never depart from thine house."

All backsliders should be aware of the attention of their children who watch them. People may receive pardon from a forgiving God, but even such forgiveness cannot repair the damage done within families by parents who provide terrible examples. When people lose sight of the Lord, problems arise.

A SAFE SANCTUARY

And when Joab heard the sound of the trumpet, he said, Wherefore is this noise of the city being in an uproar?. . . And Jonathan answered and said to Adonijah, Verily, our lord king David hath made Solomon king. . . . And all the guests that were with Adonijah were afraid, and rose up, and went every man his way. And Adonijah feared because of Solomon, and arose, and went, and caught hold on the horns of the altar (vv. 41-50).

Expository Notes on Adonijah's Wise Decision

Adonijah's bubble of prosperity had burst! The throne of Israel, which had apparently been his, had become unreachable. His enthusiastic followers were worried, and even the old warrior Joab was ominously silent. The congratulatory speeches had not been delivered, and the sumptuous banquet was unattractive. Then, a chair was pushed backwards as a guest asked to be excused. Others followed so that the would-be king was abandoned within minutes by his closest associates. A terrible dread overwhelmed the desperate man. The moment of his supreme triumph had been ruined, and death seemed imminent. What could be done to prevent that catastrophe? If he fled, Solomon would follow and find him; his crime was so unpardonable that any request for clemency would be rejected. Then, a ray of hope suddenly shone into the darkness of his tortured mind. There was a place where even Solomon had sought forgiveness. Perhaps, after all, there was a way to avoid the deserved retribution. "And Adonijah. . . went, and caught hold on the horns of the altar" (note the following homily).

HOMILIES FOR PREACHERS AND TEACHERS

Study No. 20

**ADONIJAH . . . From Whose Coronation Party the Guests Ran Away
(1 Kings 1:45-50)**

Adonijah, the would-be king, was in great danger and knew it! Before him stood the tables of his coronation banquet, and all around the spacious chamber, distinguished guests sat in their places of honor. The high priest and Joab, commander of the army, sat on either side of the throne, and many noblemen graced the gathering. Yet, a grim silence had hushed the congratulatory speeches. Jonathan, the son of the high priest, had entered the hall to announce the latest news from the city. He told that King David had heard of Adonijah's plan to steal the kingdom and had prevented it by commissioning the prophet Nathan immediately to crown Prince Solomon. A great congregation of Israel had already witnessed the ceremony and had shouted, "Long live the king." This announcement brought deadly fear to the gathering, and the guests hurried one after another from the room. Finally, Adonijah was left alone.

THE MAN AND HIS PROBLEM

The guilty pretender to the throne considered his predicament and made three startling discoveries. First, he recognized that according to the law of the land, he was a great sinner. He had known of David's intention concerning a successor to the throne, but had rebelled against the appointment of Solomon. His heart had cried, "I will not have this man to reign over me," and he had carefully laid his plans to assume the kingship. He had failed in his attempt and was obviously guilty of treason. Secondly, he recognized that he was a sinner *in very great danger.* The law knew so little of mercy that as soon as Solomon became acquainted with the evil intentions of the usurper, he would undertake a great manhunt until Adonijah had been found and executed. Thirdly, he recognized that if he intended to seek safety, there was need to hurry. Soon all chance of escape would disappear. To linger complacently would reveal folly of the most serious kind. He had to do something and do it quickly.

THE MAN AND HIS PERCEPTION

What could he do? Where could he flee? He realized that although he took the wings of the morning to fly to the end of the earth, the long arm of his brother's vengeance would ultimately reach out and take him. If he sought a hiding place, his brother's servants would never rest until they had tracked him down. What then could he do? To remain inactive while hoping that events would take a turn for the better was out of the question. He knew that his position was most critical, for he stood condemned as a traitor and fully deserved the fate about to overtake him. Then, as he desperately faced his problem, a possible way of escape opened up before him. While ruthlessly slaying any vestige of pride remaining in his heart, he "feared because of Solomon, and arose, and went, and caught hold on the horns of the altar." He knew that his only chance of escape lay in taking hold of the place which testified of sacrifice and forgiveness. He ran quickly to the sanctuary, and climbing on the altar, he wrapped his arms around the place where the blood of the offering had been sprinkled and then adamantly refused to descend.

THE MAN AND HIS PARDON

"And it was told Solomon, saying, Behold Adonijah feareth king Solomon: for, lo, he hath caught hold on the horns of the altar. . . . And Solomon said, If he will shew himself a worthy man, there shall not an hair of him fall to the earth: but if wickedness shall be found in him, he shall die. . . . And he came and bowed himself to king Solomon" (1 Kings 1:51-53). Thus a guilty man received his pardon. It is easy to discover in this ancient account another evidence of the inspiration of Scripture. Only God who is able to see the end of things from the beginning, could ever express in history the gospel message yet to be revealed. Old Testament altars were finger-posts pointing onward to the glorious fulfillment of all prophetic utterances. The Lord Jesus came to take away sin, and the work which the Father had given Him to do, He completed at the Cross. There alone can the guilty find pardon. If man has already discovered his threefold need, he has only to hasten to this place of supreme sacrifice and in faith lay hold on God's altar. There the grace of God dispenses forgiveness; there the guilty find rest. (Homily reprinted from the author's book, *Bible Cameos*, pp. 45-46.)

Episode 45

THEME: *David's Last Words*

SCRIPTURE: 1 Kings 2:1-11

KEY VERSES:

> And keep the charge of the LORD thy God, to walk in his ways, to keep his statutes, and his commandments, and his judgments, and his testimonies, as it is written in the law of Moses, that thou mayest prosper in all that thou doest, and whithersoever thou turnest thyself; that the LORD may continue his word which he spake concerning me, saying, If thy children take heed to their way, to walk before me in truth with all their heart, and with all their soul, there shall not fail thee (said he) a man on the throne of Israel (vv. 3-4).

OUTLINE:
- I. The Famous Charge (Verses 1-4)
- II. The Foolish Commandment (Verses 5-6; 8-9)
- III. The Friendly Commitment (Verse 7)
- IV. The Final Call (Verses 10-11)

THE FAMOUS CHARGE

Now the days of David drew nigh that he should die; and he charged Solomon his son, saying, I go the way of all the earth: be thou strong therefore, and shew thyself a man . . . and . . . there shall not fail thee . . . a man on the throne of Israel (vv. 1-4).

Expository Notes on David's Last Message to Solomon

The people at David's bedside were solemn and silent; their lord the king was dying. Everyone knew it would only be a matter of time before their ruler left them. The physicians could do no more for everything now rested in the hands of the Almighty. Then, David suddenly stirred, and a nurse hastened to his side. As she leaned over him, she heard, "I wish to speak with Solomon—now!" When the stately young prince whispered, "I am here, my father," David sighed as though a heavy load had been lifted from his mind. "My son, I shall soon be leaving you, and the kingdom will belong to you. I have made many mistakes which I hope you will avoid. Yes, I think I should give you advice, for this will be our last meeting. Be thou strong, and shew thyself a man. The throne of Israel should never be occupied by immaturity. My son, let God be first in your life, your decisions, and your government. His Word should always be in your mind. His sovereignty should supersede your pleasures; His purposes must be your guide. Solomon, if you have difficulty knowing how to act, consult the laws of Moses and never hesitate to obey the commandments of God. So shall you prosper and have continuing success. My son, never compromise with evil as did your father. Follow the Lord with all your heart and walk before Him in truth. If you do this, my final bidding, there will always be a man on the throne of Israel." David was becoming tired. Nevertheless, as a loving father, he desired to help his boy. Yet, even as he instructed Solomon, he probably thought, "I wish I had lived according to these standards. Had I exemplified these truths, I would have avoided the pitfalls into which I stumbled." Unfortunately David's words only reached Solomon's mind because his example had ruined his morals. It has been said that a fence on the top of a cliff is better than an ambulance at the bottom! David unfortunately forgot to erect such a barrier.

THE FOOLISH COMMANDMENT

Moreover thou knowest also what Joab the son of Zeruiah did to me, and what he did to the two captains of the hosts of Israel, unto Abner. . . and unto Amasa. . . . Do therefore according to thy wisdom, and let not his hoar head go down to the grave in peace. . . . And, behold, thou hast with thee Shimei. . . which cursed me with a grievous curse. . . when I went to Mahanaim: but he came down to meet me at Jordan, and I sware to him by the LORD, saying, I will not put thee to death with the sword. Now therefore hold him not guiltless. . . but his hoar head bring thou down to the grave with blood (vv. 5-6 and 8-9).

Expository Notes on David's Commandments to Solomon

David was doubtless very exhausted as he lay on his bed. He had given his blessing to his successor. Then, his eyes suddenly became bleak; he was reminiscing. The watching prince wondered what occupied his father's mind. Where had he wandered in thought? David suddenly scowled as he whispered,

"Yes, I remember."

"What is it father?" asked Solomon.

The king quietly whispered, "Joab and Shimei—the scoundrels! I shall never forget what they did to me. Yes, son, I would like to believe that you will pay my debt. Joab killed two of my captains—Abner and Amasa—without permission. Anyone might think that he is the king of Israel; he is self-opinionated and too big for his shoes! I detest him. Solomon, I know that you will be able to handle him. I do not care how you do it, but do not let his gray head go down to the grave in peace!

"And, while I think of it, son, there is another fellow in the kingdom whom I have never forgotten. His name is Shimei. Do you remember him? He cursed and stoned me when I fled from Absalom, your brother. He took advantage of my circumstances and shamed me. Yes, I remember that terrible day. When I returned to Jerusalem, I was obliged to forgive him, for otherwise his execution would have marred my homecoming. That wretched man escaped easily, but, Solomon, all these years I have remembered him. Maybe I did forgive him, but I never forgot what he did. No man can say that I broke my word to that wretch, but nothing can change the fact that he cursed and stoned me in the time of my adversity."

When the king paused, Solomon's countenance had hardened; his expression was frightening when he asked, "Father, what would you like me to do?"

David hesitated, and then replied: "Now therefore, do not hold him guiltless, for you are a wise man and know what you ought to do, but you should bring his gray head down to the grave with blood." It might have been better had David expired before expressing that desire. The sweet singer of Israel finished his life on a discord. (See the homily, "Shimei. . . and the Ghost That Killed Him," p. 312.)

THE FRIENDLY COMMITMENT

But shew kindness unto the sons of Barzillai the Gileadite, and let them be of those that eat at thy table: for so they came to me when I fled because of Absalom thy brother (v. 7).

Expository Notes on a Belated Reward to the Sons of Barzillai

It is remarkable that during David's final moments on earth, he remembered his old friend Barzillai, who had preceded him into the hereafter. His statement to Solomon supplies interesting information. He said that the sons of Barzillai came to his aid when he fled from Absalom. The earlier account mentioned only two other generous donors, Shobi and Machir (see 2 Samuel 17:27-29). The historian also wrote that when Barzillai later refused to accept David's magnanimous offer of residence in the royal palace, the aged friend asked that the king's kindness be extended to Chimham, who might have been the son of Barzillai (see 2 Samuel 19:37-38). The king gladly acceded to that request and apparently gave to Chimham some of his estate close to Bethlehem (see Jeremiah 41:17). There was never mention of the *other sons* of Barzillai being part of the company which brought provisions to the fugitive David. Perhaps at the time, they were young and insignificant, thus playing only a minor role in the benevolent gesture of their father. It is noteworthy, therefore, that David remembered those boys when other people had forgotten them. His request (1 Kings 2:7) that *these men* be considered worthy of distinction among the elite of Solomon's kingdom is amazing. This would have been appreciated if they had performed spectacular acts of bravery, but they had only been faithful in doing something which was neither recognized nor mentioned until David recalled his flight from Absalom.

The other brothers could have been jealous when only the service of Chimham gained official recognition. Yet, it is more likely that they emulated their father's example and rejoiced in serving the king whom they adored. Their belated reward should inspire all who serve David's far greater Son. The Savior enunciated the same principles when He said, "Thou hast been faithful over a few things, I will make thee ruler over many things" (Matthew 25:21).

THE FINAL CALL

So David slept with his fathers, and was buried in the city of David. And the days that David reigned over Israel were forty years: seven years reigned he in Hebron, and thirty and three years reigned he in Jerusalem (vv. 10-11).

Expository Notes on the Death of David

The funeral of David was truly a magnificent occasion upon which Solomon lavished extreme devotion and attention. The elite of the nation doubtless attended the burial, and the description written by Josephus provides many fascinating facts. He wrote: "David was buried by his son Solomon in Jerusalem with great magnificence, and with all the other funeral pomp which kings used to be buried with; moreover he had great and immense wealth buried with him, the vastness of which may be easily conjectured by what I shall now say. 1300 years afterward Hyreanus the high priest; when he was besieged by Antiochus, that was called Pious, the son of Demetrius, and was desirous of giving him money to get him to raise the seige, and draw off his army, and having no other method of compassing the money, opened one room of David's sepulchre, and took out 3000 talents and gave part of that sum to Antiochus, and by this means caused the seige to be raised. . . . After him, and that many years, Herod the king opened another room, and took away a great deal of money, and yet neither of them came at the coffins of the kings themselves, for their bodies were buried under the earth so artfully, that they did not appear even to those that entered into their monuments" (Josephus, *The Complete Works of Flavius Josephus*. Book 7, Chapter 15, Paragraph 3).

The last words spoken by dying people are often repeated many times by relatives present at the bedside. Nevertheless, it would be wonderful to know the unspoken thoughts of those about to leave this world. Perhaps the final thoughts of David were expressed in Psalm 16:9-11:

Therefore my heart is glad, and my glory rejoiceth: my flesh also shall rest in hope. For thou wilt not leave my soul in hell [sheol]; neither wilt thou suffer thine Holy One to see corruption. Thou wilt shew me the path of life: in thy presence is fullness of joy; at thy right hand there are pleasures for evermore.

David's wisdom and vision of death were extremely different from the modern concept. He considered death to be a beginning, not an ending, and an entrance into a new and better world, not merely a termination of mortality. David was aware of the natural process of decay, and yet, he joyfully exclaimed, "For thou wilt not leave my soul in hell [sheol]; neither. . . thine Holy One to see corruption." It is now recognized that the king's statement has messianic significance, but the statement also reveals the faith of the dying monarch. He had much in common with Job, who said: "And though after my skin worms destroy this body, yet in my flesh shall I see God: whom I shall see for myself, and mine eyes shall behold" (Job 19:26-27). It is not possible to determine when David wrote the twenty-third psalm, for there were numerous occasions when death appeared to be imminent. Yet, the immortal poem expressed the assurance of a man who knew that death was a highway to a better world.

HOMILIES FOR PREACHERS AND TEACHERS

Study No. 21

DAVID . . . and His Apple of Gold in a Picture of Silver (Psalm 23:4)

King Solomon once said, "A word fitly spoken is like apples of gold in pictures of silver" (Proverbs 25:11). He probably had access to his father's writings, and Psalm 23:4 perhaps appeared to him to be the greatest of all words fitly spoken. This great verse probably seemed like an apple of gold in a silver setting amid the magnificent grandeur of the entire psalm.

HOW DELIBERATE HIS STEPS. . . "Yea, though I walk"

David realized that the end of his earthly journey was quickly approaching and that soon he would be required to tread the pilgrim path into a new world. Others in a similar position might have become a prey to panic. Fear would have destroyed their confidence and peace. Yet the man of

God looked calmly along the road to see the termination of life's long journey. Unruffled, he proceeded one step at a time. His footsteps did not drag; neither did he hasten with false emotionalism. The man who had walked with God for many years continued to do so until the end.

HOW DISCERNING HIS SIGHT. . . "through the valley of the shadow"

A small window may become a lookout to an entire world. This proposition is a window through which we are able to see the extent of the psalmist's vision. He did not speak of walking *in* the valley or even of walking *to* the valley. He said, "Yea, though I walk *through* the valley." His destination lay beyond it, and his was a pilgrim's path. Death was not a termination on life's journey for him; it was more like a junction where the traveler changed from mortality to immortality in order to continue the journey into higher and grander scenery.

HOW DECIDED HIS SOUL. . . "the valley of the shadow of death"

Shadows are harmless. They may appear to be very frightening, and many nervous people may shrink in dread before them. Yet the fact remains that a shadow will not hurt anyone. The shadow of a dog will not bite, nor will the shadow of a tree hurt any upon whom it is cast. David realized that he would not be passing through the clutches of the monster called death; his pathway merely ran *through* its shadow. Shadows are not possible unless a light is shining somewhere, and this shadow was cast across the valley by the Light of the World, who was waiting to welcome the homecoming pilgrim.

HOW DELIVERED HIS SPIRIT. . . "I will fear no evil"

"Perfect love casteth out fear" (1 John 4:18), and David loved the Lord with all his heart. Oppression was unknown in his spirit, for communion had transformed his outlook. There had been days when he had been forced to cry, "Why are thou cast down, O my soul?. . . hope thou in God: for I shall yet praise him" (Psalm 42:5). But now, all such experiences belonged to the past. A perfect peace had settled upon his soul; a calm had banished unrest from his mind—all was well.

HOW DEPENDABLE HIS SAVIOR. . . "for thou art with me"

David's history had been rather checkered. His best friends had failed him, and on two occasions members of his own family had threatened his life. Yet in spite of these distressing events, he had continually known the companionship of his God. In all of the changing scenes of life, the Lord had been true to His covenant promises, and now that death was near, the psalmist had no doubt that God would be with him in the valley.

HOW DELIGHTFUL HIS SONG. . . "thy rod and thy staff they comfort me"

And so David once again remembered the days of his childhood when as a shepherd boy he had owned both rod and staff. He had resolutely protected his flock, he had gently reproved the obstinate ones among his sheep, and every day he had led them to new pastures and sparking waters. He smiled as he wrote, "The LORD is my shepherd; I shall not want" (Psa. 23:1). Eternal love had been manifested in all of God's dealings. As David had cared for his flock, so the great Shepherd loved every human sheep. The psalmist meditated upon these sublime facts and, as comfort flooded his soul, exclaimed, "Surely goodness and mercy shall follow me all the days of my life: and I will dwell in the house of the LORD for ever" (Psa. 23:6). (Homily reprinted from the author's book, *Bible Pinnacles*, pp. 67-68).

BIBLIOGRAPHY

Amplified Bible. Grand Rapids: Zondervan Publishing House, 1965.

The Bethany Parallel Commentary on the Old Testament. Minneapolis: Bethany House Publishers, 1985.

Clarke, Adam. *Commentary on the Bible*. Nashville: Abingdon Press, n.d.

Conder, C. *Tenting in Palestine*. London, England: Richard Bentley and Son, 1879.

Doan, Eleanor. *The Speaker's Sourcebook*. Grand Rapids: Zondervan Publishing House, 1960.

Exell, Joseph, ed. *Pulpit Commentary*. Grand Rapids: William B. Eerdmans Publishing Company, 1950.

Henry, Matthew. *Commentary on the Whole Bible*. New York: Fleming H. Revell, n.d.

Jamieson, Robert, Fausett, A. R., and Brown, David. *A Commentary, Critical, Exegetical, and Practical on the Old and New Testaments*. Grand Rapids: Wm. B. Eerdmans Publishing Company, 1984.

Josephus, Flavius. *The Complete Works of Flavius Josephus*. Grand Rapids: Kregel Publications, 1960.

Kitto, John. *Kitto's Daily Bible Illustrations*. Grand Rapids: Kregel Publications, 1981.

Meyer, F. B. *Great Verses Through the Bible*. Grand Rapids: Zondervan Publishing House, 1982.

Pink, Arthur W. *Life of David*. Grand Rapids: Baker Book House, 1981.

Powell, Ivor. *Bible Cameos*. Grand Rapids: Kregel Publications, 1985.

————. *Bible Pinnacles*. Grand Rapids: Kregel Publications, 1985.

————. *Bible Treasures*. Grand Rapids: Kregel Publications, 1985.

Thomson, W. M. *The Land and the Book*. New York: Harper and Brothers, 1869.

Wilson, William. *New Wilson's Old Testament Word Studies*. Grand Rapids: Kregel Publications, 1987.